Apocalypse Later
Books by Hal C. F. Astell

<u>Cinematic Hell Series</u>
Huh? An A-Z of Why Classic American Bad Movies Were Made

<u>Filmography Series</u>
Velvet Glove Cast in Iron: The Films of Tura Satana
Charlie Chaplin Centennial: The Keystone Year

<u>Festival Series</u>
The International Horror & Sci-Fi Film Festival: The Transition Years

Apocalypse Later
Festival Series

The International
Horror & Sci-Fi Film Festival:

The Transition Years

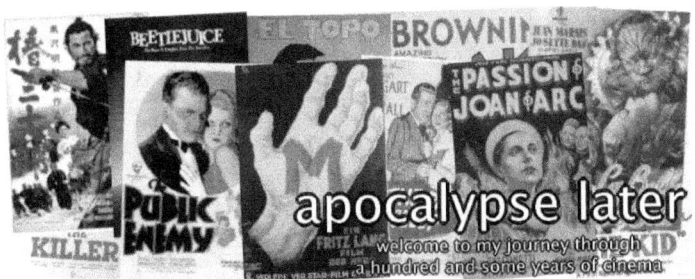

Apocalypse Later Press
Phoenix, AZ

Apocalypse Later Festival Series
The International Horror & Sci-Fi Film Festival: The Transition Years

ISBN-10: 0989461327
ISBN-13: 978-0-9894613-2-0
Apocalypse Later Press catalogue number: ALP004

Reviews by Hal C. F. Astell

These reviews originally appeared, albeit
in evolutionary form, at Apocalypse Later
http://www.apocalypselaterfilm.com/

Cover by Marty Freetage
http://www.freetage.com/

Published through CreateSpace
https://www.createspace.com/

Typeset in Gentium
http://scripts.sil.org/FontDownloadsGentium

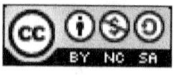

Dedication

This book was always going to be for Jason Carney, even before I started compiling reviews to start putting it together.

He is the most obvious and recognisable face of the Phoenix Film Foundation and therefore, by extension, also the most obvious and recognisable face of everything that the foundation runs. Let's see! That's the Phoenix Film Festival, the International Horror & Sci-Fi Film Festival, the Arizona Student Film Festival, IFP Phoenix (which includes three filmmaker challenges per year and Filmmaker Fusion events, among others) and the Phoenix Film Society. Whew! With no attempt to downplay the efforts of the smörgåsbord of other important and talented people in the local film scene, Jason is often the first key professional that local filmmakers meet.

I can't remember when I met him first, but it was a long time ago. Since that long forgotten moment, most of my interaction with the Phoenix Film Foundation has been through Jason, whether that be as a critic reviewing films that screened at the festivals mentioned above or as a screener of submissions for some of the same festivals. This book certainly could not have been completed without access to the Phoenix Film Foundation library, whose gatekeeper is, you guessed it, Jason Carney.

So thank you, Jason, for doing everything that you do, for doing it for so long and for putting up with people like me while you do it, always with a happy face. I hope your reaction to this book is your trademark, "Sweet!"

Acknowledgements

No book is ever created by one person, regardless of whose name is on the cover. Many other people deserve credit, along with my undying gratitude and appreciation, for their part in bringing this one to print. Thank you, one and all!

Most obviously, thanks to Dee Astell, my long suffering better half, not entirely because she goes to film festivals with me and buys popcorn with extra butter. As always, she watched every film reviewed in this book along with me and performed much needed literary troubleshooting as I read my reviews aloud to her.

Thanks to Mike Flanagan, the man behind *Absentia*, which is both the first review in this book and my favourite movie of the last decade, for kindly contributing the foreword.

Thanks to Andrea Canales (formerly Beesley-Brown), the Midnite Movie Mamacita, who graciously agreed to write the afterword.

Thanks to Melanie at Dog-Eared Pages in Phoenix for allowing my books onto her hallowed shelves. I'm all for replacing our pop culture idols with librarians and independent bookstore owners.

Thanks to Darryl Dawson, Marty and Alice at Massoglia Books, Bob and Sharon at Brick Cave Media, Michael and Becky Bradley, Ron C. Tobin and T. M. Williams, Patti Hultstrand of AZ Publishing Services, Brain Damage Films, Duncan Rittschof of Duncan's Books & More, Chris and Jim McLennan of Phoenix FearCon and Jasper and Caryn of FreakyWearz, all of whom have kindly sold my books from their tables or booths at conventions.

Thanks to the Stampeding Herd (Gini, Lisa, Barb, Lynn, Marci and Sue at this point) who spurred my word counts and helped me to get this book finished.

Special thanks to Chris Lamont, Jason Carney and everyone at the Phoenix Film Foundation, who put on this festival every year; to Brian Pulido, the Baron Frankenstein who brought it to life to begin with ("It's alive, I tell you, alive!"); to Andrea Canales, the festival director who picks the showcase material; and to the programmers who craft the genre tracks: author Michael Stackpole for the sci-fi side and, for horror, the dynamic duo from *I Can Smell Your Brains!*, Danny Marianino and Brandon Kinchen.

Contents

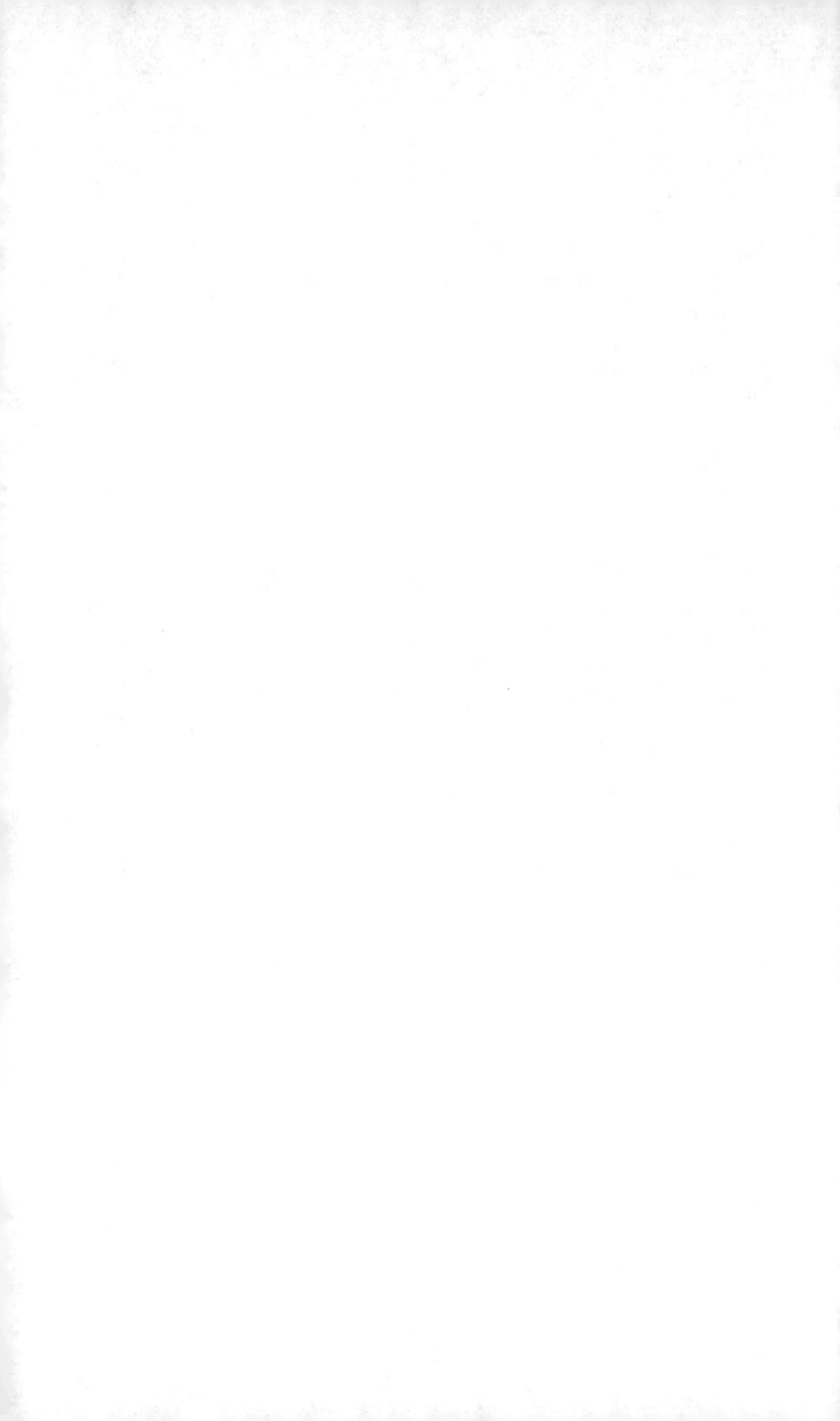

Foreword
by Mike Flanagan

I first heard of the International Horror & Sci-Fi Film Festival in 2011, when we were submitting my film, *Absentia*, to genre festivals across the country. I've had two of my films screen at the festival since then and they represent two remarkably different (but both oddly positive) experiences.

Absentia was a tiny little indie feature, shot for $70k and funded on Kickstarter with the sincere hope that it could finally kick down the door to the industry and launch my directing career. (I always pictured those doors as looking very much like the gates in *Jurassic Park*, except there are snipers. And at least one *Monty Python*-esque heckler.)

Like thousands of similar hopefuls, we targeted genre festivals as we began submitting the film, and the International Horror & Sci-Fi Film Fest popped up on the search engine. It was as simple as that.

Both festivals (this one had been merged with the Phoenix Film Festival by the time we were accepted) had positive word of mouth on the Internet (otherwise known as "the only reliable means of vetting festivals"), and Phoenix was a short enough drive from Los Angeles that we felt it would be worth the trip.

When we were accepted into the festival, the producers and I decided we'd like to attend.

It should be said that I am wary of film festivals.

Since my debut feature, *Makebelieve*, premièred at the Maryland Film Festival in 2000, I've attended dozens and dozens of fests, varying in scope and quality from the very small (the Annapolis Film Festival), to the very big (T.I.F.F., SXSW) and the very-likely-to-be-indicted-for-fraud (the New York Independent Film and Video Festival). If the festival marketplace is a big family, N.Y.I.F.V.F. is the shady, creepy uncle who's either trying to grab your ass or your wallet whenever you see him.

Our experiences with *Absentia* ran the same gamut that I'd become accustomed to over the years. We played to empty houses in some of the smaller fests; we packed multiple screenings in others. We met buyers, producers and fans at some festivals; we realized the only people in the seats were cast/crew/friends of the programmed films at others.

So when we arrived in Phoenix, we were hoping for the best but actively reserving judgment. The festival was engaging from the start... it had taken over a legitimate multiplex, and seemed to have a very enthusiastic crowd. It was well-attended, and there was that intangible energy in the air that you hope to experience when you get to a festival... excitement to *see movies*.

You can tell. You can feel it, at a festival, if it's there... *a love of movies*.

That's a powerful thing and it isn't always the case.

I remember one festival, located in the heart of California's Central Coast wine country. I couldn't wait to attend, as I really wanted to hit some vineyards, take in the sights, and drink some good wine. I wasn't alone in that, it turns out... seemingly everyone attending the festival had the same idea. The tasting rooms were packed with festival badges, but the screenings were deserted. Like, tumbleweed deserted. It was a great fest, but the last thing anyone was interested in was watching movies.

Phoenix was different right away. We made our way out of the check-in and into the giant party tent a little ways down from the theatre. It was packed. Vendors, filmmakers, and a genuinely enthusiastic general audience buzzed through the place, talking about the movies they've seen and pounding the last of their drinks so they wouldn't be late for the next screening.

It was a terrific energy.

A man approached me a few minutes after we'd arrived. He had a camera for a head. I decided I liked this festival.

Absentia was screening a few times, if I recall, but we were only going to be attending our evening screening. That was the big one, and man, were we excited to put the movie in front of such an enthusiastic audience.

We screened the film and the house was packed. Someone from the festival stepped out in front of the screen with a wireless microphone and introduced the film. The crowd quieted. The host stepped outside and the movie started...

And then the trouble began.

It sounded *terrible*. And I mean TERRIBLE.

It was like nothing I'd ever heard... there was a painful, high-pitched feedback shrieking through the speakers. Everything seemed to echo, and underlying every frame of picture was a soft but undeniable *humming sound*, as though the movie itself was preparing to self-destruct.

I ran for the projection booth.

"There's something wrong with the sound," I said.

"I know, it sounds awful," said the helpful projectionist. He looked at his board. He looked at the connections. He listened. He thought. He hit some buttons. And then he looked at me and said the only thing he could have said in that moment to truly, truly enrage a filmmaker: "Everything's good here, it's got to be on your master."

My blood boiled. No, it wasn't on my master. I mixed my movie myself. I sat through the playback. I tech-checked each of our masters. *Twice.* This was my livelihood. This movie was supposed to be my calling card. This was supposed to kick open the doors of Hollywood, pacify the snipers and silence the wall-heckler.

"No, it isn't a problem with my master. My master is perfectly calibrated. We've screened it at half a dozen festivals in the last month. It is *fine.* Whatever is happening, it's on your end."

A great standoff ensued. He continued to check connections. I paced and fumed. Through the tiny window, I watched the audience shrugging, *wincing,* shifting uncomfortably in their seats as their ears were assaulted.

My movie... my baby, my little cinematic engine that could... it was *assaulting people.* In their ears!!! How was this possible?!

After an exhaustive examination of the connections for the audio, there wasn't anything more to do. It was a mystery. The theater hadn't had a single problem so far that day (or so we were told at the time) and there was nothing to be done.

God, it seemed, had intervened. It was Written. Somewhere between my pristine master and the speakers of the auditorium, God had inserted himself into the proceedings for reasons we'd never know... and he was a vengeful god. A god who didn't like my movie, and wasn't gonna let us screen it without the constant death buzz.

I walked back into the theater. I looked at my movie, watched my actors going through their scenes, and tried to convince myself that the audience might still enjoy it regardless. They might still get it, it might not be that big a deal...

It'd be the same argument I'd make if I had to make a public appearance with a Alaskan King Crab perched on my shoulder. Or if I had to do a Q&A with an epic, unstoppable nostril-bleed. "This is bad, sure, but maybe no one will notice...?"

Five more minutes in, I couldn't take it any more. I did something I'd never done, not one time, since I first started showing my student films in class in 1996. I did something I've never done again.

I left the screening.

I complained and complained to the poor festival volunteers stationed near our theater, begging them to please figure out what went wrong... or if they couldn't, please bring me a flux capacitor and a DeLorean, because the only thing that could save this screening was time travel.

They were perplexed, regretful, and – I could tell right away – very embarrassed.

I finally gave up on the whole endeavor and went to the tent.

Where I drank.

I returned to the theater for the Q&A, my anger having given way to a philosophical resignation (the beer helped with that). I'd politely go through the questions and stress as many times as I could that the movie didn't *really* sound like an army of fingernails was gang-banging a chalkboard... something was just very wrong with the sound.

The mystery was solved, if I remember correctly, as we began to get ready for the Q&A. The wireless microphone that had been used to introduce the film, ninety minutes, four beers and one mental breakdown ago... had been *left on*.

The microphone had been *left on*, placed on a table to wait for the Q&A... and its feed was pumping into the speakers of the theater, creating a catastrophic loop of feedback, static and noise.

A story like this could easily end here. While the festival seemed terrific, our screening had been a technological blunder of epic proportions. I could have left the theater and never come back to Phoenix.

But that's not what happened.

The festival programmers were as mortified as I was. But the audience, it turned out, *did sit through the movie.* Not only that, *they liked it anyway!*

They had deduced that something was wrong early on and had recalibrated their viewing experience in an effort to see the film *past* the noise. That requires not only a love of movies, but also an inherent familiarity with how movies are supposed to sound... and they took that ride. They didn't have to, they chose to.

It was an expression of the same enthusiasm that we'd felt when we first entered the festival tent a few hours prior. An enthusiasm born out of a deep and real desire to see, experience and love cinema.

Absentia ended up winning Best Horror Feature at the festival that year. My producer was present to accept the award, but I'd had to return to L. A. for work. I was surprised and grateful for the reception, particularly considering the problematic screening. While the technological hiccup was about as unfortunate as possible in a festival, the way it was handled – by both the festival staff and by the audience – left me feeling grateful and impressed.

Fast forward three years.

It's 2014 and I'm on my way to Phoenix again. It turned out, in part thanks to the reception that *Absentia* got at festivals like the International Horror and Sci-Fi Film Fest, that my little movie did indeed pave the way for the career I'd always wanted.

I'd made a film called *Oculus*, which was my first "big" movie. It had premiered at TIFF the previous September, been acquired by Relativity Media and Blumhouse and was about to be released wide on 2,400 screens across the country.

As I was traveling with the movie for our publicity tour prior to its wide release, I learned that we would be screening at IHSFFF. I smiled.

I arrived in Phoenix, excited to see how the festival had grown in the few years since I'd taken that long, depressed walk from the theater to the party tent while my movie screened to a confused audience.

I went to dinner with Jason Blum, who was there promoting

Oculus as well, and Ti West, who was screening *The Sacrament* at the festival. They both told me how excited they were for the screenings, how much they loved this festival. I told them the truth... it was a great festival, with a great audience. It was run by great people. And it represents the only time in my career I've ever walked out of my own screening.

After dinner we headed to the theater together, and I got to see some familiar faces. Not only the festival programmers and staff, but friends and fans who I had met in 2011 with *Absentia*. People I still kept up with. People who had become regular correspondents on social media and email.

It was such a thrill to screen *Oculus* there, for them. For that audience, so enthusiastic and generous. For that festival, so dedicated to their cause and earnest about bringing movies they love to audiences they believe will love them.

After the screening was over, I was touched and delighted to shake hands, pose for pictures and have terrific conversations with some of the very same people who had seen *Absentia* at the fest in 2011.

Later still, a number of us found ourselves at a local bar sharing a drink (the party tent was sadly absent, and I did miss it).

Both screening experiences were very different, but both ultimately very positive. As I heard more about some of the challenges that the festival faced in 2011, during what was by all accounts a difficult transition for the fest, I found myself increasingly impressed with the dedication and spirit of the people behind the festival.

I said as much to Andrea as she joined us for a drink after the *Oculus* screening... it was a real pleasure to be back.

And it truly was.

Mike Flanagan
June 2015

Introduction

I believe that it was *Dara* which sowed the seed that eventually became this book.

It's a stylish 22 minute Indonesian slasher that I saw as part of the second of three sets of horror shorts at the International Horror & Sci-Fi Film Festival in 2007, its year of release. It was directed by Kimo Stamboel and Timo Tjahjanto, who were both also writers and producers, and the startling leading lady was Shareefa Daanish.

Today, it's easy to see because Tjahjanto uploaded it to Vimeo, where it can be watched for free. Partly, that's because he and Stamboel had expanded it into a feature in 2009, known as *Rumah Dara* in Indonesia and *Macabre* in the English speaking world.

Back in 2007, it wasn't so easy. Either you went to a festival that screened it or you didn't see it at all.

In fact, not only was the short not online back then but neither was any information about it. There was no official website. Nobody had reviewed it and Google didn't turn up anything useful. There wasn't even an IMDb page. The International Horror & Sci-Fi Film Festival, like most such film festivals, doesn't archive past events on its website, so there wasn't anything there to help either.

The only thing to confirm that this picture even existed, beyond my memory of it and appreciation for it, was the festival program, which also wasn't online.

Of course, that was 2007, a generation or two back in internet years, and, as I mentioned, the situation has since been addressed: *Dara* is now all over the web.

So, we're good? Well, not quite.

When I saw *Dara* back in 2007, I was attending the International Horror & Sci-Fi Film Festival as a complete newbie. I'd made the right Google search at the right time and thought that it looked like a lot of fun, so my better half and I waltzed over to the Harkins Centerpoint in Tempe and found ourselves in the Twilight Zone.

Just getting our tickets, we met the genial Brian Pulido, creator of *Lady Death*, who had co-founded the festival two years earlier with Chris Lamont, the president of the Phoenix Film Foundation. As we found our way into the venue, we crossed paths with Michael Beck from *The Warriors*. We enjoyed showcase screenings of *The Exorcist* and *The Hidden*, as well as the accompanying Q&A sessions with Linda Blair and Claudia Christian. Leaving one film, we bumped into the creators of another, *Long Pigs*, talking to fans and answering questions in the hallway. We saw all three sets of horror shorts and as many other films as we could.

Clearly we were overwhelmed but we survived the event, only a little shellshocked by the experience. Best of all, we'd become the beneficiaries of a glorious mistake. While we didn't know anyone at the event, someone overheard my English voice and, assuming I was from New Zealand, promptly introduced me to a friend of his, Andrea Beesley-Brown (now Canales), because "she was a Kiwi too". We didn't share a nationality, but we did share a common taste in movies and we became fast friends. Dee and I immediately became regulars at her Midnite Movie Mamacita screenings at Chandler Cinemas and followed her when that closed.

The rest fell naturally into place. Many of our closest friends nowadays are people we met through this festival and this scene. I'd already started reviewing movies at Apocalypse Later, but that soon grew, in both number or reviews and their scope. We started screening submissions for this festival, which we still do today, and we're doing the same for a few others now as well. I've covered the last few events under press credentials and expanded outwards there too to cover other festivals, not to mention the local film scene at large. We've got to know many filmmakers and meet many famous and not-so-famous names. Nowadays I'm programming film festivals of my own, at conventions in Arizona and California, and helping out others by bringing in films to ensure they have strong programming. Of course, I'm also writing books like this one.

So this festival isn't only an enjoyable event for me. It changed who I am in so many ways that it's difficult to even count them.

And here's where *Dara* comes back in. A great deal of that change happened because I'd seen that one Indonesian horror short and loved it but was frustrated to find nothing at all about it online to back up my memories or allow me to see it again. Over the years, I found that it was far from alone in this situation and I gradually found myself offended that in this internet age where everything is supposed to be online, films like *Dara* can effectively cease to be.

Many films screen at festivals to appreciative audiences. They win acclaim and awards. Filmmakers travel hundreds or thousands of miles to these events to meet fans and react to their questions and applause. These films are *something*.

And then they often start to fade. The filmmakers move on to other projects and let the domains behind their official sites lapse. The festivals move on to their next year's programming and replace their old sites with new ones hawking what's to come but rarely remembering what had been. If nobody had set up an IMDb page or uploaded a video file to Vimeo or YouTube by this point, then any chance that they might do so later only decreases over time. Short films are rarely released on DVD, so we can rarely buy them. And if nobody can see them, nobody is going to review them.

So I started doing exactly that. I started to review every film that played the International Horror & Sci-Fi Film Festival, every short and every feature, however prominent and however obscure, to at least draw a line in the sand that said, "This film existed. It played at a festival on a big screen and people saw it. It deserves to not be forgotten."

One of the greatest joys in my life is when a filmmaker finds my review of their creation and thanks me for drawing that line in the sand. More than once, I've been informed that my review is the *only* review anywhere online and I've confirmed that through Google. At this point, it doesn't even matter whether I liked the film or not. It matters that I've shouted from the ramparts that it exists.

Each time that happens, I redouble my efforts to keep up to date with my festival coverage, to catch up (because I'm always behind) and to draw more lines in the sand. This book is merely the next step in that process.

Originally, each book in this series was going to cover a single year of the International Horror & Sci-Fi Film Festival, but I came to realise over time that it made more sense to cover it in sets of three years, because the festival falls naturally into them.

This event debuted in 2005 at the Harkins Centerpoint in Tempe, with some screenings that first year at the Valley Art on the other side of Mill Avenue. It stayed at the Centerpoint for two more years as it gradually found its identity, but then Harkins sold the venue and it had to move. I call 2005 to 2007 "the Early Years".

After that came "the Indie Years", when the festival took to the road, playing independent venues and epitomising the indie spirit of genre festivals. 2008's event was at Chandler Cinemas in, well, Chandler, but then that theatre closed too, so it returned to Tempe. Plans to turn the Centerpoint into a hotel had floundered in the economic downturn, so the building was leased for a dollar a year to a non-profit organisation which chose to relaunch it as MADCAP Theatres. It housed the festival for two glorious years.

Unfortunately, circumstances beyond anybody's control had led preparations for 2010 to be notably behind schedule. The festival went off swimmingly, but audiences were down because of a lack of publicity. The Phoenix Film Foundation, which also runs the larger Phoenix Film Festival, was finding that it was tough to host two big events each year. And so these two big events merged in 2011, with the International Horror & Sci-Fi Film Festival becoming a sort of late night track for the Phoenix Film Festival at that event's regular location, the Harkins Ciné Capri on the border with Scottsdale.

So began "the Transition Years", in which it had to find itself all over again, at a historic multiplex, at a different time of year and in the shadow of the most prominent film festival in the state.

2011 was a strange year indeed. It featured some of the very best films ever to be screened at the event, but few of them and mostly opposite each other so that it was hard to see many. Nine features played, compared to seventeen the year before. *Triple Hit* won as Best Sci-Fi Feature because it was the *only* one in competition. The four sets of short films in 2010 dropped to three in 2011. The only official guest was Heather Langenkamp, there with a documentary rather than a classic. To make matters worse, technical problems plagued the event, which felt less like a going concern and more like a red-headed stepchild. The future did not seem bright.

But that red-headed stepchild refused to behave. 2012 was bigger and better than 2011, with twelve features and three sets of shorts and a neatly varied set of films on show, not to mention Michael Biehn bringing his low budget throwback, *The Victim*. 2013 grew yet again, up to fourteen features, with six of them in competition, three in each track. There were still three sets of shorts, but they were better than ever, especially on the sci-fi side. The number of major guests expanded too, headed by the wonderful Meg Foster. Each year saw better variety, better scheduling and better support.

2011 was the worst year in the festival's history. The mutterings that underpinned its failure decreased in 2012 but didn't go away. Only with a second strong year of growth in 2013 did they become applause again and pride in a event that was strong once more.

I'm blissfully happy to report that 2014 lived up to this promise for the festival's tenth anniversary, perhaps the very best year yet. Numbers were up again, to the seventeen features and four sets of shorts that we'd enjoyed in 2010, but with even more prestigious titles and guests. We're now at the start of a new set of three years, but we'll need to wait to find out what they'll be called.

So, with the International Horror & Sci-Fi Film Festival ten years old and thriving once more, it's time for me to celebrate by looking back at the lines in the sand that I've drawn over the years.

The volume you hold in your hand includes reviews of every film, whether feature or short, that played during those three Transition Years from 2011 to 2013, as the festival was eaten by its bigger sister but carved its bloody way back out of her belly to scream at us that it was reborn. Maybe it arrived at the Harkins Ciné Capri as a red shirt, all ready to be sacrificed in front of its more prominent peer, but it soon enforced that it was really a survivor and that shirt was merely drenched in blood. The films deserve to survive too.

If you're reading this and you attended the International Horror & Sci-Fi Film Festival during these Transition Years, don't let these films die. Tell people about them. Write about them. Especially let the filmmakers know what you thought about their work. Do what you can to keep these films alive. I'm proud to be the first review for some of these titles, but I don't need to be the only one.

And if you attend the event in future years, please come and say hi. I'll be there in my kilt and Apocalypse Later shirt watching the next batch of films to review.

Hal C. F. Astell
October 2014

The International Horror & Sci-Fi Film Festival

2011

Horror Features

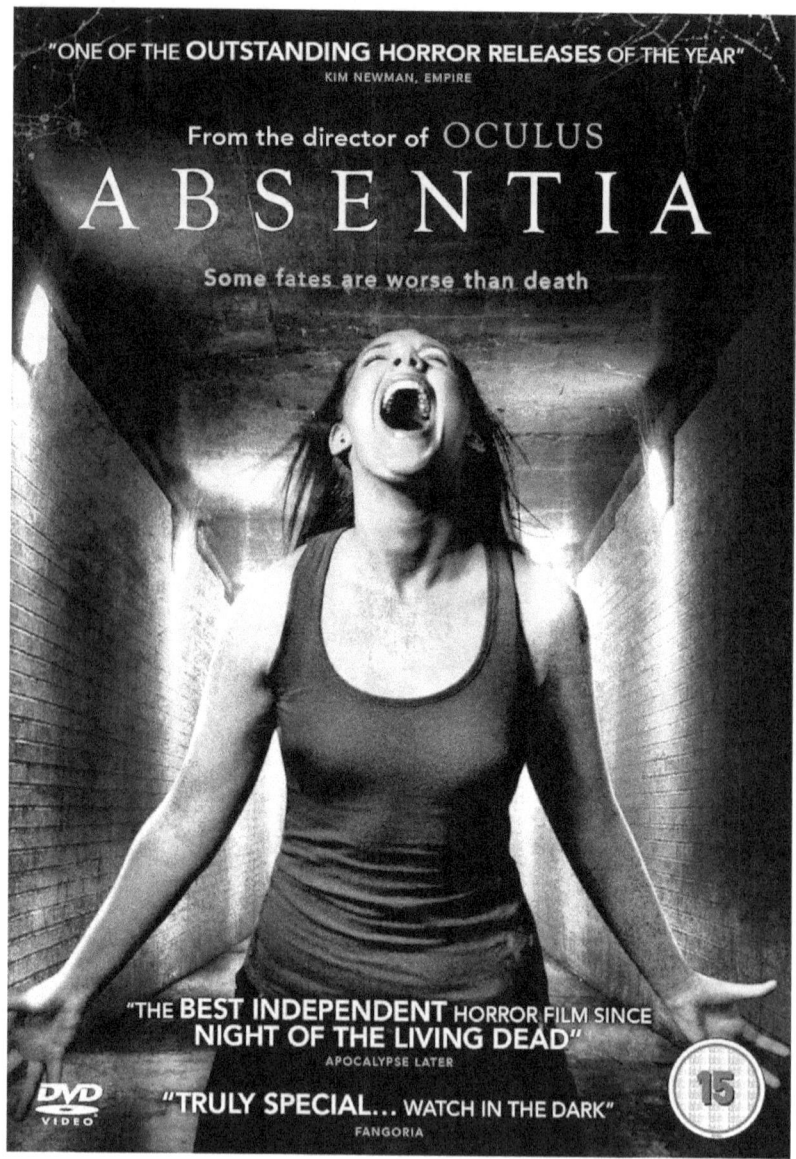

Absentia (2011)

Director: Mike Flanagan
Writer: Mike Flanagan
Stars: Katie Parker, Courtney Bell, David Levine, Morgan Peter Brown, Justin Gordon and James Flanagan

I watch as many low budget, independent horror movies as I can get my hands on.

One reason is that I just love the genre, but the main reason I have such an enduring fascination with them is that they have traditionally acted as a training ground, teaching filmmakers the arts of cinema so that they can move onto the next level and become someone special. There's a third reason though: every now and again someone appears out of the blue who has already done that, and they are the most special of all because not only do they work their magic for us to wonder at, they do so without moving on to the mainstream quite yet. That tends to leave us something that will be talked about for years: a low budget, indie genre flick that surpasses every expectation and leaves all its slick, professional competition in the dust.

I'll say this outright: this is the best horror movie I've seen since *Let the Right One In* and the best independent horror since *Night of the Living Dead*. It carries the biggest emotional impact of any horror film since... well, since I can remember. [Since my original review, part of this quote was used on the British DVD and BluRay covers of *Absentia* and I am truly honoured to see my words there alongside those of a genre legend like Kim Newman.]

Absentia achieves this by throwing out the modern rulebook and stepping back in time to the days of character, suspense and subtlety. This is the sort of film that Val Lewton would be making if he were still alive today.

The mysteries begin with the film. Daniel Riley is missing and his pregnant wife Tricia is stapling up fresh flyers onto telegraph poles to replace older ragged ones. She's using up the last of them because he's been gone now for seven years and back home is an application for death in absentia which may or may not bring the closure she hasn't found thus far. She's a complex character twisted by a whole slew of emotions, most obviously guilt, which is hardly diminishing now that she's about to have her husband declared dead while bearing another man's child. This renewal of posters is as much ritual for her as burning the ones she brings back. There are more subtle rituals in this film than anything else I can think of outside the work of John Ford.

When she gets home, her sister, Callie Russel, is there waiting. Writer/director Mike Flanagan doesn't just break the rules of convention to give us a female lead, he gives us two, who appear achingly real and who serve as a fascinating dynamic. They're very different characters, perhaps the only things they share being hidden strength and the fact that they clearly care deeply about each other, enough to mention taboo subjects but not to harp on about them.

Tricia is settled being unsettled, unable to leave her home and its memories even when she wants to. Callie is younger and full of wanderlust, having apparently travelled and lived everywhere, not just physically either as the box she slides under the bed testifies. They haven't seen each other for five years, but Callie has grown and discovered a conscience with religion, so has come to help her sister through a tough time. Why now instead of five years earlier is merely another depth to her character.

Courtney Bell and Katie Parker are the actors tasked with these delicate portrayals and had they not been up to the task, this film would not be the success it is. Neither have much experience, it would seem, but they make every bit count, aided by realistic, well written dialogue and by Ryan David Leick's almost minimalist soundtrack, a pointer from moment one to the film's subtlety as a whole.

Everything is psychological at this point, most obviously our first views of Daniel within Tricia's thoughts of what might have happened. Initially she just thought he left due to a fight, but that turns to amnesia and eventually alien abduction or other esoteric rationalisations. And that's just year one of seven. Great writing and great acting really embue this with emotion. It all matters, just as if we were part of the family. Finally, of course, is the inevitability of death, but that's the toughest to really believe, right? As Tricia says, it's hard to come back from that one.

Watching a second time, I caught a few clever hints in the early scenes that I'd missed the first time around and I'm still finding odd things I missed on what might be my tenth viewing, but none affect the overall experience. This is an accomplished screenplay with clear bookends, a pivot halfway through and a set of three well defined acts, along with a host of nuances that make sense on a first viewing but add depth on a second, once we know exactly what Flanagan has in store for us in the later acts.

I'm still in awe at how he twists the viewers and characters both, not least because the twists are emotional things here, not some sort of self-righteous M. Night Shyamalan intellectualism. All that unfolds in this film is utterly consistent with the story as a whole, and the various readings that can be made of it, but the events that lead us into the second and third acts are truly emotionally powerful. A third of the way in, Flanagan rooked me between the eyes and I felt my gut twist at the power of what he had done. Another third and he did it again.

This also means that I can only summarise a fraction of the story because if I go beyond the first act I'll be throwing out spoilers, something that wouldn't happen with many films until the finalé.

I can tell you about the tunnel, of course, because that's at the core of the film, a tunnel close to Tricia's house that leads to a park on the other side. Callie jogs through it in the morning, finding that the missing posters over there are about small pets rather than people. On her way back through, she wakes up a freakishly thin man who lies in the way and rambles on about nothing. "It's sleeping," he says. What, he doesn't seem to know, but he wants to trade with her.

He's a bizarrely cool character but the most awesome thing about him is that he's he's played by Doug Jones. Yes, Doug Frickin' Jones from *Pan's Labyrinth* and *Hellboy*. Flanagan funded this movie through Kickstarter and yet he managed to cast the Silver Surfer. Some things are very right with the world of film.

Also building the freakiness of this film are the hallucinations Tricia starts having about Daniel, whether she's awake or asleep. Her therapist thinks they're lucid dreams caused by the stress of declaring her husband dead, which makes sense. They're nicely done too, neat manipulations of the laws of physics. Discussing their meaning actually has meaning, which doesn't happen too often. I can't highlight just how much I despise therapist sessions in movies, but this one is spot on and it underpins much of the story, because the whole thing can be read in a number of ways. Every event has a few possible explanations, though the characters find the ones that work for them, in itself a message because that's precisely what we do as viewers, whether watching this film or going about our daily lives. This realisation heightens the tension as we seriously wonder what we would do in these situations.

There's much more that I shouldn't go into because you should discover it for yourself. Honestly, you deserve to be rooked between the eyes too. Cheap thrills are fine but every once in a while you owe it to yourself to experience the real deal, something that makes you wonder and squirm and think all at the same time.

Somehow the freakiest thing in the first third of the film happens because of a good deed. Cassie, performing a Christian act, took food to the freaky dude in the tunnel only to find him gone. She leaves it there for him but, the next day, she finds that he's left something in return on her doorstep, what looks like a collection of keys and odd jewellery. After she takes it back to the tunnel, even when cautioned not to by a young passerby, it reappears that night, under her bedcovers. In most films this would be a cheap shock moment, but here it's merely the final underline to enforce that we're in new territory, we're not in control and whatever is going on is scary as hell.

Flanagan didn't have a lot of money to play with here but he achieves well beyond his meagre budget. He raised about $25,000 through Kickstarter, enough to appeal to private investors who added another $40,000. He used it wisely, starting with what he had and building from there. He knew the actresses who play the leads well, so well that he could write the parts for them and incorporate some of their own personalities into the characters. Courtney Bell, who plays Tricia, really was pregnant during filming, but she didn't have to travel far to work because Flanagan is the father, their apartment is where they shot most of the movie and the tunnel is really that close. "I've been looking at it for four years," Flanagan told me, "and wanted to find a good story for a horror movie to feature it." He found one and in doing so he also found another way to keep costs down.

Another way came through growing experience. Flanagan is a director at heart but his credits are all over the map, most obviously in editing as that's what pays the bills. Usually when people dismiss the art of editing, I point them at Russ Meyer movies, as all his wild motion is conjured up through editing because he never moved his camera. Now, I think I'll point them at *Absentia*, as an object lesson.

Before his career as an editor took off, Flanagan made three features as a writer/director and the first cut of each ran well over two hours, only to be trimmed down as far as 80 minutes. His third feature, *Ghosts of Hamilton Street*, shrank from 140 to 106, but when he made *Absentia*, he experienced his "sensibilities as an editor driving the script and the directing," meaning that he effectively edited in camera, a trick Hitchcock did deliberately to avoid studio interference. The first cut of *Absentia* ran 95 minutes and it ended up at 91. Needless to say, the editing is exactly what it should be, leaving us with a slow burner of a movie without an ounce of fat that never loses our interest for a second.

A second viewing does outline a few flaws, but even here I think Flanagan found luck on his side. Some of the camerawork is a little shaky, though that may actually help provide an edge, a mere hint at the immediacy that found footage provides but without all the motion sickness. The lighting isn't perfect but again, that often works in the film's favour. From outside, for instance, the tunnel is just a tunnel. Even looking out from a few yards in, it's just a tunnel. However the further inside you go, the more surreal it gets as it seems to shift somewhere else, perhaps outside of space and time, helped to no small degree by the fact that the ends are nothing but light. We're not in Kansas any more, Dorothy. As the story unfolds and we start to realise different interpretations are possible, this all helps, even if it was merely a byproduct of the budget.

The cast help too, every one of them adding something notable to the film. The two leads serve as the grounding for the story but the supporting cast back them up ably. Morgan Peter Brown is particularly excellent as Daniel, even though very little of his role involves speech. He's the actor I've followed since to other films, like *Biology 101*, a local Arizona feature co-written by Liz Bradley, who had worked as a production assistant on *Absentia*. Dave Levine is solid as Det. Mallory, powerful and unmoving but not always knowing. Justin Gordon is as solid as his partner, Det. Lonergan, thoroughly different but just as good. They play well off each other, just as Parker and Bell play well off each other as Tricia and Callie.

Flanagan only got Doug Jones for a day but that was enough for him to become a very powerful presence in the picture. He's the only hugely experienced member of the cast, the rest ranging from very little to not much in the way of credits, which come often only or predominantly from Flanagan films. It doesn't matter. Nobody lets the side down.

I have much more that I want to say about this film, but can't, beyond the emphatic suggestion that you find a way to see it. For a while it seemed to be one of those features that critics rave about but audiences don't see, but Flanagan moved on to bigger things with his next feature, *Oculus*, and the publicity machine behind it thankfully caught *Absentia* back up in its wake.

For me, it's become the movie I recommend to everyone who visits Apocalypse Later and asks me what they should see that they've never heard of. Often, I'll watch it with them. It's awesome, freaky, fascinating stuff, character driven from moment one, full of ideas and worthy of many interpretations. Watching *Absentia* is a privilege and a pleasure and I look forward to introducing many people to it for many years to come.

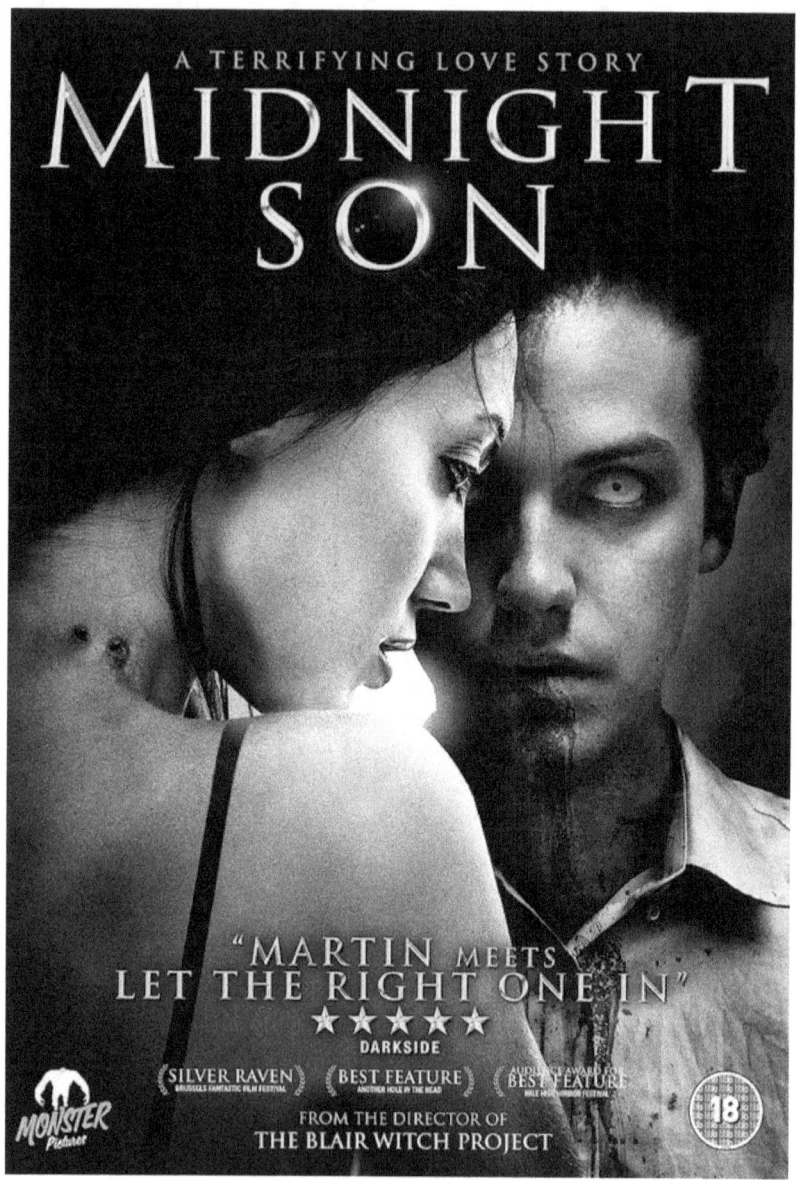

Midnight Son (2011)

Director: Scott Leberecht
Writer: Scott Leberecht
Stars: Zak Kilberg, Maya Parish, Jo D. Jonz, Arlen Escarpeta, Larry Cedar, Juanita Jennings and Tracey Walter

Scott Leberecht, who wrote, produced and directed *Midnight Son*, is much better known for being a visual effects arts director at Industrial Light and Magic. Having films like *Eraser, 101 Dalmations* and *Sleepy Hollow* behind you can hardly be seen as a bad training ground for a start in making the films you really want to make. He wrote and directed a short film in 2003 called *Underdog*, around the time he also directed a couple of other shorts that he didn't write, but this is his debut feature as a writer/director, one that perhaps took him eight years to get going.

It's a solid film too that made a few ripples on the festival circuit back in 2011. Perhaps its biggest problem is that it doesn't feel like a 2011 movie, more like the sort of novel that more ambitious horror authors were trying to write back in the eighties when vampires were being reinvented. It's slow, careful and thoughtful. It has a strangely hopeful ending. It's a vampire movie that only mentions the V word once and only ever hints at the possibility of showing us fangs. And no, nothing sparkles.

Our hero, if such a word is remotely appropriate here, is Jacob Gray, who works security for a faceless corporation. It's very apparent that something is wrong with him, not only because he soon collapses in the lobby but because he does so while listening to Gary the janitor's heartbeat from a few feet away, over the noise of the floor polisher, even over conversation. He's showing signs of malnourishment, although he eats a lot of junk food; the doctor thinks cirrhosis, jaundice and anaemia and recommends tests. He's very pale and he suffers from a serious skin condition, serious enough that he burns in sunlight, and I do mean burns, not just turns a little red. Only when he drinks the bloody juices from an undercooked steak does his stomach begin to feel happy. He may not have much of a clue what's happening to his body, but it's pretty obvious to us with ninety years of vampire movies behind us. He already works nights, third shift. "It's like you're a vampire," a girl tells him and it's something he's obviously thought about.

Why it manifests itself now is the real question and the only hint we get in that direction comes from the janitor, who is a believable fount of hidden knowledge because he's played by Tracey Walter, Miller from *Repo Man*. When Jacob tells him that he's 24, Gary replies that the human body stops growing at 25, so he must be in the last stages of something, not the early ones. Maybe he's "like a caterpillar turning into a butterfly."

That's how this film is phrased: there are no undead armies, no Transylvanian counts, not a single dubious accent; it's about Jacob struggling to find himself when he's not like anyone else around him. After half an hour I realised I wasn't even thinking of this as a horror movie, more like a coming of age story, merely a little later in the protagonist's life than usual. It's a romance, a thriller, a drama. It's a drug movie, one whose drug happens to be blood rather than cocaine or heroin. It could even be seen as a nature film, a lost animal discovering his potential and transforming into what he could be.

It's only hokey briefly, as Jacob rents *Fright Night* (on VHS, no less, our only hint at a timeframe) to test the lore. None of it proves accurate. He can see himself in the mirror. He sticks a cross on his forehead but nothing happens. We never see fangs.

We do see other things though, like how the film is sparsely populated as if to highlight how sparsely populated Jacob's life is. We wonder a lot about him, not only about what he is right now and what he's becoming but about what he used to be like. It doesn't seem to come up, apparent only in a few photos, knick-knacks and an abiding memory of the sun which he paints from photographs. He lives in a basement apartment with a heavy blanket over the door, which doesn't seem unusual to him. Gary the janitor and Mary, a girl he meets outside a club, are the only people he connects with and then not easily. He's likeable but he's just not a social creature. He seems to have drifted thoughtlessly into self medication as his condition worsened. He simply got used to it.

Mary proves to be as much a catalyst for change as Jacob's condition. Zak Kilberg, an experienced but hardly prolific actor who seems to be transitioning into production, underplays Jacob throughout the film because he's a nonentity. He isn't anyone we would be watching a feature about if he wasn't becoming some sort of vampire butterfly.

The differences between him and Mary are major from the moment we first see her, hawking candy and cigarettes. He's dressed simply in black and white; she's colourfully adorned with bangles, ribbons and a varied assortment of glowing things. She's experienced; she works multiple jobs, she smokes and does drugs, she's had and ended relationships. He's done none of the above. Maya Parish, another experienced but not prolific actor, plays Mary as someone who has been there, done that often enough to be confident but still remain somehow empty. Meeting Jacob is an opportunity for her to change too. He's nice and he's different. He's a way out of a life she isn't particularly happy about.

It's through Maya that we find an analogy between vampirism and drug addiction. Realising how much animal blood agrees with him, he starts drinking it out of coffee cups, hiding his drug of choice; it only wanes when he inadvertently gets a taste of human blood for the first time. At Jacob's for a date, Maya snorts some coke in his bathroom and gets a nosebleed while making out. His reaction shakes her and prompts her to stop doing drugs, but it also prompts him to escalate, to the point where he scavenges from the biohazard trash at a hospital. An orderly called Marcus rumbles him, but gives him an expired blood pack with the promise of more, at $150 each. The drug analogy couldn't be more obvious at this point, but it's continued. Later when his shirt is splashed with blood he cuts a piece out to suck, like an acid dot. We even see production, the ever-opportunistic Marcus draining a man in a wheelchair. Jacob tries to go legal after that, looking up blood sales online, but it isn't quite that simple, as you might imagine.

Leberecht achieves much with *Midnight Son* but I'm not sure quite what he aimed it to be. I saw it at a horror film festival, perhaps appropriately given that it revolves around a man who can only be seen as a vampire, even if all the usual supernatural elements have been excised. It may well appeal to fans of more unusual vampire movies as *Near Dark*, *Grace* or *Let the Right One In*, but it's certainly not for the usual horror throngs.

It probably plays best as a drama, with strong acting and a slow but sure progression as Jacob discovers who and what he really is. Yet the people who watch dramas don't tend to expect to be given a vampire as a lead character, however much it avoids the use of the word. Perhaps I'm seeing all this as a potential issue because it feels out of time. Nowadays, pictures like *Let the Right One In* have found an audience that appreciates artistic filmmaking, whatever the subject. *Midnight Son* plays like it was made in the late eighties but took 25 years to find a release. Back then, "genre" was a dirty word.

From some angles Zak Kilberg has a Brendan Fraser thing going for him, albeit a rather anorexic Fraser, maybe crossed with Richard E. Grant; from others there's some early Russell Crowe. Yet he's grounded, appearing like an everyday person rather than some A-list movie star. He doesn't have the charisma for that but he does have the acting chops to draw us into his plight anyway, like a new face in a random TV show that you find yourself watching more than the leads; yet an hour later, you'd walk past him on the street without even thinking. This may not have the star power of *Zombie Strippers!*, his most recognisable film, but it's surely a number of notches up on the quality scale.

Maya Parish also has plenty of talent and promise. She gets a substantial role here, not remotely close to the average character for a leading lady. Sure, she's the love interest, but she's also the driving force for the story in a number of different ways, often far more than the more passive Jacob. It falls more to Parish to push it forward than to Kilberg.

The supporting cast are generally capable too. Jo D. Jonz and Aren Escarpeta fit the same category as Kilberg and Parish; they're both experienced but neither has made it big yet. Like them, this film can't hurt to be an entry on their respective resumes and they will surely make themselves noticed in the future. While *Midnight Son* firmly belongs to the two leads, Jonz and Escarpeta bring depth to their characters as Marcus and his brother Russell. They also grow well, even without a substantial amount of screen time. The most recognisable name is Tracey Walter, but he gets very little to do; it's a reassurance that he does a lot with it. Juanita Jennings and Larry Cedar are also both highly experienced, but their characters are restricted to subplots as Liz, the proprietor of an art gallery, who Mary persuades to exhibit Jacob's paintings, and Det. Ginslegh, a cop investigating a string of murders which may or may not lead back to Jacob. All of them could easily have done more and done it well, but expanding their roles would have detracted from the core story.

And that all comes back to Jacob Gray, who remains an enigma even past the end credits. We discover much about his condition as the film runs on, but not so much about him, not through any fault of Kilberg but because Leberecht obviously didn't want to tell. Everyone Jacob bites becomes like him and those who don't learn to survive, as he did, soon burn instead; this is consistent throughout, so helps us to find a grounding in what is to come, but it doesn't explain how Gray managed to make it this far.

The difference is clearly that he was made a vampire at a much younger age, maybe even at birth, but we're shown none of that so it's all conjecture. How did he survive as a vampire child? How did he make it to the point where he could self medicate by closing off the windows, putting up the blankets and taking a job working nights? Who are his parents and where are they? Why didn't they prepare him? Leberecht could easily make a prequel to explain to us where Jacob came from; perhaps that was always the idea. I'm certainly not averse to it.

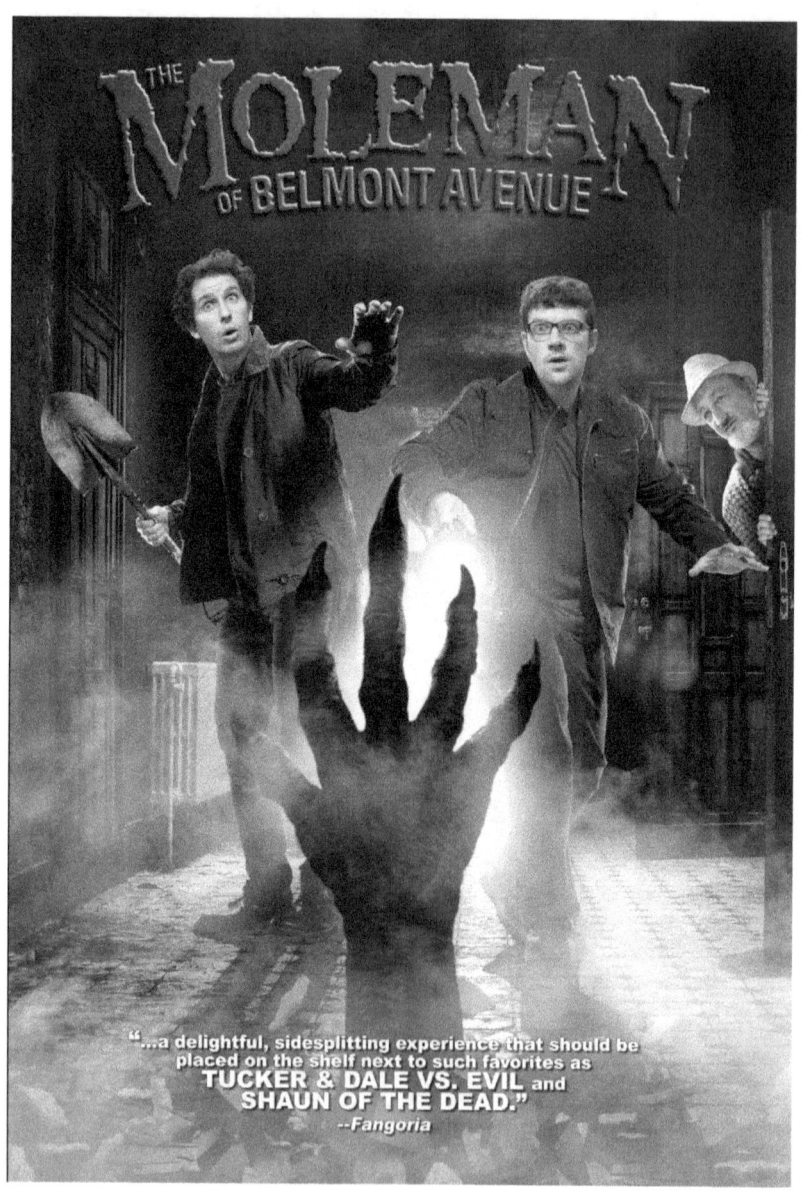

The Mole Man of Belmont Avenue (2010)

Directors: Mike Bradecich and John LaFlamboy
Writers: Mike Bradecich and John LaFlamboy
Stars: Mike Bradecich, John LaFlamboy, Susan Messing, Nicholas Barron, Justin DiGiacomo, Tim Kazurinsky, David Pasquesi, T. J. Jagodowski, Mary Seibel, Xzanthia and Robert Englund

No movie with a title like *The Mole Man of Belmont Avenue* is ever going to be high art and, frankly, it isn't going to care.

It may have been up for competition in the horror track at the International Horror & Sci-Fi Film Festival, but it's really a comedy. Sure, there are horror elements, but the balance between comedy and horror is so biased towards the former that I wouldn't even call it a comedy horror, merely a comedy.

Now, regular readers at Apocalypse Later will know that I don't have much of a soft spot for modern comedy, which far too often tends towards the lowest common denominator, but I found that I enjoyed this, however often it's happy to get stupid. Perhaps my lack of depth with the modern comedy stars is a good thing in this instance, because it means I have no idea quite how much Mike Bradecich is ripping off Seth Rogen and John LaFlamboy is ripping off Ben Stiller. Viewers a decade or two younger than me see it instantly (and I did check, trust me), but I'm otherwise blissful in my generational comedy ignorance.

They're the Mugg brothers, a rather appropriately named pair of incorrigible slackers who are doing a stunningly bad job of running the apartment complex on Belmont Avenue in Chicago that they inherited from their mother. Well, Marion is doing a stunningly bad job, while Jarmon arrives back to join in at the beginning of the film after failing to breed llamas some place else.

He picked a terrible time to return home, as the whole place is a complete nightmare. Tenants are leaving, their pets are vanishing without a trace and Marion has been stealing electricity from the church next door because he's apparently unable to pay any bills at all. As Mrs. Habershackle, their oldest tenant, astutely points out, the place died along with their mother. The Muggs' standard response to this sort of pressure, indeed any sort of pressure, is to go to the bar, which in their case is the Bootleggers Run downstairs. The bartender is as dry as the Muggs and even funnier. She's K. C. and she suggests that the place's glory days date all the way back to the prohibition era when it was a brothel and a speakeasy. She's probably not wrong.

And, of course, they have a Mole Man, as the title suggests, who is, of course, the strange monster spiriting away all the pets. We catch sight of him just before the Muggs do, ahead of the ten minute mark, as he tries to steal a Yorkie through the letter box of one of the apartments. I got the impression that he'd have shown up sooner if only the comedians running the show hadn't written an infuriatingly catchy song that needed a sort of music video to wake us all up, but it's still early enough that any mystery is lost. We clearly know whodunit and we can hazard a pretty good guess as to why because, as a running joke suggests, there really isn't any other way to describe him but "mole man". What we're left with is less about how the landlords are going to stop the creature and save the building's remaining pets and more about whether these mildly sympathetic idiots will ever get round to it. Their mole man is successful not only because he's good at disappearing but because they're morons, albeit a cut above some of their tenants.

Fortunately these tenants are a varied bunch, who add some character to proceedings. Danny and his family leave at the outset, but they're the only normal ones. There's Mrs. Habershackle, the crotchetty old lady with her beloved cat, Mr. Marshmallow; she's played by a former vice president of the Screen Actors Guild, Mary Seibel. The other elderly tenant is a libidinous old codger named Hezekiah Confab, capably played by Robert Englund in a supporting role for a change. Eliza is a dreadlocked and heavily tattooed sex worker who runs her business out of her apartment and walks around topless without a single care in the world; she's played to perfection by alternative model XZanthia, also a businesswoman who owns a nudist colony with a makerspace. T. J. Jagodowski is drug addled Paulie, such a dedicated slacker that he even wears a shirt that says "slacker" on it; he has four others living in his apartment that aren't on the lease. That leaves Dave the Hermit, who we naturally don't meet for quite a while.

In and amongst this quirky chaos, there's a mildly serious theme, namely that the Mugg Brothers' worst enemy isn't the Mole Man but themselves. Certainly they quickly realise what they need to do but take a heck of a lot longer to get round to actually doing it, as they spend far more of their energy avoiding it than would have taken care of the job to begin with. It could be argued that between them, they're like Gary Cooper in *High Noon*, somehow finding the strength to face a major threat even though nobody around them is willing to help. If you can somehow imagine and get a laugh out of the ludicrous replacement of Gary Cooper with a pair of cowardly weaklings and the subtextual threat of the Communist witchhunts with a mole man, then this might just be a film for you. Much of its success arises from their setting up horrible schemes, only to feel bad about them and eventually sabotaging their own efforts. This builds sympathy for characters who didn't start out with much of it and draws us into their plight.

It certainly doesn't hurt that, even though they're undeniably derivative, Bradecich and LaFlamboy have some excellent comedic timing and that they're surrounded by many of their favourite Chicago comedians. They were also heavily invested in the project, not only as its stars but also as its writers, producers and directors, their first time in any of these roles on a feature film.

For first timers, albeit first timers with a solid amount of useful experience in theatre, storytelling, sketch comedy and haunted house production design, they did a lot right. Their film has a great title, a great retro menu on the DVD and a great opening pair of lines. The monster is a refreshingly different creature, however ridiculous it is and even if we see too much of it early on and too little towards the end. Justin DiGiacomo, the actor in the suit, makes the mole man lithe and quick and it's no stretch to imagine him anywhere and everywhere: floor, ceiling, walls, you name it. He provides some solid scares in a picture that plays far more for laughs.

The characters are enjoyably diverse, albeit perhaps too deliberately so; I wonder how such folk would get along if they were forced to share apartments in the same brownstone for real. If I was stuck here, I'd spend most of my time at Bootleggers Run, just like the Muggs, but for no apparent reason their tenants seem to avoid it like the plague. One of the less successful aspects of the film is that each of these supporting characters is tasked with being quirky and different from the others but never to contribute anything substantial to the story. It's clearly the Mugg Brothers' show and their tenants are as much props as the pets.

On the other hand, the gimmicky sections of the picture, like the musical number and the drug trip, are effective, surprisingly so given that they're precisely the sort of egocentric asides that usually detract from a movie, even if they work well in isolation. I especially liked how Nicholas, K. C.'s resident musician, provides an effective in film commentary in his soundtrack that the Muggs would have done well to listen to.

However much they did right, Bradecich and LaFlamboy apparently struggled to get their film released. When I saw it in competition at the International Horror & Sci-Fi Film Festival in 2011, it was dated 2010 and the press kit still hopes in 2014 for a 2011 release. However IMDb now has it listed as a 2013 picture. To emphasise what that delay means, Brian Boland, who plays K. C.'s boyfriend here, made two *Paranormal Activity* films and appeared in archive footage in a third, entirely within the timeframe between this film being made and released.

I wonder why it was such a struggle; perhaps it was too comedic for the horror set but a little too scary for comedy fans, but that seems like a stretch. Maybe the humour goes to darker places than distributors might have felt comfortable with. Police brutality is played for laughs here and that's a tough joke to sell in the era of U. C. Davis and Occupy Wall Street. Black humour surrounding pets is also particularly risky in a comedy that wants to find more than a niche audience, however hilarious it happens to be.

I hope it finds that audience, as it deserves one. As a clearly low budget film, apparently shot mostly on church property with a crew as inexperienced as the double act running the show, it demonstrates surprising technical proficiency. The comedy is a less surprising success, given the cast's substantial experience, however unknown many of them are outside of Chicago. The script ends up being the weakest link with its tendency to veer off into improv territory instead of moving the story forward. That the improv scenes are enjoyable, often because of T. J. Jagodowski's hilarious turn as Paulie, the lead stoner, hides the script's weaknesses to a large degree, but they're still there. The pace lags in the middle and again during the third act as the Mugg Brothers finally step up to the plate, but they do get great arguments in the process.

That Bradecich and LaFlamboy have known each other forever is obvious, as they're an effective double act. I just hope more people see this film and get to know them too.

The International Horror & Sci-Fi Film Festival

2011

Sci-Fi Features

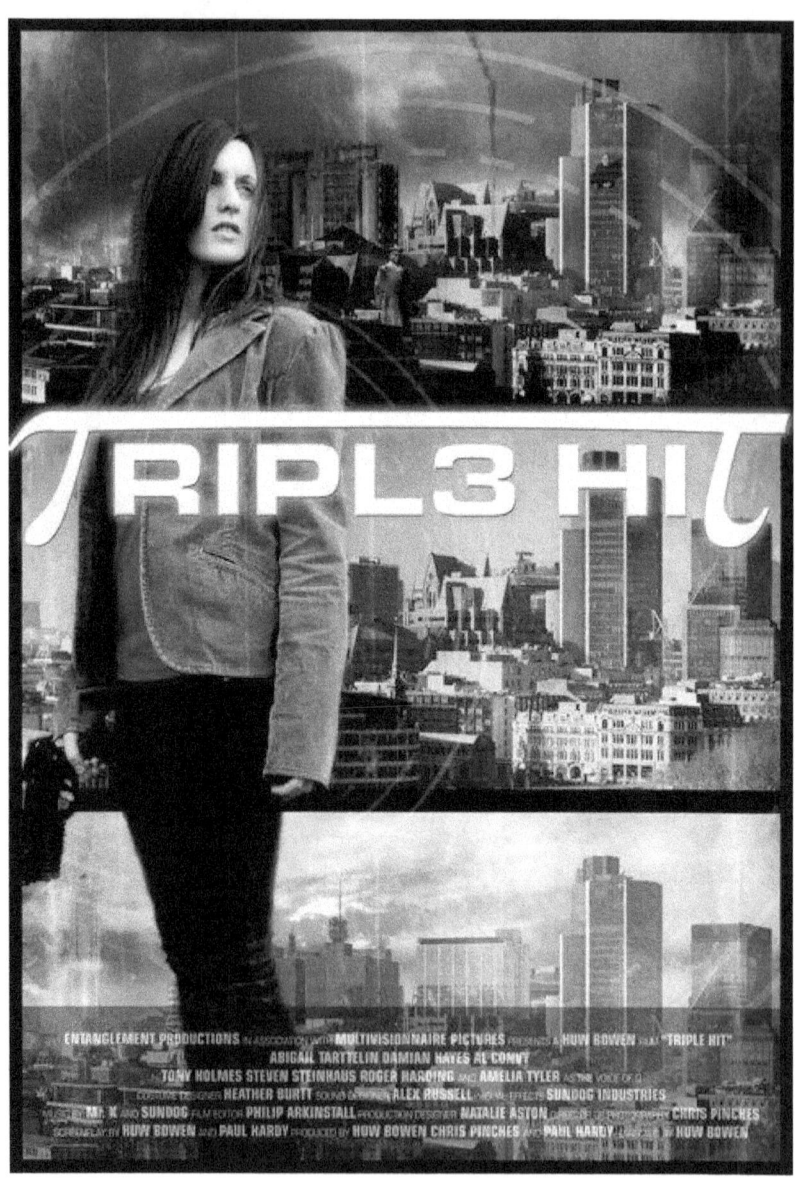

Triple Hit (2009)

Director: Huw Bowen
Writers: Huw Bowen and Paul Hardy
Stars: Abigail Tarttelin, Alan Convy, Damian Hayes, Roger Harding, Tony Holmes, Stephen Steinhaus and Amelia Tyler

Triple Hit, formerly titled *Schrödinger's Girl*, is one of those movies that epitomises how hard it is for indie film to get really noticed. Better by far than most indie features, especially on technical grounds, it impressed on the festival circuit and gained a good deal of attention. Unfortunately that meant that it got to duke it out with the big boys in the real world, where many viewers, used to the sort of slick product that the big studios lavish tens, if not hundreds, of millions of dollars onto, found it lacking.

Most criticism was hurled at the quality of the acting, which is understandable. There are no big stars here for a start, each of the lead actors being relatively inexperienced, but four of them also accepted a rather ambitious challenge; they weren't merely tasked with playing a lead role, they're each tasked with playing three different versions of those lead roles within three different parallel universes. They had to appear enough alike to be recognisable as the story starts shifting between universes, but different enough to be easily delineated when the story starts throwing them together. Their success was variable.

It begins well, with a catchy hook and a notably energetic set of credits. "How did it start?" a girl is asked during an interview on Alpha Station about "recent disturbances in parallel universes". "With me being a genius," she replies. Already it feels like a British sci-fi television show, with the usual limited budget but a lot of imagination, and that remains a fair description throughout.

Then the script, written by Paul Hardy and director Huw Bowen, knuckles down to that attempt to introduce us to three different versions of four fundamental characters without confusing us to death. They do better than the actors do, conjuring up a trio of easily delineated parallel universes, each apparently next to each other in the dimensional stack.

7829-097 is the United Kingdom, either the one in our world or something believably close to it. However, next door in 7829-098, it's the U. N. Administrative Division, Western Europe, far more advanced than us. One step further into 7829-099, it's the People's Republic of Great Britain, a muted Soviet state.

As we might expect, each of these characters is shaped by their environments. The most important is the girl being interviewed at the beginning, who is perhaps deliberately younger than we would expect a genius to be. In 097 she's Dr. Rebecca Hunter, a rough and ready quantum physicist with a natural air and character enough for us to buy into that genius status. That isn't on show in 098, where she's Prof. Sarah Hunter-Gibson, played capably but without any real authority. She feels far more like a project manager who knows how to deliver but has no real knowledge to go any deeper. In 099, where she's Science Director Anastasia Hunter, she ought to be as callous as she is intelligent, but she comes over more as prissy and that unfortunately deflates her power somewhat. The actor is Abigail Tartellin, making her debut as a lead in a feature, after a supporting role in *The Butterfly Tattoo* and the other sort of parts that show up early in an actor's career. She's promising but this complexity was beyond her at this point.

In each of these universes, she's running experiments in quantum tunnelling using a machine known as Q. In 097, the quirky, slapdash version of modern Britain, it's clearly under the radar, given that Dr. Hunter is her own test subject, using black market pharmaceuticals and an illegal botnet. In 098, Prof. Hunter-Gibson is demonstrating the Casimir Effect that allows parallel universes to interact to a university class using overtly advanced technology; here, the Q unit is an unseen biological supercomputer with the expected melodious female voice. Over in 099, Science Director Hunter is running a state-sanctioned biocomputer by hooking up human livestock.

As you can imagine, these worlds are highly delineated. 097 is believably natural with kludged together tech and relaxed, down to earth characters, while 098 is clean, slick and polite and overlaid with CGI. 099 is shot in muted colours that approach black and white, with radation exclusion zones, severe uniforms, mutations, famines, statues, commissars, the cold war era works.

Each of these universes shares a few other key players. Closest in each is the man who assists the respective leads and built the respective Q machines. He's Matt, Matthew and Mateus, played by Damian Hayes, the son of the much loved Melvyn Hayes, of *It Ain't Half Hot Mum* fame. While Tarttelin is more obvious and has a particularly strong presence in 097, Hayes remains more consistent across the parallel universes. His delineation appears to be through a moral compass; his versions are good, evil and bland, depending on the universe, but he's always capable and clearly ready to be more important than he seems. He's also the most overt seventies *Doctor Who* character. Also present is Dave, David and Dmitri, played by Alan Convy, who is the black market dealer in 097, the husband (visible by video link from his space station, no less) in 098 and the naysaying pharmacologist in 099. Behind them all is Theodore, Theo and Fyodor, the establishment figure in each universe, played reliably by Roger Harding.

That's a lot of setup for a feature and we surely have to pay attention or something will slip past us and confuse us later. Of course, there's more than that to come, as Bowen and Hardy start to play with the framework they've built and have these characters interact outside their own universe.

When I first saw *Triple Hit*, at the International Horror & Sci-Fi Film Festival in 2011, some of it felt highly reminiscent of where the TV show *Fringe* was starting to go. However, while it most closely resembles the third season of *Fringe*, it actually both predates it and goes a step further, adding a third parallel universe to the mix; *Fringe* worked with only a pair of them. Some of the interactions between characters felt similar, as did the collisions between universes, especially with icons shifting from one to another, like the vast statue of Stalin or the airships suddenly appearing in the recognisable United Kingdom. Obviously, this picture didn't have the luxury of a 22 episode season to flesh out its ideas, just the usual hour and a half.

While *Triple Hit* predates the similar seasons of *Fringe*, it does make a few deliberate nods to classic sci-fi television; my favourite was when Dr. Hunter meets Science Director Hunter in 099, at a rather tense moment, immediately takes a shot at the old two Kirks routine and fails utterly. This is appropriate, because the whole film feels like it would fit better on television than in a movie theatre, especially with some of where it decides to go towards the end. I think of the film rather like a well written six episode story of the classic *Doctor Who*, that plays with scientific concepts in a clever way but nonetheless manages to wrap itself up suspiciously quickly and, in doing so, transforms a new character into a new companion. Of course, there's no Doctor here, his role taken by a little and large double act of men in black by the names of Officers Slip and Hand, effectively parallel universe cops, tasked with retrieving Dr. Hunter for interdimensional trespassing and cleaning up the mess she's inadvertently caused.

Slip and Hand are engaging characters, though hilariously they're not played by the expected jobbing actors who usually filled such quintessentially seventies sci-fi roles on TV. Mr. Slip is Tony Holmes, who left acting for academia and currently serves as the Geographic Information Systems Officer for Warwickshire County Council. I'm glad Bowen talked him back into doing this one. Mr. Hand is a bouncer turned poet called Stephen Steinhaus, who fronts the enticingly named Dr. Teeth Big Band and has an MPhil degree in Shakespeare Studies. I adore these backgrounds, which are at once utterly unexpected but somehow perfect for the roles they play. As we find, Alpha Station hires the best from the most unlikely sources, and they get the job done. That they appear as a British TV version of the double act of Bob Hoskins and Derrick O'Connor in Terry Gilliam's *Brazil* is icing on the cake. I kept wishing that Steinhaus had ignored the dialogue he was given here in the way O'Connor did to mimic his partner's lines instead. That would have been priceless.

How you'll receive *Triple Hit* is probably going to depend on how you approach it. It's not a blockbuster with $200m and a major studio behind it; it's a story based film that does a lot with a little, elevating it from the usual indie fare and explaining why it's done well on the festival circuit. It doesn't have the sort of awesome effects that improve every summer, but it does capably enough; some are good and some are really good but a few are still notably flat. Unfortunately the final one is the worst, which won't help naysayers to leave the film well. There are minor technical downsides: sound that occasionally echoes a little, a bad wound effect here or a poorly choreographed fight there. A few lines are lost in transitions. I also noticed a few little details that rang untrue second time through; such as why a genius scientist would say something redundant like "threshold limit" or why an apparently callous science director would look away during an injection, but its story is, at least, rather more ambitious than the dreck Hollywood tends to conjure up.

Mostly it needed a stronger set of actors than it found. The story is ambitious and notably complex, so needed an insanely talented cast to sell each of the parallel universes and the characters they play in them. It has a talented cast, far more so than some of the reviews that I've read might suggest, but they're not experienced enough to meet the challenge fully. This renders the film capable rather than stunning and it needed that extra push to really make a difference. Abigail Tarttelin in particular could be much worse than she is and she really doesn't deserve the flak she's received at IMDb, especially given that her performance as the main lead, the one in parallel universe 097, is by far her strongest, but it's fair to say that she could have been much better too.

Really, the same goes for the movie as a whole. It's a refreshing ride through parallel universe shenanigans, story based but fast paced and action oriented. I've seen better, but I've seen a heck of a lot worse too and I'd certainly watch it again.

The International Horror & Sci-Fi Film Festival

2011

Showcase Features

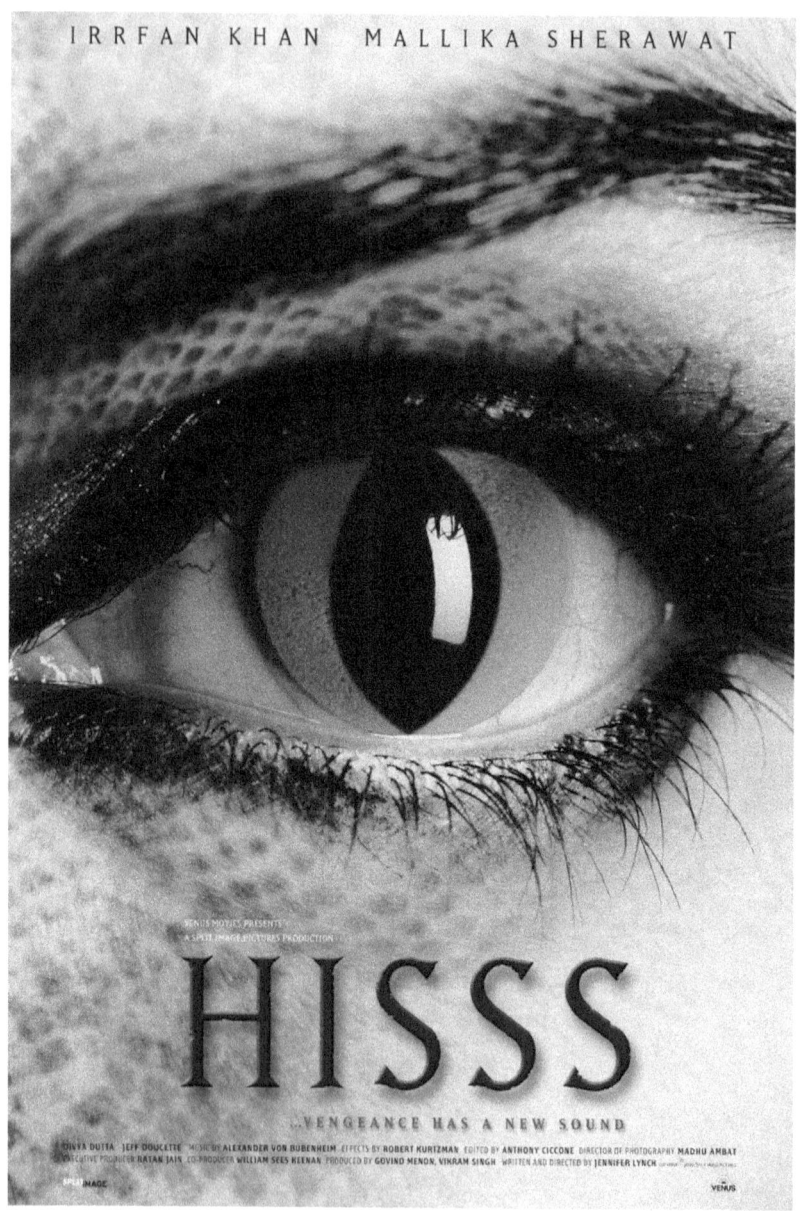

Hisss (2010)

Director: Jennifer Chambers Lynch
Writer: Jennifer Chambers Lynch, with dialogue by Gulfam Khan
Stars: Mallika Sherawat, Irrfan Khan, Jeff Doucette, Divya Dutta, Raman Trika, Mahmood Babai and Laxmi Bai

It's a little depressing that, until this film, my only experience of Jennifer Chambers Lynch's directorial talent was from an episode of *Warehouse 13*, especially given that she began learning her trade on the sets of her father, David Lynch, as far back as being a P.A. on 1986's *Blue Velvet*.

Her debut as a director, *Boxing Helena*, based on her own script, was an unmitigated disaster, if the press and legal activity are to be trusted, and it took fifteen years for her to take a second shot. Perhaps because *Surveillance* was well received, albeit with many detractors, she was soon attached to *Nagin* in 2008 as both writer and director. It's an unusual movie about a nagin, or snake woman, that would be shot in five languages in India with a mostly native cast, Jeff Doucette the notable exception.

It finally saw release in 2010 under the horrendous title of *Hisss*, but in nowhere near the form that Lynch wanted. Far better received was a documentary by Penny Vozniak, *Despite the Gods*, about Lynch's uphill struggle to make the film.

I haven't seen *Despite the Gods* yet, but I have seen the trailer and read the press kit and it looks like a fascinating journey through the deterioration of a project "doomed from the start" with a subject who is "the kind of natural performer documakers dream of."

There's no doubt that any film would suffer from what *Hisss* experienced (a technician strike and a cyclone, for starters), but the biggest reason for the mess it became is surely the clash between western and Indian styles of filmmaking that led to Lynch's part in proceedings deteriorating from director to cheerleader. Of course, none of these can be used as an excuse; the film is what it is and it has to stand on its own merits.

What it eventually turned out to be is an odd picture indeed, an insubstantial and convenient set of B-movie clichés elevated by scenes of cinematic bliss, especially in its many outdoor scenes of ethereal beauty. Shots in the jungle feel like meditative art but scenes in the city are more like routine, lowest common denominator stuff.

We begin with a prologue that's edited like a trailer, with many moments to draw us in, but also lots of fades, hints and soaring music. We're in ancient India, "a time when legends were created to explain the unknown", with an overblown narration to fill western audiences in on the "shapeshifting cobra goddess, the nagin" and telegraph the entire plot, because we just know that this is going to become one of the sort of lessons that the ignorant are ever doomed to repeat.

The key here is the naagmani, "a stone of immortality" carried within the nagin, which is bound to cause trouble. Naturally, the narrator explains how and why because we're surely too dense to figure it out. "Many a man out of sickness or greed has tried to otain the naagmani by holding her lover for ransom, ignorant of the vengeance she would bring to both guilty and innocent." Ah yes. That trouble. "For then it is learned that only gods have the power to give or take, to create or destroy." Can we guess where this is going after five minutes?

Enter George States, an obnoxious American with stage three brain cancer and six months to live, who has hired a trio of guides to find him the nagin and her mate in the Ghats Jungle. He's not a subtle man, as his opening lines suggest: "I may have brain cancer but I can still piss like a racehorse. Up and at 'em, dotheads, it's snake huntin' time." It's no surprise to find him killing an unwilling assistant and making faces at the captured nagin in its tank.

So far, so awful, a blatant bunch of clichés and unimpressive CGI; the snakes look pretty good up close but pretty terrible waving around in the distance. Doucette makes a memorable villain, but he's as blatant as blatant can be, apparently doing everything he can to make sure that we can't possibly find a single shred of sympathy for his condition. Meanwhile back in town, police inspector Vinkram Gupta prepares to go to work, even though his wife's locked in the bathroom losing their baby. He underwhelms from moment one, both as an actor and a character.

Fortunately, it's at this point that we start to see some interesting visuals. While the townsfolk of Naichi celebrate Holi, the beginning of spring, by spraying paint everywhere and dancing in the multicoloured chaos, the nagin turns into a woman. Her transformation is far better than the dancing CGI snakes could ever have suggested, morphing through both physical and CGI effects. She sprouts legs like a crocodile, then contorts into a woman in a snakeskin suit, with excellent contact lenses and a wild flicking tongue, finally emerging as a beautiful and naked Indian woman, who swallows crocodile eggs whole just like a snake.

The actress is Mallika Sherawat, a Bollywood star known both for her bold characters on screen and her bold ambition to break beyond India's borders by appearing in the Chinese film, *The Myth*, and the American *Politics of Love*, even a Bruno Mars music video. The choral accompaniment hints at what Lynch may have aimed for with her "admiration of sensual, sexual female bravery".

These outdoor scenes in the Ghats Jungle are impressive, artistically shot and beautifully framed in well selected locations. They jar with the rest, which is maybe the point, the city perhaps being seen by this goddess as an unwelcome encroachment on nature.

Their clash is reflected in the lead characters: the routine cop in his routine office, the emphatically unlikeable villain in his empty warehouse lair and the sensual goddess finding her way slowly towards civilisation. Even when she gets there, she's the point of attention. There's a wonderful scene where she strips naked and climbs a lamppost to sleep by the light; it begins like soft porn but doesn't end that way. It's beautifully shot and a credit to the film, just like her first scene in the city, where she falls under the spell of a snakecharmer, her undulations matching his. Of course, they have to lower the tone, by having a pair of pissant rapists entice her into their house to have their wicked ways with her, only for the tables to be turned in precisely the way you might expect.

The portrayal of the Indian characters, which is to say almost all of them, feels notably poor to me, not only one dimensional but stereotypical. The only exception is the cop, who has potential but is so underplayed by Irrfan Khan that he's lost in the background, thoroughly inconsequential in a film about female power.

He's another established Bollywood actor who has spread his

wings further afield, playing major roles in films as well known as *Slumdog Millionnaire*, *The Amazing Spider-Man* and *Life of Pi*. His admirable restraint is sadly not mirrored in the supporting cast, especially his new partner, Navin, who is an annoying stereotype, incessantly jabbering in polite, heavily accented English with a stupid grin on his face. We also see far more overt acting as a succession of vile men rape, beat and abuse women, then receive their violent reward at the metaphorical hands of the nagin. The recurrent theme seems to be that all Indian men want either sex or money by force, except the cop, who doesn't feel like an Indian character.

Another recurrent theme is surely closer to what Lynch aimed for, namely the empowerment of women. Beyond the all-powerful monster of the film being a goddess, she manifests for much of it as a beautiful young lady, clearly the personification of beauty with power. There's a particular abiding visual of the burqa clad nagin chasing the snake charmer through the streets of Naichi. It feels like the epitome of female empowerment, with the nagin caught frequently in slow motion in what could only be described as superhero poses.

Even Insp. Gupta's mother-in-law, for most of the film a bizarre character who can't acknowledge him as anything but an ugly woman whom nobody will look at, eventually finds a purpose in an important way that grants her power too. It's a strange shift for her, given that she's presumably the comic relief of the piece, somewhat like a bloated Roman senator played by John Belushi in drag, but it underlines the power of the goddess and by extension the power of women.

There's a potentially great picture in here, but it's buried so deeply that we're only given periodic hints at its wonder. What sits on the surface is a film so annoyingly routine that we keep wanting to give up on it, only to be drawn back in by another blissful visual treat.

If only the story hadn't been so incessantly convenient. Guess who ends up with the nagin after she's reported to the police as "very distressed"? He takes her home so that his mourning wife can take care of her as therapy for both of them. Now guess whose mother worships the snake goddess, praying to her frequently for grandchildren. Isn't it convenient how all these varied plot strands coalesce in one household?

I wonder what would have happened if Lynch had kept the power to make the film she wanted. Maybe that will come clear when we finally get to see *Despite the Gods* and gain a better understanding of the balance between Lynch's obvious strengths and weaknesses. In the meantime, this picture is best approached with all due caution.

You know, like a nagin.

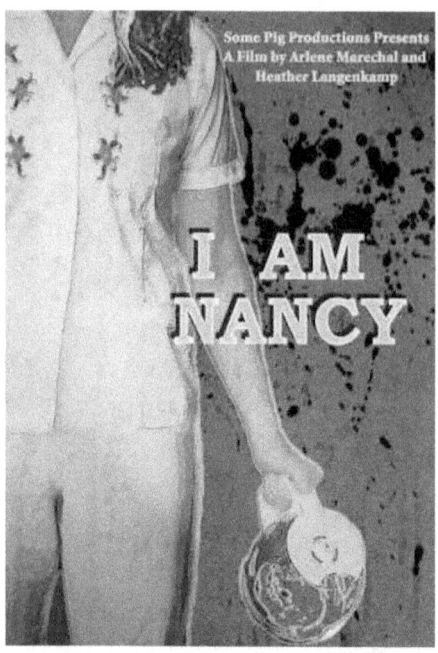

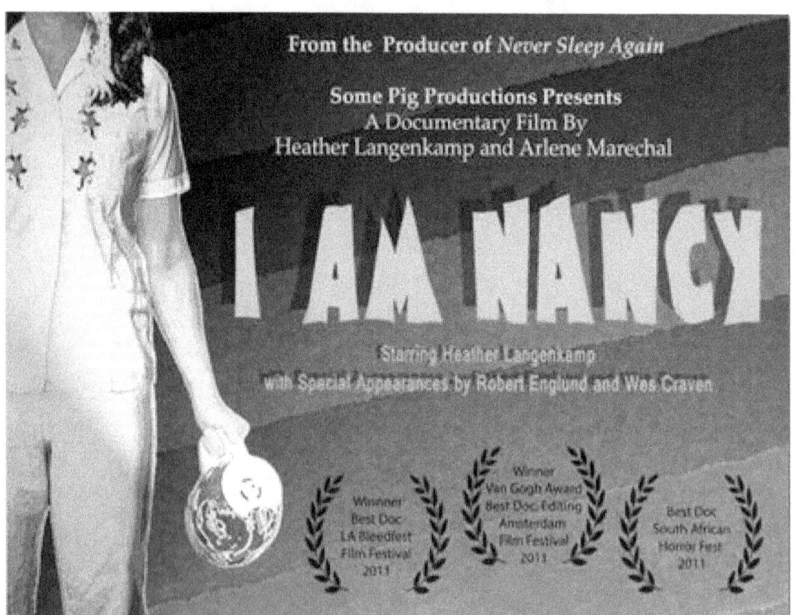

I am Nancy (2011)

Director: Arlene Marechal
Star: Heather Langenkamp

I missed *I am Nancy* at the 2011 festival for a variety of reasons, but I wasn't heartbroken about it as it really didn't appear to be a particularly important documentary, even if its subject was there in person as a special guest.

Sure, Heather Langenkamp played a pivotal character in modern horror, Nancy Thompson, the heroine of *A Nightmare on Elm Street*, but she hadn't done a heck of a lot else. She returned to this franchise twice, reprising her character in *A Nightmare on Elm Street 3: Dream Warriors* and starring as herself in the later meta version, *New Nightmare*, but didn't spin that into other work. By this point, she'd appeared in only eight other pictures over almost three decades. Counting screen time alone, she worked more on the TV show *Just the Ten of Us*, a spinoff from *Growing Pains*, than the entire rest of her film career combined. She'd shifted mostly off screen into make up effects work, running the special effects shop AFX Studio with her husband, David Anderson.

So when I finally caught up with *I am Nancy*, I found that I ran through a little of what Langenkamp ran through while making the movie, which was an enlightening experience.

It's a surprising documentary, which has a massively different approach to 2010's far more traditional *Never Sleep Again: The Elm Street Legacy*, which Langenkamp narrated and executive produced. That one was an exhaustive four hour sweep through the entire franchise to coincide with its reboot after a quarter of a century. This looks very specifically at the character of Nancy Thompson and at Langenkamp herself, as she reengages with the character and the franchise just ahead of its silver anniversary and struggles with her part in its legacy.

It's a far more personal approach that prompts the film to appear to be insubstantial fluff for most of its running time, but there's substance waiting to creep in as it moves forward. It even has a story arc, as we follow Langenkamp on what could fairly be called a voyage of discovery without hyperbole.

After a well set up opening, in which Freddy Krueger pops in the VHS of *A Nightmare on Elm Street* for us to see video clips of how he's affected popular culture, and the opening credits, which unfold neatly through the assistance of Langenkamp, her silver Sharpie and a set of 8x10s, we settle in to the first of three acts.

The first one initially seems to be the most insubstantial, but it's highlighting how far out of the picture she'd actually got. We're at the superbly named Clandestine Rabbit, where a tattoo artist called Twelve is inking Freddy Krueger onto the leg of a horror nut, Mikey Rotella. No doubt you're wondering why I'm including all this detail, but it's to highlight how I was wondering why the picture includes all this detail as it was doing so. Initially it appears that it's only because Rotella works at AFX Studio and thus has a direct connection to Langenkamp, his boss, who pops in to watch. Only later do we realise that it's the quirk of circumstance that brought her into contact with the legacy of her character.

In and amongst meandering discussions with Rotella and others, we get to why the entire *It Began with a Tattoo* section is included. It's just to point out that everyone in horror fandom cares about Freddy while nobody cares about Nancy. Like duh. To Langenkamp's credit, her disappointment is clear but not overt and she merely comes off a little whiny as she asks questions like whether Rotella would follow up with a Nancy tattoo and gets awkward silences in response.

This sort of thing continues on throughout the film, but especially this early third, as she goes out on tour to celebrate 25 years of *A Nightmare on Elm Street* with six conventions in three countries. We continue to wonder how substantial this material really is as we discover a lot more about conventions in general than we do about either Heather or Nancy and very little of it is remotely new to anyone who's ever attended one. Do we really care that some dedicated fans fly out from Kuwait to see the stars, or that one man sold plasma for eight weeks to finance his trip?

There's a lot more character here than substance, but the character is on the other side of the table to what we might expect in a film called *I am Nancy*. Langenkamp appears to be discovering this world or at least questioning it for the first time, while joking that her career might have been more substantial had Nancy's wardrobe been more revealing, but that's about it. Her character shows mostly in how she handles the disappointing answers to her questions about Nancy's, and by extension her, impact on the world and in how the editing of the movie demonstrates a notable sense of humour.

There's a running joke about how the merchandising is clearly centred around Freddy Krueger, whether it's brought to her table to sign or whether she's hilariously asking the event vendors. There's a wonderful moment where she finally discovers a Nancy toy, the 2008 one from Mezco that depicts the famous bath scene in the first movie, only for the vendor to point out that it's discontinued and the editing to cut into a comedy skit.

And so on it goes. Freddy gets the merchandise; Robert Englund gets the applause and the lines. Nancy may have been an important character in the original film and the series, but Langenkamp seems to be an extra in the minds of the fans. To be fair, so are many of the other celebrities manning tables but this isn't their film.

What unfolds is fundamentally sad and depressing, but lightened considerably by the clever editing and Langenkamp's frequent quips, such as when she suggests to one attendee that her signing a Freddy action figure may decrease its value. These moments are often simultaneously funny and sad, especially as there's a truth in the quips; Langenkamp is only half kidding. I enjoyed these scenes, which are often personable and engaging, but, even as I enjoyed them, I wondered why we were being consistently hammered over the head with the same point. We get it! Few remember the heroes in horror movies; the villains are the iconic ones who return time after time and so dominate our memories.

Ironically, for perhaps three quarters of an hour, Langenkamp does little to suggest that we'll remember her here either, in a movie which, after all, is supposedly all about her. We're more likely to remember some of the fans who come up to her table, even if they often do so because they have nothing else to do while they wait for their number to come up in Robert Englund's line. Some are memorable because they're odd, like the girl who takes pictures of herself with celery or the guy whose girl is moving out at that very moment; others are memorable because they're different, like the deaf girl or the amputee in a wheelchair. Again, their scenes are enjoyable, highlighting the diversity of conventions and breaking the stereotypical view of them, but they don't seem to have any real purpose in this film. At least some of these scenes are phrased in an interesting way, such as the neatly edited responses to the question of how old people were when they first saw *A Nightmare on Elm Street*. How low can they go?

The substance finally starts to arrive in the third act, as Langenkamp talks with other key players in the series, such as its star, Robert Englund, and its creator, Wes Craven.

Englund is lucid and interesting, though grounded enough to highlight the nerd sin his former co-star is committing by ripping open her new toy purchases so he can sign the figures rather than the boxes. Craven, who wrote and directed the original *A Nightmare on Elm Street* and whose involvement in the ensuing series was restricted to the same three movies Langenkamp starred in, is still more insightful, expounding on the philosophy that underpinned the picture.

There's even a neat anecdote to explain Nancy's derivation; watching an earlier Wes Craven movie, *Swamp Thing*, his daughter Jessica was upset that Adrienne Barbeau tripped while being chased. She asked him why girls always tripped and he took it to heart, writing a strong female hero for *A Nightmare on Elm Street* who didn't trip because she was able to stand up and face truth and fear. It's a feminist reading of an anomalous character in '80s horror.

And here, finally, is where this documentary finds its feet and adds some perspective to all that's gone before. One of the toughest human truths, explains Craven, is that you can only save yourself and that individualistic spirit is what both Nancy Thompson and Heather Langenkamp epitomise in these movies. This is a far different legacy to that of Freddy Krueger but it's a fundamentally more important one, as we soon see manifested in the form of Jude, the convention goer in a wheelchair.

Parts of her story are reminiscent of Freddy's (she came back from being clinically dead after a car accident that left her in need of skin grafts), but she turns out to be the personification of Nancy instead. The surprisingly cheerful take she has on a horrific event brings tears to Langenkamp, as she listens to the mirror image of her character, summing up what Nancy Thompson's legacy is in a single, telling, emphatic sentence: "You just have to face it, man." Langenkamp has described it since as "a mantra of strength".

This scene has clearly stayed with her and she's called it out in interviews. "It's the best part," she explained to Steven Murray at BellaOnline, "It's the very, very best part."

Not only is it the best part but it's precisely what I am Nancy needed. In one scene, Jude gives the entire film a purpose and explains to us why the structure was so strange. You can't begin a voyage of discovery with the discovery; you have to find a starting point and work your way to it. So it went for Heather Langenkamp, a minor celebrity interested in finding her part in the legacy of a film she made decades earlier and which refuses to die. She doesn't find what she wants, though perhaps she finds what she expects, until we get to Jude and everything she's learned up until that point is rocked. No, Nancy is never going to get the attention that Freddy gets, but she has changed people in startling ways and the title of the film gains a double meaning. It's true that Langenkamp is Nancy, but as she finds, she's not the only one.

I am Nancy, indeed.

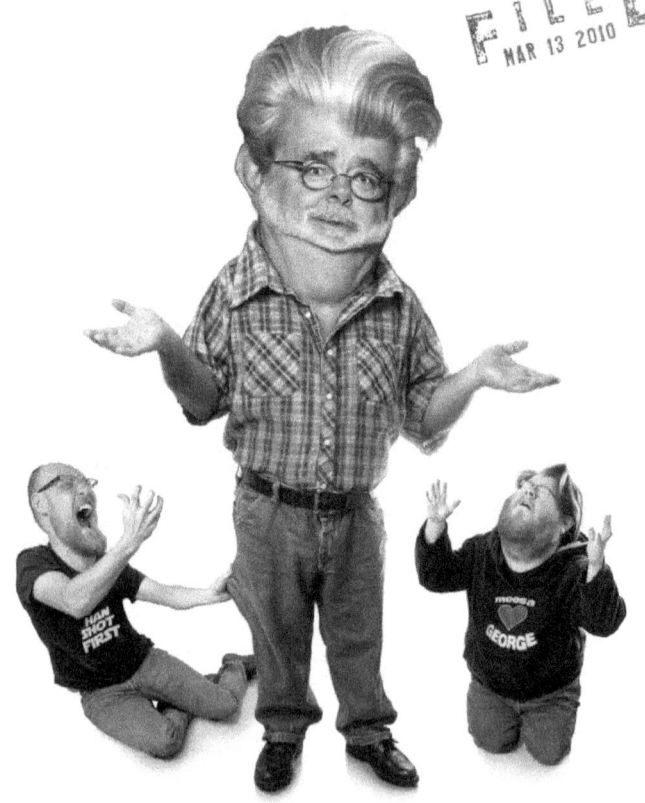

The People vs. George Lucas (2010)

Director: Alexandre O. Philippe
Writer: Alexander O. Philippe

One of the most unconventional documentaries on film, *The People vs. George Lucas* isn't successful at all it aims to do but it's an interesting ride nonetheless and it's only going to become more relevant over the coming decades.

Right now, many of the arguments that Alexandre O. Philippe, the writer and director, hauls out of the nerd forums or convention panels to which they've long been relegated are, for the most part, only about *Star Wars*, details that only the most dedicated fanatics really care about. Yet, as technology progresses and a wider set of filmmakers, distributors and copyright holders continue along the slippery slopes set in motion by George Lucas, this will become a much wider issue. These are already becoming much wider issues and these arguments will only become more relevant and more important to mainstream culture and the ongoing fight to preserve it for the public domain. In many ways, Philippe is documenting the easy to discount tip of an iceberg that will over time become a serious danger to how we will be able to collectively interact with culture.

The biggest problem his film has is that it's far from impartial. It's not really propaganda, but it finds itself unable to stay in the middle ground because there is no middle ground. There's the side of the public, the consumers, the creators of culture and then there's the side of the corporations, which exist entirely to make money off art.

Before *Star Wars*, when George Lucas was an auteur filmmaker, shooting features like *THX 1138* and *American Graffiti*, he was on the same side as us. He was a lucky film nerd who was able to play with the biggest and best electric train set of them all, to paraphrase Orson Welles, which, of course, is Hollywood. After *Star Wars*, however, he gradually became the thing he most hated: he became the corporation. In 1988, when Ted Turner was releasing colorised versions of classic black and white films, Lucas testified to the

United States Congress to push for legislation that would preserve cultural artefacts like films so that the public, who eventually owns them, would continue to be able to see them as they were intended.

He was lucid and convincing. "A copyright is held in trust by its owner until it ultimately reverts to public domain," he outlined. "American works of art belong to the American public; they are part of our cultural history." He even went so far as to suggest that, "People who alter or destroy works of art and our cultural heritage for profit or as an exercise of power are barbarians."

Yet his words weren't heeded, nor were those of many of his esteemed colleagues. While the U.S. did eventually recognise the Berne Convention for the Protection of Literary and Artistic Works, it did not apply it to films because of the inherently collaborative nature of their creation. Therefore, rather ironically, his failure to persuade the American government to protect motion pictures is the only reason that he was then subsequently able not only to fundamentally change the *Star Wars* films whenever he wanted but also to suppress their original versions, thus effectively changing history.

Unfortunately, George Lucas himself only appears here in archive footage. He is not present to put his new case against his old self.

Like the *Star Wars* films, it's phrased like a trilogy. The first episode, *A Nerf Herder from Modesto*, is by far the most conventional, outlining where *Star Wars* came from and how George Lucas got to that point. It's also the least substantial, skimming the surface to get through the material quickly.

Where it starts to find validity is in explaining how and why the first *Star Wars* movie was fundamentally different from anything else that had come before. To do so, it casts its net particularly wide, hauling in writers like Joe Haldeman and Neil Gaiman; the editor of *Empire* and the director of *Troops*; fans from Spain, Japan or the UK; a very wide range of interview subjects indeed. The key, it appears, is the unprecedented merchandising, which transformed it from merely a feature film into what Henry Jenkins describes as "participatory culture". The clips from fan films and productions, old and new, obscure to *Star Wars Uncut*, are another plus point, as they all serve as a substantial underline to the point that Philippe is making.

Unfortunately and inevitably for one short segment in an hour and a half feature, it merely scratches the surface. I'd like to have seen more than teasing frames of Lucas's early short films. I'd like to have seen a good deal more than one line of dialogue about his relationship with Francis Ford Coppola. I'd like to have seen more about his struggles with the mainstream studio system and his part in the New Hollywood of the 1970s, but that's a different movie.

It seems fair to forgive Philippe for avoiding an odd detour into territory that deserves its own documentary (and already has it, in the 2003 adaptation of Peter Biskind's excellent book, *Easy Riders, Raging Bulls*). However, on the flipside, he really can't then get away with extending his sweep of *Star Wars* fan films into *Raiders of the Lost Ark: The Adaptation*. I'm very thankful to him for making that production known to the world at large, me included, but it stands out as footage that should have been better used by more to the point material. It's far from the only instance of that here too.

If there's material in the first section that seems superfluous, that's not the case with the second. When Philippe introduces the New Edition of *A New Hope* that Lucas released to theatres in 1997 in *The Great Tinkerer*, the aptly named second section, things get very serious very quickly and *The People vs. George Lucas* suddenly finds itself.

While the archive footage Lucas pushes this as what he'd always aimed to do but couldn't because he didn't have the money twenty years earlier, everyone else in the film unites in opposition. Many are on board with the updating of the special effects or the fleshing out of backgrounds with new technology, which is what the publicity for this anniversary edition pushed, though others highlight how disrespectful this is to the original artists who won Oscars for their special effects work in 1977. However, the publicity didn't mention other changes and that's when the united front forms. "The other versions will disappear," Lucas said outright in an interview with *American Cinematographer* magazine and everyone hated him for it.

Every since that release, the fanboys have debated the pointless new scene to introduce Jabba the Hutt and decried the change that Han no longer shot first. The mainstream public laughs at this stuff, what an interview subject describes as "super nerd nitpicking over something that's not important." But it is important. As another retorts, "It's not geeky nitpicking when you go into the heart of a character and you do something that changes that character's dynamic. That's destroying story. That's betrayal."

I was especially taken by the comments of Steven Vrooman, an Associate Professor of Communication Studies at Texas Lutheran University. His take is that Lucas made a fan film, oddly because it's a fan film based on his own work. In changing his own material, he explains, "George Lucas took away your sandbox, he took away your colouring book and said, 'No, no no! It belongs to me again and I'm going to continue to rewrite my stories.'" Many comments stand out here, like "It's going to take the edge of *Star Wars* and make it a safer, dumber place." In other words, it's revisionism.

And here's where the film really ceases to be *The People vs. George Lucas* and becomes 1988 George Lucas vs. 1997 George Lucas and all the many interview subjects who speak for "The People" become redundant. If the man himself testified to Congress to stop people like he would become doing what he would go on to do, we really don't need the reinforcement.

I enjoyed it anyway, of course, because Philippe edits down crazy amounts of hours of footage to golden nuggets like, "Thanks to Lucas, VHS is still alive." One speaker here gloriously underlines the disconnect between the law and the moral high ground by explaining that fans created digital files from laserdiscs and then released them for free online. "Certainly this is illegal," he points out, "but from a moral standpoint they are preserving our cultural heritage." And with a Lucasfilm letter stating that the original negatives were destroyed to make the New Edition, Philippe wisely quotes 1988 Lucas citing this precise future. "Our cultural history must not be allowed to be rewritten," he testified.

This second section is so strong that it deserves to be its own documentary. In fact, it deserves to be this documentary, but it's sadly only a small part of it. It especially deserves to be this documentary because the discussion in how this shift in Lucas's morals happened leads to a natural conclusion, the matching bookend to the one that began the story with his early days. We see here that the change in his outlook coincided with him becoming the Man, the Machine, the Corporation that he always hated.

Rather than keep his burgeoning career as a massively important filmmaker going, he instead transformed into "a producer, an entrepreneur", "the evil genius of marketing", the end result of what inevitably happened when "the storyteller went away and the businessman took over."

We've now seen Lucas's story arc, his rise, his success and his fall, echoing Anakin to Vader, but Philippe has a different structure in mind that really prompts the beginning of a new documentary. His pivot, almost to the precise second, is the announcement of *The Phantom Menace*.

Don't get me wrong, I enjoyed the second half of this picture, especially the early parts that accompany the insane hype that surrounded the release of *Episode I*. It's tough to imagine anything that underlines the success of *Star Wars* more than people lining up around the block to buy tickets to films they don't care about and that they won't even watch, entirely so that they can see the two minute trailer to *The Phantom Menace*.

That's as eye-opening to me, writing in the age of YouTube, as the realisation that back in 1977, an underestimation of demand meant that fans bought empty boxes that would be later populated by action figures when the toy companies actually caught up with the production demand.

It's frankly hilarious to watch those who travelled from continent to continent to see *The Phantom Menace* being asked in line, "What are you going to do if the movie really sucks?" That it wouldn't was a given, an article of faith. People were seriously going to enjoy a moment that they would be able to tell their kids about. How's that going now?

There are moments of substance in this third section, *Revenge of the Geeks*, about how people went back to see *Episode 1* time and time again to come to terms with their abuse, to convince themselves that they had somehow missed a point first time around or to desperately hold on to the possibility that they might just come to like it, but mostly it's fluff compared to *The Great Tinkerer* section. In fact, the best parts of the second half emphasise or enhance it. Talk about Jar Jar Binks and racial stereotyping, mitichlorians and the shift from spirituality to biology, those sorts of slaps in the face pale when compared to the talk about control, like Lucas stating in interviews that he doesn't want anyone else messing with his stuff. What Philippe achieves here is to remind us that even *The Star Wars Holiday Special* should be preserved, as it isn't merely George Lucas's history, it's also Jefferson Starship's history, Art Carney's history, even American history.

And, don't just take that from me or from Philippe. Take it from George Lucas himself, who testified as such to Congress. That irony is what riddles this documentary through and deserves to be shouted from the rafters.

Perhaps Philippe should have made a real trilogy instead of a standalone documentary. As it happens, he is currently working on a sequel, *The People vs. George Lucas: Episode II*, sparked by the sale of Lucasfilm to Disney, which will focus on the question, unimaginable at the time he made this film, of what the *Star Wars* franchise will look like without Lucas at the helm. It's very possible that, by the time we see it, some of the concerns highlighted in this first film will have been addressed.

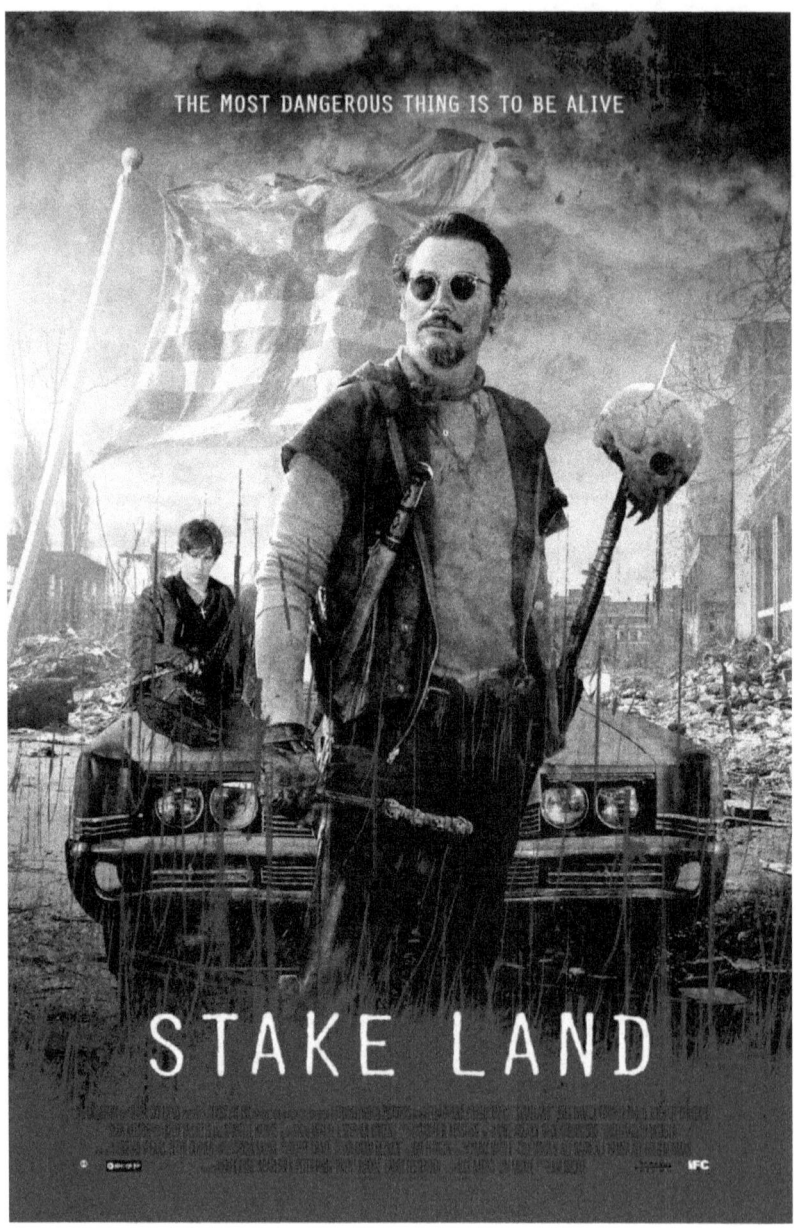

Stake Land (2010)

Director: Jim Mickle
Writers: Nick Damici and Jim Mickle
Stars: Nick Damici, Connor Paolo, Michael Cerveris, Sean Nelson, Kelly McGillis and Danielle Harris

No, this isn't a vampire version of *Zombieland*, a much more prominent film with a much bigger budget that was released the year before. However there are similarities if we ignore the tone and the money.

At $625,000, this didn't cost much more than the rounding error introduced if I cited *Zombieland* as costing $24m instead of $23.6m, while the tone is utterly serious, with no Bill Murray cameo, no Twinkie search and no David Letterman-esque list of rules. Otherwise, it might feel familiar, as the plot has a young man, taken under the wing of a pseudonymous anti-hero experienced in the art of hunting monsters, narrating their travels through the remnants of America in search of somewhere safe where they can live free of the plague that's taken down the nation. On the road, they encounter a number of other survivors, good and bad, who shape their journey. *Zombieland* would feel like a spoof of *Stake Land*, if only it hadn't arrived first, while its more serious twin, *The Walking Dead*, didn't launch until a month after this film. Of course, the comic book series which that show was adapted from predate this too.

Even though this is a vampire picture, I was surprised to find that it started with vampires, or at least a vampire hunter, as the religious subtext is so prominent that I expected to find that the genre side grew out of it. The writers, Jim Mickle (who also directed) and Nick Damici (who stars as that pseudonymous anti-hero), had served the same roles on a post-apocalyptic feature with an even lower budget in 2006.

Mulberry Street, which also avoided zombies in favour of mutant ratmen, cost only $60,000 but garnered a host of great reviews from the genre press. Eager to work together again, they thought up a web series that they could shoot on weekends for cheap and wrote forty eight-minute scripts that actor turned producer Larry Fessenden suggested should be turned into a feature instead. He strongly affected the development of the tone too, pressing Mickle to give it a heart and emphasise feelings of isolation over bloodshed. "It's a road movie and a western," he explained to the *New York Times*. "It should never be horror for horror's sake."

What came much later was the religious angle which infects the film like a virus. Initially they just aimed for something that felt real, rather than make another movie with what Mickle described to *Crave Online* as "super over-stylized over-choreographed zombie vampire action". They also wanted a strong post-9/11 feel as they remembered the way that everyone came together then rather than bicker the way they tended to do in such situations on film, but, perhaps inevitably, "the extremists come along and fuck it up."

I found the religious angle stronger than anything here because it grounds this approach. With the country they know gone, people team up to try to rebuild what they love and they often make a pretty good go of it, but they just as often want the approval of a higher power first. There's also always someone out there who takes it in another direction, often someone who got their approval from a different higher power. We hear old time gospel music before we even see a visual in this movie, so it's no surprise to find so many religious references dotted throughout and religious extremists hijacking the plot just as they try to hijack the survivors in it.

First we're introduced to the little picture. Martin, a telling name for a lead character in a vampire movie, is a young man who lives with his parents who are massacred by a vampire shortly into the apocalypse, even as the radio is explaining what's coming and they're preparing to escape it. He's saved by Mister, a passing vampire hunter who lends a hand. It shrugs off a pitchfork through the neck, a shotgun blast and a pounding by a car bonnet, but it doesn't survive the stake that Martin pounds into its heart. That's one heck of a coming of age moment for Martin, who then has to witness his father ask Mister to save him as the last words before he's taken down too. It's a bloody, horrific and traumatising wake-up call, one that's emphasised by the training opportunity that Mister gives him as we build to the opening title. He traps a vampire in the boot of his car, then dresses Martin up in American football armour and gives him a spear to defend himself. "Welcome to Stake Land, kid," he tells him as he opens the boot.

We're given no explanation of why this apocalypse came about, thrown into this new world just as Martin is. All he and Mister know is to keep travelling north, to escape the chaos that the southern states turned into. "Cults spread like wildfire," Martin tells us, "waiting for the messiah, but he never came. Death came instead. He came with teeth." North is where the possibly mythical New Eden is supposed to be, which is the only real hope they can cling to. They avoid the cities, of course, taking the back roads and spending time with the clumps of civilisation which banded together to survive. For a while they fall into a routine. They keep on northward. They pick up supplies wherever they can find them. Mister trains Martin as best he can, both combat training and survival skills. Each is as important as the other in this post-apocalyptic landscape where you can starve as easily as you can fall prey to a vampire. In fact, the numbers we see suggest that the former is even more likely than the latter.

And always there's that religious undercurrent. The shots of abandoned America are evocative ones, the location scout perhaps doing as important work as the set decorator. I'd guess that the latter is the most responsible for the little notes and signs we see everywhere, like one reading "And God Smote the World Asunder" that decorates a corpse hanging by a roadside, but they're so quintessentially southern gothic that many could well be real. In another time, so would the corpses.

We see a lot of religious people and a lot of religious signs. We see religious communities, which are usually seen in a more cynical light than those comprised of people merely banding together for the common good. The cynicism is encapsulated into Martin's observation that, "In desperate times, false Gods abound. People put their faith in the loudest preacher and hope they're right." Here, in a horror take on a western road movie, that extends to the Brotherhood, a fundamentalist militia which sees vampires as sent by God to cleanse the world for them.

When the religious subtext reaches the point where a pair of these Brotherhood nutjobs attempt to rape a nun, we can't help but believe that it's no longer a subtext, it's the text and vampires are merely a means to tell it. This nun, known only as Sister, is a key player in the film, even as she flits peripherally through it. She escapes her would be rapists when Mister kills them both without warning. Unfortunately, one of the pair turns out to be the son of Jebedia Loven, leader of the Brotherhood, which prompts the redirection of their trek north for a while.

The actress in the nun's habit is also the most famous name in the film, Nick Damici building his reputation here and Connor Paolo best known at this point for a supporting role in the TV show, *Gossip Girl*. Horror fans ought to recognise Danielle Harris, though Mickle apparently knew her more from sitcoms. Sister, however, is played by Kelly McGillis, looking more like my mum than the hot chick in *Top Gun*. This marked her return to the big screen after nine years and she brought some power with her.

Not everything is solid. Some scenes are too obviously set up, like the little girl vampire hiding upstairs in a house they stay in. Some of the effects work is obvious, such as a bloody cross carved into a back to be a homing beacon for vampires clearly not breaking the skin in the slightest. The camerawork is strong for the most part, with a lot of good composition of frame, but occasionally it aims for a gritty feel with some handheld footage that actually distracts instead of helps. Unfortunately, this tends to be married to dark scenes, which become doubly awkward, though flares do help. The pace is slow, deliberately so but with the inevitably depressing tone and the sadness inherent in Martin's narration, even when he's aiming at hopeful, it can be a little much. Strangely, the second half is slower than the first, though perhaps this is partly due to the progression of their trek north and the focusing of the dangers around them from wider, open ones to narrower, more defined ones. Some of these dangers are not surprising at all.

For the most part though, this is a capable, thoughtful and well grounded attempt to recount the zombie apocalypse without zombies and, in a major way, not even as a horror movie. The vampires aren't really villains, they're just obstacles. The real villains are the religious nutjobs, who manipulate a disaster into their own personal deliverance and, in so doing, only serve to make survival even tougher for the decent folk who try to salvage something of civilisation for the future.

Change the vampires into aliens and it's a sci-fi movie; into Apaches and it would be a straight western; into sharks and you'd have a SyFy Channel Original. It's really not a genre movie at all, merely a drama surrounding the universal quest for a better life, with a strong anti-religious undercurrent. This makes it a clear analogy for modern America, even more so than on its release four years ago.

The good news for those of us living here is that there is always hope; the bad is that happy endings aren't always what we expect. Respect is due for that observation as much as for the film.

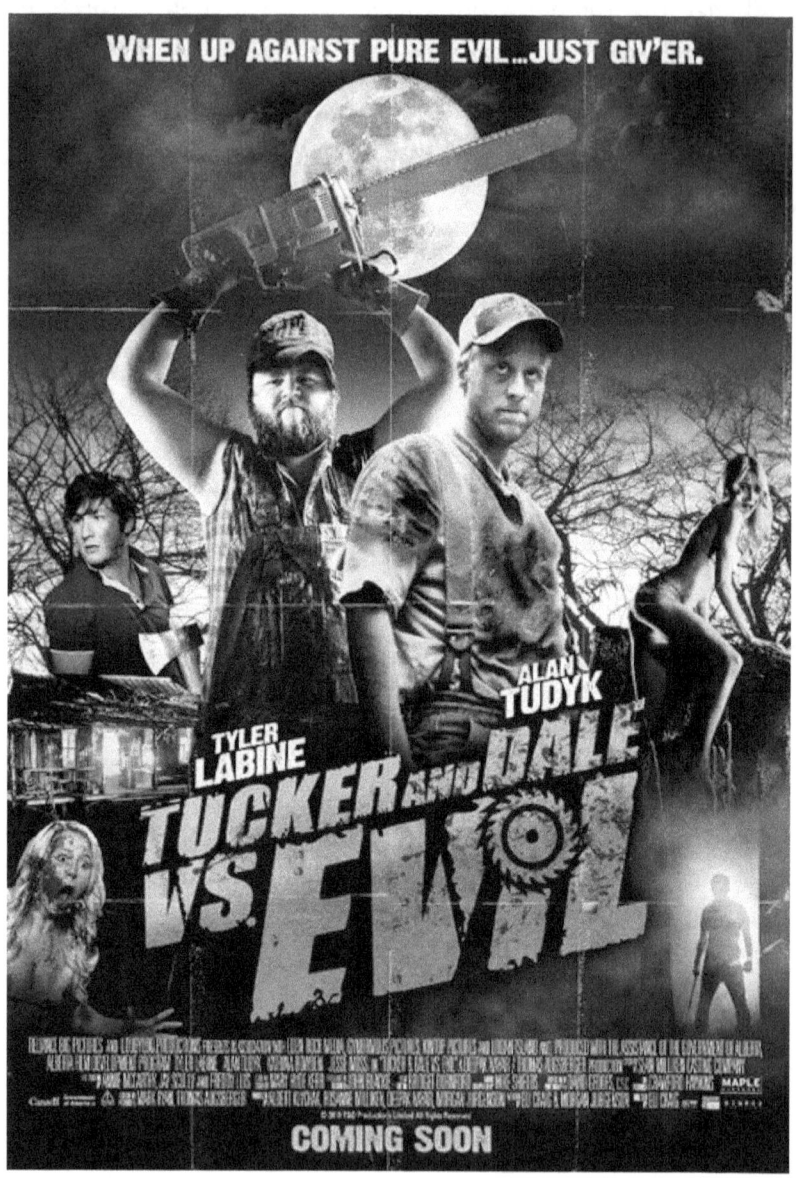

Tucker and Dale vs. Evil (2010)

Director: Eli Craig
Writers: Eli Craig and Morgan Jurgenson
Stars: Tyler Labine, Alan Tudyk, Katrina Bowden and Jesse Moss

For about five minutes, *Tucker and Dale vs. Evil* is the painfully clichéd and stereotypical nonsense I had a sneaking feeling it was going to be from the little I knew about it beforehand. Tucker and Dale are creepy rednecks passed on an Appalachian country road by a gaggle of loud college kids. You'll hardly be surprised to find that the girls are gorgeous, the guys are assholes and they're all about beer, sex and dope, not to mention bad fireside ghost stories. We've all seen this a hundred times before, down to every little detail. It's only the names that ever change, right? Allie is the lead hot chick in this version; Chad is the entitled asshole who dominates the rest of the guys from Omega Beta.

Well, what changes here is that the whole thing is turned neatly around to be a revisionist take where the hillbillies are the heroes, even if Tucker is happy to drink and drive, and the annoying college kids are... well, amazingly enough they're exactly the same as always, except for the one who becomes the villain of the piece.

It's outside Last Chance Gas that the reversal takes effect and Dale is shown to be a sympathetic lead. It's when he builds his confidence to approach the college girls and smile and laugh with a scythe in his hand that it gets funny. By the time they're pulled over by a deputy with Dale's head in Tucker's lap, it becomes priceless. Unfortunately it doesn't manage to stay there for the rest of the film because director Eli Craig, who wrote the script with Morgan Jurgenson, isn't quite sure what he really wants it to be.

This works best as the revisionist slasher movie, delightfully playing on the preconceived notions of the characters just as it played on those of the audience as it began. It works well as a comedy horror flick too, working its agreeably gory way through a progression of cleverly contrived and neatly outrageous splatstick setpieces. However, while the mix of comedy and horror works well, the mix of comedy and drama isn't as successful and the mix of comedy and romance falls somewhere in between. The eventual shift to pure parody is particularly unworthy.

Tucker and Dale are brought to life by Alan Tudyk and Tyler Labine respectively, two experienced actors who are easily able to render them sympathetic leads who nonetheless can look a little creepy whenever the script calls for some conclusion jumping. I've been a fan of Tudyk's for quite a while now, mostly from his work on major Whedonverse shows like *Firefly* and *Dollhouse* but also from as far back as *A Knight's Tale* and as obscure as the pilot episode of *Airship Dracula*, which I was able to screen at Wild Wild West Con this year. By comparison, I only knew Labine from the TV show *Reaper*, at least at this point in time. I gave up on that quickly, even though he and Ray Wise were superb; maybe if its humour had been more like the humour here, I might have stuck with it.

He and Tudyk comprise a capable double act with strong comedic timing, whether they're merely lying in the dirt or running with chainsaws. Like Kevin Bacon and Fred Ward did in *Tremors*, they go beyond the comedy to shine in the tender moments too. They dominate proceedings here, to the degree that almost everyone else in the film fades emphatically into the background just as much as the trees in the forest surrounding their new vacation home.

Allison and Chad are the only other characters to really establish themselves, the former when she's startled in the creek, falls into both the water and unconsciousness and is rescued by Dale, and the latter when he perceives this as a kidnapping and reason enough to spark a bloody trail of vengeance.

Katrina Bowden is an endearing leading lady, enough to remind me that I should get round to *Piranha DD*, but Allie really isn't a good part. With the romance angle sidelined into being a given, she's mostly restricted to being a MacGuffin, the reason why everyone in the movie does what they do. As much as I'd have enjoyed more of her in the film, she could easily have delivered everything she brings to it with much less screen time. Sadly, her biggest scene is also one of the weakest of the picture, though that isn't her fault.

She still comes out of it all better than Jesse Moss, another of the surprisingly experienced young actors in the film (Tyler Labine is a lot older than I expected). He's Chad, the nutjob college kid who sets up the whole second half of the film by outing himself as the "evil" in *Tucker and Dale vs. Evil*. He actually does a really good job with what he's given, but sadly he's given nothing but clichés. He's annoying to start with but manages to get progressively more annoying as the picture runs on, apparently living a dream to be voted onto the island in *Lord of the Flies*. Like the rest of this, he's best when subverting expectations at the beginning. While Tucker and Dale appear to be stereotypical hillbillies, Chad appears to be somehow both the jock and the nerd, an annoying but forgettably average college kid, everyday right down to his inhaler. That he becomes the villain is as enjoyable as Tucker and Dale becoming the heroes. Sadly most of his part comes after that, leading the charge to turn this into yet another slasher parody.

Each trip I take through *Tucker and Dale vs. Evil* emphasises how enjoyable the role reversal approach is and how much fun the splatstick action, but also how disappointing the final act. Even on a first screening, it felt like an easy way out that betrayed the promise of everything that had gone before, especially the early scenes. After all, I had sympathy for the hillbillies not only because they weren't what slasher flicks usually make them but because everyone else is. It felt good to hate the obnoxious college kids and yet be on the side of the writers. I cheered when Tucker and Dale discovered their ramshackle holiday home, almost the epitome of creepiness, but saw only the possibility of the place.

This isn't revisionism on the scale of *Grendel*, but it's good stuff that highlights how villains have their own untold stories that may show that they're not even villains. But then it falls into its own trap and introduces a routine villain with a routine story whose every fibre is woven from cliché. It didn't need to go that far.

It's not quite as simple as saying that the revisionism succeeds while the parody fails, because there are strong parody scenes in and amidst the revisionism. While the homage to *The Texas Chain Saw Massacre* may mark the point at which the role reversal grounding shifts from comedic believability to outrageous setpieces shoehorned into the script to force a laugh from the audience, it is at least superbly done with Tucker chainsawing his way into a beehive, which naturally prompts his running around like a complete maniac.

In a way, I wish there were two different *Tucker and Dale vs. Evil* pictures: one which goes utterly hog wild with all the splatstick insanity, progressing ever further into inspired lunacy until it reaches its memorably outrageous finalé, and another which ratchets down the comedy and maintains a believable grounding in misconception and misunderstanding to serve as a firm counter to the American slasher movie and, in so doing, explain to us why we so often find ourselves siding with the monsters. Neither would turn into *Scooby-Doo* like this, though.

When I wrote my original review, I suggested that it wasn't difficult to shrug off this weak ending "after perhaps 80 minutes of the funniest gore movie since *Braindead*." I've seen the film a couple more times since and I'm finding it harder to shrug it off, perhaps because movies like *Dead Snow: Red vs. Dead*, the splatstick insanity movie of my dreams, have claimed that sort of epithet far more successfully, but partly because it's not just poor, it's wrong.

If it only served to weaken the film perhaps we could shrug it off, but it spoils it too. When Craig and Jurgenson tell us that the obvious villains aren't really villains, we're with them. When they show us the obvious victims doing it to themselves, we're more than with them. Both times, they're subverting what slasher movies do, neatly and effectively. But when they decide to bring in an actual villain they're not subverting anything, they're just going through the same old song and dance.

And for what? Weak parody?

After the inventiveness of the chainsaw and woodchipper scenes, the humour of the sprung trap and the suicide pact, the sympathy of Jangers the dog and the Trivi-UP game, not to mention some magic dialogue and the sheer genius that pervades the scene when the cop found by the college kids shows up at Tucker and Dale's holiday home at precisely the worst moment, we get weak parody to finish up?

I'm sure that Craig and Jurgenson felt that they were continuing down the road on which they started but they took a wrong turn and left the insight behind. Instead of continuing their insightful twist on slasher tropes, they start to hurl out cliché after cliché in an attempt to highlight how Hollywood endings are full of trite flashbacks, plot conveniences and banal threats. Well, guess what? We know. You're preaching to the choir and you're far from the first to do it.

The first two thirds of *Tucker and Dale vs Evil* is original, worthy and insightful, something we haven't seen before. The first ten minutes is especially great because it plays with our expectations as much as it does those of its characters, without ever laughing at us. But the end... no, it deserved much better.

This is ten minutes of a great movie but sadly only two thirds of a good one.

The International Horror & Sci-Fi Film Festival

2011

Horror Shorts

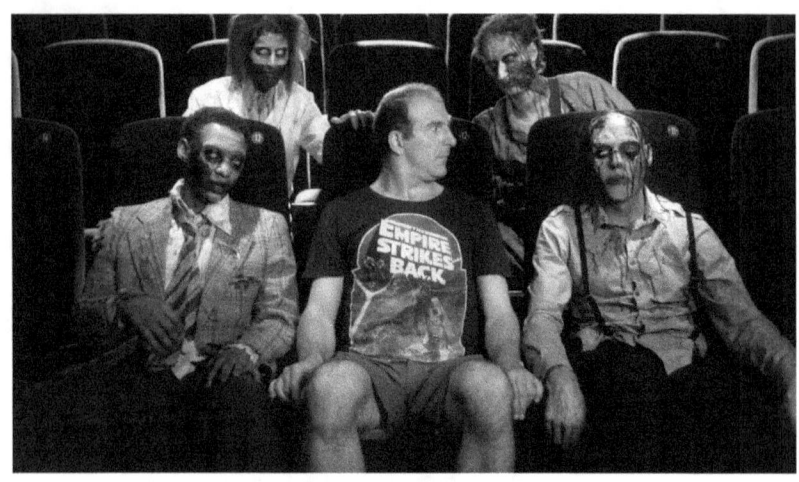

Zombiefication

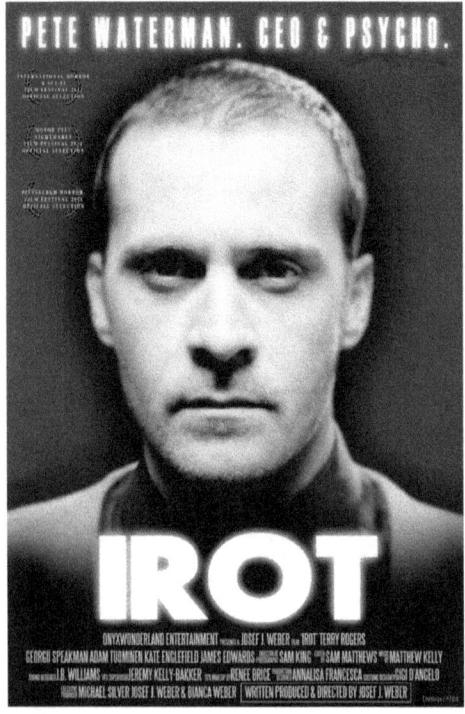

Zombiefication (2010)

Director: Stefan Lukacs
Writer: Stefan Lukacs
Stars: Lauren Cooke, Alexander T. T. Mueller, Lee Oscar Kirchberger and Ursula Weichhart

This Austrian short is almost the definitive way to open a set of horror shorts at a film festival, as indeed it did at both FearCon and the International Horror & Sci-Fi Film Festival in Phoenix in 2011.

It's a faux infomercial that spoofs the spiel that we get from stewardesses at the beginning of flights. Instead of the dangers that might befall us at thirty thousand feet, this entry in the fictional but desirable Total Security Safety Films series addresses the threat of zombies. In the theatre. Yeah, this explains how to identify the living dead in the seats around you and what you can do about it if you find them. I wonder how many people who saw this in theatres really checked under their seats to see if they'd been left a chainsaw or baseball bat, you know, just in case.

The catch, of course, is that it's a one joke movie, so while it can't fail to raise a smile on first viewing and prompt theatre owners to sign it up to precede all future screenings, it doesn't stand up too well to too many repeat viewings.

Beyond the strong idea and the perfect choice of backing muzak, what makes it work so well is the young lady who presents these instructions. She's Lauren Cooke, credited as a flight-attendant, even though that's really just the inspiration for her presentation, and she looks and sounds precisely as she should, never losing her composure even in the face of serious adversity. IMDb suggests that she was dubbed by Claudia Kottal, who isn't credited at the end of the film; if that's true she did an amazingly seamless job. Whoever the voice does belong to, it's the only one we hear throughout, suggesting that this is an Australian rather than an Austrian film.

The script, written by director Stefan Lukacs, is agreeably funny, if inevitably predictable, and the effects work, always a key factor in any zombie flick, is strong, except for the obvious contact lenses. Cooke aside, it's really not the sort of picture that has opportunities for actors, but David Wurawa and Markus Scholze (I presume) make their presence known as living dead theatregoers.

The downside is that the piece is slow and sedate, the approach inevitably forcing proceedings to stay safe and free of tension. It's not as internally consistent as it could be, possibly because it deliberately plays for laughs, whatever they might cost the script. I wonder how much better this could have been had Lukacs put the consistency first, with its reanimated corpses there but safely restrained, and built the laughs out of that. Instead he stays relatively close to the flight model, going so far as to translate some parts of the stewardess spiel almost intact, with merely the threat changed to fit. "Please watch carefully," she tells us, "even if you've been a regular victim of zombiefication."

It seems a little unfair, though, to delve deeply into something that's clearly meant to raise a laugh and land the opening slot on horror short selections at festivals the world over. On that front it's a notable success, ensuring that people showing up late with popcorn find their seats pretty quickly, shut up and enjoy the show.

I Rot (2010)

Director: Josef J. Weber
Writer: Josef J. Weber
Stars: Terry Rogers, Georgii Speakman, Adam Tuominen, Kate Englefield and James Edwards

I first read the title for this Australian horror short as *iRot*, so expected some sort of rotten Apple spoof commercial. It's really *I Rot* and I'm still not sure exactly why, because what we're given is a corporate drama that uses zombiefication as a metaphor for everything negative about human nature, where all that might fester inside unseen instead festers outside with the assistance of make up effects and CGI flies.

It's set at Perfect Touch Cosmetics, a multinational corporation with offices in London, Paris and Tokyo and a boss from Hell called Peter Waterman. He looks like an ass from the first moment we see him and he only underlines it as we follow him through the Perfect

Touch building on the way to his office. He insults a young lady who shares his lift, apparently because she had the audacity to smile at him, and then fires another he passes because he doesn't like her cheap perfume. With each negative deed and thought, his external appearance gradually becomes a mirror of his internal state.

With Waterman such an obvious candidate for the character we'll love to hate, who's going to show up that's sympathetic? Well, the supporting four are just as bad, in fact they're junior versions of Pete, two male and two female. They're all ruthless, brown nosed climbers of the corporate ladder and they're eager to figure out what's going to happen in the upcoming restructure or, more accurately, to manipulate how they're going to benefit from it. He invites them to dinner at his place that night, and... well, let's just say that he has more experience being ruthless than they do. The cool curved dagger in his briefcase suggests how far he might be willing to go to hold on to his spot at the top.

And, if you're wondering who you might want to root for in this short, I'll confirm that the answer is absolutely nobody, at least nobody important enough to be given a name. The two girls at the beginning seemed nice; if it takes wearing cheap perfume to piss off an obnoxious boss, I should have tried it on my last one.

This is a horror film mostly because Pete rots through most of it, but what's notable is that he's the only one who ever brings it up. None of the asskissers do, even though they're clearly nasty pieces of work who have ample opportunity. It's all just metaphorical, an outward visual of what Waterman feels inside.

It works well enough as a general concept but I'm not sure what writer/director Josef J Weber aimed at. Was it just negativity in general or a more overt target like eighties style yuppiedom? Was it a specific feeling like jealousy or fear of being replaced? Surely there's a reason that Pete rots while Deacon, Kashia, Dana or Aysh don't, at least one that goes beyond it being his movie. The idea seems good, however elusive its details, but I'd have preferred a sympathetic character somewhere to provide us engagement, even a supporting one like a long suffering wife or secretary. Without one, this runs long and slips away from us.

There may be a great movie somewhere in this concept but, unfortunately, *I Rot* is only a fair one.

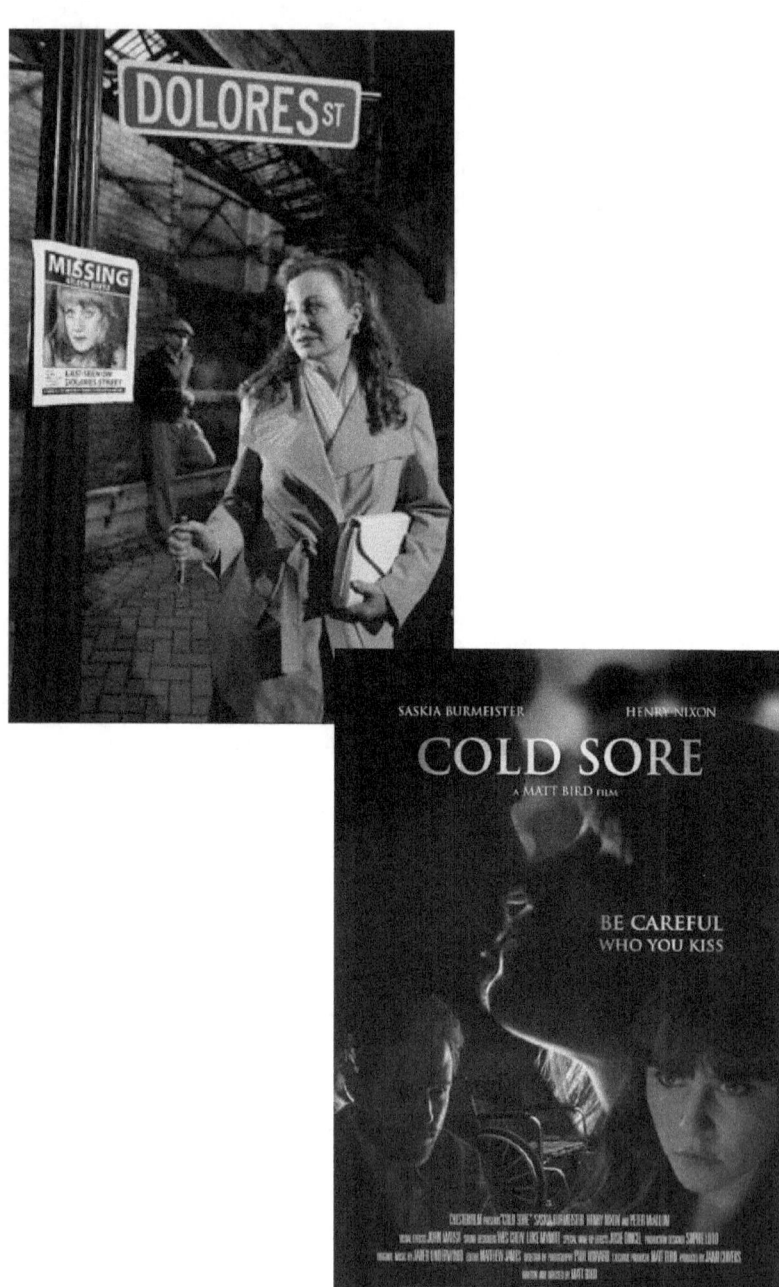

Last Seen on Dolores Street (2010)

Directrix: Devi Snively
Writer: Devi Snively
Stars: Cynthia Dane, Roxie Schaller, Circus-Szalewski, Eileen Grubba, Ken Dusek Jr. and Max Roush

I enjoyed Devi Snively's 2011 horror comedy *Trippin'* and was delighted to see a quote from my review on the cover of the 2-disc DVD alongside another from the indefatigable Jim McLennan, the scholar and gentleman from Trash City. I was even more impressed by Snively herself, who brought her cast for the *Trippin'* screening at Phoenix Fear Fest 3. Beyond being a clearly capable film director (or directrix as she has it), surely a good thing given that she now teaches the subject at the University of Notre Dame, she's also a thoroughly grounded one, as professional a young lady as I've met.

I'm not sure why it took me this long to catch up with one of her short films, as it's just as solid, albeit not very long. I mean, sure, it's a short film, but it's a really short short film, running only just over three and a half minutes, even including the credits; yet it never feels rushed. It's a twist movie, as so many short shorts are, and there's no time to do anything except set up the story and then hit us with the twist. Luckily for us, Snively and her crew do both well.

Not a shot is wasted, with some gorgeous composition of frame, much of it reminiscent of old films noir, even though it's shot in colour. The old time feel is enhanced by the fact that there's only a single line of dialogue throughout the entire picture. "Do you have anybody?" the vet asks our unnamed leading lady, after he puts her dog to sleep. She's credited as Cyn and we can see from her tag that the dog's name is Eileen, as is the lady whose face adorns the missing poster outside the vet's surgery. The lowlife who follows Cyn as she walks off into the night is Kenny and... well, you'll need to watch the film to figure out where everything goes.

I mention all the names because they're also the names of the actors who flesh out the roles. Cyn is played by Cynthia Dane and Kenny by Ken Dusek Jr. Even the vet, Dr. Szalewski, is played by Circus-Szalewski. The reason is that it's apparently a very personal film for Snively, who spent a year in Los Angeles and apparently didn't have a particularly great time of it.

In interviews she has said that she "got mired amidst the bottom feeders and carelessly lost my soul", a viable synopsis for a film noir if ever I've heard one. She adds that "luckily it grew back," but for a while, long enough to shoot this film at least, she clearly felt like she was one of the myriad victims of forties cinema. We're fortunate that she dreamed of being the femme fatale rather than the victim, so this story grew out of her experiences and into a cute and hopefully cathartic little short.

It was received well, playing a whole string of horror festivals, including the International Horror & Sci-Fi Festival here in Phoenix in 2011. Visiting it now tells me that I've waited far too long to catch up with Snively's short work and suggests that I should get on with it and track them down. At least that shouldn't be much of a chore, given that this film, along with six others, which include such gloriously titled shorts as *Confederate Zombie Massacre* and *I Spit on Eli Roth*, are on disc two of that DVD set. You know, the one with an Apocalypse Later quote on the front.

Cold Sore (2010)

Director: Matt Bird
Writer: Matt Bird
Stars: Saskia Burmeister, Henry Nixon and Peter McAllum

Another Aussie movie, *Cold Sore* is more consistent than *I Rot*, it has a more agreeably off kilter feel and it's more likely to stay with you. Then again, this was one of the short films I saw a couple of times back in 2011 but, less than three years later, I couldn't quite remember how it went until it got there.

It's the story of a boy and a girl who meet at a party and the cold sores that both acquire there during a brief snogging session. She's Jenna, who sits on her own, looking completely out of place; he's Guy, who has a lot more confidence, so hones in on her in a neat piece of cinematography. She points out that she's waiting for someone; he adds that he's been stood up by a friend. And so he buys a couple of mojitos for them, which I now realise were always everywhere in movies and I just didn't realise it until I saw *Burn Notice*, and they're all set for a night of it. What doesn't happen is what we might expect, because Guy bails on her after a friend calls him at the party. That's a little odd but hey, maybe he's taking it slow... no, it's a little odd.

What does happen is the title. Jenna wakes up in the morning, next to a mostly empty glass of wine and someone else's name badge, with a cold sore on her top lip. We know that this is going to have some serious meaning and Jenna seems to think so too, going to the doctor to have tests run. Perhaps she's just overly sensitive to anything medical, given that she has some weird scars on her body and there's a wheelchair in her apartment. Guy rings, of course, and she puts him off until Friday, to give it a chance to heal up, but when he arrives, he has one too. Dr. Darvas rings with the results at a highly inappropriate moment, but it's the results themselves that explain where we're going.

Or at least we think so. The end of *Cold Sore* is a neatly powerful one that benefits from the slow buildup and hints at misdirection. This is one of those scenarios that might just invade our dreams and turn them into nightmares because it's never overt, it moves gradually like a creeping thing to fester cleverly in our minds.

I liked the performances by Saskia Burmeister and Henry Nixon, as well as Jared Underwood's capable score which draws them along throughout. I was less impressed by the pacing of the film; while the dénouement deserves a slow build to deliver its shivers, what it gets isn't as consistently grown as it could have been. I wished less that the film would have been shorter (at eighteen minutes, it's longer than usually makes it into horror shorts sets at this festival) and more that the first fifteen would have built more emphatically. As it is, there are a few slow points where little happens and which could have been harnessed to build the tone; perhaps Matt Bird, the writer/director, intended them to. He's aware that the tone is the film's bedrock, but I wanted it to be heightened more dramatically, whether through a stronger sound design or just a quirkier visual aesthetic, something notable to haul *Cold Sore* out of the everyday before it lets us in on its odd little secret.

I liked this film but it could have been more.

Bugbaby (2010)

Director: Rebecca Lorenne
Writer: Dan Spurgeon
Stars: Lara Fisher, Jared Martzell and Mink Stole

It's utterly obvious that co-producers Rebecca Lorenne (who also directed) and Dan Spurgeon (who also wrote the script) are fans of John Waters. Casting Mink Stole as a busybody adoption agency prude is a giveaway, but the darkly comedic tone, kitsch fifties Americana setting and "adventurous" approach to mass murder are quintessential Waters too. Add in throwaway references to flipper babies, Communism and dialogue such as, "People like you make me sick!" and you might be surprised to see anyone else's name on *Bugbaby*.

However, Waters isn't the only influence; Peter Jackson's gorefest *Braindead* (aka *Dead Alive*) is another film that springs to mind. It was set in the same era, albeit in New Zealand, the other side of the world from Baltimore, in which most Waters pictures are set, but it's simultaneously far more polite and far more bloody. The title character, the mostly unseen MacGuffin of the piece, is Samson, a six week old baby who reminded me in many ways of Selwyn, the bizarre zombie baby in *Braindead*.

Whatever their influences, Lorenne and Spurgeon conjured up a delicious slice of fifties apple pie with a thoroughly average couple whose baby is anything but. We discover that fact before the the memorable title reaches the screen in just as memorable a fashion, captured with great timing right before six week old Sammy grabs Mrs. Johnson's cat as a pre-dinner snack.

There are plenty of hints here as to how odd Sammy is, hints which continue throughout the movie even though the title gives it all away. Yes, he's less of a baby and more of a bug but somehow a combination of the two. His parents, the Gregorys, aren't even convinced he's human, though Mrs. Tottifot from the adoption agency, has a lot more tolerance (or blind devotion to all children). They've invited her over because things are getting a little out of hand, but of course we ain't seen nothin' yet. Out of hand is a mild euphemism for where things end up, in delightfully horrible fashion. If Mink Stole gets a line like, "It's positively disgusting!" you just know that it's going to be hilariously wrong.

Bugbaby won the Best Horror Short award at 2011 festival, though it's not quite as strong as that might suggest. It was a weaker year for horror shorts, though conversely it was a strong one indeed for horror features.

The chief joys are in the setting, which gets increasingly surreal, and in the dialogue, which remains blissfully happy throughout, regardless what calamities descend on the Gregory house. These are well fleshed out, the pastel colours and little background details a solid grounding for the insanity that erupts.

However we don't see much of Sammy, just hints here and there with a few Sammycam shots from his compound eyes, and there's only a modicum of mangling. Would a few gallons of gore have hurt the film? I doubt it, especially with filmmakers this capable to put them to good use. I also wanted to know what happened next. There's surely a full feature in the next ninety minutes, but it has to play out in our head. We can fever dream, right?

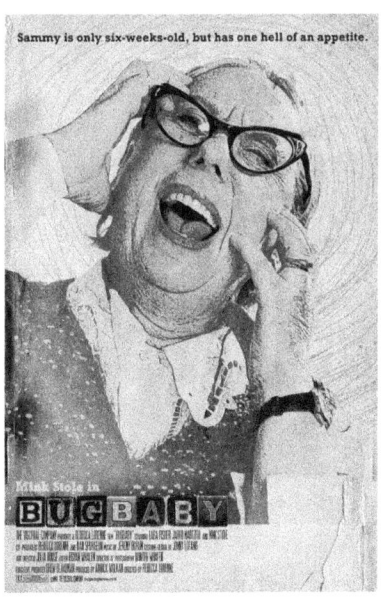

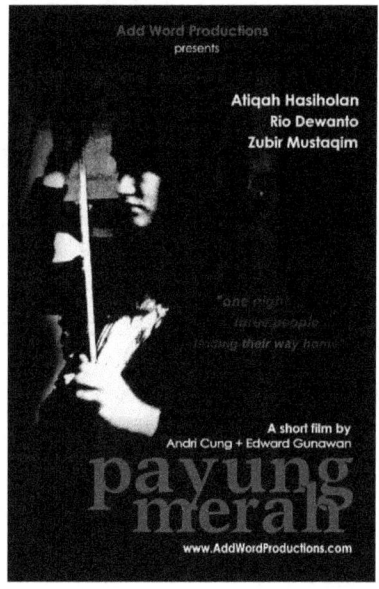

Red Umbrella (2010)

Directors: Andri Cung and Edward Gunawan
Writer: Edward Gunawan
Stars: Atiqah Hasiholan, Rio Dewanto and Zubir Mustaqim

The most obvious flaw that Red Umbrella has is that it's entirely predictable to anyone who's seen more than a few Asian horror movies. To be fair, it's probably entirely predictable to anyone else watching too, but fortunately it's constructed with panache, so it's little hardship to watch through the story one more time.

It's also played out entirely as a drama without a single effect. While judicious use of an effect or two might have enhanced the film technically, it would have rendered it even more of a cliché. Playing it straight and keeping it down to ten minutes means that it becomes something like the taxi ride we see: safe and reliable.

It shows up in the middle of a horror shorts selection, something that could easily be equated to the bad side of town, draws us in until we realise where we're going, lets us out safely at the end with a decent memory of the ride, then stays with us, at least for a little while, to fade away into the graveyard of memories until another short film comes along with the same story.

We know we're in Indonesia because the sign on the top of Mohammad Raza's vehicle reads "TAKSI" not "TAXI"; I think every Indonesian movie I've seen features a taksi in it somewhere. He's nearing the end of his shift, clearly knackered, and his better half is pressuring him by phone to come home. On his way through Cawang, though, he stops for a young lady who flags him down in the dark. She's under a red umbrella, even though it isn't raining out, and something tells him to take her home to Bintaro, even though it's not on his way.

They talk about the usual things: whether she has a boyfriend and how dangerous it is for young ladies to wait for a taksi alone in a bad neighbourhood like Cawang. Even if she's not worried about local hoodlums, what about ghosts? And on we go until we get to Bintaro, which frankly doesn't look any more safe than Cawang, and we're given, along with Raza, the explanation of the story that we figured out long ago merely by reading between the lines.

I liked this story of *Payung Merah* or *Red Umbrella*, even though it offered no surprises. Most movies that tell an oft retold story are annoying precisely because they're so familiar, but this one feels more like an old friend stopped by for ten minutes to say hello. Perhaps it's because Atiqah Hasiholan is so inherently likeable as the girl with the red umbrella, or because Rio Dewanto manages to find his character so capably and so immediately. If she's the sort of customer taksi drivers want to pick up, he's certainly the sort of ride girls want to flag down.

The camera is hardly ambitious, given that almost the entire piece takes place inside a taksi on the road, but it picks up a lot of colour; we absorb in delight the neighbourhood's flavour through its reflection in Raza's face. There's little opportunity for anything clever, as the story keeps moving along mostly through some efficient editing and through Dewanto's voice.

We become his passengers too, tired but comfortable, in an agreeable state because of his chatter, patiently listening to an old story told yet again.

Cell Phone Psycho (2010)

Director: David S. White
Star: Billy Slaughter

I can't argue too much with a picture made by a production company named Evil Penguin Films. That's awesome and their logo is just as cool. If this surreal homage to Alfred Hitchcock's *Psycho*, made in the form of a public service announcement, is anything to go by, they're surely fun people to hang with. I'd say that even before seeing their other short on Vimeo, *Marigny Bywater Ladies Tea Auxiliary Sunday Demolition Society*, which surely confirms it.

Cell Phone Psycho is another of those shorts designed to kick off short film selections at film festivals. I'm sure that's where the International Horror & Sci-Fi Film Festival would have put it too, if only *Zombiefication* hadn't landed the slot first. There can be only one, right? Well, this one's versatile enough, and short enough at only three and a half minutes, to meet the need and it even ends with a neat breaking of the fourth wall that would warrant a smile even on the hundredth viewing. If it lost thirty seconds more in the middle, it would be blissful.

The star is Billy Slaughter, an unfortunate name for an actor given the circumstances. The concept is to have him watch a movie in a theatre, while simultaneously doing all the things that we all hate people doing when they're watching movies in theatres. You know, like leaving his mobile phone on, answering it during the movie and chatting through the whole thing. He throws out spoilers and even has the gall to tell his fellow moviegoers to shh.

To emphasise that this is a P.S.A., there are text overlays to show us where we're going, but they need to combine with the title to really highlight where we're really going. It's the shower scene, of course, because "WE WILL FIND YOU" and the Evil Penguin folk do so in surreal magnificence. Movie fans will deconstruct this scene in their heads to check off all the shots that mimic the original, subverted neatly of course, and probably miss what else is on show. That's why theatres should play this before every screening, so we can catch it all through repetition.

I'm not sure precisely what the rest of the cast are supposed to be, beyond people who find people who run through the litany of movie faux pas. The credits call them the Noisician Coalition and their website describes them as "a loosely confederated alliance of very loud people, including, but not limited to, The Krewe of Joyful Noise, The Buttonmen, The Big NONO, The Spasmodic Marching All-Stars, Vermillion Lies and other shadowy organizations about whom little, if anything, is known."

In other words, they're what New Orleans is all about and they must liven up those 430 party days a year that they celebrate in the Big Easy. Their costumes are awesome, an unholy hybrid of Día de los Muertos, steampunk and marching band, along with half a dozen other fashion trends neatly subverted into something wildly original, and they appear to have the character to make it work.

My suggestion is that this collective should be cloned and paid to accompany this P.S.A. before every screening at every theatre in the country. Surely it wouldn't be expensive. They're from New Orleans; we can pay them in beads, right?

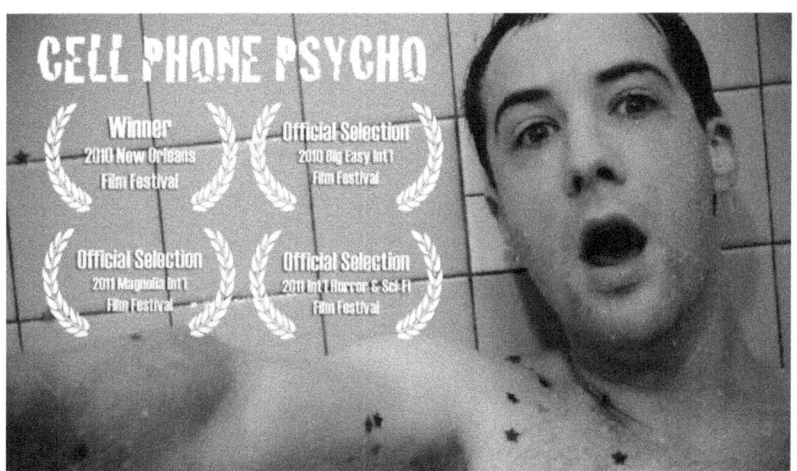

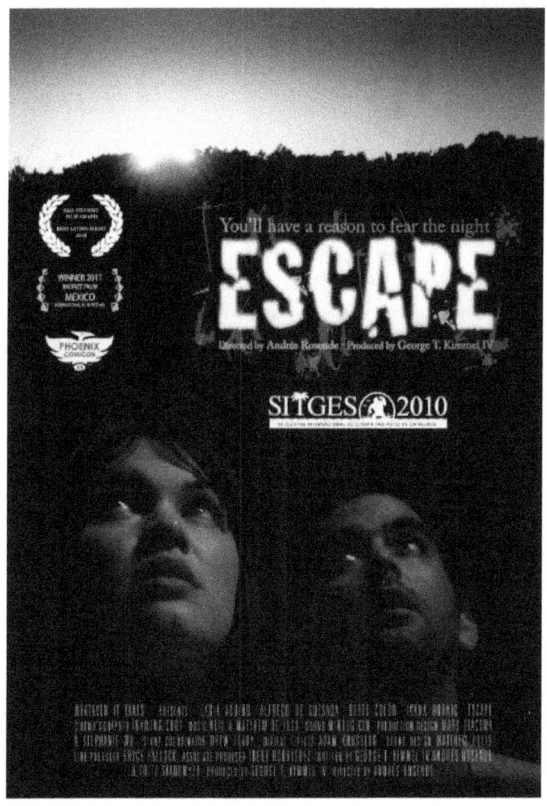

Escape (2010)

Director: Andrés Rosende
Writers: George T. Kimmel IV, Andrés Rosende and Fritz Staudmyer
Stars: Lydia Aquino, Alfred de Quesada, Berto Colón and Ivana Horonic

Escape, a capably made picture from a company called W.I.T. or Whatever It Takes, is one of those films that is weighed down by its metaphor and its message.

With no background for us to explore to find a moral compass, we're given two sets of people who must therefore be seen as good guys and bad guys. Because we always support the underdog, the bad guys are surely the ones driving around at night in pickup trucks with bright searchlights to help them shoot the good guys with crossbows. Those good guys are the ones running as fast as they can to remain alive.

Well, maybe not alive, but in one piece at least. There are two other clear observations that we can't fail to make from the opening minute and one of them is that the good guys are fanged. Usually, vampires avoiding the rising sun aren't the good guys, but we can vaguely buy it here because, hey, at least they don't sparkle. The other observation is that these vampires are Latinos who speak Spanish, while the hunters are Caucasian and speak English. Here's where the metaphor jumps in to slap us in the face.

This short film isn't badly written but it struggles with this metaphor because it refuses to allow us to delve any deeper than the surface. We're effectively told to trust the angle from which the story is told and there's nothing here that allows us to deviate from that without acquiring a vaguely guilty feeling about doing so; it's never good for a message movie to play for guilt because it can backfire so easily.

Fortunately Lydia Aquino, the lead actress, gets a story arc that almost makes up for it. She's a Latino vampire called Alicia, who makes it safely to to a building with Guillermo, her significant other of some description. Already there is Martin, who is doing as well as can be imagined with a couple of arrows in him. They spend their time bemoaning their lot and arguing about what they should do next, until their pursuers catch up with them and it all becomes real again. Guillermo wants to leave the country; Alicia sees it as their home and refuses to yield to oppression. You can see where this metaphor is going.

It never really comes out to state that cornered vampires tearing the throats out of the people hunting them with stakes is somehow morally equivalent to illegal immigrants taking a stand against racism, but it does feel like it's what Andrés Rosende, the director and co-writer, took here. It all works much better as a drama than a message.

It's good to see Spanish speaking vampires in an American film, though, as it's been rare even with an early start like 1931's *Drácula*, Universal's Spanish language version with Carlos Villarías as the Count, shot at night on the very same sets that Béla Lugosi was making history on during the day.

The differences in Alicia's and Guillermo's reactions to these circumstances are explored well and Alicia's character has a fairly believable progression within a short amount of time. With the metaphor toned way down, this could play well as the beginning of a feature, one where the opening credits and title screen arrive as this ends, to be followed by a bigger, better story, which would bring needed background and depth.

The International Horror & Sci-Fi Film Festival

2011

Sci-Fi Shorts A

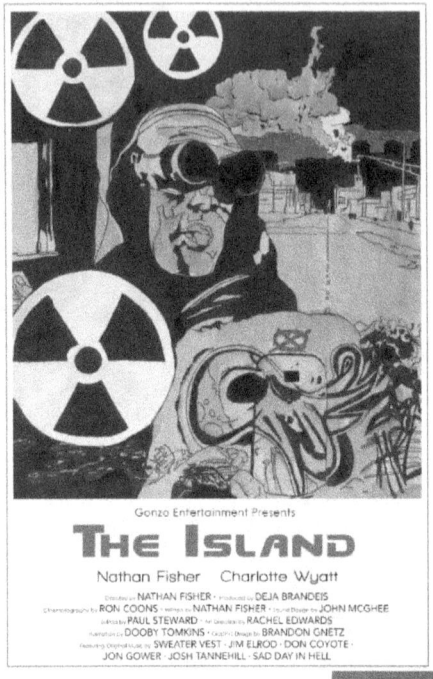

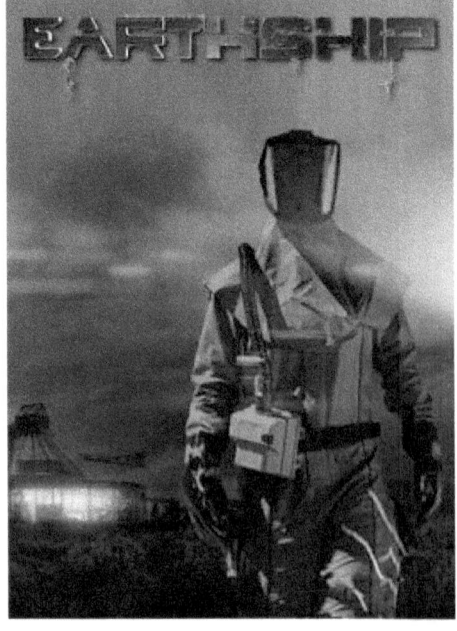

The Island (2010)

Director: Nathan Fisher
Writer: Nathan Fisher
Stars: Nathan Fisher and Charlotte Wyatt

I got a real kick out of *The Island*, a short science fiction film with a deliciously dark tone that could easily be seen as the flipside of *Earthship*, the short that followed it.

Like *Earthship* (and indeed the entire set of four films which it began), it's set in a post-apocalyptic world but refuses to conjure up a budget to show us whatever mutants, zombies or triffids thrive in the ashes of civilisation, instead situating us firmly inside a self-sufficient home used to wait out the fall of mankind and hinting at the situation out there with sound and hearsay. Unlike *Earthship*, however, there's only one survivor here and he goes by Tom.

He seems a decent enough chap, very calm and collected, but just a little off, as we soon discover when someone pounds on his door, pleading for help, and his response is to put a noisy album onto his record player and settle down with a book. The six inches of steel in his bank vault of a door and the two feet of reinforced concrete in which it's set allow him to ignore the world as much as he likes. The title of the film clearly refers to his bunker, an island of peace in a world of chaos.

Tom is played by Nathan Fisher, which explains how comfortable he is in the setting, because Fisher is the driving force behind the film, as its writer, producer, director and star. There are only three actors on screen throughout the entire film and he's the one we see the most of, which is plenty in a 25 minute short entirely set in a single room.

Apparently unwilling to deal with the world outside, he's able to sit back in his chair and frankly ignore it because he has everything he needs around him. He has food stacked up against a wall in labelled boxes and a stove to cook it on. He has oodles of bottled water. He rolls his own cigarettes. He has a chair, a bed and a toilet. He generates electricity by pedalling a bicycle that's hooked up to batteries. He has books, records and puzzles to keep him busy and he's teaching himself how to play chess. He only goes outside to dump the trash and even then he has a pair of goggles to deal with the light and a set of concussion grenades to deal with anything he might find within it. In short, he has everything he might need.

Well, not quite. What he doesn't have is company, a lady friend with which to pass his abundant time. He has to make do with the scantily clad models on his album covers, at least until we reach the seven minute mark and one comes knocking on his door, one who's young, pretty and very scared. This time he opens the door and the real story begins.

For a while things are polite, with this new female guest stunned at the comparative luxury he enjoys. Katie hasn't eaten in days, but Tom has enough water to wash in, so she's shocked and amazed, not to mention wary about the possibility that her dream has come true. All this would soon be echoed in *Earthship*, but here's where the two pictures diverge. This is a science fiction story, but Fisher's obvious passion is with the cosmic horror of H. P. Lovecraft; his first picture was a direct adaptation of *Beyond the Walls of Sleep*, but he followed up with this, an original story that is merely influenced by the master.

Purely as a science fiction film it was promising, but it's the shift to the dark side that makes it such an enjoyable piece, even if it's only peripherally Lovecraftian. Katie's description of the aftermath of the apocalypse is very reminiscent: "they're starving and turning on each other and worshipping those things"; what sort of things is hinted at in the fantastic graffiti octopus plastooned across the door of the bunker. While the elder gods might be raging outside in a mythos world, we're voted onto the island with Tom and Katie to witness a study of sedate madness, a theme Lovecraft played with often. Secure in his fortress of solitude, amidst the terrors of a dying race, what must Tom do to stay sane? How will Katie adapt to his claustrophobic existence and her apparent salvation? What cool records are racked within Tom's admirably varied collection? These are the questions that *The Island* attempts to answer and to find out what Fisher has in mind for Tom, Katie and us, you'll need to watch the film yourself.

I liked it from the opening scene, where the camera zooms in slowly towards the octopus on Tom's vault door and a man scuttles around before being scared away by gunshots. It's deceptively slow, with little apparently happening but Fisher builds his character well, so we sympathise with Tom's situation and even envy it, given the context, but nonetheless realise that we don't know everything.

The underlying concept and Fisher's performance are the strong points but there are weaker ones too. Charlotte Wyatt does a fair job as Katie but it's no shock to find that this was her screen debut. She's also too clean and her leggings are too neatly ripped, more like a fashion statement than battle damage. We get that Tom has a well stocked bunker, but he'll also need regular deliveries of toilet paper and concussion grenades to survive more than a week at his rate of use.

Back in 2010, Fisher had plans to turn this into a feature, though it hasn't happened; I'd be happy to see that. The short has depths and different readings; I'd love to see how it might expand.

Earthship (2010)

Director: David K. Wilson
Writer: David K. Wilson
Stars: Brian Leahy, Genia Michaela, Gavin McClure and James Loren

As someone who has read quite a lot about earthships and other sustainable housing projects and one day plans to live in one, I was overjoyed to see a short science fiction film that revolves so much about the concept that it provides the title of the film.

It has a decent story too, albeit a relatively simple one that follows an obvious creation arc. When faced with an earthship, any creative soul will want to conjure up a story; what story would apply to a residence so self-sufficient that its occupants could live there in comfort indefinitely whatever else happens outside its walls? Well, a post-apocalyptic story, naturally, which is precisely what we get, one which director David K. Wilson wrote cleverly enough to be thoroughly believable without ever requiring what was surely a low initial budget to swell into something more substantial. This was his thesis film at the University of Southern

California's School of Cinematic Arts and it worked well enough to make its way to at least 32 different film festivals, including the 2011 International Horror & Sci-Fi Film Festival, of course.

Wilson places us into a post-apocalyptic Canada, supposedly in the desert outside what remains of the city of Vancouver ('Couver here), though it was shot in and around the Phoenix House in the Earthship Biotecture Community in Taos, NM. There's plenty of time for global devastation to have arrived, given that we're at least as far out as the year 2047, which is marked on Mary Whitmore's gravestone as the date when she left her family without a female presence. No wonder tensions are running high!

Other than that, the family is doing pretty well, at least when compared to the rest of the world. The Whitmores shifted over to the earthship after civilisation fell and survived there for twenty years; living off the grid might be enticing today, but it's even more enticing when there's no longer a grid. They grow their own food, capture and recycle their water, without ever needing to venture back to what remains of 'Couver for anything at all. Theoretically they could stay in their self-sufficient earthship forever.

One obvious catch is that three men do not a new civilisation make, at least not without outside help, but that isn't where this film begins; instead the triggers here come from not knowing. Allan and Mary Whitmore had two sons, and the younger, Dax, has never experienced civilisation. He's young enough to have spent his entire life in this earthship, isolated from everything and everyone, and he's simply burning to go out and see the world, or at least what's left of it.

Needless to say, this causes conflict, especially with his elder brother, Brian, and they're fighting about whether Dax should leave or not when the plot stumbles over the horizon and collapses in the desert just ahead of them. It's another human being, perhaps the first Dax has ever seen, hidden from view by a black airtight suit marked Belial Corp. No wonder he runs to help, as Brian holds back with ingrained caution, and thus the brotherly conflict continues on throughout. Dax is ever fearless, with no real experience to draw from, while Brian remembers the end of the world.

It's no spoiler to point out that this new arrival is a woman, as you wouldn't expect any different. She's Isis, played by Genia

Michaela, and she's very good at providing believable reactions to waking inside the Whitmores' comfortable earthship after decades of dubious post-apocalyptic survival. We're back in the territory that *The Island* explored, at least for a while. This is an unknown and unimaginable world to her, one in which Dax reads Shakespeare and the Whitmores stargaze with telescopes, plural. What's more, they have a shower, with running water, no less. Isis cries as it cascades down onto her.

To be fair, Michaela owns the film mostly because she's the wide eyed guest who gets scenes like this one, even as Brian Leahy does well otherwise as the inquisitive and carefree Dax. Gavin McClure isn't allowed to do much as Brian except bitch at his brother, so it's no great slight that he fades quickly. James Loren overplayed Allan consistently in his emotional scenes, leaving the picture to the youngsters and the story to the ending that some clever twists only hint won't show up eventually.

It's a cliché that reviewers always ask for good short films to be extended into features, but *Earthship* could certainly have done with more length, if not quite that much. Wilson did a lot here with not a lot and I'd be interested in where he could have taken his concept.

The earthship is such a great location for a science fiction film, rather like an earthbound version of Bruce Dern's memorable spaceship in *Silent Running*, but any overt comparisons to that film would need to tie to its isolation, which Wilson refuses to go for. Rather he builds up its isolation as a temporary state of affairs and sets his story at the point where that ends.

His thinking is that the Whitmores have been living their lives in a protective bubble, which Isis promptly pops as she arrives, thus becoming a catalyst for change. Wilson's story therefore becomes a lost world story in reverse, where the roaming savages discover a little pocket of civilisation. I really like the possibilities inherent in that approach, but unfortunately little of the potential depth can be addressed in eighteen minutes, making the credits somewhat like an alarm clock ending a promising dream.

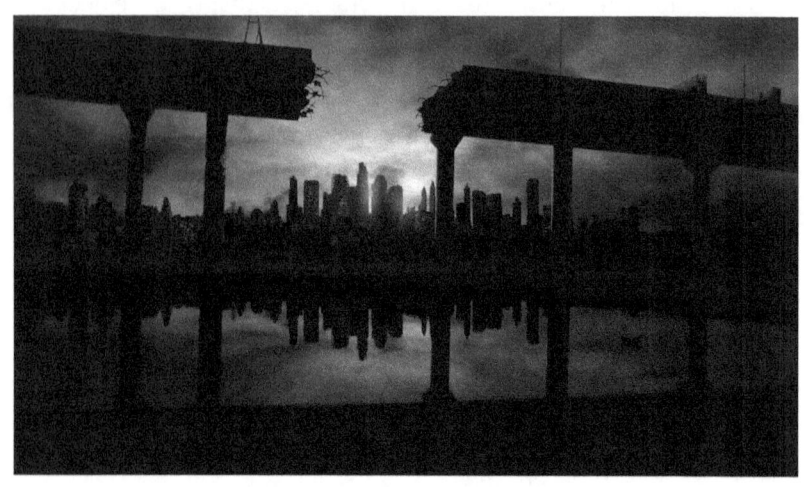

Picture Show at the End of the World

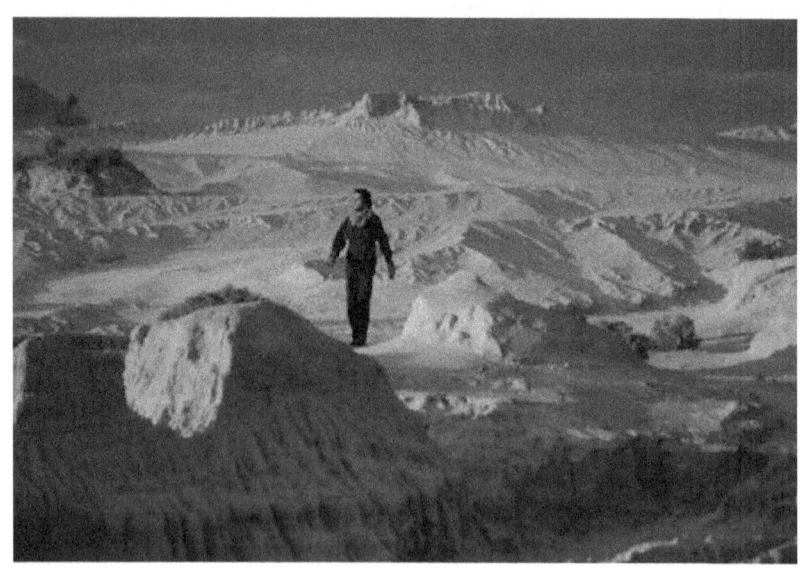

Roman's Ark

Picture Show at the End of the World (2009)

Director: David Rusanow
Writer: David Rusanow
Stars: Peter Barron and Hannah Jones

I wasn't quite as sold on *Picture Show at the End of the World* as the International Horror & Sci-Fi Film Festival judges in 2011, who chose this as the Best Sci-Fi Short Film of the festival. That isn't to say I didn't like it, because I liked it rather a lot.

It's an interesting little picture that speaks as much to what cinema means to we audience members as any science fiction concept. In fact, if this wasn't set in the sort of post-apocalyptic landscape that dominated the Sci-Fi Shorts A block, it might not even be seen as a science fiction film at all. Perhaps the setting in time might qualify it too, as its concentration on the silent era of cinema and the costumes and music conjured up to evoke that age suggest that this particular apocalypse took place in the past rather than the future, an alternate 1920s where movies never found a voice and 35mm film was never replaced. It's disturbing to imagine this world in which the last 90 years worth of motion pictures would never be made.

It begins stylishly with a dusty old car sputtering along some sort of manmade canal until it peters out. The driver, B. K., is in a gas mask, while his passenger, Pandora, covers her mouth with a makeshift fan. Otherwise they wear formal attire, as if they might be on their way to the opera rather than to search the wasteland in an increasingly desperate attempt to find one working movie theatre that can screen the reel of film they carry around with them like a prized possession. The desperation springs from the young lady being in bad shape; Pandora is weak and coughs up blood. I'd suggest that she might have tuberculosis if this wasn't a science fiction movie; here I presume she's afflicted with whatever calamity ravaged the planet.

In an interesting approach that deliberately mirrors the era of cinema that the film reprises, B. K. and Pandora never speak, for reasons which become very apparent later, but few of the other survivors they encounter during their quest have any lines either.

As Norma Desmond famously said in *Sunset Boulevard*, "We didn't need dialogue. We had faces!" Peter Barron, who plays B. K., fits that epithet perfectly. He might not look like a silent screen idol, but he has the sort of face that was designed for movies. He has that classic chiselled visage always required of British leading men in romantic comedies but with a darker edge that suggests that if you met him in the street you might wonder if you've ever seen him play James Bond. He's actually an Australian actor, as this is an Australian film, but Hollywood's inability to place accents lends him strong potential for a future in a lot bigger picture than this. He's kept mildly busy racking up roles here and there, but doesn't seem to have made his mark yet. Of course, on the basis of this film alone, I have no idea what he sounds like. His co-star, Hannah Jones, debuted here, which isn't surprising. She's fair as Pandora and certainly fits the part, as a vague Louise Brooks lookalike, but she doesn't carry the sort of depth that Barron does.

The key name behind *Picture Show at the End of the World* is that of David Rusanow, which is all over the credits like a rash. He wrote and directed, for a start, but he also edited both the film and its sound and provided its visual effects. Bizarrely he didn't shoot the picture, given that most of his varied credits were earned for cinematography; he handed that role here to Graeme McMahon. IMDb lists this as Rusanow's third short film as a director and it's an assured piece that would fit well in anyone's portfolio.

My problems with it mostly tied to its middle, which felt hollow and inconsequential. What we see is decent enough and the cast and crew did their jobs well, but I had a strong feeling that the middle ten minutes could have been anything. I couldn't help but visualise a stack of parallel universes where the beginning and end of this film remain identical, while the middle plays consistently and unrecognisably differently in each of them. None would lose the overriding drive of the piece, which is contained entirely in its bookends.

Would this be better as a five minute film or as a feature? I wasn't quite able to decide.

Roman's Ark (2011)

Director: Seth Larney
Writer: Jonathan Samiec, from a story by Jonathan Samiec and Troy Darben
Stars: Damon Gameau, Robin McLeavy and Ingrid Kleinig

Roman's Ark wrapped up a particularly strong set of four long post-apocalyptic shorts at the 2011 festival, where it took a rather different approach to the subgenre to the other three movies which went before it.

The commonality shared by *Earthship*, *The Island*, *Picture Show at the End of the World* and *Roman's Ark* is that civilisation had already fallen before the opening credits ran, the reasons behind the calamity are left unexplained and the characters to which we're introduced have already come to terms with it.

Where *Roman's Ark* stands unique is with the prescience of its lead and its choice of timeframe. Instead of characters who found ways to survive in a reactive fashion, a Russian scientist called Roman foresaw the end of the world and proactively prepared to survive it, to out-wait radiation through cryosleep and thus live on to the point where he could help the world heal and begin afresh. If mankind can reach the point where it destroys itself, the least Roman can do is provide an undo button.

We're never told quite how much time has passed from the holocaust to the beginning of the film, but it's long enough for Roman's muscles to have atrophied a little from his sleep within a nutrient tank of green liquid and, as we soon discover, this awakening is not his first.

Once ready, he emerges from his secure underground bunker to face a stark desert world, as captured perfectly by the astounding dry lakes of Mungo National Park in the southeastern Australian state of New South Wales. We see the tops of lamp-posts, otherwise buried in sand, leading up to broken skyscrapers. Memorably, there's a boat on top of a cliff, suggesting just how violent the devastation must have been to sear our planet dry. He takes a sample of dirt in a little glass vial and takes it back to the lab in his bunker to test, but the chemical he uses turns the soil red, as we clearly see it did on each prior trip. We don't know how many he's made, as the vials extend off screen, but he's certainly been a busy botanist. With nothing to find on the radio, it's back into the tank for Roman.

Thus far it's been eight minutes and it's only when a song kicks in to accompany his descent back into suspended animation that we realise that they were entirely without human voice. Damon Gameau is believable as this driven scientist, the only human being we've seen thus far except for his wife, who had occupied the next tank and didn't make it, but the idea and the scenery carried us on their own.

Then Jonathan Samiec, who co-wrote the original story with Troy Darben and adapted it into a script, decides to hit us with tension, an impressive feat given that we're at the end of the world with only a single character. 140 years later, an emergency alarm causes Roman to burst out of his tank and stab himself in the heart with some sort of medication. Something has clearly gone horribly wrong and life support has gone offline, along with much of the power. This time, however, Roman is not alone when he leaves the bunker to obtain his soil sample. To say any more would constitute a spoiler.

Roman's Ark is a substantial and mature film that deserves a lot more attention that it appears to have garnered, perhaps because 25 minutes is a tough length to sell to film festivals. It played a diverse set of them in 2011 and 2012, the International Horror & Sci-Fi Film Festival being the first, but only picked up one award, at the St. Kilda Film Festival for its sound. That's surprising, because it's a picture to stay with the viewer. It certainly stayed with me over three years and, revisiting this set of post-apocalyptic shorts, I realise that it wraps it all up with a touch of class. It's the obvious choice to finish up a selection of short films or even a festival, because its wonderful ending is precisely the sort of uplifting experience that stays with filmgoers as they leave the theatre. However pessimistic the film's initial concept might seem, and it does posit the near extinction of the human race which is almost as pessimistic as it gets, it not only doesn't get us down, it leaves us with a strong and abiding feeling of hope.

It's also refreshing to discover that the film and the strong ecological message that it carries also has a strong connection to the land it features so strongly. Elders of both the Ngyiampaa and Paakantyi aboriginal tribes of Australia had "generously invited, welcomed and nurtured" the production, as well as providing the striking extras that we see in the radioactive wasteland. The ties that both tribes have to Lake Mungo and what is now the national park surrounding it date back over 40,000 years, a timeframe that dwarfs the already ambitious one visualised in *Roman's Ark*. Their presence in the project, a rare dramatic one to shoot in this area, grounds it in history and anchors its journey into the future. What those tribes have seen in these lands over the millennia is the sort of conjecture usually reserved for science fiction, making it all the more appropriate that Chaotic Pictures made and fostered those connections.

Please ignore the mushroom cloud shot, which is a frustratingly clichéd moment; the rest of the film deserves to be seen.

The International
Horror & Sci-Fi Film Festival

2011

Sci-Fi Shorts B

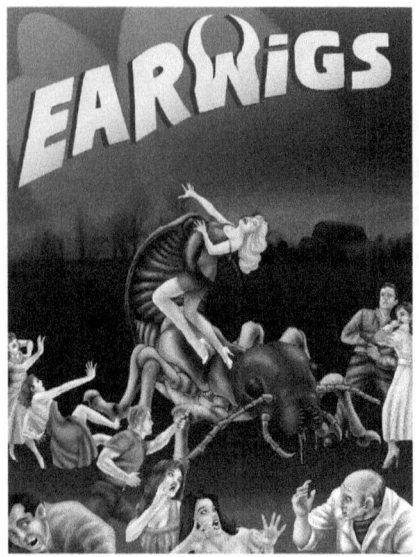
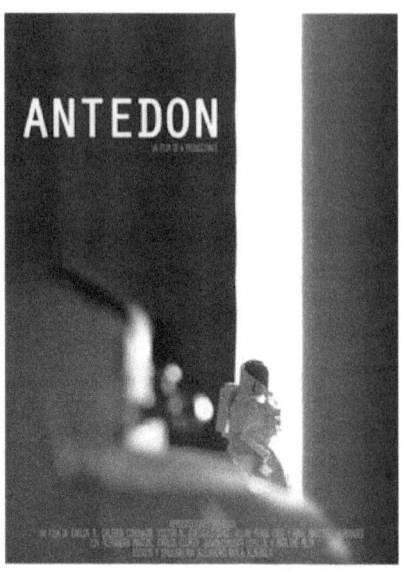

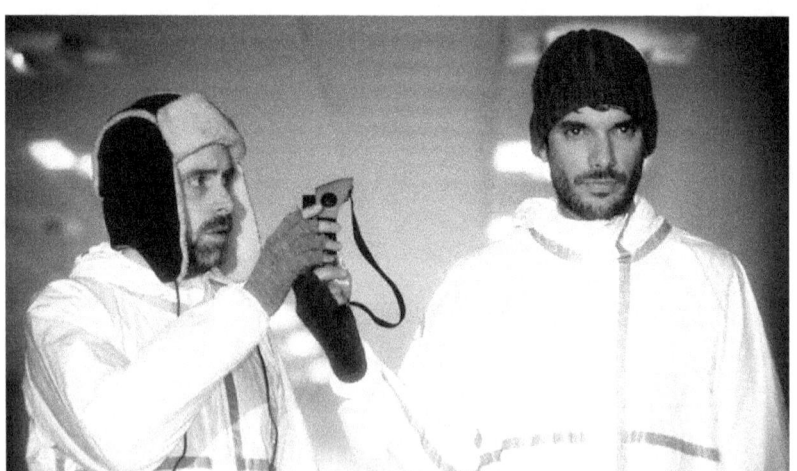

The Hollow Men

Earwigs (2010)

Director: Bruce Legrow
Writer: Bruce Legrow

Regular attendees of genre film festivals may be excused for believing that there's a rule nowadays that requires the first film in any selection of horror shorts to be a faux trailer for an outrageous throwback of a movie. I've certainly followed it myself on occasion and *Earwigs* would fit the bill magnificently.

It was shot specifically for a trailer contest called Silver Wave but, at the 2011 festival, it opened up a set of sci-fi shorts instead. Hey, fifties monster movies were horror and sci-fi all at the same time, so I'm not complaining!

From that single comment, though, if you have any background in the genre, you'll be able to visualise precisely what Bruce Legrow does with his two minutes. The bad news is that there's nothing else here at all, but the good news is that he does it very capably indeed. His anonymous actors don't just act the part, they look the part too, well cast as the stereotypes we expect, and it's not difficult to figure out how the imaginary movie that Legrow never made to expand upon this trailer would play out. Just in case we don't have that background, there's a synopsis online that goes a lot deeper.

The scientist working on a serum to alter the human brain and unleash its "full potential for empathy and compassion" is Dr. Rutherford, who has a calamitous home life with a gossip of a wife. Once he adds in a "caring gene" from an earwig, "the great mothers of the solitary insect world", he's ready to leave it all by drinking the serum with his sexy assistant, Diana, so they can start "a new loving life together". She baulks though, so it's only Rutherford who turns into a giant earwig, prowling the city for women with whom to create a new family and using his newly acquired psychic powers to capture them and turn them into mindless slaves. Meanwhile, Private Buck, Diana's boyfriend, is eager to save her and soon gets his chance as the military take on the giant earwig's lair, a conveniently abandoned barn on the edge of town, with tanks and artillery. They might be Communists, right?

Legrow does well in capturing the essence of fifties monster movies, even if the overblown advertising he slathers onto the screen is obviously digital rather than analogue. Other than that minor slip, the details are strong. It's shot in 16mm with costumes and cars that look appropriate for the era. Either he and his crew sourced well from thrift stores and antique shops or they built glorious props like the general's huge field telephone with an astute eye for detail. Even the anomalies are mostly appropriate, like the young lady in her nightgown who is tormented outside for no apparent reason. The only one that seems a little out of place is the parade of villagers with torches and pitchforks, which ought to fit far better within an homage to Universal horrors than sci-fi B-movies. The stock footage, with inevitably different grain, is a nice touch, as I've seen that many times. The lighting, the subservient women, the use of garbage sacks as costumes, all help to add authenticity to the piece.

Hey, I'd definitely watch this feature!

Antedon (2010)

Director: Alejandro Ayala Alberola
Writer: Alejandro Ayala Alberola
Stars: Alexandra Martín and Jorge Clorio

They may well have separate IMDb pages, but the slightest online research suggests that at least four of the seven Alejandro Ayala Alberolas there are the same person.

Antedon was made by Alberola (III), while *Dry Gulch*, the creation of Alberola (VI), marked the return of his work to the International Horror & Sci-Fi Film Festival two years later. Merely looking at the other films that he's uploaded to Vimeo and YouTube highlight that he's also the Alberola (IV) responsible for *Guerra de Papel*, made the same year as this, and the Alberola (V) behind *Petropolis* a year later. Why he's ending up with a new IMDb page for each new film he makes, I have no idea, but perhaps there's a nefarious plot down in Mexico to clone Alejandro Ayala Alberolas to churn out animated science fiction films.

I'm all for it in principle, but I have to say that I much prefer *Dry Gulch* to *Antedon*. The two were made using very different animation styles, but the former has a lush and enticing presence to it while this one feels empty.

Dry Gulch also had a story, of sorts, while I'm really not sure what this one has. A large spaceship arrives in orbit around the moon of a planet and sends a shuttle down so a couple of stop motion astronauts can explore the surface. If I'm picking up what happens properly, they send up a flare and discover some sort of statue. There's a skeleton nearby. And then, perhaps looking into some sort of milky black surface, one of them becomes convinced that he's watching a prancing unicorn. As the surface opens to bathe him in inviting light, he enters and the end credits roll.

It's that experimental and I have no clue what it's trying to say. The names don't seem to suggest any meaning. "Antedon" is a genus of stemless crinoids or water lilies, so that's presumably a dead end. The ship's name is another; "Thebes" could refer to any number of ancient cities, most notably the former capital of Egypt. I initially thought the male astronaut was named Alejate, but that's merely the Spanish for "Get away!" For some reason, both switch to English for their final lines.

If I don't understand what *Antedon* is trying to tell us, I can at least appreciate the unique approach that Alberola and his team of animators and filmmakers took to make this picture. Stop motion is rarely used nowadays because it's so damn time consuming, but I'm always happy when someone devotes that time. The motion is a little jerky, but I'm not sure how much of that is due to the number of frames in the animation itself and how much is the compression of the digital version available online. The outfits look subtly odd, probably because they're partially built out of Lego, but with the faces of real people overlaid inside them with the requisite heads up displays.

I liked the look, but I did want to know what Alberola was aiming for them to do. I imagined *2001: A Space Odyssey* and *Blade Runner* homages, but apparently the piece was inspired instead by the myth of the Sphinx, as depicted in *Oedipus Rex*, the classic tragedy by Sophocles. As that was about reason's victory over religion, I'm unsure how it applies here. *Dry Gulch* is far more accessible.

The Hollow Men (2010)

Director: Ashley Denton
Writer: Ashley Denton
Stars: James Harwood and Jerome Quiles

I had problems with *The Hollow Men* when I first saw it, but it stayed with me and eventually made itself known as one of those films that draws you in and makes you think.

Any filmmaker can refuse to dot his i's and cross his t's for the sake of cinematic ambiguity, but it's easy to lose the audience when doing so. What Ashley Denton achieves here is a film that we don't get, but is enticing enough to make us want to explore it and figure out the puzzle.

Ironically, in doing that, he does to us precisely what the story does to his characters and I believe that's the key to understand what's going on. I have no idea how long it took me to figure out the ending, but I think I'm finally there and *The Hollow Men* plays all the better now I have my own theory as to what it means. I should emphasise that while my theory holds true, as far as I can tell, it is just a theory and Denton may have aimed at something else entirely or even to create a film that has no answer but prompts its audience to theorise.

Two scientists walk into their laboratory for the umpteenth time, entirely familiar with their surroundings, moving through the routine steps they need to set up their new day, bickering at each other about their methodologies as they do so. Oli is the shorter one in the flying helmet that ought to look completely out of place but somehow fits with the delightfully analogue equipment with all their switches and dials. Charlie is the taller, more arrogant one who clearly believes he's in charge, whether he is or not. The word of the day is surely "comfortable", but something is different and eventually they notice. There's some kind of burning vision at the end of a corridor, a sort of artificial sun that just sits there radiating light, waiting for them to notice it and ask questions. "What did you change?" Charlie asks Oli and they're off and running.

What it is we're never really told, though it's apparently an unexpected overflow of their experiment to generate something. Its blinding light hides a doorway, which it has also metaphorically become.

And as they walk towards it, the movie restarts. They're back at the beginning, arguing as they walk into the lab. It isn't a straight repetition, of course. While their actions and dialogue are mostly identical, there are changes which change all the more as Oli and Charlie gradually realise that they've done this before.

We aren't told how often they've been through this time loop already or how long it took before déjà vu set in, but they keep on restarting. We don't know how it's triggered or how large an area is affected. We have little data to go on, but we find a crucial point which sets up the dynamics of how they can jump the loop and move forward. What I find most fascinating about this is the irony with which the entire film is constructed. The scientists' job is clinical and methodical, but the reason they're watchable is that they're human beings, creating drama. The very stuff that makes the movie for us is what in them creates the opportunity for it to exist; when it goes away, so does the film. In a way, this is the purest and truest movie ending ever.

Denton's chief inspiration was Shane Carruth's *Primer*. "Seeing *Primer* for the first time was like a kick in the soul," he wrote on the film's website as part of a larger explanation that's well worth reading. Each of the points he makes there stood out for me as major successes for the film. The unexplained science was appropriate, to the degree that both Oli and Charlie appropriately mumble through their routine. Not showing "the machine" was a great choice, but so was not explaining it. Something as unreal as this MacGuffin is rendered all the more realistic by the characters not focusing their dialogue for the audience's benefit. A collection of tech donated by a ham radio nut grounds the whole thing.

Even the major omission Denton cites is spot on; I wondered why there were so few cables. Sure, the old tech would have been designed to house them, but not so the bigger or more modern equipment. There are flaws, as the staticky editing was certainly overdone, but it's powerful, if not a film for everyone. Let's see if it grabs you too.

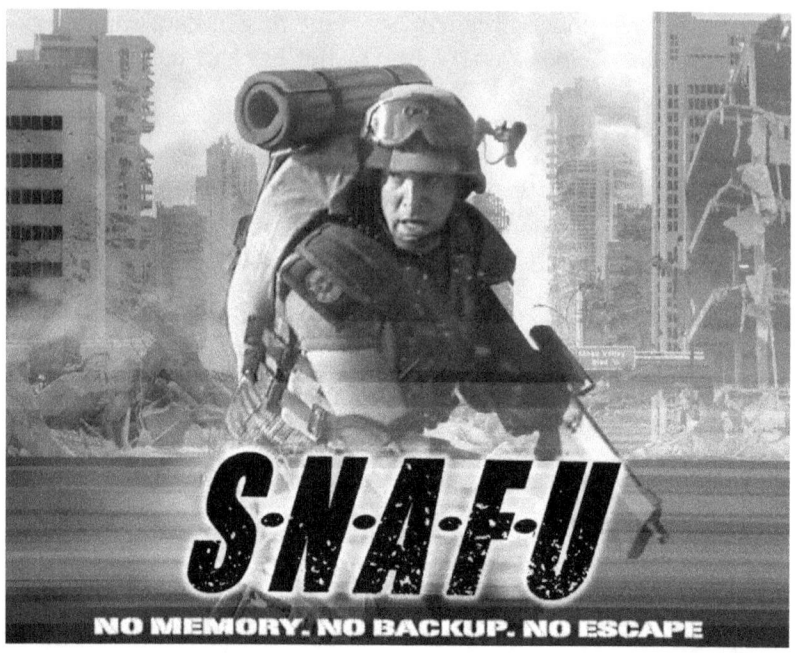

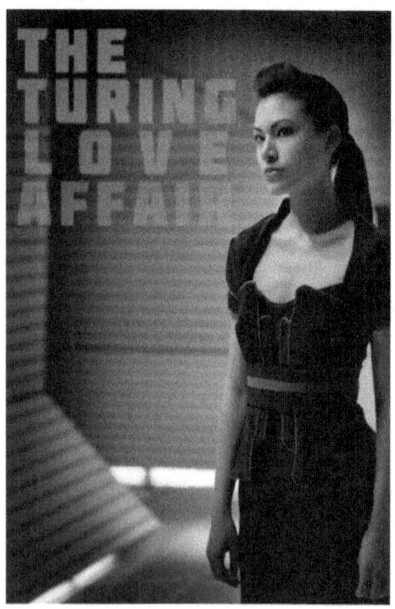

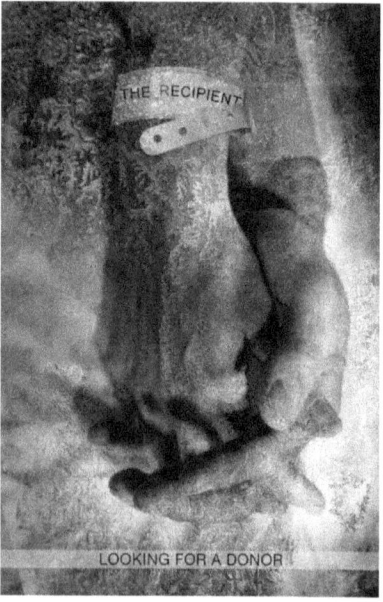

S.N.A.F.U. (2010)

Director: Julian Caldow
Writer: Julian Caldow
Stars: Eric Loren, Tom Sangster and Marshall Griffin

I enjoyed *S.N.A.F.U.* a lot, though it didn't take me long to figure out where it was going. That I continued to enjoy it, even after figuring out where it was going, says quite a lot because the twist isn't the be all and end all to the movie.

There's a lot more here, especially on the visual front, where the effects look great but how they're woven into the film is even more important. For instance, the short opens with a serene shot of the majesty of creation, a moon slowly orbiting a planet, then the peace of the universe is raped by the violence of a spacecraft going down hard because an unnamed soldier is about to crash onto an alien world. That shot also highlights the playfulness, appropriately as it turns out, that keeps a particularly dark story engaging, especially as it could easily have been rendered much darker still. It was intriguing to revisit it, as I'd forgotten the film over three years but its ideas had stayed relentlessly with me. When I caught up with *Edge of Tomorrow*, for instance, I saw *S.N.A.F.U.*, even though there were other ways to read it.

The soldier survives, apparently intact except for his memory. As he walks out of the mist on the surface, he narrates to us how he can't remember anything from before the crash: not his name, not his rank, not his reason for being there. He doesn't even know what the I.P.M.C. on his insignia stands for. He appears to be lucid now, with one driving thought that comes out of the haze: get to zone four. So off he goes, as a soldier is trained to do his duty, after all, whatever the circumstances. He discovers that he's not alone when he leaps into a foxhole to avoid some hover-tanks out on patrol, but the soldier there dressed in a similar uniform is a corpse with no face. He keeps on towards the destroyed city in the distance, whose roadsigns and construction appear quintessentially Earthlike even if the heavenly bodies in the sky tell us otherwise. He tracks down other soldiers, but the only one on his side is quickly killed by men from the other. An I.P.M.C. cylinder lands in the street, so he takes down a sniper nest and heads over to see what's in it.

And, after finding that it's a trap, he's shot dead by a laser installation that emerges from the ground. So much for our sole protagonist. But then, we start again. He wakes up out in the desert and heads back to town. "It's a stuck record," he narrates, "and I don't think I like the groove."

If we weren't paying attention to all the weirdness that was going down before, we can't fail to do so now. He'd watched as the soldier was killed, but a blink later they were all gone. One of the enemies, who dies in front of him, apparently can't remember anything before the crash either, and he has a great line of dialogue, albeit one hijacked from *RoboCop*. "I killed you," he says. There are a few ways that this can go, as déjà vu shows up and the soldier questions his environment and his connection to it, but I was with the right one all the way. After a fresh viewing, that may well be because I once wrote a short story that had major similarities to where it takes us after the initial twist is revealed. If so, this may play a little more surprising for you.

S.N.A.F.U. was a team effort, especially on the visual side, but the man behind it is clearly Julian Caldow, the writer, producer and director. He also scored the short, something that is surely due to one of the two influences that he cites, John Carpenter, with Sergio Leone being the other. Certainly the end credits feel very much like what Carpenter might have conjured up, not only because of the music but because of the choice of font, even its colour. The end of the film is reminiscent of Carpenter too, as is the use of a narration that feels much more hardboiled detective than standard science fiction. The coarse acting of Eric Loren fits too, though mostly through the archetypal action approach rather than through his channelling any particular Carpenter actor; he isn't trying to be Kurt Russell, for instance, not really. Clearly the sequel, if Caldow ever makes one, would move totally into Carpenter territory, but that's the sequel. I didn't see a lot of Leone though, maybe the lack of actors in detailed landscapes being the closest, but even then the vision was different.

Given the strong visual aesthetic, which is consistently fantastic for a film which runs a short 27 minutes, it's no surprise to discover

Caldow's background. He debuted here as a writer, producer and director, possibly as a composer too, but he has a major history in cinematic art, whether that be storyboarding, creature design or concept illustration. He started as a draughtsman on Tim Burton's *Batman*, and is still in the business, with films as prominent as *Gravity*, *Prometheus* and *X-Men: First Class* on his resume, as well as *Game of Thrones* for television.

With such a visual background, I was more surprised to find that his script stands up so well within the world he creates here. The only thing missing is population, as more enemies would have made a lot of sense and fleshed out his vision better. Perhaps Marshall Griffin could only bring life to so many of the Bluehawk Horde within the shooting schedule, but extras are generally easy to come by.

At the end of the day, it's a well rounded piece from a man who really should find time to make another short film of his own.

The Turing Love Affair (2010)

Director: Natasha Kermani
Writer: Natasha Kermani
Stars: Stefanie Woodburn, Brandon Wardell, Randy Spence and Grayson Brannen

I wanted to like *The Turing Love Affair* a lot more than I found myself able to, because it looks gorgeous and it's unashamedly geeky. Unfortunately the story it finds to unfold in this gorgeous and unashamedly geeky environment is far too weak to stand up to much attention, which is a real shame.

For those who have no idea what the title means, Alan Turing was a British mathematician who contributed so strongly to the field of computer science that he's been called "the father of artificial intelligence". During World War II, his work to break the codes of the German navy prompted no less a name than Winston Churchill to claim that he "made the single biggest contribution to Allied victory". Sadly, the reward he was given in 1952 for his service was to be chemically castrated after successful prosecution for being gay; he committed suicide two years later. He's in the title because of his Turing test, which famously defined the standard for a machine to be considered intelligent as being the point at which a human being, through conversation, proves unable to distinguish it from another human being.

As the title suggests, we're presented not only with a particular conversation between a human and a machine, but a conversation that moves into far more emotional territory.

The human is Harry Zelazny, probably a portmanteau of homages to science fiction writers Harry Harrison and Roger Zelazny. He's a musician, an important one if the magazine cover mounted onto the wall in his room at the Elizabeth Space Station is anything to go by. It calls him the "new face of modern music". Why he's staying on the Elizabeth we have no idea, but it's halfway between the inner system and the outer colonies, placing us firmly in both the future and the middle of nowhere. Perhaps he's trying to escape something, usually the case in the films noir that provide the look and feel of the piece. This is presented in colour, but a sepia-toned colour that often reminds of *Blade Runner*, itself a science fiction neo-noir. We quickly discover that Zelazny won't be leaving the Elizabeth, not ever, because someone or something has broken his neck in two places.

So in come the homicide investigators, Det. Anya Greenwood and Dr. Sam Tarkov, to ask questions of what seems to be the only suspect, Charlotte CA110, the stewardess responsible for taking care of Zelazny on the Elizabeth. She's a cyborg, one of 25 that maintain the station, and it's pretty obvious that she's not a human being. She looks great, but she moves too deliberately and has an odd melodic but artificial voice.

There's a lot that's derivative in the story, which is an archetypal one for science fiction literature, so the Lije Baley stories of Isaac Asimov, detective tales set in a world where humans and robots are very close to being indistinguishable, leap as quickly to mind as a reference point as does the Voight-Kampff test which Deckard and his colleagues administer in *Blade Runner* to delineate humans from replicants, itself based on a science fiction novel, Philip K. Dick's *Do Androids Dream of Electric Sheep?* Whatever we call the test, it's a Turing test, though here there's another level: has the known cyborg found consciousness?

And here the script has us watch two stories unfold. In flashback, we watch Charlotte CA110 talk with the man she's tasked to steward, conversation that goes far beyond what might be expected for her job. She listens to him play his music, which may be part of why she appears to fall for him in ways a cyborg isn't supposed to be able to do. This flashback shows us what led up to Zelazny's murder while, in the present, the Nucorp interrogators try to figure it out by questioning the stewardess.

I find it admirable that writer Natasha Kermani, who directed the film too, aimed to tell a human story in addition to the one more overtly rooted in science fiction, because Greenwood and Tarkov approach the interrogation very differently, something that builds them as characters and a dynamic between them. There's an important story hiding in here about the origins of consciousness, one important enough to frame the film and provide its title, but its actual exploration is surprisingly only hinted at.

I'm not calling for this to be a feature, but it deserves to be a much longer short film as fifteen minutes is not enough to do it justice. While Kermani started down all the right roads, none of them get to where she aims to reach, leaving us dazzled by the visuals but frustrated by the script. It's almost a Hollywood trope that time honoured ideas be trumped by the look and feel of a film, but this doesn't feel like Hollywood, it just feels incomplete.

I'll happily praise a host of crew members for their contributions to the visuals: Seth Hagenstein for his cinematography which plays very nicely indeed with angles and lighting; Raquel Cedar for her production design, as she nails both the sterility of the space station and its film noir atmosphere; Brendan Bellomo and hs visual effects team, the former something of an International Horror & Sci-Fi Film Festival regular with *Bohemibot* and *Sol* also under his belt; even Lauren Bates Jaffe for her make up work. If we could watch this in a half hour version, perhaps Kermani's script could explore enough to catch up to their standards.

The Recipient (2010)

Director: Javier Bermúdez
Writers: David Norris and Javier Bermúdez
Stars: Zack Zublena, Marigló Vizcarrondo, Cristina Sesto, Terry Muñiz, Lydia Aquino and Alfredo DeQuesada

While many of its peers within the Sci-Fi Shorts B set at the 2011 festival were complex affairs, worthy of a great deal of discussion, *The Recipient* would seem to be a simpler, much more focused piece.

Simple that is, until the very last line, an absolute peach that prompts the reevaluation of everything that has gone before. That's superlative writing from David Norris, who also shot the film, and Javier Bermúdez, who also directed it; both of them also served as its producers. Until that last line, Pierre Gautier seems a relatively straightforward lead character, the man referenced in the film's tagline: "How far will a man go when he finds out that the only way to save his wife is to end the life of another?" Until that last line, what he goes through is something we can all imagine, empathise with or even remember, at least to a degree; Pierre does go a little further than most of us would, after all. Surely, whatever depth of pain we might discover after the loss of our respective spouses, most of us would still set limits on what we might do about it.

However, Pierre Gautier is especially devoted and, as a company C.E.O., he has some resources to bring to bear in the matter. Norris and Bermúdez set him up as a good man, who isn't just clearly in love with his wife on the wedding video he watches as the film begins; he still is, however many years that it's been since. He also appears to be a good man in that, even from the pinnacle of his company's power structure, he's willing to take the time to chat with the man who cleans his office.

Of course, as the story moves on and we find out what he's willing to do to save his wife, he shifts consistently into darker territory. The people he's working with to bring her back from cryogenic storage are not regular scientists. He has to provide a large payment, of course, but sign no formal contract. There are serious requirements for secrecy and no guarantees that the process will work. He also has to provide a donor, by kidnapping one. These are the people of last resort, providing an underground service at a serious financial and moral cost.

While the film works on the level of the question it poses, the lengths we would knowingly go to in order to save someone we love, there's a little more here that's worthy of discussion.

Pierre Gautier is clearly an important man, not just because he's a C.E.O. and because he can raise a large sum of money very quickly, but in the way he carries himself. Zack Zublena, a French actor fluent in the English language, makes him feel like he's important because of who he is, someone with natural power, from which his position naturally springs. A poor man could have kidnapped a donor and stolen the money, but he couldn't have had the inherent power to make him appropriate for this story. So, while this is no moral judgement on the 1%, it is at least a meditation on what "power" means.

And, of course, that's highlighted by the blistering finalé that's delivered by Mariglo Vizcarrondo in what appears to be her only film role. I won't spoil this, but I will recommend that, now Fanatico Films have made the film available online, you should experience this amazing ending for yourselves.

Carry Tiger to the Mountain (2011)

Directors: Bennett Lieberman and Arnold Barkus
Writers: Bennett Lieberman and Arnold Barkus
Stars: Xin Li and James Rich

I've seen many films with titles sourced from odd places, but I don't think I've ever seen a science fiction film named for a tai chi position before.

It makes sense here, because this short film has the rather ambitious goal of merging two ostensibly incompatible concepts: time travel, the science fiction staple, and tai chi, a Chinese martial art practiced as much for inner tranquility and health benefits as for any of its pointers to self defence. Why writers and directors Bennett Lieberman and Arnold Barkus thought these would merge well, I have no idea, but that starting point provides all the good points to this short film, as well as all the bad points too. Marrying science to spirituality is a noble goal but also an impossible task and we leave the film as confused as to what we just watched as entertained by some of what went down. In the end, it's a human story about two people who don't know they're in love yet surrounded by a sci-fi attempt to spice up how they figure it out. Yet even that doesn't really work, so I'm unsure as to what's left.

Initially it comes over as scientific gibberish painted over a hippie backdrop. I'm still not quite convinced that it really leaves that by the time the end credits roll, because the more I try to fathom the answers to what it raises, the less I'm sure as to what the questions actually were. It's the sort of movie that continually moves around to keep us interested but without ever seeming to actually do anything.

Certainly it's almost stereotypically insubstantial to begin with, with an enticing narration all about time and dreams and transdimensional gateways. It may be as much freeform poetry as it is science hinted at by on screen mathematical formulae that may or may not attempt to describe the deliberately slowly edited living world they overlay. "Dreams originate on the space-time manifold of cosmic consciousness," expounds the eager narrator who seems unable to stop. "They're forged in a turbulent furnace by quantum mechanical fields percolating bubbles of time into ever expanding oceans of simultaneous being and nothingness." Yeah, baby! Right on!

To be fair, it does get more grounded as we begin the film proper and watch Ali try to chat up Ming. He's a nerd but not outrageously so. He wears glasses and Tesla shirts and has that sort of constantly happy demeanour that makes us want to punch him. Ming, on the other hand, is a free spirit. The camera floats around her and she floats around him and it in a sort of dance. It's odd to see her during the staccato editing phases where the goal appears to be to capture moments of time and skip forward through them rather than let them unfold at normal speed. That seems somehow right for him, as a scientist aiming to figure out how to travel through time, but utterly wrong for her as nothing ought to contain her, even deliberate editing. Eventually they connect through tai chi, because she knows what she's doing and he doesn't, perfecting pratfalls but not postures. Apparently he's figured out that tai chi is the way to travel through time, though we're never quite let in on that secret. Carry Tiger to the Mountain is the move that presumably works.

And off he goes, blinking into nothingness and scaring the crap out of Ming. When he comes back only a few moments later, he's talking backwards and convinced that they're an item. The rest of the story may or may not explain any of why.

And here's the real problem of the film. I can watch Ali because he's good at being a wacky sort of charmer with an undercurrent, half science and half new age, that prompts us to wonder which side of those strange bedfellows he sleeps with. I can watch Ming all day because she's a pretty Chinese girl who sunbathes on the roof and knows tai chi, and because, while she doesn't appear to actually do anything, she does hint that there's substance there waiting to be found. James Rich and Xin Li aren't the most talented actors I've ever seen but they fit the story well, people caught up in something magical and never losing their sense of joy. So, while the sci-fi pretends to be substantial, it plays much more like a large slice of meaningless jabber.

And as a quirky romance, it's well, quirky. New age time travel: A+ for ambition at least.

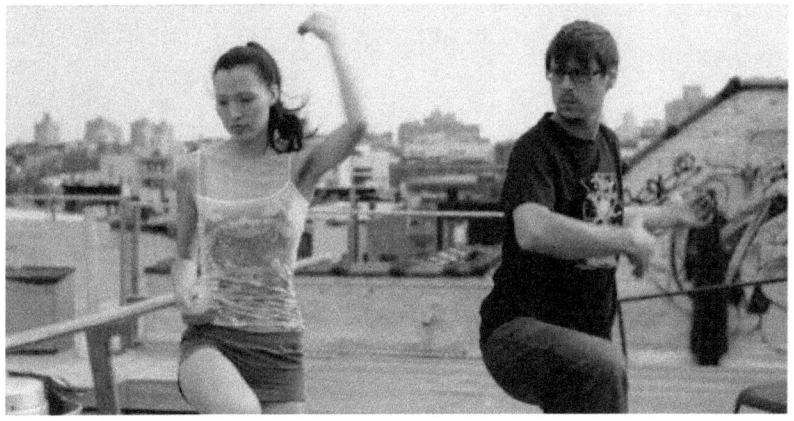

Carry Tiger to the Mountain

The International Horror & Sci-Fi Film Festival

2012

Horror Features

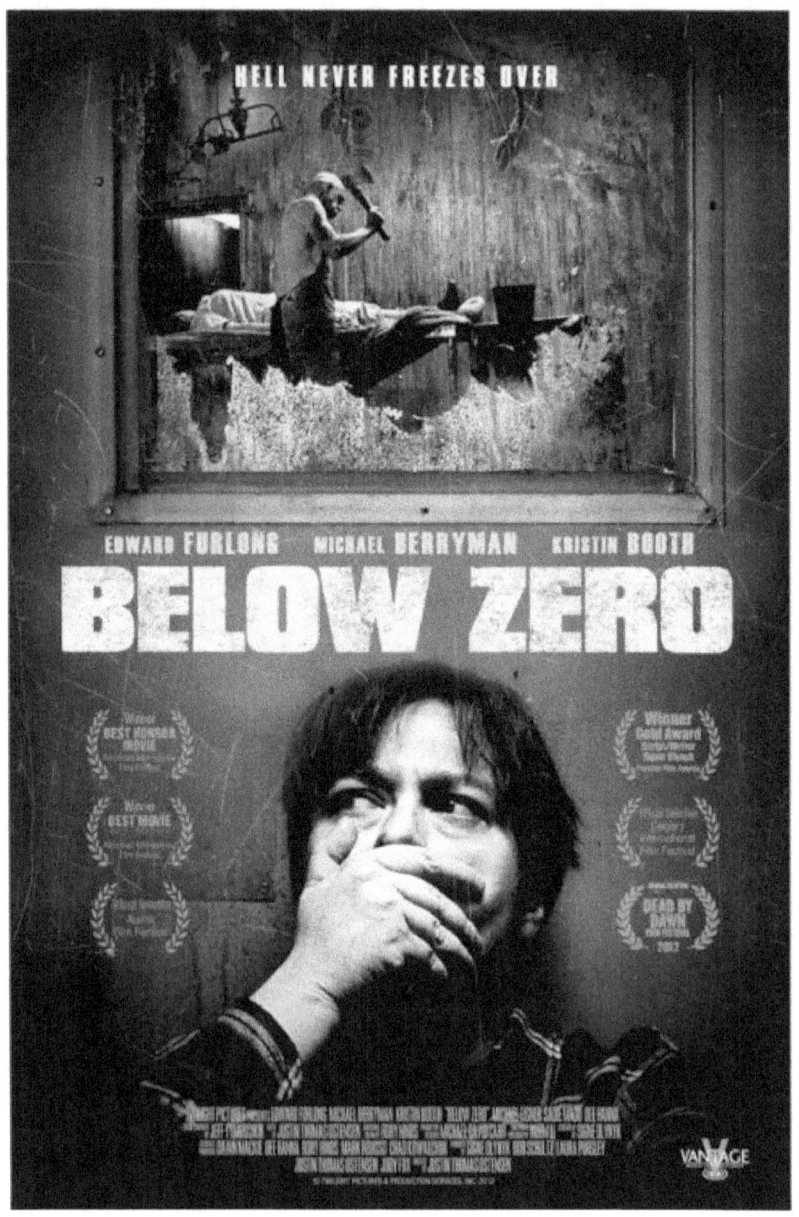

Below Zero (2011)

Director: Justin Thomas Ostensen
Writer: Signe Olynyk
Stars: Edward Furlong, Michael Berryman and Kristin Booth

Below Zero is a Twilight Picture, apparently, but not a *Twilight* picture. Let me make that clear right off the bat! You'd really think they'd change their name.

More promising as it kicks off are the setting, which is firmly in the middle of Canadian nowhere, and the cast, which isn't big but is impressive. Kristin Booth plays Penny, a small town single mother who's desperately trying to be Frances McDormand in *Fargo* and doing a pretty decent job of it. She picks up Edward Furlong, who's a screenwriter from California known to one and all as Jack the Hack.

He's suffering from writer's block and his agent is going to drop him if he can't produce a script in a week, so what can he do? Well, perhaps being locked inside an Alberta meat freezer might do the trick. Jack tries to pass it off as method writing, but he really doesn't have a choice: Penny isn't to let him out until he's done. The orders are strict.

I get the concept, which is an enticing one, especially to a writer. So does the screenwriter of this film, Signe Olynyk, far more than anyone, because she apparently did for real what Jack only gets to do in the movie, and she did it in the same meat freezer to boot.

Given that we can't fail to merge the two of them within our imaginations as we watch the product of theirs, it seems surprising that Olynyk writes Jack as pretty much a waste of space. Sure, he has a successful movie behind him, but that was four years ago, which is forever in Hollywood. What's more, Penny saw it. "But I'm sure this one'll be good," she tells him.

The cleverest thing Jack says throughout the entire picture is its tagline: "There's nothing scarier than a blank page." It sounds like he's said it many times before and to many different people; his nickname is presumably a lot truer than he'd like it to be.

He's just as lacking outside of work as well. While Penny is taking good care of her son, the silent Cole who she calls "a good kid, just different", Jack hasn't seen his son in three years, a particular shock when he realises it. For my part, I was shocked to realise that this film marks a full two decades since *Terminator 2: Judgment Day*, but Furlong has worked his way through *American History X*, *The Crow: Wicked Prayer* and *Detroit Rock City* to end up looking somewhat like a young Sam Raimi.

And so off we go. Penny has set everything up as per his agent's instructions; he gets a bed, a set of books and a school desk to put his laptop on. There's food, of course, but no toilet, just a bucket. There's no internet and the only phone is broken. A cork board, a goldfish in a bowl and Elvis the dead pig hanging from the ceiling will apparently be less distracting. How a dead pig hanging from a ceiling could be less distracting than anything, I have no idea, but I'm thankful that Elvis is in the movie. Jack does get a ball, which was all Steve McQueen ever needed in *The Great Escape* during his isolation time. And there's also a screenplay Penny wrote, just in case he gets bored.

He may well need it because, without it, all that he manages to conjure up to begin his script is, "What if someone was accidentally locked in a meat freezer by a serial killer... who doesn't know he's in there?" That's all the setup we get. She locks him in and we're all ready to be stuck with Jack and his writer's block for five full days. Really that isn't promising, as it sounds a lot cooler than it's ever likely to look, something that feels more like a novel than a feature length film, as inherently as it ties to a writer's state of mind and work ethic. Clocks ticking in movies are annoying and so, usually, are empty rooms and tiny casts.

What we get instead is a neat blurring of reality and imagination, as we see what Jack starts to conjure up. I was quickly reminded of Tom Waits. "Some songs come out of the ground just like a potato," he explained to Edna Gundersen of *USA Today* back in 1999 about his inspirations. "Others you have to make out of things around the house like your mother's pool cue and your neighbor's ostrich and your grandma's purse." Another version the same year showed up as he introduced *Tango 'Til They're Sore* during his *VH1 Storytellers* episode, with examples like "your dad's Army buddy, your sister's wristwatch, and that type of thing." The point is that you just have to look around you to find the ingredients to your literary stew. Waits has the luxury of time, of course, while Jack the Hack is stuck in a meat freezer with Elvis the dead pig and the most important deadline of his life. It sounds just like the next version.

There's not a lot to find, by deliberate design, so he naturally builds his screenplay out of the things he, and we, saw in the first twenty minutes: hooks, cows, a tarp, a silent little kid and a locking door. Of course, he imagines a decor that's dirtier, grittier, darker, you know, more horror movie. The walls become bloody, with partial skeletons impaled on those hooks, a woman hung from the ceiling along with the pigs.

Oh, and Michael Berryman, of course, from *The Hills Have Eyes* and a whole shelf worth of other horror movies that all capitalised on his hypohidrotic ectodermal dysplasia, a rare medical condition that means that he has no hair, fingernails, teeth or even sweat glands, and occasionally even made good use of his acting skills too. I'm not sure if his inclusion here tells us that Jack the Hack might not be quite so much of the latter after all, because he's perfectly cast for this part, or whether he's all hack because, hey, Michael Berryman's recognisable features are pretty safe imagery for any writer trying to visualise a horror movie. Doesn't Jack's imagination stretch any further than safe imagery?

I focused far more on the approach, which is notably interesting, especially when you factor in the real life layer. Just as Signe Olynyk apparently imagined her own self into Jack the Hack, Jack in turn imagines himself into Frank, a tow truck driver who's a take on Cole's mysterious and absent father. It's relatively predictable, but it's capable enough. Of course, the silent child is a fictionalised version of Cole, called Golem. The woman hanging from the ceiling is Paige, a social worker investigating him.

Just as Furlong plays both Jack and Frank, Kristin Booth plays both Penny and Paige and Sadie Madu plays both Cole and Golem. The latter is an Edmonton local, only nine years old and cast in this role because she knew the location very well, having visited the slaughterhouse for Hallowe'en parties. The film's website suggests that her experiences making this film inspired her to join a youth theatre group, which transforms *Below Zero* into a pretty cool way to start a career. Now I need to be shocked to realise it's 2031 so I can look back at her achievements.

There are a couple of new characters joining the story, so that we don't just watch Furlong for an hour and a half. Michael Eisner (no, not the billionaire former Disney C.E.O.) gets a little screen time as Morty, Frank's colleague in the towing business, but it can't be a shock when Berryman gets much more.

He channels a Karloff as the Mummy vibe as Gunnar, who's a completely cuckoo serial killer in a leather butcher's apron. He's always worth watching, whatever the material, but Berryman can do freaky in his sleep; his condition ensures that on its own but he also has a lot of experience in figuring out how to use that to his advantage and ratchet up the unease. To stand out against anything else in his filmography, though, this film would need substance, much more than what we get from Jack rewinding the footage he imagines to slip in new plot devices.

Some substance does arrive the moment we shift back to reality, only to discover that Jack is his own worst enemy as we realise that he's not there alone; he's been locked into this meat freezer with his inner demons, who blur the line between his reality and his imagination as they torment him. They also seriously boost Jack the Hack as a character, which was just as seriously needed.

What follows turns out to be less of a horror movie and more of an exploration of the writing process and how hard it is to write, especially when the flow isn't there but a deadline is. It's not only about writer's block, it's about everything that sits behind it: doubt, motivation, integrity and a special brand of insanity which only writers will recognise. While Edgar Allan Poe may never actually have said, "I'm a writer, therefore I am not sane," contrary to a recent internet meme, the sentiment still rings true. He certainly did write in a letter to George Washington Eveleth that, "I became insane, with long intervals of horrible sanity" and that line could easily be described as the bedrock on which the entire horror genre was forged.

It's this last third of the film that will matter most when people determine what they think of it, as the first two acts are pretty accessible and straightforward. The first is all setup, played entirely straight, while the second reimagines the reality as fiction and begins to blur the two together. The third ratchets it all up a notch, as you might expect, but it also convolutes the story and makes us unsure how much of what we see is real or imagined.

When a fictional version of the film's writer imagines a fictional version of a character real to him and she tells him that a further fictional version of herself who has been interacting with a fictional version of himself could really be fictional to his fictional self, it may just be one little step too far.

I felt that the last act started out well but lost itself and I watched the film twice to be sure. It got to the point where I started to wonder whether any of this was real or whether the key to it all is Jack's T-shirt, which reads simply "Insanity". Perhaps we're back to Poe again. I see the cues that tell us what's real and what's not, but I'm not convinced that they're the only ones. A second viewing did help and I won't discount the possibility that a third might clear up the rest, but somehow I doubt it. I think I may now have got out of the film what was put in.

I wonder how much of an idea Signe Olynyk had about what she was going to write before getting locked in that real meat freezer, but maybe she took a journey inside her head, just like Jack does, and found herself a good story, only to lose it again before she could wrap it up.

At least it isn't B.O.S.H., the term Penny uses to highlight how Jack's work is the same ol' same ol'. It stands, rather neatly, for Bunch Of Shit Happens.

Whatever else this is, at least it isn't B.O.S.H.

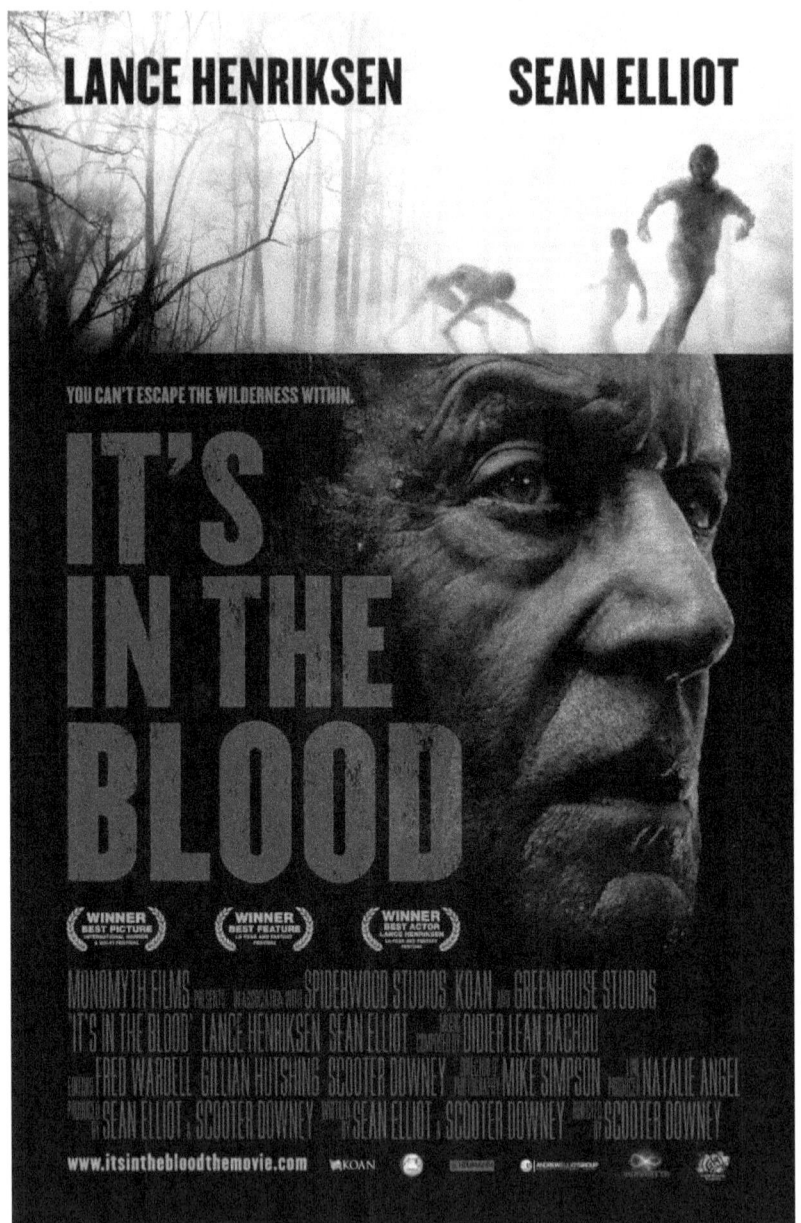

It's in the Blood (2012)

Director: Scooter Downey
Writers: Scooter Downey and Sean Elliot
Stars: Lance Henriksen and Sean Elliot

There were no less than three new Lance Henriksen pictures on show at the 2012 festival, making it more his event than that of anyone who actually showed up. The special guest that year was Michael Biehn, only represented by one film, *The Victim*, even if he was its writer, director and star and the head of the production company that made it. Ironically, Henriksen was the special guest a couple of years earlier in 2010, when he was only represented by a retro showcase feature, *Aliens*.

In 2012, he found his way into three tracks, as *Monster Brawl* was a showcase feature, while *Ambush* was up for competition as a horror short and *It's in the Blood* as a horror feature. *Monster Brawl* can be safely ignored for everything except Henriksen's tiny contribution while *Ambush* was a really interesting short, but this was his key title of the year and it fairly took home the Best Horror Film award.

It's an indie feature from Monomyth Films and it's far from the usual schlock horror, but it still elevated itself considerably when it landed such a prestigious name. What's more, Henriksen, always a reliable actor, gives one of the more impressive performances of his career to emphasise the film even more.

If Henriksen is the big name and the powerhouse on screen, he's perhaps less important in the grand scheme of things than his co-star, Sean Elliot, of whom precious few had heard until this picture.

He started his career in 2008 in a bit part in a sequel shot for TV, then played a little further up the credits in a couple of features. Here, though, he's half of what's close to being a two man cast in a picture that calls for serious depth from his performance, even as he plays opposite a major actor with major experience, and he's responsible for half of that depth. Now he surely understood his character particularly well, because he co-wrote and co-produced the film too. but it still highlights that where Elliot goes next will perhaps depend more than anything else on how far he wants to reach. His future should be very open indeed, even if two years on he hasn't earned himself a single further credit. I wonder why.

Elliot plays October, a man with an eidetic memory who reads an entire medical book while hitching his way home to go on a hiking trip with his dad. It's particularly fortuitous because he has to put his newfound knowledge to use as soon as he gets there, because Cairo, his father's dog, was caught in a trap.

Dad is Russell, a fourth generation Texan sheriff, but October not being the fifth is only one of the reasons why they're apparently not very close. He hasn't lived up to his father's expectations, that's overtly clear, but there's also a more specific history between them. We soon discover that it ties to a girl named Iris but the details are teasingly withheld and revealed gradually, in keeping with the psychological nature of this story.

Both here at the beginning and throughout the film, we wonder how much of what we see is external plot and how much just the history of these two finding its way off their chests after all these years, but really it's the latter manifested onto the former. The question of the day is this: when you fight your demons, how real can they be? Here, they're very real indeed.

Initially, at least, it's clearly all about the relationship. It took October a year to answer his father's call and he still isn't really sure why he did. He calls him Russell or Old Man, never Dad, and the back and forth editing as they argue ably emphasises the distance between them. Yet at points, they're still able to find common ground and connect. They can even pee together. The first long scene they share has Russell teaching October how to drive stick and it's a joyous scene, outrageously set up as an overt sexual metaphor.

Driving stick is one of those things Russell never got round to teaching him, like shooting a rifle or drinking 150 proof, though as we soon discover, the clock is ticking. This dramatic approach works particularly well. Russell, who has nothing left of substance in his life, wants to start teaching his kid the things he should have done long ago. October, who has wandered the country trying to escape from his past, is on board with that but, tellingly, not one of the skills he uses here is sourced from his dad.

The two sides of the film merge quickly, as Russell and October reach the woods through which they're planning to hike together. Their history raises its ugly head in their very first argument. "Are we going to talk about what happened," asks October, "or are we going to keep pretending there's nothing wrong?" Russell is sure of his side. "What's done is done," he states.

Rather tellingly, it's as this clash really begins that Russell sees something in the woods that shocks him, fires his rifle in reaction and falls off a bluff, breaking his leg very badly indeed. Now, instead of hiking together, because that's clearly not going to happen, they share in the aftermath of this event and the one that won't stay in their past. We don't really know what that something is that's out there in the woods, but we can be pretty sure that it isn't what we see. We're shown what Russell and October see, visions shaped by their personal demons and shrouded in metaphorical fog. "See what you want to see," one vision tells October late in the film and that's meant for us as much as it is for him.

While *It's in the Blood* felt very fresh on a first viewing, it didn't gel the way it did on a second, where it played far more consistently for me. The writing has depth that doesn't all surface the first time through but makes itself very clear when we watch again with knowledge of where things are going to go.

What was clear immediately was that the two leads do justice to substantial, well nuanced parts. Henriksen is sorely underrated, whether he's undeservedly slighted by being perceived as a genre actor or hindered by the weight of so many awful movies that he's carried over the years, but I've never seen him quite so deep as he is here. He gets a lot of opportunity to be tough, hardly a stretch for him, but a lot more to be weak too and it ably demonstrates how broad his range truly is. Sean Elliot may well have this part because he wrote it, but if he wasn't worthy, Henriksen would have stolen this whole thing out from under him without even trying. That he fought hard enough for the two to be seen on equal terms speaks volumes. Rose Sima and Jimmy Gonzales only exist in the back story that we see in flashback but they do fine work nonetheless.

A perennial question at film festivals, one that is rarely answered for all sorts of reasons, is to ask the size of the budget, especially with indie pictures. While the revelation of a tiny sum can lead to astonishment at how much was achieved with so little, it often ends up becoming an albatross. How can a film that cost a mere X dollars be fairly compared with another movie that cost ten times X or ten thousand times as much? As much as I appreciate the reasons why many filmmakers don't answer that question, I'm often intrigued to figure it out. This is one of those films where I didn't want to know at the time, because it stands up so well on its own merits that I didn't want a number to flavour it. Looking back from the hindsight of a couple of years, I see that it cost an estimated three million dollars which is right in the sweet spot of indie budgets, enough to do what they want but not enough to allow sloppiness.

It's put to good use. Nothing much here warranted a sizable cost, beyond perhaps Henriksen's salary, but three million meant that we don't find ourselves trying to figure out where the filmmakers avoided spending money. Perhaps they could have put a little into a camera with a better steadicam, but they certainly didn't need to throw money at the effects. This is one of those monster movies where the monster is even more of a McGuffin than usual. We don't need to know what it is because it doesn't matter, only what it stands for.

It's a frequently dark film, but the lighting (or the lack of it) fits the tone. We see everything we need to see. The camerawork is annoyingly handheld at points for a non-handheld movie, but the composition of frame is very careful and artistically set, starting with the very first shot, which is of an upside down stick insect, of all things. Many subsequent shots would work well as photographs, even before movement is factored in. The effects are appropriate, whether they're the impressionistic monsters, part Bigfoot and part Grey and all freaky weirdness, or Russell's rapidly deteriorating leg.

Elliot's cohort as writer and producer, Scooter Downey, also served as director and editor and is capable in all those varied roles, even though he surprisingly has even less experience than Elliot. Amazingly, this is his first feature outside of an internship on a Frank Langella movie in 2005, *How You Look to Me*. The maturity of the film, given the lack of experience of its key players, is truly astonishing. At least Downey has gone on to other work, with three further titles to his name since this one.

I'm guessing it was Elliot who brought the ambition, though it may have been him and Downey both. Heaping a psychological overlay of internal demons onto an external threat isn't your usual sort of horror movie, let alone a debut. To see it superbly handled is more than refreshing.

I found myself less consistently impressed by the use of October's eidetic memory though. Initially it felt like a deus ex machina, a particularly convenient way for him to have the knowledge that he needed later on in the picture but, as the story evolved, it became more substantial as a real plot element. Russell explains to him that "everything fades" but, of course, it won't if you have photographic memory. Suddenly it ceases to be a powerful boon and becomes a constant irritant. From that odd angle, trauma is a powerful thing indeed and this story is an excellent framework to explore that concept.

What didn't find itself is the fact that October is a cutter. Why would a man who can't forget cut himself to remember? Maybe I'm not reading that imagery as it was intended, but I can't see another way to read it. It just looks cool? Surely not.

Maybe there's more waiting for me in a third viewing; it wouldn't surprise me. There seem to be many detractors of the film, but they consistently read it as a survival story, a monster movie or some other conventional thing. On that level, I would echo their disdain, but that's not the level this film works at. *It's in the Blood* may be the title, appropriately when you consider more than one meaning of "blood", but really it's in the mind.

The International Horror & Sci-Fi Film Festival

2012

Sci-Fi Features

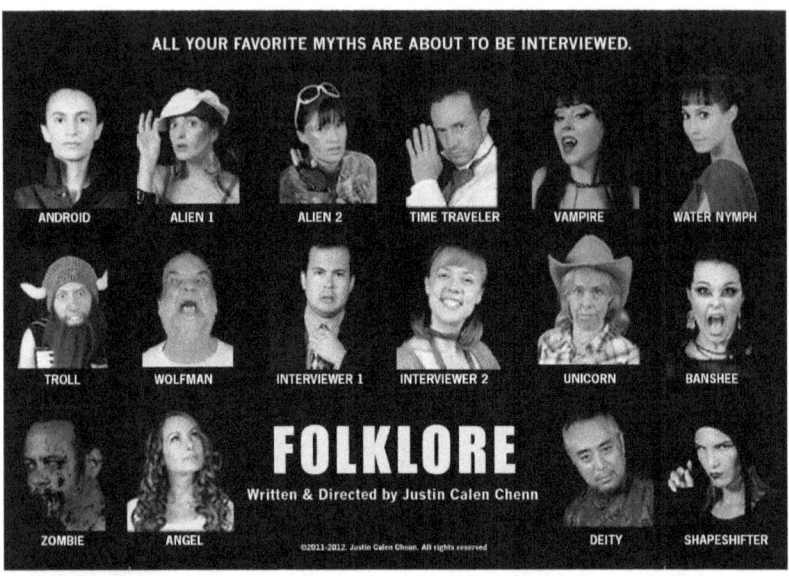

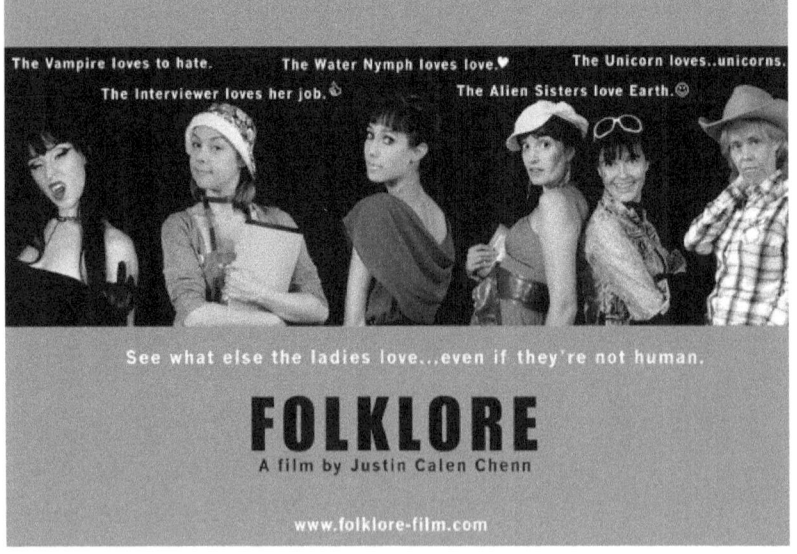

Folklore (2012)

Director: Justin Calen Chenn
Writer: Justin Calen Chenn
Stars: Laura Waddell and Brad Roller

Of all the many movies I saw at the Phoenix Film Festival in 2012, not just the genre side of it but from any track, this was perhaps the one that I enjoyed the most.

Now, it wasn't the best picture or the deepest. It was far from the most outrageous or provocative. It wouldn't even make a shortlist for the most expensive. Yet it was 81 minutes of pure enjoyment that I still think back on with a big grin, because that's what was plastered across my face for the entire running time.

Shot in a mere eight days after a more substantial project fell through, with a Kickstarter budget a tad shy of not a heck of a lot, *Folklore* is something of a textbook on how to achieve a lot with only a little. There's an empty office floor near LAX that ably doubles for a set of corporate looking conference rooms and corridors. There's a smattering of props to break up that empty space. There's a vague concept of a story setting rather than a traditional plot. That's not much to build a feature film out of, huh? But with great actors and great writing, not to mention great comedic timing, it comes alive.

And that's exactly what we have here: a multinational ensemble cast of character actors who all have a blast with their roles and a script that bubbles with the sort of quirky British humour I grew up with back in England.

The biggest surprise is that writer/director Justin Calen Chenn, a mere thirty years old at the time, is Taiwanese American. He's a Californian native, born and bred, even if he happens to be fluent in Mandarin, but you'd think he came from the other side of the pond, so natural is he with the traditional British sense of humour. He cites Mike Leigh and Ken Loach as primary directorial influences, with *Monty Python's Flying Circus*, *This is Spinal Tap* and even *Minority Report* more specific to this script, but I have a feeling he could cite three other influences at every screening he attends and never come up dry. His script is something of a distillation of the history of British comedy: the surreality of the Pythons, the dry wit of the Ealing comedies, the satire of the news quizzes, the perspective shifts of Douglas Adams, and of course the frustrations of no end of BBC sitcoms.

Out of this cauldron of comedic influence comes a simple idea for a movie. The Quartz Agency is a government department that attempts to keep track of the various supernatural entities which populate our planet, through periodic interviews. We're treated to a single day's worth of them, conducted by new guy Collins Jahn. He's struggling through his first day on the job without either the right paperwork or the classifications of the fourteen subjects he's scheduled to interview. Pretty much all he has to ground him is the joyously inappropriate Merle Eppis to assist.

His struggles are framed as a set of recurring vignettes which are rarely tied together, so if you're here for a plot you're going to be sadly disappointed, though some do eventually join together to hint at subplots on occasion. The joy here comes from the vignettes themselves, the situation comedy that underpins them and the character actors who give them life. This may sound like a flimsy base for a feature film and, to be brutally honest, it is, but in these hands it could easily drive a sketch comedy series for years, never mind just eighty minutes.

In many ways, Jahn is the least watchable of the bunch because he's almost the only actor in the entire film who plays it straight. Brad Roller does a capable job but being the only character without quirks in a picture that thrives on quirkiness does tend to shift him inexorably into the background. I'd like to see him in something where he has the opportunity to be more dynamic.

Certainly, he's overshadowed by his assistant, Merle Eppis, because actor Laura Waddell is as natural a clown as I've ever seen. She steals a great deal of the show here, even when sharing the screen with talented scenestealers, as Eppis has no restraint and Waddell has perfect comedic timing, along with a smile that has no conception of how to quit. It makes her entire face light up and it's acutely contagious. Simply visualising that smile has the magic power to turn bad days into good ones and the memory of the blush that arrived when I told her that, a couple of days after seeing the film, in the hallways of the Harkins Ciné Capri, is a treasured bonus for me. If she's given the right opportunity in the right sitcom, she'll be a superstar in no time flat. Watch this space.

Jahn and Eppis are the grounding for the entire film and their chalk and cheese characterisations are what everything else is built on. In many ways the rest of the cast are merely props for them to work with, my favourite scene perhaps being one where a French android is tasked merely with keeping a straight face while Eppis leans into frame for more inappropriate monologue.

Yet a few of them are gifted with their own opportunities too and, while some do shine brighter than others, not one lets the side down. It's hard to tell which is more diverse: the sampling of beings from folklore, the origins of the actors who portray them or the notably different comedic approaches which they apply to their roles. Fourteen actors from ten countries play thirteen different beings and the most important crew member after Chenn would surely be casting director Stephon Frost, if only that wasn't him too. I can't imagine anyone else in these parts, even the ones with little screen time.

All this diversity gives me the impression that any random sampling of viewers would manifest a wide range of favourite characters. I'm pretty sure mine wouldn't stay constant for long.

During the film itself, I'd probably have gone with the black clad shapeshifter Freda Gomo, who knocks herself out trying to shift in a performance that owes much to mime. Half an hour later I might have switched to the Ipsett sisters, a twin alien double act who continually finish each other's sentences, even when they're mad at each other. Tomorrow it might be the dominatrix vampire who can slap people with her mind. Or the surreal time traveller who channels Shakespearean dialogue in a truly outrageous outfit. Or the Icelandic troll with an accordion. Or... let's just say that I'm likely to play *Folklore* so much when it comes out on DVD (which it annoyingly still hasn't done) to discover my favourite that I should buy two copies so that I don't have to slow down when the first one wears out.

While we're drawn into the characters rather than the actors, the folk who gift them with life deserve credit. Chenn wrote the script but his writing was improvised on by some of the actors, making their portrayals a collaborative effort.

The shapeshifter is Tracy Bjelland, one of the few inexperienced members of the cast, judging from her credits list. Beyond mere dialogue, I loved how she acted with her face and body. The Ipsett twins are Sherill Turner and Rachel Rath, who share incredible chemistry as a double act, even though one is English and the other Irish. Taryn Kamus, time traveller, is Napoleon Ryan, who I'm seriously amazed managed to keep a straight face reading such pompous dialogue. Garrett Liggett plays the troll and he's priceless, though he gets little to do. Ruth Connell is the haughty lady vampire. Also worthy of mention are Paris Benjamin as the stoic French android Annabelle Sein and Paulie Rojas, who channels Audrey Hepburn as ethereal water nymph Nairie Sleen.

I'm eager to follow many of these actors to other roles in other pictures, because I want to know how much of themselves they put into these characters and how much they conjured out of the material. I knew one already, though I couldn't place her at the time. Maria Olsen, a backwoods Texan unicorn here, was the bloody nurse I enjoyed so much in the underrated indie horror movie, *Shellter*. She's less impressive here but utterly different and she serves as the point at which I began to wonder about the story.

There's no budget for effects here, so we can't safely assume we're watching what we're told we're watching. You won't see the werewolf transform or the shapechanger change, for instance, let alone the time traveller travel in time. Until Eatha Haemm, the backwoods unicorn, I took it all as given, but after her I began to wonder whether it was all really unfolding in a lunatic asylum with Jahn merely a doctor playing along with his patients' delusions. Certainly one character is not what he claims to be, but I wondered about a few others too.

Since *Folklore* I've also seen Laura Waddell in an odd web series called *Divine White's Introduction to Hollywood*, which is more British humour but very different to this and she's by far the best thing in it. At this point she was best known for the *William & Kate* TV movie, in which she attracted attention in a small role as Kate's boss. Her future looks brighter though, as she's in an upcoming Guillermo del Toro movie, *Crimson Peak*, and a couple of other features I'm looking forward too, most notably a Jennifer Tilly picture called *Renaissance Girl* in which she plays a pixie.

Following this up with earlier Chenn movies, I saw a few of these actors in the interesting *Embers of the Sky*, a themed set of serious science fiction shorts. I was particularly interested in seeing if the Ipsett twins, Sherill Turner and Rachel Rath, would be as good apart as they are together, but I was intrigued as to what Napoleon Ryan could do outside of the time traveller, Taryn Kamus and Maria Olsen also added yet another wild character to her portfolio. I found myself impressed with each of them and am eagerly following Chenn's career to see what else he conjures up with these folk from *Folklore*.

He's a particularly interesting character. He came late to film, a troubled young man searching for a way to slay his many demons through the art of filmmaking. His debut feature, *The Way of Snow*, dates back to 2007 with Chenn saving as much money as he could by doing almost everything himself, not only serving as writer and director and sundry other crew roles but as lead actor too. Then again, it is sourced from his own life, so that's highly appropriate. He followed up with the science fiction shorts that eventually grew into *Embers of the Sky*. *Folklore* makes something very different again, an overt comedy to follow drama and serious science fiction. Next up are a set of short films adapted from video games and they've been interesting pieces thus far.

I have no doubt that he'll make better films than this one, but his real challenge is in trying to make something that's more fun. That'll be tough.

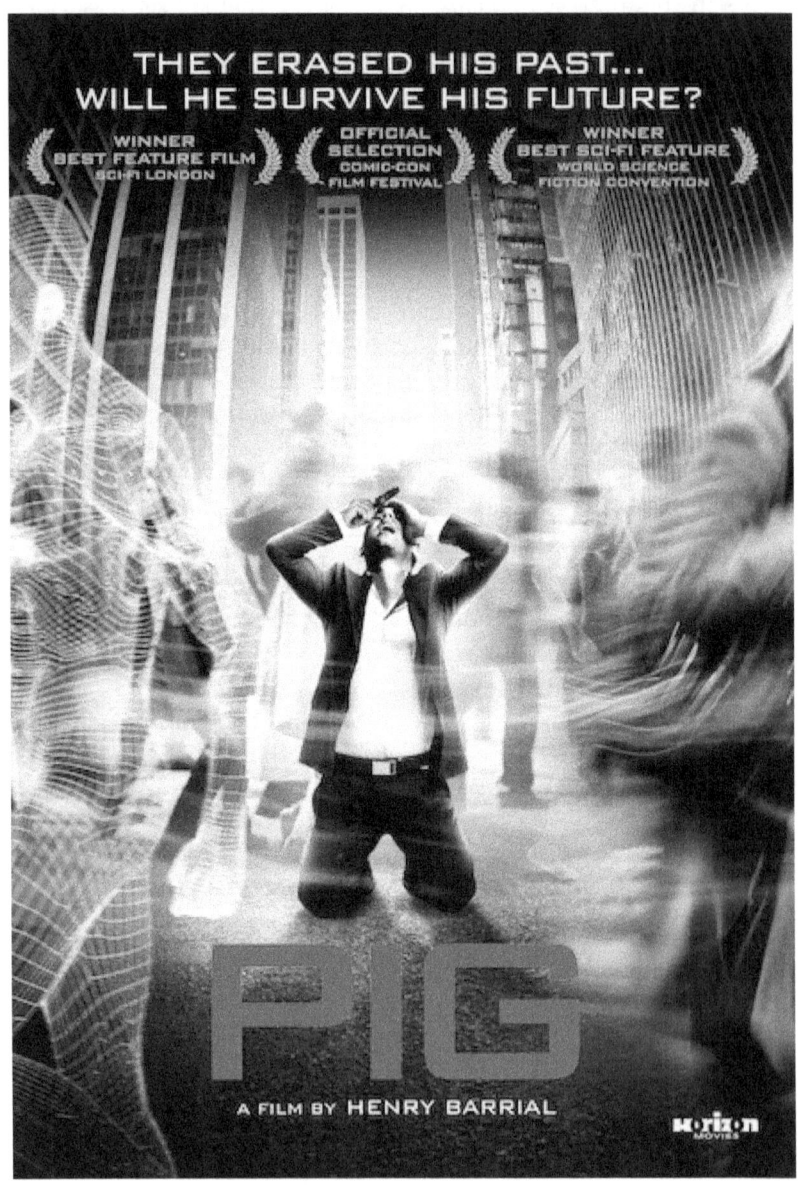

Pig (2011)

Director: Henry Barrial
Writer: Henry Barrial
Stars: Rudolf Martin, Heather Ankeny, Keith Diamond and Ines Dali

In one of the more accurate plot synopses at IMDb, "a man wakes up alone in the middle of the desert with a black hood on his head and his hands tied behind his back." He has amnesia with mere glimpses of memory. A slip of paper in his pocket reads "Manny Elder", which may or may not be his own name: he doesn't even remember that much, let alone what might have led him there.

Isabel, a young mother who finds him in the desert and nurses him back to health at her home in remote Page, AZ, understands from experience that drug smugglers do that sort of thing, as her dead husband was one such victim. Our mystery man doesn't know what he does, but this is good an explanation as anything he can bring to bear. Obviously something is going on, but we're not in on the secret either and we have as little idea of who is as him. We're forced to rediscover this man's past along with him and, as we have no idea where discovery might come from, we have to pay a great deal of attention.

What's important here? Should we focus on the little details that he can remember or those that he can't? Snippets do come back to him, like the tune to *London Bridge is Falling Down* or a figure of a knight in stained glass at Isabel's house, but nothing that's either substantial or apparently useful. On the flipside, he's forgotten that "Cheers!" is a toast or that bees sting. Is it notable that wine and pain elicit similar reactions in him? They carry shock and bring a memory that he can't quite define. Is it important that he doesn't dream? Certainly he's completely functional: he speaks English, he can read and write, even draw. He knows what things are, for the most part, and he's at home with his bodily functions. If this was deliberately done to him, who might have done it? All we see is Isabel and her young son, Jason, along with some quick visits from a local doctor to tend to his immediate wounds. The only real clue is that name in his pocket: Manny Elder.

Isabel searches online and finds that a Manny Elder runs a hotel called the Continental in Los Angeles, so off he goes to see what a conversation with him might bring. However, before Elder's door even opens, suddenly he's back in the desert in those plastic cuffs and that black hood. We're thirty minutes into the picture, yet it's apparently starting again.

And again. As the audience, we're only given the benefit of one detail that the man living through this bizarre process doesn't see: the numbers at the corner of the screen that appear each time everything reboots. It was 1.2 when the film began, then it became 1.3 and 1.4, always counting up.

We aren't forced to run through everything again in detail though, we find ourselves right back at the Continental to discover that Manny Elder is a friend, that our guy is called Justin Reeves and that he's subscribed to a substitute teacher agency. Surely it isn't an accidental irony that he likes puzzles, given that he himself is now his own biggest puzzle.

What makes this film special is that, as answers arrive in a flood they only bring more questions flowing along with them. With each fresh discovery Reeves makes about who he is and why this might be happening to him, we make that discovery with him and we can't help but realise that they don't all seem to be compatible with each other. Initially they're just subtle inconsistencies but they escalate in grandeur, to the point that, while he's enjoying some fresh air in L.A., a lady in a car calls out to him in German, in which language he promptly answers her. She tells him that he speaks German because, like her, he was born in East Berlin and his name is Lukas Ernst. By now, we're forced into a constant reevaluation of each piece of evidence we're given, juggling it with every other piece to try to build a coherent bigger picture. Increasingly, it feels like we're looking at pieces from two different puzzles, but we try to reconcile everything to being one.

The name behind *Pig* is Henry Barrial, who wrote and directed, and it was surprising to find that he doesn't have a large body of work behind him. While this features no major stars and obviously doesn't enjoy a major budget, it's a complex film that doesn't feel like it could have sprung fully formed out of nowhere. Certainly the actors are experienced and some are recognisable. Rudolf Martin, who plays the mystery man at the heart of the film, has many credits going back to 1993, including Hollywood features like *Bedazzled* and *Swordfish*. I recognised him only from television, where he played Ziva's half-brother Ari on *N.C.I.S.* All three of the major supporting cast, Heather Ankeny, Keith Diamond and Ines Dali, have similar experience in varying quantities. The production values are high, budget notwithstanding, and there are few issues with the technical side. My biggest complaint was an annoying spelling mistake that reoccurred a few times towards the end of the film, hardly a showstopper.

While Barrial's credits are varied, this would seem to be a natural extension of his core focus as a writer/director. *Pig* is his fourth feature as a director, three of which he also wrote, and while I hadn't seen any of his other films at this point, it was clear merely from their synopses that they're are all about relationships. *Some Body* is a search for something beyond sex in the singles scene, *Heartland* has to do with a girl looking after a brother with Downs syndrome, and *True Love* examines three couples at different stages of their respective relationships. Indeed, his next film, *The House That Jack Built*, which won a number of awards at the Phoenix Film Festival in 2014, revolves around a young drug dealer who buys an apartment building and moves in his dysfunctional family.

While *Pig* may seem to be something of a departure, it really isn't, as at heart it's about a man's relationship with himself at its most strained. It's a science fiction movie without a single spaceship, ray gun or monster, but it's still science fiction, which at it's best and purest is about tweaking the world in a single scientific way to see how everything else changes because of it. That's exactly what Barrial does here.

To my mind, it's Barrial's script that most obviously succeeds here but not completely. He frames the science fiction as a mystery, not to be obtuse but to keep us engaged in the puzzle, and like all the best puzzles it continues to make us think even once we've solved it.

Some will figure out what's going on sooner than others, but nobody will leave wondering what happened. Instead, they'll be wondering about that single tweak itself, initially about whether it's a good thing or a bad thing, but then, when they realise that, like most changes, it's intrinsically neither good nor bad, they'll wonder about the morality of the concept instead, whether it's ethical or not and how it could or would be abused. If it isn't black or white, how grey does it get?

The ending itself is a good one, though it isn't nearly as iconically phrased as other provocative movie endings like those of *Brazil* or *One Flew Over the Cuckoo's Nest*, which still spark debate today.

Rudolf Martin is deceptively great here. As the story is entirely about him, he has to carry it and he proves up to the task, even though he's in a state of confusion for most of it and is frequently missing dialogue because he has no memory to provide answers to people's questions. He becomes more grounded as the film runs on, with each discovery about who he is, who he was and why he's in this story to begin with, but he plays it more subtly and with less flash than Guy Pearce did in *Memento*, another puzzle picture.

The three main supporting actors back him up well, though their respective stories are fleshed out to different degrees. As Anouk, the German lady who finds an old friend by chance, Dali's is most naturally contained. Diamond's as Manny Elder has a wider scope but it's fairly covered too. It was Ankeny's role that satisfied me least, not for her acting, which is excellent, but for where Barrial takes, or rather doesn't take, her character.

I had a lot more questions about Isabel than are ever spoken to, as she's a complex and pivotal character worthy of much more exploration than is attempted here. Perhaps it would be tough to include that without detracting from the central character, but I think the fault may be with just how far Barrial was willing to let the science fiction aspect of this story take him. The big reveal, if it could be called that, comes too early to be seen as a twist ending, but too late to shape how the rest of the film goes with any real depth. I felt that Barrial's background with straight drama made him see this as an insular story about one man, but the science fiction approach is bigger than that and once that door is opened it really can't be closed again. Barrial is good at setting up questions but the answers he provides don't complete the puzzle. He isn't willing to take a crack at the new world he's created, remaining content instead to focus on one man within it.

It's not surprising that *Pig* won for Best Science Fiction Feature at the International Horror and Sci-Fi Film Festival in 2011, and it's not surprising that it's won a whole slew of other awards at other film festivals across the map. Sadly there are few enough serious science fiction features made at this level that when a good one shows up, it's almost guaranteed to accumulate laurels like there's no tomorrow. This is certainly a good one, but it's not a great one and it shouldn't have been the shoe in that it was.

I thoroughly enjoyed and was affected by Barrial's subsequent film, *The House That Jack Built*, which is as ostensibly different from this as could be imagined and have his earlier films ready to go. All are straight dramas and it's the dramatic side of this film at which he shined brightest. If he comes back to the science fiction genre, I hope he'll be willing to look beyond the dramatic to address the wider questions of change, not just to an individual person or a couple but also to society at large.

The International Horror & Sci-Fi Film Festival

2012

Showcase Features

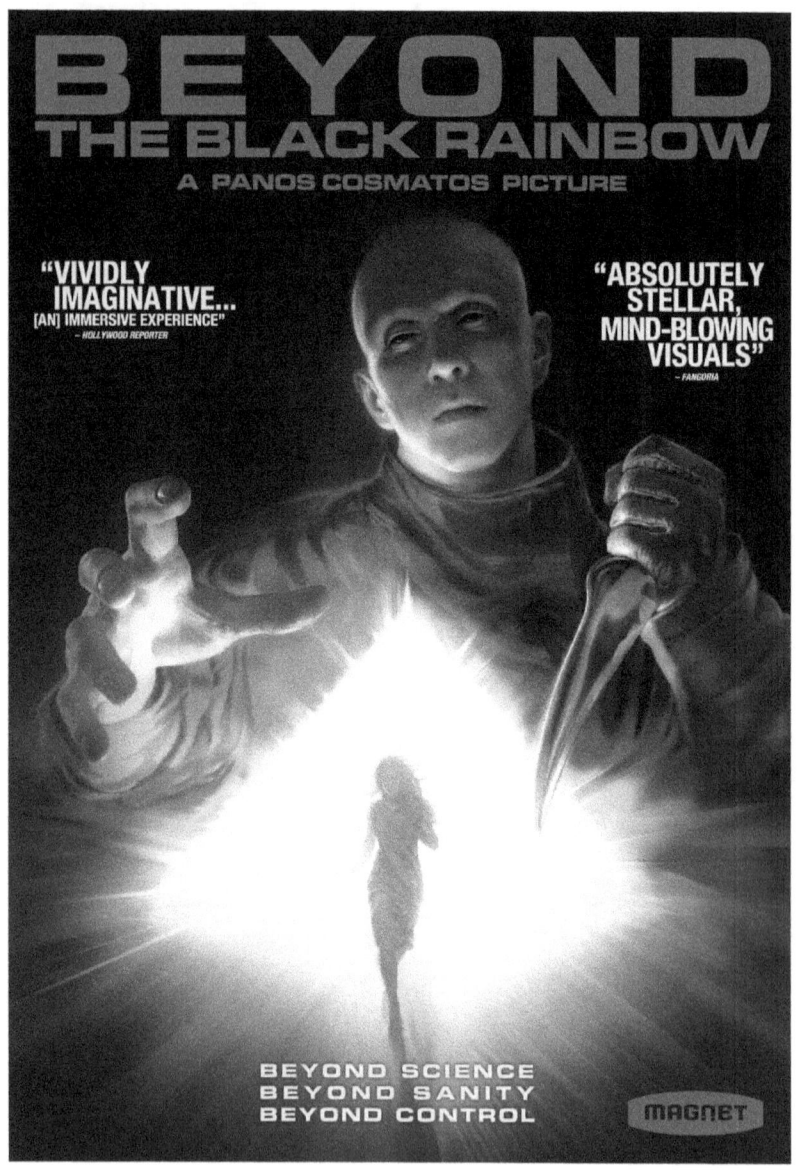

Beyond the Black Rainbow (2010)

Director: Panos Cosmatos
Writer: Panos Cosmatos
Stars: Michael Rogers, Scott Hylands and Eva Allen

Surely the most uncompromising vision of recent years, this debut feature from second generation filmmaker Panos Cosmatos was immediately acclaimed and decried.

Aiming to create a film that could believably date to 1983, the year *Beyond the Black Rainbow* is set, he deliberately and surprisingly ignored the notable output of his father, George P Cosmatos, as an influence, though his films like *Cobra, Rambo: First Blood Part II* and *Leviathan,* are quintessentially eighties. Instead the key influence he built from was an abstract and very personal concept. As a child he remembers visiting a rental store called Video Addict, but being too young to actually watch the many enticing horror/sci-fi movies available, he imagined his own versions of them, entirely from their covers and the blurb on the back of their boxes. If this film has a direct provenance, it's to all those imaginary takes on real movies that he conjured up as a youngster, albeit combined with some of the actual films that he saw years later.

There is a story, though it's a very simple one and it's drawn out through the power of art to much longer than would normally be the case and with a deliberate absence of detail, right down to the exquisitely clinical architecture of the Arboria Institute in which we spend the majority of the film, so that everything here can be read in more than one way.

Put simply, a young lady named Elena has mysterious powers but has been trapped in a near catatonic state within this institute, which is ironically dedicated to the goal of happiness; its motto reads, "Serenity through technology". She's the captive of Dr. Barry Nyle, its sinister head of research, and her powers are dampened by a mysterious pyramid at the heart of the institute. She may or may not be Nyle's own daughter and she may or may not have been at Arboria since the moment she was born. As Nyle focuses on her growing resemblance to her mother, she may or may not also be a sexual obsession for him.

All this is kept ambiguous, but it does become clearer on repeat viewings. It's far more likely that Elena is really the daughter of Dr. Mercurio Arboria, the founder of the institute, and his wife, Anna. Elena certainly asks Nyle telepathically to let her see her father, suggesting that she doesn't believe it's him. However it's still possible, given the obvious connections between Nyle and Anna during a failed pharmacological experiment which we see during a flashback scene to 1966. Does Anna spurn Nyle before he kills her or do they conceive Elena, supposedly intended to be the beginning of a new age of enlightenment, which of course fails to materialise? Indeed it may not be too much of a stretch to see Elena as the real experiment, created by Nyle through his obsession with Anna and using her as the means. However, it's Dr. Arboria's death and the subsequent transfer of knowledge to her that allows Elena the means to overcome Nyle and the pyramid and make her escape.

In most films, delving that deeply into the storyline would mean providing spoilers, especially for a film released so recently. Here though, everything is kept so deliberately ambiguous and open to personal interpretation that I could tell you frankly what happens in any scene you like and it still wouldn't constitute a spoiler. While the story is there and perhaps enough repeat viewings can fully nail it down, it's hardly the most important part of the film. It's the feel of that story and the means by which it's told that Cosmatos was obviously aiming for most.

You could easily call it style over substance, unashamedly so, but there is, at least, some substance beneath the style. What makes this film so discussable is that as many arguments could be waged over the influences of the look and feel of the piece as to what it all actually means. The last film to truly fit that category may be *2001: A Space Odyssey*, which was ironically 42 years old when this was released.

There's no doubt that Stanley Kubrick was a major influence. The precise visual style, the deliberate pace and the careful use of sound are very reminiscent of Kubrick. The colour is too, with Elena a white symbol of purity throughout and Nyle frequently red, the Devil's colour. The fades to red are surely a nod to *A Clockwork Orange*. Most obviously, the set and furniture design is so clearly channelled from Kubrick that many of the scenes that feature them most prominently could easily have been shot in discarded sets from *2001: A Space Odyssey*. They're deceptively functional too, but in a subversive way; rather than provide function, as would be the norm, they restrict it. There are no clocks so we're kept outside the flow of time, just in the year of 1983. Beyond not knowing where the Arboria Institute is, we have no idea of its internal geography either, even after an hour and a half, as the consistently sparse and sterile design frees us from spacial recognition too. We're as lost in time and space as Nyle within his acid trip.

David Cronenberg is another obvious influence, with ideas borrowed from many of the films he made as the seventies became the eighties. When the pyramid's influence is dialled down, Elena has the psychic power to explode heads, a concept borrowed from *Scanners*. Most of the characters here only connect to the outside world through television, something inspired by *Videodrome*, and the ending is an overt nod to that picture too. The idea of hacking the human body as a way to enhance our control of it is a frequent Cronenberg theme, perhaps the predominant one. That's explored here in a great number of ways, most overtly through the Arboria Institute's dream of using "benign pharmacology, sensory therapy and energy sculpting" in order to create "a different way to think, a new way to live, a perfect way to believe." Merely re-reading these quotes, I can't help but hear them in Cronenberg's voice, through which they were not delivered. The fear of physical transformation is another of his common themes, manifested here in the changes we see within Dr. Nyle later in the film. Of course, Cronenberg often merges the psychological with the physical, as this does too. While I don't have a list, I'd be astounded if those films which Cosmatos couldn't watch at Video Addict didn't include more than a few of Cronenberg pictures, not least because they have a shared Canadian nationality, Cosmatos being from Vancouver Island and Cronenberg from Toronto.

For all the many connections, this isn't merely sourced from Cronenberg pictures though. The first half is mostly seventies science fiction, both American films like *Silent Running* and *THX 1138* and Russian ones like *Solaris* and *Stalker*. The locations of all of those films are referenced in the isolation and sparse population of the

Arboria Institute and many of their settings and themes are touched upon also. Then, the second half turns into an eighties slasher movie, but with the style of the first half allowed to bleed through into it. The Cronenberg angles both overlay and underpin all that, as befits the filmmaker who originated the sci-fi/horror hybrids of the era at which Cosmatos deliberately aimed.

No discussion of *Beyond the Black Rainbow* can fail to acknowledge the huge impact on the film of its score. Unlike any other picture I can name since the death of Kubrick, it's an intrinsical part of the piece. Given the visual style and the sparse dialogue, it might be an interesting experiment to watch the film on mute to see how much is lost. I'm sure it would be a notably lesser film but conversely, listening to the film without visuals is certainly a surreal but oddly enjoyable experience. I don't mean a soundtrack album, I mean listening to the movie rather than watching it. I let it play on my laptop in a different workspace while I wrote up my notes on the film and found it fascinating. Ironically, it allows us to imagine our own movie from it, just as Cosmatos did from those videotapes.

The score was created using analogue synthesizers, but runs the gamut from ambient to krautrock via Italian prog, John Carpenter's film themes and lots of drone. Seamlessly merging with Eric Paul's clever sound design to mimic the power of the pyramid, it also incorporates the analogue clicks and beeps of the props, even Nyle's voice. Every piece of audio contributes not only to the movie itself but also to the score.

In the end, the film's biggest success is in how all these elements work together as an immersive experience. While the stubbornly sedate pace, which could also be fairly described as "glacial", makes it tough to pay attention and, on its own, will alienate most of its audience, I found myself utterly engrossed. The ambient music ties so closely to the sounds and, by extension, to the delightfully wild variety of delightfully analogue interfaces that are the antithesis of the technology seen in most modern films that I found myself just as engrossed by the little details as the big picture. Even the actors could be seen in this light, although they do magnificent work, especially given that only Michael Rogers has much dialogue as Nyle and even then far less than the average. They all have to compensate with body language, especially Eva Allen as Elena, who gets a large amount of screen time but is rarely allowed to speak. That makes them all something akin to moving props for puppet master Cosmatos to manipulate along with everything else we see. It really is an accomplished piece. Sure, it's uncompromising and not remotely commercial, but Cosmatos self-financed it and frankly doesn't care. He knew what he wanted to capture on film and he achieved that.

There's nothing here whatsoever to suggest that this isn't a lost film from 1983; it's "a sort of imagining of an old film that doesn't exist", as Cosmatos would have it, enhanced by shooting on two thirds 35mm using an authentic period Panavision camera, with exposure techniques used to raise the grain. In particular, Michael Rogers looks like he stepped right out of the eighties; I'm surely not alone in noticing a particularly strong resemblance between the controlling Dr. Barry Nyle and the controlling Steve Jobs, who was a notable icon of the eighties even if he attained his real pop culture godhood later.

Perhaps the key can be found in Nyle's very deliberate choice of words. "I know who I am," he explains to Elena. "It's what gives me my confidence and my power." While we may not understand all that Cosmatos tells us here, he certainly does and he tells it with confidence and power.

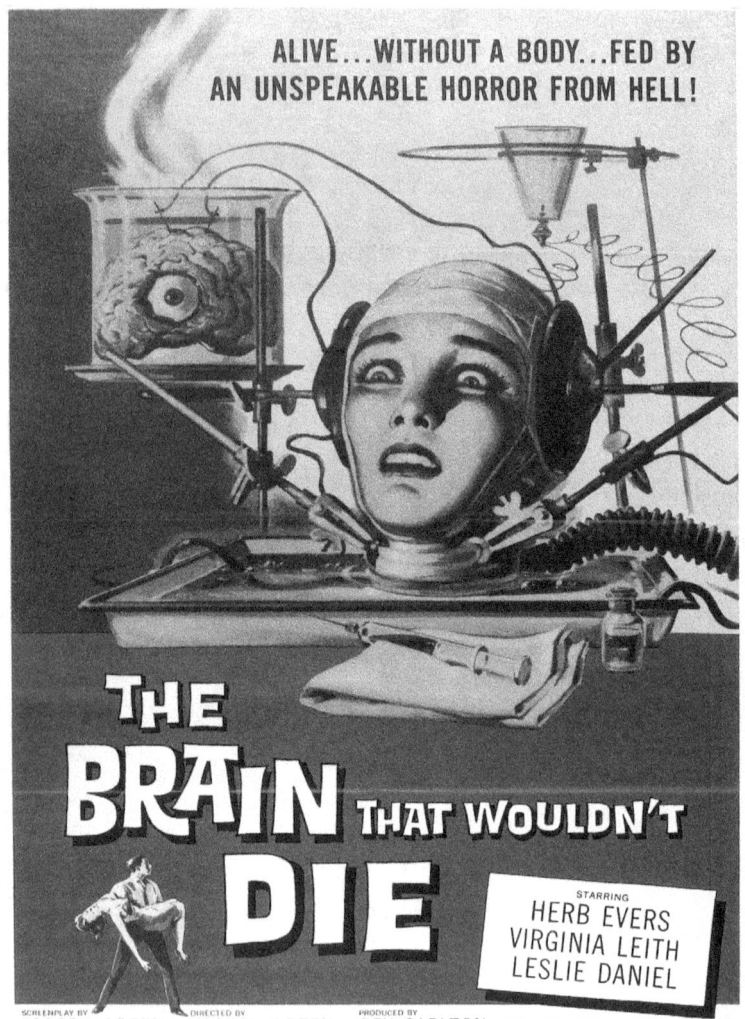

The Brain That Wouldn't Die (1962)

Director: Joseph Green
Writer: Joseph Green, from a story by Rex Carlton and Joseph Green
Stars: Herb Evers, Virginia Leith and Leslie Daniels

"Let me die!" pleads a woman's voice before the opening credits begin, in fact before we see anything at all. It's a disembodied voice out of nowhere that suggests a female version of *Johnny Got His Gun*.

It's all very promising but sadly it's all downhill from there, which possibly explains why this film was completed in 1959 under the title of *The Black Door* but wasn't released for three years and then with its current, far more lurid, title. It isn't without merit, as it does contain a number of memorable cult moments, not least one of the most abiding images of all sixties genre cinema, but it still can't live up to the title.

It's another mad scientist movie from an era bogged down with the things, but unlike *Frankenstein*, their common progenitor, which remains as timeless as ever, this has already been superceded as the unholy transplantation of limbs and organs that it rages against is routinely beneficial today.

I find it fascinating to witness public opinion, as distilled through the scriptwriters of old horror movies, change over the decades. This film is only half a century old but it already seems quaint and dated to the many of us who have benefitted from or know people who have benefitted from the very transplant techniques that are derided by its characters as immoral, unethical and/or insane.

Sure, science is constantly moving forward and the best writers follow it, but Joseph Green clearly couldn't give a transplanted rat's ass about science. He clearly fits with the mass of schlocky writers who wrote schlocky genre movie in the fifties or sixties who began with "Burn the witch!" and worked backwards from there to build a salacious heap of scientific gobbledygook.

At least Green, adapting a story he wrote with Rex Carlton, does make a token effort to explain where Dr. Bill Cortner, our central character, is coming from. His first scene involves him failing to save the life of a patient and asking the lead doctor if he could try something new. Medical ethics are thrown immediately out of the window, where they're devoured by vultures.

"He's dead," he explains. "I can't do any harm,"

"Very well, the corpse is yours," volunteers his superior. "Do what you want to do."

So our rogue doctor, too polite to be either Henry Frankenstein or Herbert West, starts massaging the heart and applying electric current to the exposed brain. The corpse returns to life and with a steady pulse. "Nothing's unbelievable if you have the nerve to experiment," he gloats to the nurse. He's been working on this new technique for weeks. Yes, weeks.

In other words, Dr. Bill Cortner is a visionary. He views the idea of being a surgeon as more than being a carpenter or a plumber and he dreams of transplants that can save the lives of many. "It can be done!" he reiterates to his disbelieving superior, who isn't having any of it but tolerates Bill because he's his father. Yes, these folks are all tied together by far more than just a patient. The boss is Dr. Cortner too, Bill's father, and the nurse is Jan Compton, Senior's secretary and Junior's fiancée.

With this grounding, we're then given a hint at where we're going. "The line between scientific genius and obsessive fanaticism is a thin one," explains father to son. "I want you on the right side!" We just know that that's a revelation trigger. "Sure, I've made a few mistakes," answers Bill, who has been stealing limbs from amputee victims to perform wild transplant experiments on people and we quickly find out out what mistakes and how wild.

Something terrible has happened at the country place where Bill struts his experimental stuff, so he races off with Jan to see what's up, merely a little too quickly. We see the warning signs, literally, as Bill makes it past a set of "winding road", "stop" and "curve" before he crashes horribly. He is thrown free, at least, and lands heavily on soft ground but Jan isn't so lucky, as we discover from a glorious exploitation shot from inside the burning wreck of the car with only her hand grasping up for help to show us that she's in there. He reaches down inside to retrieve something with his jacket and then runs for the country place, his eyes wide like Johnny Rotten's. It's a long run too, so much so that it becomes a stumble by the time he gets there.

The scenery chewing is flamboyant and outstanding. I'm not sure if actor Jason Evers pictured himself as an American football player weaving through invisible opponents as he flounders through the woods and up the long steps, or whether he was looking around eagerly for more scenery to chew. He falls, he stumbles, he rests. It's all almost beyond him. It's supposed to be suspenseful, but we're just wondering how long the detached body part that he surely has wrapped up in his jacket can survive and to where the inevitable gouts of blood have all vanished.

Amazingly, Evers is outdone as an unashamed chewer of scenery by Leslie Daniels, who gives life to his assistant, Kurt. Evers reserves his most outrageous chewing for the most outrageous scenes, at least, but Daniels has no such restraint. Perhaps he'd picked up his over-emotional acting style on the continent given that most of his eight films were shot in Italy. He only acted in one more before moving sideways into the niche job of writing English dialogue for Italian movies, then directing the dubbing work.

Evers appeared in more prominent movies, including *The Green Berets* and *The Illustrated Man*, but was better known on television where he guested on what may be every American show ever made.

It's Virginia Leith who steals this entire film though, starting at the twenty minute mark when she becomes something more than merely nurse and fiancée Jan Compton. She had acted for Kubrick in *Fear and Desire* and was decent in *Violent Saturday* but she'll always be remembered most for playing Jan in the Pan.

Jan in the Pan is the great description the *Mystery Science Theater 3000* folk gave to what we find after a long sequence of Bill hooking up tubes and vials and other scientific gadgetry. Eventually we see the severed head of Jan Compton wrapped up in a swimming cap and sitting in a pan of Bill's special compound. It's a great cult shot and it only gets better because Jan remains the most important character in the entire film, even though she never gets out of the pan. She hasn't a scar or a blemish on her, except for the lack of a body, which makes her head perfect to transplant onto someone else's body. The only catch is that he Bill doesn't have one. Yet.

Here's where Green's drive to be horrific renders the film utterly inconsistent. Bill is more of a magician than a surgeon, given that

Jan in the Pan can talk wonderfully even though she doesn't have lungs or a throat or any other means of generating sound. Yet he has a horrible track record otherwise. There's a monster in the closet gibbering away in some maniacal tongue, so horrible that we aren't even allowed to see it. Kurt has a withered and deformed left arm because Bill can't keep it healthy. In this world, grafting a replacement arm is much tougher than running the gauntlet on an invisible field for ten minutes with a severed head under your arm, then miraculously bringing it back to life without a body. Either that or he just can't be bothered to return to his early failure now that he has AdrenoSerum™ to bring to bear. It's all about how much you care, I guess. Sorry, Kurt.

What Bill cares about is a body for Jan, especially as he reckons he has only fifty hours before surgery becomes non-viable. Where would he find a body worthy of his bride to be? How about the local burlesque joint where sultry strippers dance to sultry saxophone music and some guy sings "jiggy jiggy" at odd moments? Perhaps a Miss Body Beautiful contest, where he literally shops for bodies. Maybe a man-hating actress called Doris with an acid-scarred face! At least that's a notably efficient approach, even if the body belongs short and scrawny actress, Adele Lamont.

What's most hilarious here is that Bill is entirely honest with his intentions. He tells the blonde bimbo at the strip club that he's just looking around and once he's done looking, he'll operate. When the other stripper asks him to come back later because she'll remember him, he points out that it's what he's afraid of. He tells Adele that he'll cut her face off and give her body away. "'Do I look like a maniac who goes around killing girls?" he asks before giving her a sedative. "Here's to your future," he tells her. "Whatever it may be."

In case anyone watching might believe that this is Bill's movie, these scenes are alternated with Jan in the Pan developing acute psychic powers which allow her to play telekinetic tricks on Kurt and converse with the monster in the closet (Jan with a questioning rasp, the monster with one knock for yes and two for no). You can't help but admire a movie where the leading lady is reduced to being an almost immobile head but is tasked with acting through body language! She's enforcing control so far that she's tuned into her fiancé's thoughts throughout his search for a body and tells him that she doesn't want Doris's undernourished frame. He shuts her up in the most outrageously male fashion imaginable, by literally taping her mouth shut with duct tape!

Of course, her newfound psychic powers set up the finalé which was supposed to be shot in gory colour but was presumably too expensive to be viable. Shot over less than a fortnight, mostly in the basement of a New York hotel, there's no doubt that the film would have benefited from a longer finalé. There are additional gore scenes but they were trimmed when AIP picked the film up for release. In fact, had it screened as intended, it would have beaten out Herschell Gordon Lewis's *Blood Feast* as the progenitor of the modern gore movie by a year, even accounting for its three year wait in limbo because of legal issues and problems with the censors.

It also has much that *Blood Feast* didn't have. It had Eddie Carmel, the 7' 6¾" Jewish Giant, who nobody will be surprised portrays the monster in the closet. It has a catfight in a strip club, also trimmed for the AIP release, albeit one that's mangled by the addition of a very human meow and a shot of two calendar cats on a wall. It has the most overdone death scene in cinema, as Kurt's arm is ripped off and Leslie Daniels drags the bloody stump over every wall in the house while Jan in the Pan laugh hysterically at his contortions.

It also has a lot of joyous B-movie dialogue. "Together we're both more than things," Jan explains to Kurt. "We're a power as hideous as our deformities. Together we'll take our revenge. I shall create power and you will enforce it! You're the thing outside and I'm the thing in here." Ed Wood would mouth these words. My favourite speech is Kurt's explanation to Jan of what's in the closet. "Horror no normal mind could imagine, something even more terrible than you. Parts of experimentation twist and turn through mountains of miscalculation and often lose themselves in error and darkness. Behind that door is the sum total of Dr Cortner's mistakes."

So *The Brain That Couldn't Die* is an awful movie, but one with real cult appeal. The underwhelming ending also leaves it open for a sequel, which is always possible, given that Virginia Leith is still alive. If *Manos: The Hands of Fate*, *The Beast of Yucca Flats* and *The Killer Shrews* have seen sequels, but this could be see the most fun sequel of them all. Instead it became a couple of stage musicals, the fate du jour of classic bad movies.

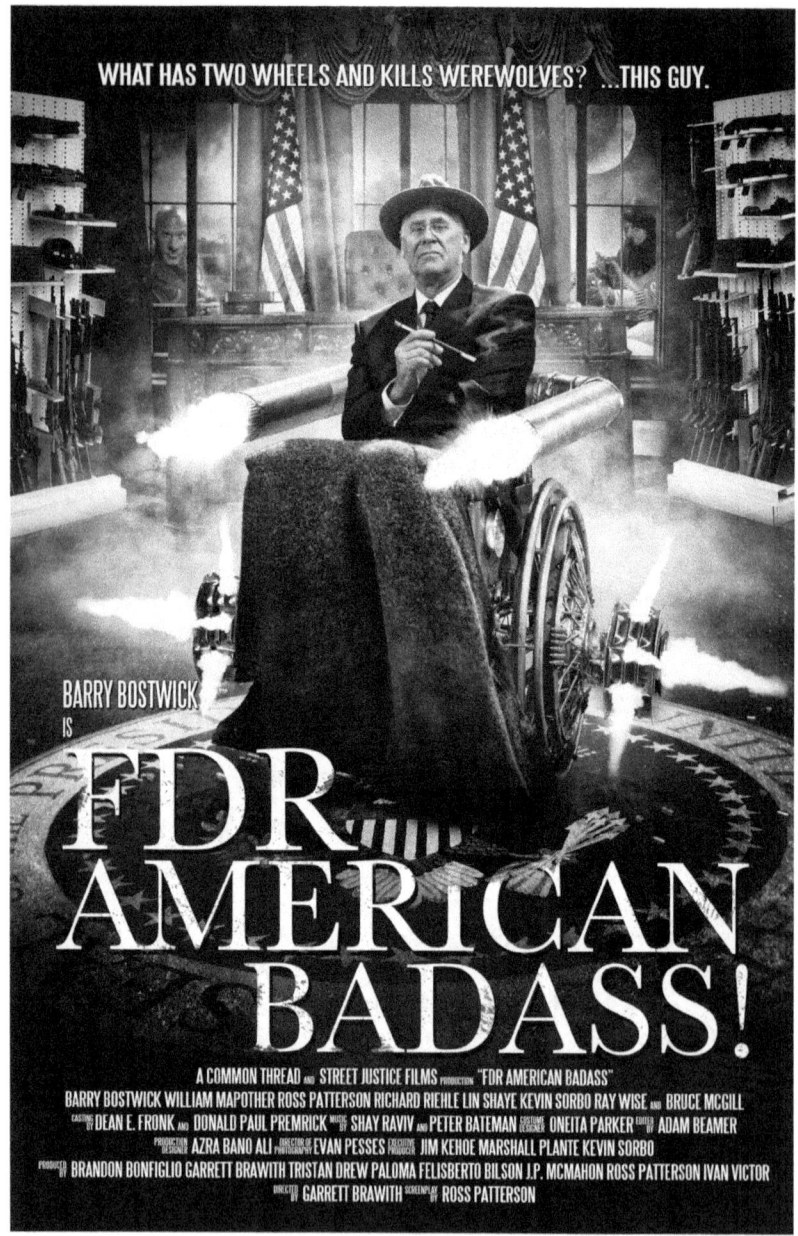

F.D.R.: American Badass! (2012)

Director: Garrett Brawith
Writer: Ross Patterson
Stars: Barry Bostwick, Lin Shaye, Bruce McGill, Ray Wise and Kevin Sorbo

After seeing the trailers online for *Poolboy: Drowning Out the Fury* and *F.D.R.: American Badass!* (they were both viral hits in that friends and family who aren't necessarily into film shared them with me), I knew I had to see these films, a rare sentiment for me given that modern American comedies are more likely to have me curling up in a ball and pretending the outside world is a figment of my twisted imagination. Having opened up my Phoenix Film Festival experience in 2012 with the latter, I realise what drew me to them and I wonder if I've stumbled into one of those game changing moments in film history that can only be truly acknowledged in hindsight.

The key player is Ross Patterson, a former stand up comedian and small time Hollywood actor, who may just become a household name if he can maintain the momentum that he's building right now. Through his production company, Street Justice Films, he's utilising modern technology to generate strong publicity to build his fanbase, then following up in a very old school way: making cheap movies and keeping them coming.

It's a gamble but it's one that will surely pay off for him. While Hollywood is spending more and more money to make tired movies with tired stars who believe they're still funny, then raising ticket prices and suing their own customers to maximise their profit potential, Patterson is going the other way.

He's spending less money on his films, writing and shooting quick B-movies on standing sets with Roger Corman's efficiency and a dash of Ed Wood's confidence that the audience won't care about the goofs. There are few stars, but quite a few talented people who we already recognise and some we will in the future. His tongue is firmly in his cheek as he throws enough wacky ideas at the screen to ensure that at least some of them will stick. Best of all, he has his actors play their ludicrous parts delightfully straight. He understands comedy in ways that the big studios don't. If he understands business too, It may just make him the next Mel Brooks and a prolific Mel Brooks is something to dream about.

Now, *F.D.R.: American Badass!* is most certainly not for everyone. It's lewd and crude, more politically incorrect than anything I can remember, and it revels in slaying sacred cows. It's knowingly and outrageously over the top, as much so as any Troma movie I've seen. It's utterly irreverent, not just playing with history but with actual historical figures with wild abandon. There's everything the moral majority finds grossly offensive: not merely foul language, sexual innuendo and great gouts of violence, but even gags about cripples and gas chambers too. There's even more period sexism than in the campaigning during this year's Republican primaries. In short, it's pretty much guaranteed to offend everyone, but how it offends is the key. A lot of people may walk out of this film, but I'd bet money they'd all walk out within the first five minutes. Anyone who lasts that long won't be able to leave for laughing so hard and Patterson never slows down enough for you to stop.

In the year that's later brought us a disappointing big budget adaptation of Seth Grahame-Smith's thematically similar *Abraham Lincoln, Vampire Hunter*, Patterson already delivered an even more sacrilegious mashup that Tim Burton and Timur Bekmambetov couldn't top, even though they had $69m to play with.

You all know F.D.R.: the 32nd President of the United States, the bringer of the New Deal, the most famous polio survivor of all time. But do you know what gave him polio? How about a Nazi werewolf?

That's Patterson's revisionist take on things and he opens up with the scene where it happens. In and amongst the historical anecdotes and foul language, all made up of course, Gov. Roosevelt's hunting party is attacked. One of his friends is eaten alive, with gore galore. F.D.R. takes down the werewolf but doesn't have silver bullets so has to follow up with his fists. "Shit goblins," he exclaims. Waking up in hospital, he feels like "a bag of dicks at a lesbian convention." No, this isn't a documentary. Honest.

One of the biggest successes of the film is that it never lets up. It grabs us by the throat, well, the legs, from moment one and keeps the crude laughs coming. Another is that the characters never fail to take their lines seriously, however ludicrous they get. The cast here is impeccable, Barry Bostwick and Bruce McGill nailing the parts of F.D.R. and his right hand man with aplomb. Lin Shaye is amazingly straight faced as the long suffering Eleanor Roosevelt, though Ray Wise simply can't stop from breaking up as Douglas MacArthur and it can never hurt a comedy for us to grasp that the cast were in stitches when they made it though, however many takes it took them.

Patterson keeps a major role for himself, as he tends to do in his scripts, and each of his roles confirms to me that he's a truly funny man, not just someone who can write good jokes. They should fire everyone else on *Saturday Night Live* and have him play all the parts himself.

The downsides to the film are relatively minor. Some of the jokes are more than a little forced but the gags come so hard and fast that missing a few isn't a big deal. The sexual innuendo tries for the *Family Guy* approach of beating its punchline to death until it rises again a zombie joke that's funny all over again and it doesn't always succeed. A few scenes are just plain wrong, but then just plain wrong is what Patterson does and he does it very well indeed.

After the screening he told us that some of these, including F.D.R.'s celebration after being elected president, were either improvised or extended by the cast, even beyond what he'd written for them. Yet I'm finding that in hindsight, even the scenes I didn't appreciate at the time, such as the ketchup and mustard orgy with the secretary (surely an unintentional nod to *Pink Angels*), still stick in the mind.

It's a cardinal sin of a comedy to be forgettable. Here, you can't even forget the bits you want to, which then turn around and goose you until you smile.

Most obviously, we can never ignore the low budget because we keep wondering why there are so few people on screen. Yet the picture transcends that one too, as so few other films with that problem manage to do, outside of Monty Python movies. While we watch leaders of four nations plan their war efforts, those nations themselves are conspicuously absent. Hitler just has a buxom fraulein to battle at beer pong and a messenger to shoot; Mussolini and Hirohito only have messengers.

So we're treated to gloriously insulting three way conference calls in split screen instead. This approach works here but not everywhere. In this film, the Mafia is three New York Italian werewolves in a warehouse and the US army only contains eight privates and two generals, with Albert Einstein in reserve, but I laughed my way through those scenes anyway. After a couple of weeks, I could still play them in my head, though they've faded a little now. I can even remember a lot of the lines; they're that iconically over the top.

Patterson wrote this script in ten to twelve days and director Garrett Brawith shot it in under a month. Their process seems to be to conjure up as much surreal comedic insanity as is humanly possible within set parameters and then let the cast run wild with it. None of the three of Patterson's movies that I've seen thus far are entirely consistent, but they're all as funny as all get out and he's only getting more outrageous as time goes by.

His 2010 mockumentary, *Screwball: The Ted Whitfield Story*, seemed almost tame but only because I'd worked backwards from *F.D.R.: American Badass!* through *Poolboy: Drowning Out the Fury*. If I'd found it first, I'm pretty sure I wouldn't have found all the jokes about necrophilia, child abuse and bestial rape particularly tame, but everything seems tame after this film. Somehow Patterson finds stepping over the line so natural that it even happens accidentally: his audition for a werewolf Hitler was inadvertently held on Rosh Hashanah.

It's hard to picture how this film fits into the world of American comedy. Sure, it's easy to see a link, no pun intended, to the lowest common denominator toilet humour of the last few decades, but that's just one of its facets. The fact that the cast plays everything straight means that it has much more in common with *National Lampoon's Animal House* than *Dumb and Dumber*, for instance.

There's a lot of wild imagination here too, far more than I've seen since the glory days of Mel Brooks and Monty Python in the seventies. Surely Patterson was massively influenced by both of those names, this picture containing much the relentless boundary pushing of *Blazing Saddles* and the surreal silliness of *Monty Python and the Holy Grail*.

There are overt nods to the sixties *Batman* TV series, not only but most obviously through transition effects between scenes. The lack of extras brings up *Saturday Night Live* comparisons, as does the Bon Jovi skit.

Yet the combination seems somehow new, something reenforced by seeing some of his other films, as the sheer energy and incessant ideas are as palpable there as here. There's a great deal of care given to keep the characters consistent and some of the funniest parts of the film are generated when unlikely characters meet. As much as history is rogered senseless, there's also attention paid to the period, especially in the sexism of the day. There's lots of effort given to shutting women up here, along with winking at nurses, overt homophobia and capable buns sashaying away from the camera. "Grown men conversing," F.D.R. reminds his wife at one point. "Seen not heard, Eleanor."

Patterson apparently set up Street Justice Films because he was fed up playing bullies in bad Hollywood comedies. It may well be the best decision he's ever made.

I wonder if in a decade we'll all remember our first Patterson. *F.D.R.: American Badass!* was mine.

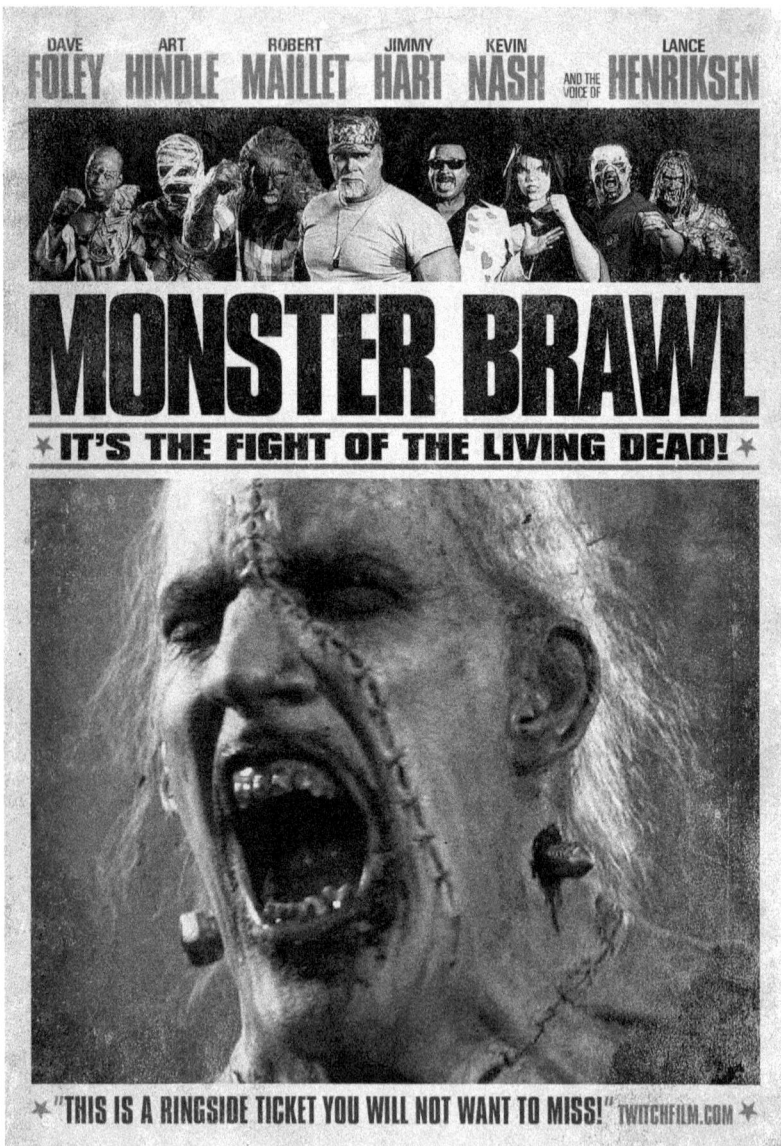

Monster Brawl (2011)

Director: Jesse T. Cook
Writer: Jesse T. Cook
Stars: Dave Foley, Art Hindle, Jimmy Hart, Robert Maillet, Herb Dean, Kevin Nash, Lance Henriksen and Jason Brown

I'll 'fess up, I really wanted to see *Monster Brawl* after seeing the trailer. I even told people I wanted to see it, a lot of people. I sent them to the trailer online. I showed them when it was playing at the International Horror and Sci-Fi Film Festival and suggested they give it a shot. Boy, did I end up looking like a prize idiot!

Sure, it looked stupid, but it looked stupid in a glorious way, like the ultimate fan film. What's more, watching the trailer afresh, after having seen the entire feature, I still want to watch the movie that it generated in my head. However, whatever that movie is, it isn't this one.

How badly did it fail to live up to its potential? Well, here's where I trawl out the sort of comment that should usually be interpreted as overdone and ignorable. You know the sort of thing. How about this: You seriously couldn't pay me to sit through *Monster Brawl* again, as I can't remember when I last felt more conscious of just how long ninety minutes can be, when my will to remain in a theatre seat was so threatened, or when I was more strongly aware that there might have been audience members watching this movie only because I'd irresponsibly suggested it. I actually formulated an exit strategy that would allow me to leave the auditorium without being lynched.

What's so sad is that it really should have been an absolute blast: a riotous, thrill-a-minute, horror comedy set up as a wrestling pay-per-view. C'mon, who wouldn't want to watch a grand pay-per-view event where eight iconic monsters battle it out for supremacy in a cursed graveyard? That's a golden idea right there and, even now, I'm grinning at the concept.

I shouldn't even have to add that there are real wrestlers on board, including Kevin "Diesel" Nash and Robert "Kurrgan" Maillet, literally two of the biggest in the business, and they're far from the only famous names who signed up for the brawl.

To introduce the match ups is the legendary Mouth of the South, Jimmy Hart, with his trademark megaphone and a couple of lovely ring girls, both of whom have appeared on *Naked News*. The referee is Herb Dean, in real life one of the most respected refs in M.M.A. There's comedian Dave Foley to call the play by play, and narrating both the film and its trailer is the ever-reliable Lance Henriksen. It stuns me, documenting that talent here, that it could be wasted so absolutely.

And yes, it really is that bad. The entire picture is almost nothing more than a consistent set of missed opportunities, an incessant barrage of missteps and lost directions, a disappointment in almost every way. It's hard to explain how the filmmakers could have gone more wrong, but in the interests of journalistic integrity, I'll try to explain the few things they got right.

For a while, Jimmy Hart's eyes steal the show. A consummate professional, he always did know just how to make himself noticed and he manages it pretty well here, regardless how effectively his ring girls flex and pose by his sides. The graphics are generally well constructed, from the opening credits to the rundowns of stats on each of the monsters via a host of intros, segues, comparisons, the works. The sound effects are solid and some of the gore effects are pretty good too, though those are less consistent. The framing shots are capable. Best of all are Lance Henriksen's *Mortal Kombat*-style voiceovers.

So it's certainly not all bad, but to compare those measly positive aspects to the overwhelming negative ones in the metaphor of the film, they'd be destroyed before they even made it to the Hillside Necropolis ring. In fact, if you exclude Henriksen's contribution, a genuine grin-inducing pleasure that could only be enhanced by the copious consumption of alcohol, thus suggesting that this entire movie should be viewed as a drinking game, all those plus points would seriously be outweighed by a single flaw: that the film is resoundingly, cavernously, echoingly empty. It's not *Monster Brawl*, it's *Monster Crawl*.

I have no doubt that its quality would double by simply adding a crowd. Real wrestlers play to their audience far more than they ever spend performing wrestling moves in the ring. How can they do that when there's no crowd? The fan film feel of the trailer does extend to the movie, but if writer/director Jesse T Cook is a fan, why in the Hulkster's name did he not rope in 500 more as extras? Like he couldn't conjure up a whole host of extras by merely telling them the concept or showing them the trailer? I'd have volunteered in a heartbeat and I'd have worked for nothing!

In the vast emptiness that this non-existent crowd constantly emphasises, Dave Foley is unenviably tasked with maintaining our interest as the match commentator, Buzz Chambers. Even though he's partnered with former champion, Sasquatch Sid Tucker, played by movie veteran Art Hindle, he fails miserably to do anything at all except make us cringe. Even though he provides us with far more detail than we ever care to discover about the fighters and his professional banter is peppered with all the expected bad puns, names and descriptions of specialty moves and backstage theatrics, he's not a highlight. His lines are slow, his timing is off and we quickly realise that all he's really doing is slowing the whole thing down, presumably because $200,000 Canadian only buys so much in the way of monster costumes and effects.

To give him a little credit, there's really not much in the way of brawling in this monster brawl for him to comment on. Amazingly, we find ourselves in Swamp Gut's swamp longer than we spend in the ring. At least it's imaginative and funny in the swamp.

It feels like forever before we get to that ring for the first match. We're stuck instead with explanations of the event's structure that go on forever, accompanied by music that doesn't remotely fit. Who cares that there are four undead characters and four legendary monsters, split up by category and by weight? We just want to see them in the squared circle, delivering some of the testosterone that the trailer promised.

When Cyclops faced off against Witch Bitch, I realised just how much better this would have been in claymation like *Celebrity Deathmatch*. The first contest is nothing but a warm up, setting the stage for the rest with a few moves, a few cheats and a finisher. Only when Lady Vampire takes on the Mummy in the second match do we really get any actual wrestling, courtesy of real wrestlers Kelly Couture and R. J. Skinner. Unfortunately it's over too soon and we don't get much more later on, merely more delaying tactics to hide that the budget was all gone.

Well, at least we're going to get to see Kevin Nash against Robert Maillet, I hear you say. I mean, it's the inevitable finalé for this pay-per-view, if only because of their sheer size.

A former W.W.F. wrestler who's carving out something of a niche in playing giant monsters in mainstream Hollywood movies, Maillet is 6' 11" tall and thus a great choice for the role of Frankenstein. Unfortunately in this odd take on Jack Pierce's iconic make-up, he looks more like Martin Landau playing Frankenstein's monster than Boris Karloff or Lon Chaney, Jr., which greatly diffuses his impact. Nash, a world champion both in W.W.F. and W.C.W., is only 6' 10", meaning that he actually has to look up at Maillet, something he can't be too used to doing. How can this match-up not happen?

Well, I won't spoil it, but I'll point out that the filmmakers do. It's nothing but promise, just as all the other hints are nothing but promise, like the missing necrophiliac serial kiler, the severe storm heading in towards Lake Michigan and Herb Deen's blood on the cursed necropolis soil. Cook's writing sets us up for so much that either never arrives or just shows up in such a way that we simply don't care any more.

With so much wrong with the film, it's hard to really focus in on the root of it all. Surely Cook has to be the prime culprit, as writer, producer and director, but then it was his imagination that set the whole thing up and really it's only that original imagination that can leave the Hillside Necropolis with its head held high. Would this have been the riot it should have been if he had conjured up all the gimmicks but hired someone else to write the script or direct the picture? I don't know but it's certainly a thought.

I'm sure it would have been a darn sight better if someone had reallocated some of the effects budget into filling up the movie with extras. I don't care how cool the cemetery set looks like, I want to see it full of fans holding up hand written signs on which a camera swooping through the audience can focus, screaming their lungs out as each of the monsters walks down to the ring and, yes, even serving as props for them to play off. This cries out for monsters crashing and burning through the ropes into the front row of the audience! However good the wrestlers, it looks really sucky when they play off invisible crowds, trust me. More wrestling wouldn't have hurt either.

A crowd would have brought a sense of life to the picture. It would have removed the need for a soundtrack, or at least most of the need. Todor Kobakov's score is unfairly tasked with keeping us awake and it can't do it. Without anything to attach to, it feels like he was told to compose a score without seeing the film it needed to accompany. Screaming fans would have stopped the film feeling like it was playing out in slow motion or I'd been roofied with speed on the way into the theatre. Having the lead commentator be bored and depressed was never a good idea either. He should have been the opposite: hopped up and hyper.

Unfortunately we don't get any of that, which does leave us wondering if the approach taken would have been more successful if the entire feature would have been crushed down to half an hour.

My thinking right now is that it shouldn't really have been a movie at all, but rather a recurring skit on *Robot Chicken*. Now that would have been legendary!

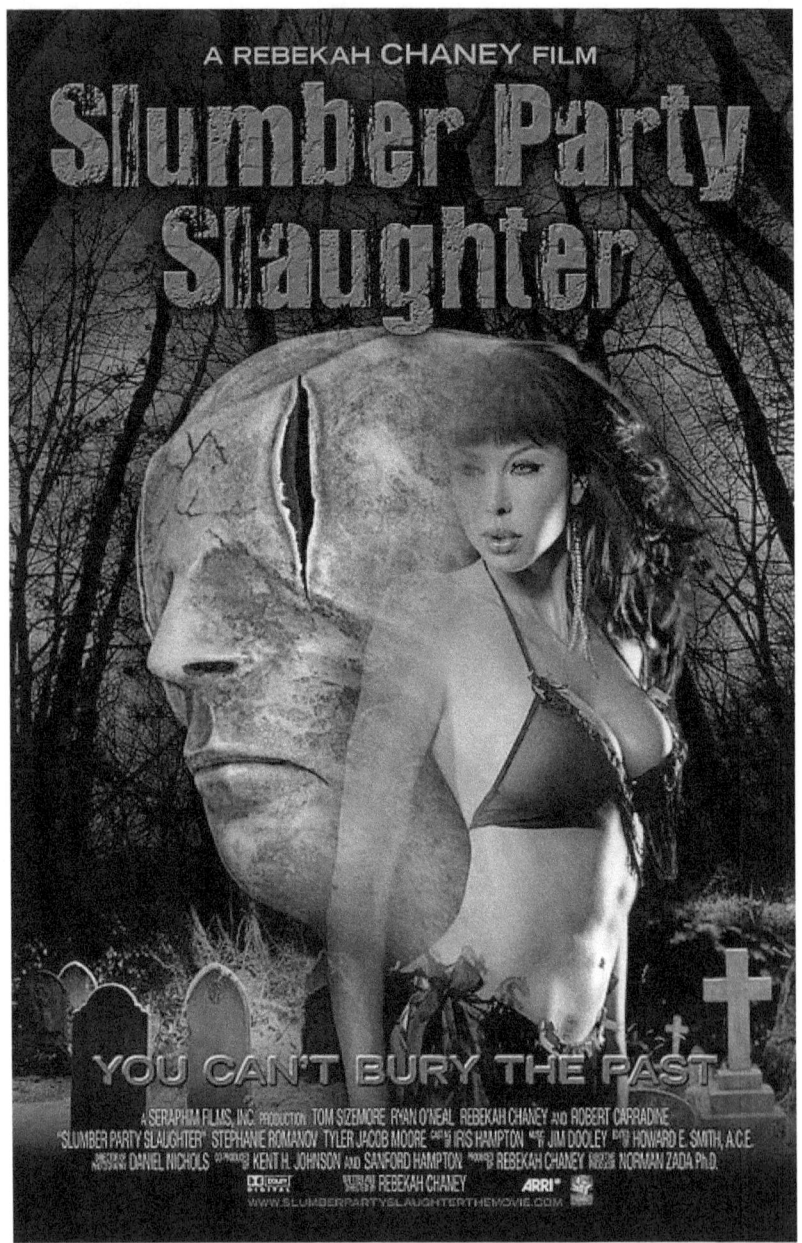

Slumber Party Slaughter (2012)

Director: Rebekah Chaney
Writer: Rebekah Chaney
Stars: Tom Sizemore, Ryan O'Neal, Rebekah Chaney and Robert Carradine

I wanted to like *Slumber Party Slaughter* a lot more than I did. It's an independent horror movie for a start. It's a debut feature from a filmmaker progressing from an award winning short, *Waste Land*. That filmmaker, Rebekah Chaney, is both young and female, neither attribute as common in the industry as it should be. Not content with merely being that rare critter, a female director, she also wrote and produced, as well as playing one of the leading roles herself. Her ambition is palpable but she didn't hog the spotlight, sharing it instead with a few other lovely ladies, as well as some recognisable men: Tom Sizemore, Robert Carradine and the actor she played opposite in *Waste Land*, Ryan O'Neal, who must have liked that film enough to return for its successor.

What's more, she may also have a major heritage to live up to, given that she's billed as the great-grandniece of Lon Chaney, the first real American horror star and very possibly the single most legendary actor in the business. I should add that I haven't seen that lineage backed up and I've talked to some of the Chaney family about it, but the claim is there nonetheless.

In other words, it ought to be my sort of movie. And, to be fair, there's much that I liked.

In the main, it's an affectionate homage to the eighties slasher genre, playing it a little gorier and with a little more substance than might be expected by those of us who grew up with the things.

The key locations are perfect for this sort of material: a strip club called the Lingerie Lounge, an Indian burial ground turned haunted cemetery and a millionaire's mansion that's sitting empty while he's at a business convention. Each of these would have been a great setting for an eighties slasher movie on its own and, to be brutally honest, they probably were; we can hardly complain when this film gives us all three of them.

It sets itself up capably, introducing us to a surprising number of characters and the very attempt highlights both how ambitious Chaney was as a scriptwriter and how the film suffers when she doesn't quite reach what she aimed for. I appreciated how she tried to build character across the board, far more than was the norm in the genre's heyday, but none of them are given enough background to become either memorable or iconic. The story follows suit, with a bundle of inventive death scenes but only fair plot twists. The eye candy is nothing to complain about either, the leading ladies (or gentlemen, depending on your personal preferences) well worth looking at.

Where it really falls down is in the consistency and the tone, perhaps because Chaney is too young to have really experienced the slasher movie as it should have been experienced. She was born alongside the genre, being a baby only two months old when John Carpenter released *Halloween*, so she's less like the babysitter from so many slashers and more like the kids being sat.

Anther oddity is that, while *Slumber Party Slaughter* generally takes aim at the eighties, it opens with very seventies aerial footage that doesn't go anywhere and there are other nods to more recent decades throughout, meaning that the camp ambience that should be everywhere simply isn't. That's the key ingredient that most will notice through its absence; anyone seeking this out for its retro feel will end up disappointed. It's too thought out to be a slasher, but too ambitious to be a postmodern homage. The subplots are all too fleshed out but the main plot isn't defined enough for us to really be sure what we're watching.

We start at the Lingerie Lounge where the strippers are easily delineated. Casey is the nice girl stuck there to support her little brother, Bobby; she'll leave as soon as opportunity knocks with Nicole, the popular girl next door type. Vicky is the statuesque blonde bitch who's been there the longest, has seen it all and is as cynical about it as she could possibly be. Bobby has a huge crush on her and she clearly knows it. That leaves Felicia, the dumb bimbo who counts her successes by how many plastic surgeries they pay for, and Nadia, the wannabe pop star whose voice is so bad that she should never be.

Watching them work is taxi driver Dave, a creepy regular, and a trio of college kids with more bravado than sense. They all get pissed off when Tom Sizemore shows up and steals all the girls, but at least he has a blast parodying himself as Tom Kingsford, a drug addled movie star who collects bad habits. That's not coincidental, as the part was apparently based on his very own appearance in celebrity rehab.

As tends to happen in horror movies, the characters that play together stay together, at least for a while. When the movie star hires all the strippers for a private party that night and they breeze off into the dark in his limo, everyone else follows and Dave shows up at precisely the worst moment, with Kingsford murdered, his chauffeur vanished and the girls figuring out what to do with the body.

Then we leap forward a year, picking the story back up as the limo is discovered at the bottom of the lake in the Indian burial ground turned haunted cemetery. At this point, Nicole has left the Lingerie Lounge for a cushier job working for millionaire art dealer William O'Toole and, as the girls start to talk about their crime, they find out that she's housesitting his mansion while he's away on business. Naturally, talk of murder and fear of discovery quickly transforms into party time, with all the same characters finding their way back into the story from wherever they'd managed to escape.

It's here that I started getting confused. Sure, we realise that O'Toole, played by near namesake Ryan O'Neal, is some sort of freaky voyeur, not away on business at all but camping out in the guesthouse watching proceedings on monitors, but did he just expect to see Nicole or the party that soon erupts? He and his sidekick sit back longer than seems natural, given that people start dying in the memorable ways that victims tend to find in slasher movies. He doesn't even call a halt when guests start to rob him blind or discover his kinky secrets. Did he set up the large but apparently retarded gardener to massacre the partygoers? Or is all of this complete coincidence?

I never could quite figure this character/subplot combo out. I couldn't figure out how Nadia had got a recording deal either, as she sounds awful, but Casey is working hard to become a cop and the other girls are still at the Lingerie Lounge, where the college kids are now as regular as Dave. We're given a lot of detail but not all of it makes sense and not all of it is important. Re-reading my review, I see a whole slew of details that, in another movie, would be spoilers, but I don't believe I've spoiled anything here.

Certainly nobody can be too surprised to find that what seems like every character we've met thus far, at least those who are still alive, conveniently shows up at O'Toole's mansion to play their part in the inevitable slaughter, with a host of romantic entanglement subplots in tow. Here, we can finally settle back to watch the fun, because even with the tone too serious and not campy enough, and the story overly-complicated and overly-convenient, there is quite a lot of fun to be had.

Felicia in particular gets a joyous death scene, combining plot conveniences galore with an inventive sense of humour and some very nice touches indeed. It's no surprise to find out she's not the only one who gets hers but I'm not going to spoil who, how or why; I'll merely point out that hers is the most memorable of the many death scenes on offer. They're all handled well for the most part, though the imagination is always in the denouement rather than the setup. It's pretty clear throughout who the next victim is going to be and how soon it's going to happen, while the actual method of dispatch and the style of the scene are much more up for grabs.

At the end of the day, there's a lot here to see but it's all on the micro scale, which means that this review probably makes the film sound more interesting than it is. It feels like one of those movies that people remember decades later for a single death scene or one freaky moment, then revisit the film and find themselves mostly disappointed because the bad never leaves the good.

The actors are consistently good but none of them are good enough to carry the picture. The characters they play are drawn better than is the norm but none of them are drawn well enough to be a real focus. The various subplots are worthy but they're all distracting from the bigger picture. And so on and so on...

What I think I'm taking away from *Slumber Party Slaughter* is that Rebekah Chaney can write and has a lot to say, but she doesn't seem to be able to stand back and see her script at a distance. To turn this into what she wanted it to be, she needed to slice off a great deal of material, some good and some not so good, in order to focus the remainder into a leaner and tighter story. So much of her potential here simply isn't realised as it gets lost in the mix.

In the end, I found myself frustrated. I enjoyed so many moments but ended up disappointed with the film itself. As time has passed, it's fading away from me. When I later chatted about the film with Robert Mukes, who played that huge, possibly retarded gardener, because he hadn't seen the film, I couldn't say much more than that he provided a strong presence to a weak picture.

However, I am hopeful for Chaney's future. If she can learn from this, her next film may be something to see, whether she's really connected to the Lon Chaney legacy or not.

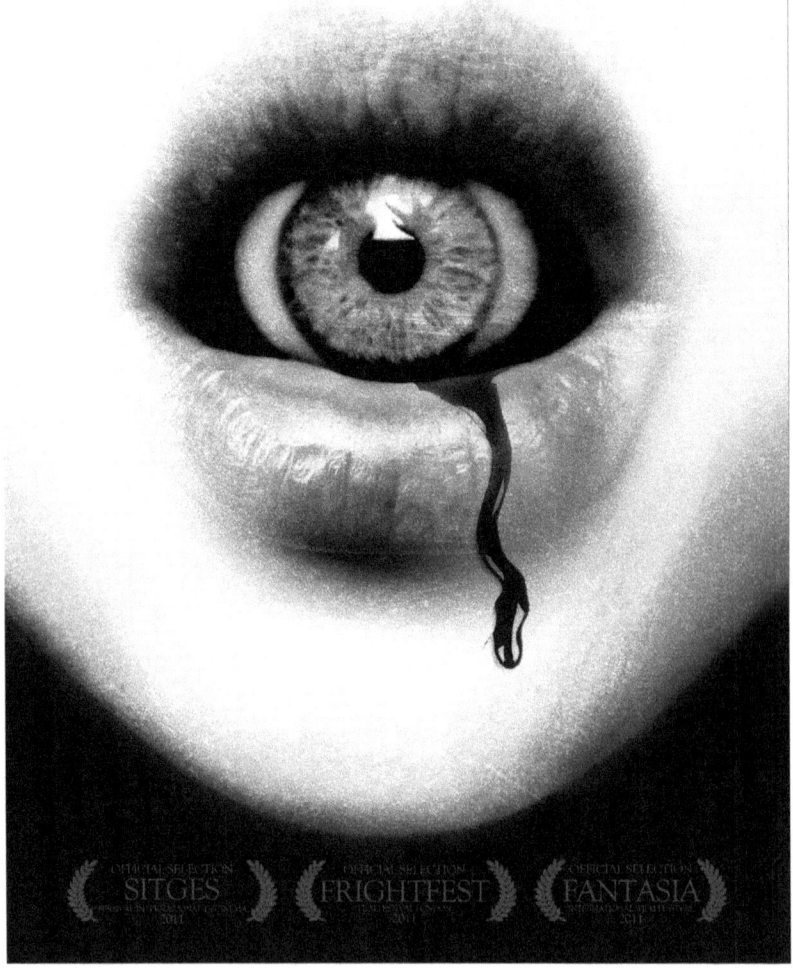

The Theatre Bizarre (2011)

Directors: Douglas Buck, Buddy Giovinazzo, David Gregory, Karim Hussain, Jeremy Kasten, Tom Savini and Richard Stanley
Writers: Zach Chassler, Richard Stanley, Scarlett Amaris, Emiliano Ranzani, Buddy Giovinazo, John Esposito, Douglas Buck, Karim Hussain and David Gregory
Stars: Udo Kier, Guilford Adams, Suzan Anbeh, Lindsay Goranson, André Hennicke, Kaniehtiio Horn, Lena Kleine, Catriona MacColl, Victoria Maurette, Virginia Newcomb, Debbie Rochon, Tom Savini and Melodie Simard

Horror anthology films are often hit and miss affairs but this one's even more hit and miss than usual.

There are six segments from six different directors and eight different writers, along with a vague framing story from another one each of each, and none of them appeared on the face of it to have any commonality with each other with regards to actors, tone or genre. Not even the choice of language is consistent. Now, there is a commonality, but it's never made obvious, either on the poster or in the film itself, so it has to be explained to us afterwards.

At the time, I wondered if it was even a real anthology at all or whether someone had merely acquired the rights to a collection of unrelated short films and shot a framing story to ostensibly link them together to the audience. I'd still believe that if I hadn't explored the credits to find the commonalities within the crew.

Douglas Buck, for instance, wrote and directed *The Accident*, but edited *Wet Dreams*, *Vision Stains* and *Sweets* too. Karim Hussain, who wrote, shot and directed *Vision Stains*, was also the cinematographer on *The Mother of Toads* and *The Accident*. And so on... so it appears to be a real project, all other evidence to the contrary, merely not an obvious anthology.

Unfortunately the first segment is by far the worst, for a number of reasons. It's *Mother of Toads*, an adaptation of an old Clark Ashton Smith story by Richard Stanley of *Hardware* and *Dust Devil* fame.

Now I'm a big fan of Smith, a contemporary of H. P. Lovecraft and a regular contributor to *Weird Tales*. What set Smith apart from other writers was his unparalleled vocabulary; reading a Smith story is a lush, immersive experience unmatched in all of weird fiction, but precisely none of that is translated to the screen here. I'm also a fan of Richard Stanley, originally of his early indie horror features but now because of his superb showing in a documentary called *Lost Soul: The Doomed Journey of Richard Stanley's Island of Dr. Moreau*, in which David Gregory (more about him later) documents how his big budget debut went quickly and horribly wrong.

So this was promising, but what we get is thoroughly routine. An anthropologist and his wife tour France, presumably chosen only because Stanley lives there, so he can do research and she can buy stuff, but they stumble upon a copy of the *Necronomicon* in the hands of a local witch and, as any reader of weird fiction knows, that never ends well.

It isn't all bad, as the imagery is decent, if not remotely new, and Catriona MacColl is fine, but it all feels flimsy and predictable and devoid of Smith's enticing vocabulary. I'll never complain about a nubile, naked witch in a movie, but this needed a good combination of freakiness and tension and only the toads in the forest come close. Stanley has done much better work elsewhere.

I Love You is an improvement, but is so utterly different that it's oddly difficult to compare. New York writer and director Buddy Giovinazzo, still best known for his debut film, *Combat Shock*, gets psychological in Berlin with a neatly arced story about Axel and Simone, an obsessive German and his former French girlfriend.

They're played by German actors, André Hennicke and Suzan Anbeh, who are much better in their native language than they are in English, obviously enough that they clearly both know it. Axel wakes up in the bathroom covered in blood, recovering from a fight that he doesn't remember. Outside is Mo, with her new boyfriend George, and our story begins when she comes in and comes clean.

It's a brutal psychological piece, which plays with our sympathies and ends well, though I did want a twist on the twist. Hennicke is excellent, like a young Polanski mixed with Robert Carlyle and a little Viggo Mortensen thrown in for good measure. I'd like to see more of his work, which is increasingly not in German.

After a Lovecraftian tale and a psychological foreign drama, next up is a more traditional horror yarn all about sex, violence and dreams. Oh, and special effects. It is directed by the legendary Tom Savini, after all.

I did like *Wet Dreams*, which is a glorious title for a horror short, but far more for the many layers of reality and dream through which it travels than for the gore, which is still agreeably solid and rarely off screen. There's much more here to remember in a short segment than in most features, beginning with a P.O.V. shot where we follow a girl in a thong and progressing through torture, genital mutilation, amputation, you name it, all done capably and, yes, quite gratuitously.

The biggest problem that *Wet Dreams* has is that it has precious little time to work with; when it tries to build a story in such a way that we aim to figure it out ahead of the ending, it fails miserably. Without intellectual engagement, it merely turns into a sequence of revelations; they're all fun ones, to be sure, but they're revelations nonetheless. The story deserves a great deal more length to allow us to explore it properly.

Slow and atmospheric from moment one, *The Accident* is a jarring shift in the pace of the film, which is a shame because it's the best segment thus far. It's beautifully shot, both in its leisurely motion and the photographic stills, it's scored well and it unfolds superbly, inevitable in plot but ambiguous in effect, which is a neat little combo to have.

"Why do people die, mummy?" the little girl asks, as the film flashes back to the title scene where a biker who waved to her drove headlong into a deer, and that's an impeccable start to a horror short.

It isn't clear on one viewing exactly what writer/director Douglas Buck, an unfortunate name given the circumstances, was aiming at here. Obviously there are many questions asked about death, not only by the little girl and not only about the biker. There's also a gruesome scene that I won't spoil that takes all this deeper. Yet I wonder if there's more: it seems notable, for instance, that the mother/daughter are in a car but the unrelated father/son are on motorbikes. I'd love to see this one again.

Almost to underline how the common thread of these segments is to not have a common thread, the fifth piece mixes science fiction and horror into a story that aims to find the secret of life in an unusual way.

The protagonist in *Vision Stains*, credited simply as "the Writer", extracts fluid from the eyes of dying women and injects it into her own. In doing so, she also extracts the important things from their lives, which presumably flash before their eyes at the moment of their death, conveniently for the Writer to document for posterity. Being a biographer is clearly a calling for her and she has a heck of a lot of notebooks.

This short is a neat take on an old idea, which calls on actress Kaniehtiio Horn to get into freaky locations and do icky things. I last saw her in *The Wild Hunt* and I appreciated her work there too, so I'll definitely keep my eyes on her in the future. Right now she's racking up credits, including a current run on TV's *Hemlock Grove*.

I'm not sure I caught everything Karim Hussain aimed at on a single viewing, but it's telling that he's known in the industry far more as a cinematographer than he is a writer/director, making him primarily a worker in the visual rather than words. His work here is notably original and it has a great escalation.

Last up is a metaphor from David Gregory, the prolific biographer in film whose work tends to be found by clicking on the "Extras" option on DVD menus rather than "Play Movie". A great exception is the wonderful documentary, *Lost Soul*, whose subtitle explains how it connects to the director of the first short in this anthology: *The Doomed Journey of Richard Stanley's Island of Dr Moreau*.

He has worked in fiction before, particularly with his excellent hillbilly horror movie, *Plague Town*, which was set with originality in Ireland. I liked that feature a great deal and I liked this short film, *Sweets*, very much too.

It has to do with a compulsive eater called Greg, who is an utter slob in a mess of a place, but who still has a lovely girlfriend in Estelle. Well, maybe not. As she wheels out all the leaving lines and he gets progressively grosser, they flashback to increasingly weird foot fetish scenes and we realise that she isn't real, or at least isn't any more.

Then we switch from Greg's suitably gross environs to a chic party, a wonderful contrast in style and setting but still very much about food fetishes and eating disorders. This is far from your average chic party, folks, and it gets progressively less so from here on out. It's a very European piece, weird but arty, and put together very well indeed.

So did you see any obvious connections between these six short stories? If you did, you're a better man than I. The only clue to be found is in the name of the theatre in which the framing story unfolds. I'd acknowledged it and knew where it came from, but still didn't put two and two together to make four.

Our host and guide is the ever-freaky Udo Kier, sharing the stage of the Theatre Guignol with a collection of automatons during the linking segments. These segments are notably weak but that name is important, as the film was apparently inspired by the legendary Grand Guignol theatre in Paris, which, at the height of its success in the early twentieth century, from 1898-1930, specialised in short and very gory plays with shocking special effects. An average of two audience members fainted every evening.

While I knew a little about the Grand Guignol, I hadn't realised that its shows varied in style quite as much as do the segments of this film, even alternating horror plays with comedies to heighten the effect. Each director built their own tribute from a consistent budget, schedule and simple directive to follow the Grand Guignol themes, but with complete artistic freedom otherwise.

And so, with each segment featuring something suitably icky or gross to focus on, this anthology would seem to be fair tribute, but it's still annoyingly disjointed and no explanation after the fact can serve to make it seem any different.

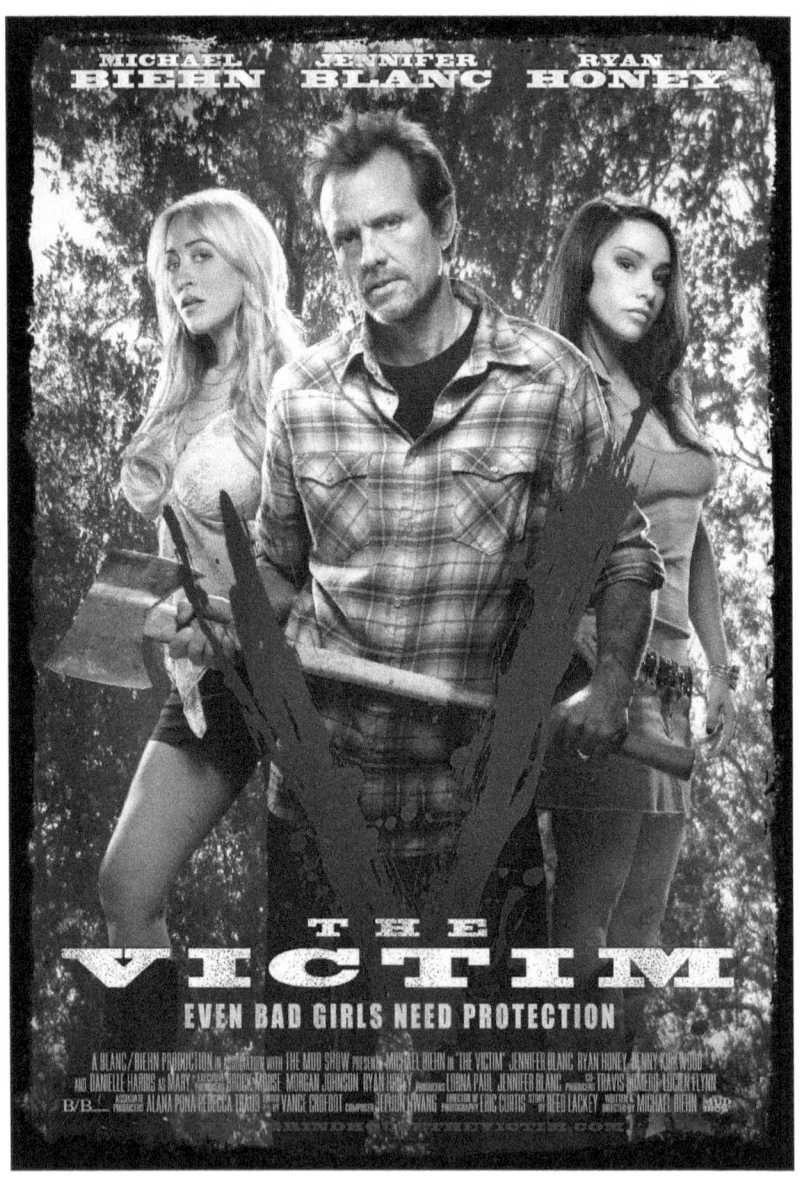

The Victim (2011)

Director: Michael Biehn
Writer: Michael Biehn, from a story by Reed Lackey
Stars: Michael Biehn, Jennifer Blanc and Ryan Honey

Introducing *The Victim* at its Arizona premiere at the Phoenix Film Festival, Michael Biehn, who grew up in the state and studied drama at the University of Arizona, so was on home ground of sorts, explained the motivation behind his second directorial effort. "It's just like cotton candy," he suggested, and he meant it. He wanted the audience to enjoy themselves, of course, but not to end up dissecting it over the water cooler at work. It's aimed at being pure escapism and only pure escapism. And here's my dissection...

First of all, I'm not sure why he highlighted that angle so much. Sure, this is far from an original story and his debut outing in the director's chair, *The Blood Bond*, made a year earlier, is apparently even less so. Perhaps he felt that the audience might have got upset at the abundant clichés if he hadn't issued a warning beforehand. Frankly, it didn't matter. However you come to it, *The Victim* is a lot of fun from the very beginning and it never lets up. It doesn't do much else but it certainly entertains.

It begins the way it means to go on: with a sex scene. We're in the woods and some guy is doing a chick from behind. He's into it, but she obviously isn't and, when she stops playing along, he snaps her neck. We soon discover that the murderer is Jim, aka Det. James Harrison. Yep, our killer is a cop, and *General Hospital* actor Ryan Honey (talk about a name meant for soap operas) plays him like a sleazy Burt Lancaster playing a sleazier Tom Selleck.

He's out in the woods with fellow detective Jonathan Cooger, who's apparently an undercover narcotics officer. Why Cooger thinks he can maintain his cover by picnicking with the man tipped to be the next sheriff, I have no idea. His excuse may be that while Jim is banging Mary, he aims to get some from Annie, a believable cause for a slip in professional ethics as she's played by Jennifer Blanc, Biehn's wife and business partner, not to mention the co-producer of this film. If that's why Mary dies and Annie lives, that's fine with me. She's sexy as hell and the camera loves her.

She's also really good at playing the victim. She isn't the greatest actress to ever grace a movie screen and this is hardly the greatest role ever given to an actress, but as she sees Mary's body and runs for her life through the Arizona woods, she's as believably scared shitless as I've seen from anyone in a long time. She may be too talented to be restricted to scream queen roles, but on the basis of this, they're screaming out for her.

Of course she finds herself at a cabin in the middle of nowhere where she pleads for help from the owner who we know is played by Biehn himself because we watched him drive there in a sequence so long that it rivalled the similar one that sat behind the non-existent opening credits in *Manos: The Hands of Fate*. Her chaos is contrasted well with his order, because he's all about peace and quiet. He's Kyle Linato and, while she's been running through the woods in abject terror, he's been reading and listening to self help lectures. For some reason he lets her in.

And that pretty much sets the stage for the entire rest of the movie, because as Biehn mentioned, this is cotton candy not *Wild Strawberries*. You could write much of the rest yourself and not be too far off what Biehn conjures up from Reed Lackey's story, both in the natural progression of the plot and in the less natural turns it takes.

For instance, when Kyle and Annie go to look for Mary's body they don't find it, so they head back to the cabin and jump in the sack. You know, like you do. Maybe it can be vaguely justified on the basis that Annie is supposed to be an idiot co-ed or some such, all about sex, power and free coke, but come on, her best friend was just murdered and she's on the run from the cops who did it. Hot monkey sex surely can't be top of her agenda at this point! It makes sense only on a different level: Biehn and Blanc are a couple, this was the first scene shot, she has a great rack and, as she says, he looks really good for 54.

To be fair, this enjoyable cinematic nonsense follows the first really good scene of the film. To begin with, Biehn didn't seem quite right. He wasn't bad, but he could easily have been better. It made me wonder whether he should really direct himself. Then the cops arrive at Kyle's cabin and ask to come in. The tension generated by the three as he refuses is delicious and from then on I saw Biehn's performance a little differently.

Kyle is an interesting character, albeit mostly through not being that interesting. He's living at his uncle's cabin deep in the woods because he's trying to keep away from trouble. We don't quite know what kind, but the impression is that he's not very bright but both very capable and down to earth. He's exactly the sort of character who might turn a simple situation into a complex one by reacting in ways that don't serve his best interests, just because. You know, like this one, where he hides the girl even though it makes him an obvious target.

To me he was overtly something else as well, though as Biehn seemed surprised when I mentioned it to him after the screening, he presumably didn't aim for it. Kyle is a very refreshing character: he unfailingly says the things we want him to say and does the things we want him to do. It doesn't matter if they're the right things or not, and they often aren't, but they're exactly what we want him to do, making him our wish fulfilment character.

For instance, when Jim breaks into his house to kidnap Annie, Kyle rescues her in his boxers and uses a heated crowbar to get the truth out of him. Frankly, nobody in their right mind is going to torture the next sheriff to get him to confess to something that he's promptly going to pretend he never confessed to, because the moment he's free he's going to shoot you in the face, but it doesn't matter. We want Kyle to do this because Jim is a slimeball and we want him to get his as a matter of principle. This is not great storytelling, but it's refreshing to have a lead character consistently give us exactly what we want.

And on it goes, continuing to entertain without trying too hard to keep things believable. There's some mild philosophy here and there, but it's nothing groundbreaking. For instance, Jim explains the slight depth behind the title in a line of dialogue: "Take life by the balls and get what you want, or you can be the victim." See, it isn't just about screaming Annie. It's about being the man or being the victim. Life's a game and Jim plays it really well, but Kyle may just play it better.

While Annie turns out to be worth a little more as a character than she's initially set up to be, this is a notably testosterone fuelled thriller. There's a lot of to and fro action suspense, as Jim and Kyle gain and lose the upper hand, done well enough for us to stay with it throughout. There's some sex, some violence, some memorably cheesy dialogue: everything you'd expect, all done well on next to no budget. It doesn't look cheap until you start to think about certain things, but we don't think too much.

There's a thank you in the end credits to Robert, and which one is hardly a surprise. Biehn had read a book by Robert Rodriguez called *Rebel without a Crew: Or How a 23-Year-Old Filmmaker with $7,000 Became a Hollywood Player*, which spoke to the techniques he developed to be able to make *El Mariaor* on a microbudget. While I haven't read it, so can't speak to what he learned, Biehn obviously paid attention because this looks like a lot more than it cost. It was shot entirely day for night with a single camera, 40 setups a day for 12 days, 12 hours a day. That sex scene was the first shot because Biehn hadn't finished the script at that point, so a dialogue free romp with his real life wife was a safe beginning. Most noticeable for me were the fights. They're very old school, tough punchfests like you'd expect in old Clint Eastwood movies, but they're also mostly outside. We don't see sets and props get broken here, because that would have cost money.

The cast were the crew, something you expect in microbudget cinema, but not necessarily from people that are recognisable. Everyone knows who Michael Biehn is, given that he took on Arnie in *The Terminator*, albeit as a different Kyle. He's a regular for James Cameron, whose budgets for single movies exceed that of entire countries. We don't expect someone like Biehn to appear in a movie that cost nothing, but then he did write and direct too and is building up his production company. It's going to pay off well for him because this is deservedly going to make a quick and decent profit, if not a vast one.

It demonstrates what can be achieved without scary money and frankly, I'd rather go to see movies like this than movies like *Avatar* or *The Avengers* that cost hundreds of millions of bucks. If this was the average Hollywood film, tickets could be five bucks a pop, I'd be seeing two or three of them every week and everyone would be making money. That's not a bad dream, is it?

It's certainly what I'm going to take away from this because, as

Biehn suggested, otherwise it's cotton candy.

There isn't much to think about, though there is a neat little twist at the end. It's mindless action, done well if not particularly originally. Biehn plays a solid hero, somewhat different from the perennial soldier roles he seems to get typecast as. In many ways he isn't even a character, he's the will of the audience taking the place of a character.

This is a *Choose Your Own Adventure* movie where you're torn away from peace and quiet by a buxom young wench who arrives in mortal peril and requires your tough and manly help to save her. Cue the sex and violence.

I'm certainly not complaining. I just wish more movies with recognisable names were like this. I'll certainly pay to see the next picture released by BlancBiehn Productions on the basis of this one, but I also hope that Biehn passes on my wish to James Cameron that at least one viewer would love to see what he could do with no budget too.

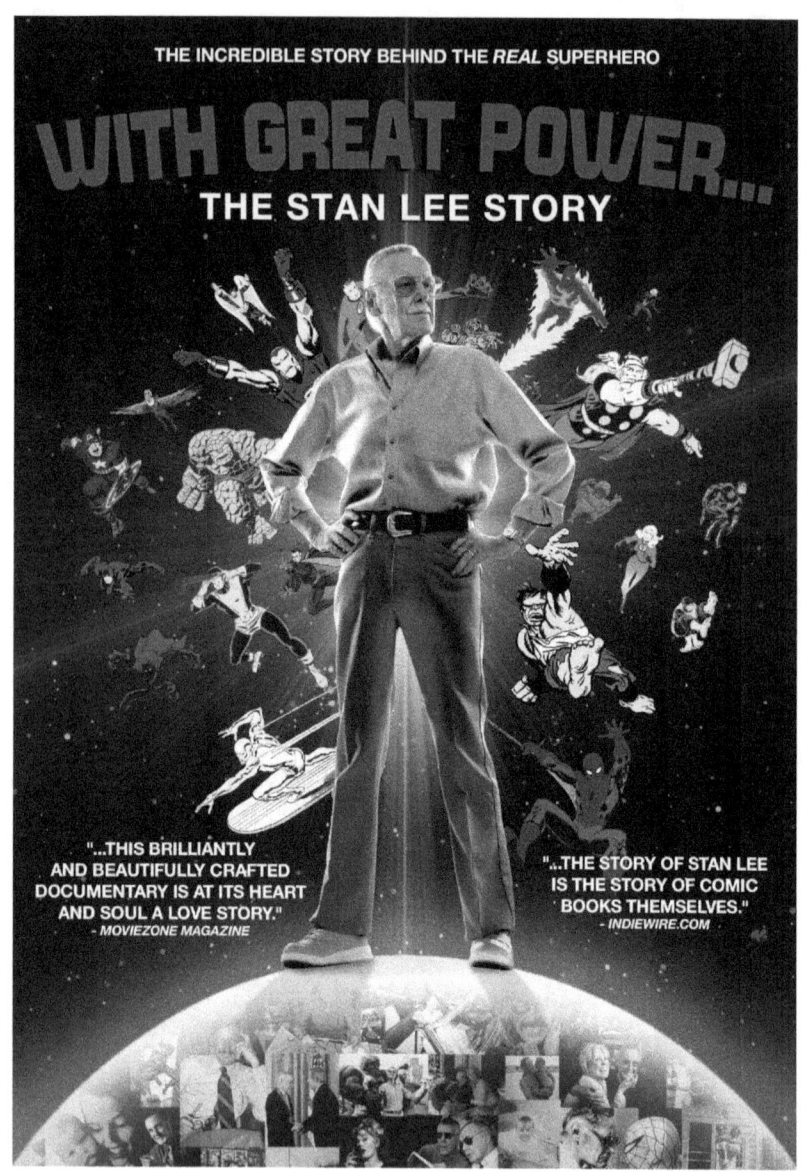

With Great Power: The Stan Lee Story (2010)

Directors: Terry Dougas, Nikki Frakes and Will Hess
Writers: William Lawrence Hess and Nikki Frakes
Star: Stan Lee

Unmistakably one of the most legendary names in the world of comic books, Stan Lee is more than worthy of getting his own documentary. In fact, I'm surprised it hasn't happened until now and it wouldn't take much argument to suggest that this is a long time overdue.

That stands however you know the man's name. You may have known him for decades from the characters he created or helped to create for Marvel Comics ("the story of Stan Lee is the story of comic books themselves," proclaims IndieWire on the film's poster). You may have discovered him more recently through the various blockbuster adaptations of those characters to the big screen (in which he invariably gets a fun cameo appearance). You may know him because he's simply a personality who magically appears at what seems like every single nerd event known to man; he even co-owns one of them, Stan Lee's Comikaze in Los Angeles, which in 2015 was voted Con of the Year by Nerd HQ.

In some ways this is a telling biography, as its best parts step back from his numerous achievements to look instead at a humble man and his wife. In others, it's a notably misleading propaganda piece, as its worst parts focus so closely on Lee that a fresh face to comic books would be excused for leaving the film with the belief that he invented the things, created every character in them and pushed them all past every evolutionary step from their establishment in 1933 to today.

Perhaps it would have been more grounded had this film been shot in the late nineties, before Stan Lee the Personality took over in many ways from Stan Lee the Talent.

I'm thinking that the sweet spot would have been before the massive success of Sam Raimi's *Spider-Man* films and before Marvel Studios began producing their own pictures, like *Iron Man* and *The Avengers*, but after Marvel Entertainment had filed for Chapter 11 bankruptcy protection and after Stan Lee Media had collapsed into bankruptcy too amid the illegal stock manipulation of his partner, Peter Paul. At that point, Lee was by no means the infallible man with the Midas touch he appears to be today and telling his story might have been more about restoring his rightful place in comic book history. Maybe, maybe not.

Instead it was shot a decade later in 2010 with Lee a household name, his powerful charisma matched only by his magical sense of childlike wonder at the world sprouting up around him and his seemingly unstoppable energy, even at 88 years young. So it's an iconic American success story seen through rose coloured glasses.

I'm far from a comic book nerd, but I do read graphic novels, I do go to conventions that are rooted in comic books and I do know a little about the history of the industry. I know enough to recognise that while what we're told in this film is no doubt the truth, it's a long way indeed from the whole truth. It's rather selective in what it wants to tell us.

This film (and a little research after watching it) taught me a lot about Lee's part in the wider story of American superheroes and the evolution of their worlds, but only because I could recognise many of the notably glaring gaps, where the contributions of others who worked before and alongside him were either omitted entirely, dismissed quickly or explained away in dubious terms that left an occasional bad taste in the mouth. These omissions are far from minor and their presence leaves all the various looks back at comic book history on shaky ground. One such omission might perhaps be excused as an unfortunate oversight but, when they're frequent and pervasive, the film turns from a viable documentary into purest propaganda.

The biggest omission surely has to be the competition. Created in 1934, DC Comics predated its biggest rival in name by 27 years and through lineage by five, given that Marvel Comics began its life as Timely Comics in 1939 and became Atlas Comics over a decade later, formally adopting its most famous name in 1961.

We're given some fascinating background into this progression, but the achievements of Marvel are not given context, even when they were made in deliberate reaction to the competition, most obviously DC. Marvel's superheroes were wildly successful in the early sixties, but they were written in response to DC's prior success. *The Fantastic Four*, for instance, was a direct response to DC's *Justice League of America*. To be fair, this is a standard hour and a half film and Lee's story is inextricably linked to Marvel's rather than DC's, but omitting the competition utterly removes any real context and makes both Lee and Marvel appear far more important than they actually were.

More galling is the treatment of a couple of other people whose names are tied more closely to Marvel's.

Jack Kirby was an artist with Timely at the beginning, while Lee was hired shortly after as an office boy, tasked with keeping the artists' inkwells full. Kirby co-created Captain America with Joe Simon, as Lee was moving up to writing filler stories. By the time superheroes were all the rage again in the sixties, Lee had become editor-in-chief and art director, but most of Marvel's most iconic characters, such as Iron Man, the Hulk and the X-Men, were joint creations of Kirby and Lee.

Those characters Kirby didn't have a hand in, such as Spider-Man, another artist called Steve Ditko did. Both Kirby and Ditko are highlighted in this film and their importance evaluated, but while Lee personally enthuses that they were every bit as important as he was, the film's tone is emphatically that he's merely being modest and that they're only equals because the far more important Lee is kind enough to throw them a bone. That's unfair.

None of this is meant to undermine Lee's own importance, merely to counter the film's viewpoint that he was the be all and end all, either at Marvel or in the wider field of comic books. Lee legitimately did change the face of the industry in a number of ways, most obviously crediting the artists and letterers, not just the writers, as well as grounding superheroes in the real world.

Peter Sanderson, a comic book historian, wrote that DC was the equivalent of the Hollywood studios, while Marvel during the early sixties was the French New Wave, shaking up the way in which these stories were told and, in doing so, revolutionising the entire industry. While DC characters lived in Gotham City or Metropolis, Marvel characters lived in New York. They fought Communists in the sixties just as they'd fought Nazis during World War II. They even dealt with everyday problems as well as the usual villains, marking the point at which superheroes became more important out of their masks than they ever were inside them. That's Lee's doing, more than anyone else.

While this picture is capable at talking up Lee's substantial contributions to his field, aided by neatly animated graphics, they're lessened through the equally substantial gaps. It succeeds better in the little details that proved fascinating to me, revealing that comic books only included two page prose layouts in order to qualify for second class mail privileges, that Lee demonstrated the poses that he wanted his artists to draw by acting them out on top of his desk or that he contributed to training films during the war, anachronistically classified by the US Army as a playwright.

It succeeds in the highs and lows of Lee's emotion: while talking about the modern blockbuster movies, he's full of energy, just like a kid in a candy store whose only enemy is time; while talking about the earlier live action movies which were almost universally awful, his frustration is palpable. Nicolas Cage may talk fairly about the deficiencies of technology at the time but that isn't the key reason, which is that only with Raimi's *Spider-Man* did those who actually understood comic books start making comic book movies. You don't hire a German speaker to make a French language movie, after all; you hire a Frenchman. Comic books have always been written in their own language and those early films were made by people who didn't speak it.

Without a doubt, the best scenes are reserved for Lee and his wife, an absolute jewel of a character who threatens to steal every scene that she's in. She's a former English hat model named Joan and she's the unsung heroine of Lee's story. While she was married when they met, he proposed after two weeks and they've been together for 65 years. They're a riot of a couple, bickering back and forth with the sort of twinkle in their eyes that can't help but raise a smile. We're privy to happy moments and sad ones, all of which feel remarkably honest, especially when placed within a frequently dishonest film. They're so intrinsically honest that the filmmakers simply aren't able to spin their words into something else, however cleverly they edit the footage or splice in interviews with others.

Writers William Lawrence Hess and Nikki Frakes, both of whom also directed alongside Terry Dougas, know exactly what they want this film to say: the movie opens with no less a cultural luminary than Larry King calling Lee "the most famous name in American comic book history" and what seems like all of Hollywood promptly agrees with him. Yet fame isn't substance and what I'll take away from this film is that, comic books and blockbuster movies aside, Stan and Joan Lee have obviously enjoyed the heck out of their lives and they're still doing it.

If the filmmakers had made Stan and Joan Lee the magnetic and very human bedrock of their documentary and allowed the legend that he has become grow out of it, through the background of comic book, film and pop culture history, *With Great Power: The Stan Lee Story* would have been a much more substantial piece. As it is, it serves as little more than an ego stroke and a reminder that those of us interested in the subject should start reading up on it instead.

The International Horror & Sci-Fi Film Festival

2012

Horror Shorts

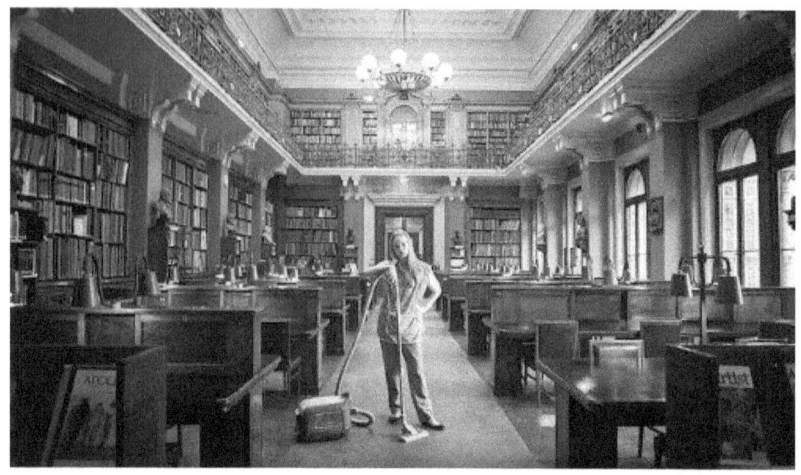

Shoreditch Slayer

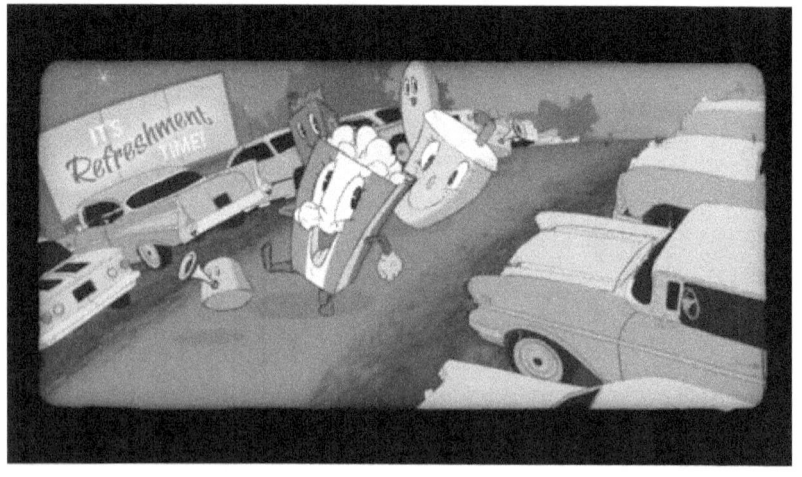

Follow the Sun!

Shoreditch Slayer (2011)

Director: Simon Levene
Writer: Simon Levene

This one caught me completely by surprise. From the title I expected some sort of microbudget British slasher movie, probably heavy on the gore. While it did turn out to be British, it's subtitled for the most part because it's shot in a number of languages, even though there's a mere three minutes to cram them all into. As for style, it's a mockumentary in which an imaginatively varied set of international vampires explain the other thing that they all have in common: a lack of decent job opportunities.

Explaining just how *Twilight* is destroying the potential for real vampires to play fake vampires in horror movies is a sure bet to go down well at a horror film festival. Talk about a gimme! That's an automatic win right there, guaranteed, with only a dragged along girlfriend or two taking mild umbrage, and at three minutes, there's not too much room to really do much else. The good news is that writer/director Simon Levene still manages to do quite a bit.

He runs through the history, explaining that the movies made it possible for vampires to make an honest living, up until *Twilight*, of course. But what next? Everyone can be a zombie, right? Well, these vampires take regular jobs instead, which are explored surprising well, given the short running time.

All the unnamed actors look great both as vampires and their menial alter egos. Beyond the mere concept of vampires taking jobs like these, there's humour built into each clip. The composition of frame and choice of locations make the footage seem artful. Levene even knows when to wrap it up.

All these successes no doubt stem from his regular work, directing TV commercials. To do that right, you have to know how to grab our attention, tell a story in a short timeframe and, most importantly, leave us wanting more. If not, we're going to prioritise taking a leak over whatever you have to say. Thankfully, Levene is good at his job and his skills are put to great use here.

Follow the Sun! (2011)

Director: MK12
Writer: MK12

Follow the Sun! isn't your usual horror short. It's a subversive and experimental animation that almost by definition would fit like a glove at the beginning of any set of horror shorts at a film festival. It's also surprisingly inevitable and I'm surprised nobody has done this sort of thing before or, if they have, why I haven't seen it.

It's a freaky take on the reels that used to screen before movies to bludgeon us into buying more refreshments by unleashing hordes of anthropomorphic drinks and hot dogs whose only purpose in life was to gleefully convince us to eat them. Come to think of it, they were pretty freaky to begin with, cannabilistic sacrifices designed to lull us into a zombie state where we hand over our dollars in a glass eyed, slack jawed stupor.

If they weren't nightmarish enough to begin with, this short adds whatever was missing, showing us in inevitable detail just what happens when things go wrong in a land where everything is inherently happy.

For a minute and a half it's horrifying only in traditional ways, the familiar imagery and hypnotic music eating into your brain like a consumerist cancer. It's well animated and neatly aged and coloured too, making it feel like a much used reel that doesn't know how to quit. Three minutes to showtime, folks! Still plenty of time to... visit the refreshment stand!

And then it happens: one cutesy mascot treads on another cutesy mascot and the tone changes utterly and irrevocably. It somehow becomes a metaphor for the fall of man, the loss of immortality and the inevitability of death. It becomes angry and helpless as these mascots, the epitome of imbecilic glee, discover that they aren't equipped to deal with anything bad. I love the hellish relentlessness of it all as they try but fail to escape, to find a happy place where no such thing exists.

Like one cute little bag of popcorn, you might just stab your eyes out with a jagged shard of crisp. But you'll love it.

Brutal Relax (2010)

Director: Adrián Cardona, Rafa Dengrá and David Muñoz
Writer: David Muñoz
Star: José María Angorrilla

Brutal Relax has won many awards, all from festivals in foreign countries with names I've never heard of, as befits a picture whose very title makes no sense in English and which was made by three directors, each with an accent somewhere within each of their names. As if to highlight his importance, the lead actor has two, because it really is all about him. And gore. Let's not forget the gore. There's more of that here than you can comfortably imagine.

First, though, there's Mr. Olivares. He's apparently recovered and is ready to leave hospital. We have precisely no idea of his condition but he's now so happy and unresponsive that he looks like he's been lobotomised. The doctor wants him to take a holiday, to somewhere beautiful where he can stay calm and relax. He gives no reply except that incessant happy face but he looks like the perfect tourist as he heads off for the sun in suitably colourful attire.

He's apart from everyone else even as he arrives. He shows up on the beach wearing a pair of tighty whities, white socks and a pair of headphones and carrying a suitcase. He plops himself down in the beach cesspool but seems very happy slathering himself with crud. And it's all neatly peaceful: calm and relaxing, just what the doctor ordered. We see families having a great time. We hear sunbathing girls giggle. But not for long.

Out of the sea comes a horde of zombies, gorgeously made up marine zombies with their scaly skin oozing neon green slime and covered in ocean detritus. They pose for a moment like a metal band doing a photo shoot and then it gets real. The tourists get very gory very quickly with some gruesomely inventive technique, but Mr. Olivares simply sits back in his puddle of crud and grins. Well, until the batteries on his Walkman run out. Then he gets angry and turns into a brutal angel of destruction, a Spanish take on the Thing.

For the most part, this is complete overkill. Eleven of the fifteen minutes constitute a marathon of special effects, gruesome gore without any semblance of plot. The beachgoers are just props for the zombies to destroy and the zombies are just props for Mr. Olivares to destroy. It might be fun to review it as some sort of spiritual journey or feminist manifesto, but it's really an excuse to go hog wild with the gore effects. That's it. There's nothing else here.

It is structured well, at least, built in five sections of vaguely three minutes each that keep ramping up. What keeps it all from becoming boring is the humour which is inherent and frequently gloriously wrong, the unusual lead and a neat contrast between happy music and outrageous gore.

On the downside, the camerawork is too jerky during the fight scenes and the choreography and greenscreen work show their seams. Really though, you won't care. If this is your thing, you'll revel in it like Mr. Olivares in crud.

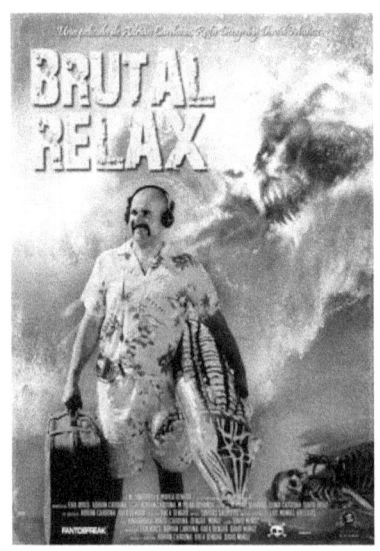

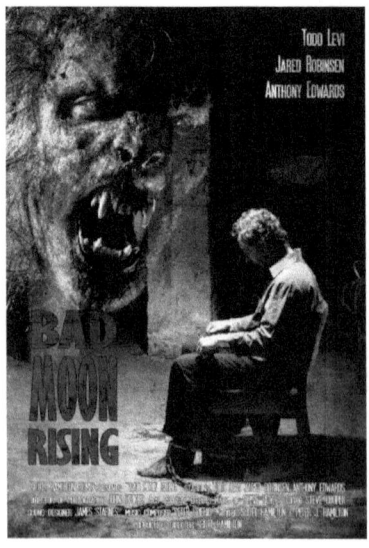

Bad Moon Rising (2010)

Director: Scott Hamilton
Writers: Scott and Peter J. Hamilton
Stars: Anthony Edwards, Todd Levi and Jared Robinsen

Only eight minutes long, this Aussie short manages to merge two genres very well indeed.

For a little while, it's a tough thriller revolving around an interrogation. The man chained to a chair in a presumably remote location is Adam and the man beating him up is Rico, who obviously relishes his work. Calling the shots is Chastel, as calm and professional as Rico is wilful and sadistic. Todd Levi and Jared Robinsen make for a believable pairing, different but consistent, and it's easy to see how they'd make a successful team in this line of work. Sure enough, Adam eventually cracks under their attentions and tells them everything they want to know, but naturally Rico carries on anyway, just for the fun of it, leaving his victim bloody and unconscious. That's when we shift from thriller to horror because the full moon shining through the bars of the window rejuvenates our hostage by transforming him into a werewolf. And so the tables are turned.

This is a simple little short with very little plot to speak of. It's much more of a vignette than a story, with the scene set immediately, a change introduced halfway and the actors tasked with changing with it. What there is is handled well. The acting is confident and assured, each of the three dealing capably with their changes in fortune, Anthony Edwards being especially solid as a believable victim who transforms well into something very different. The effects are excellent, both the creature work and the violence. The scenes in the dark are clean and well shot.

It's all done about as well as something that has so little to say can be done. Sure, some of the setups are expected but they're still done well for that and it remains stylish and effective throughout. Writers Scott and Peter Hamilton, presumably relatives, have three films behind them that look far less traditional than this one. I wonder if this was aimed at being more than just a vignette.

Ambush (2011)

Director: Joe B. Bauer
Writer: Joe Bauer
Star: Lance Henriksen

In 2010 Lance Henriksen was a special guest at the International Horror and Sci-Fi Film Festival, but not with new material; he was there to introduce a screening of *Aliens* instead. A couple of years later, he wasn't there in person but yet he was all over the screen. His feature, *It's in the Blood*, deservedly won for Best Horror Film; his voice was almost the only decent thing about *Monster Brawl*; and, most surprisingly, he was the star of an effective short action film called *Ambush*. Sure, he's a prolific actor, so much so that there's a mockumentary currently in production called *Bring Me the Head of Lance Henriksen*, in which Tim Thomerson's inability to find work leads him to seek out Henriksen, his co-star in *Near Dark* and others, to discover how he's landing every genre role for an actor over 65. Yet it was still pleasantly surprising to see him so omnipresent on the festival screen in 2012. He deserves no less, of course, as he's a gentleman offscreen and a magnetic presence on it.

This to me was the most interesting of his three films showing at the festival. It's a short film, under fifteen minutes in length, that was written and directed by a man new to both roles, but with a vast experience in film nonetheless. He's Joe Bauer, a Hollywood visual effects man with an impressive and varied filmography that runs from *Zu Warriors* to *Rise of the Silver Surfer* via *Zathura*. Yet, this is far from an effects film. It may not be as gritty as it intends to be, but it uses darkness, dubious lighting and off kilter angles to build a tone and feel that comes off as pretty effective. There should be more actors and more noise in this decaying urban landscape, but it's well envisioned in the sets, costumes and ambience. The few effects are in the news footage and in frequent views of the neighbourhood through infrared sniper scope.

Oh, and also in what goes down, of course. The title is there for a reason.

Out on the street is an old man with a flamboyant moustache

who's ripped off when he tries to cash a cheque. They take 40% of it as a fee and try for the rest later by force, but he's waiting. There is some more depth to the background but it's pretty transparent, given that the facial hair isn't enough to hide Henriksen and yet he's also on the TV as John Adams Lofgren, a massively rich public speaker and author of a book called *Take It Back: The Battle to Retake Democracy*. He wrote it because he read in the paper about an Indianapolis homeless man who had been set on fire and couldn't even be identified. On the news he asks, "Who stands up for John Doe?" On the street he tries to answer his own question.

While this works well as a short, it feels like it's part of something more, whether the pitch for a feature or the beginning of one. I'd certainly like to see more but then I always enjoy an opportunity for Henriksen to both look old and kick ass.

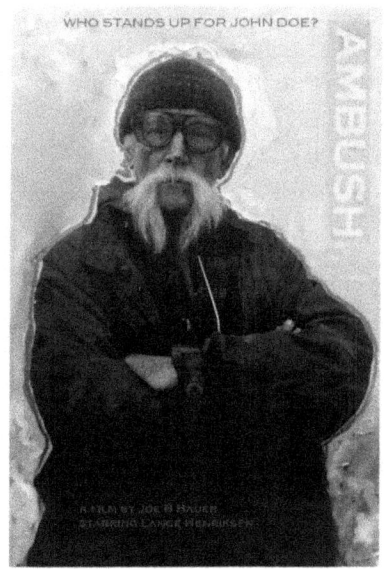
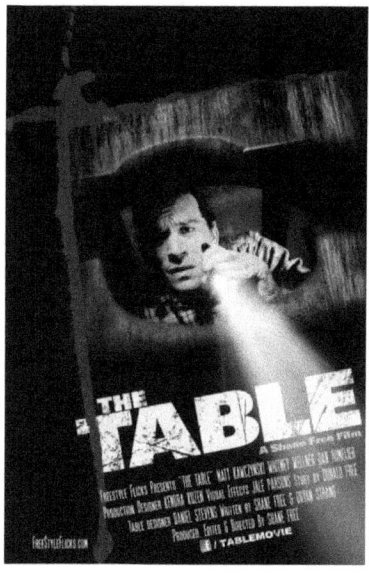

The Table (2011)

Director: Shane Free
Writer: Shane Free
Stars: Matt Kawczynski, Dan Homeijer and Whitney Wellner

A couple of guys explore an antique table that one of them bought at an estate sale, an antique table with a very deliberate hole in the middle. Now, if that doesn't already conjure up the entire rest of this short film, then you really aren't paying attention and I have some beachfront property in Arizona that I'd really like to sell you.

Yes, they fiddle around with it. Yes, one of them sticks his head up inside the hole. Yes, the other one closes the table around him. And... oh, c'mon, you honestly need help here? This pair of idiots really do deserve everything they get, but at least the stupidity that they wear like overalls is countered just a little by a young lady called Christie who reads the instructions. Well, she heads online to translate them. They are in French, after all. Oh, and handwritten. Inside a leather bound book. How many flags are going up here? Dude! There are pictures! And yet... well, let's just say that this is an exercise in inevitability. Fortunately it only has five minutes to run and, outside of being as obvious as it gets, it unfolds pretty well.

For a start, the table looks awesome, though the screws are a little anomalous. If I'd have been at that estate sale, I'd have outbid this moron for sure, though I'd like to think that I'd also notice the weight of the thing. The acting isn't even close to subtle but it fits the material; the delivery of "Dude! Put your head up through!" is never going to be better, but Dan Homeijer and Matt Kawczynski are as overt as the outcome and Whitney Wellner can only add a little more subtlety.

With the ending telegraphed from the very beginning, tension becomes of paramount importance and Shane Free, who directed and co-wrote, does a capable job on that front. It's continually obvious what's going to happen, though little details of how are fed gradually into proceedings, but we are kept interested wondering who's going to do it and when.

Roid Rage (2011)

Director: Ryan Lightbourn
Writer: Ryan Lightbourn
Stars: Zach Canfield, Ben Evans and John Russo

"Hello world," says Sammy Jenkins, like he's setting up a new website. His life was a joke, he says, but things are going to change. Let me explain that they're not going to change in any way you're likely to be comfortable with. This is far from a comfortable movie, but then that's the point. If I highlight that the title isn't referring to steroids but haemorrhoids, you might have a vague idea of how uncomfortable it's going to get.

As a pair of FBI agents follow a trail of mutilated hookers from motel to motel, they discover that the killer is far from anything that they could have comfortably imagined, I found myself torn. The concept is hardly a mature one to begin with and it quickly became clear that writer/director Ryan Lightbourn only wanted to lower that bar as the story unfolded. Yet there's some serious art in what he does with words. He has a real mastery of B-movie dialogue that frankly outstrips anything Tarantino can conjure up.

Fortunately the dialogue found me first. Agent Munroe asks his boss if the dead hooker they're looking at means that they have a serial killer on their hands. Utterly deadpan, Agent Jenkins replies, "Either that or a skull fucking maniac with flesh eating semen."

Actor John Russo (no, not the one who wrote *Night of the Living Dead*) channels Tim Thomerson and gets many of the best lines throughout. "Get on the phone and call every ass doctor in town," he orders as they discover their first lead: recurring tubes of corRectum, a haemorrhoid cream.

By this point, I was ready for another delightfully over the top modern grindhouse gem like *Machete*, *Hobo with a Shotgun* or even *The Taint*, but then it decided to aim at the *Poultrygeist* vibe when Sammy runs out of cream and has to go back to see his doctor. John Archer Lundgren is a crazed scenery chewing doc, the maturity level leaps into the toilet and everything else goes for the gross out.

And so there's much I liked and much I didn't like; well, there's a whole lot more of both.

On the acting front, Russo is a joy to behold and Ben Evans is capable as his partner, Agent Munroe. The other actors are mixed: some good, some bad, most mediocre, some bizarrely over the top. Russo rules here, but Evans is great in the trailer that accompanies the end credits.

I have no idea if this trailer will really be expanded into a feature or whether it's supposed to stand alone, but it's much more traditional grindhouse than this short, which merely tries to cram as much as it can into fourteen minutes: a little sex, a little drugs and a lot of violence, plus lots of ass jokes. There is, it seems, already *Roid Rage: The Christmas Special*, which is a stroke of genius all on its own. I have no idea what it's really like but I can imagine. This can't be unseen, after all. I'm sure I'm going to find myself wondering partway through other movies, only to find the anal facehugger appearing out of the blue in my mind's eye.

I enjoyed the gangsta subtitles. I enjoyed the spaghetti western music that accompanies the gun battle. I enjoyed the ambitious camerawork, which includes aerial photography. Even if it's stock footage, it works awesomely. I enjoyed the dialogue more than I can say. "You're nothing but a filthy ass demon and it's time I sent you back to Hell" is grindhouse gold. "I've been given a third eye that weeps shitty brown tears for humanity" is outsider poetry. Maybe if we pray, Lightbourn will be able to finance Robert de Niro for the feature. I'd pay to see that.

On the other hand, the plot progression is a shambles, far more attention given to the outrageous bits than what links them together. The whole back story is mangled and the Globotech Research scientists look less like scientists than any scientists I can think of. It takes more than a white coat, folks.

And how many ass jokes can you cram into one short film anyway? That's a rhetorical question. Honest.

The Waking (2010)

Director: John Stead
Writer: Sophie Goulet
Stars: Sophie Goulet and Jonathan Goad

The Waking is a Canadian short made in 2010 but in many ways it feels like a much older piece.

The focus is always on tension, which is managed deliciously throughout, especially through superb use of sound: not just John Rowley's score but all the sound. It's telling that, as much visual material as there is to play with, this works well even with the visuals off. You lose the fluid camerawork, the lush lighting and the careful composition, not to forget the exquisite performance of Sophie Goulet, but you gain even more creepiness in the ambience. Rowley goes for the sort of simply effective themes that John Carpenter does, but these are quieter and more subtle, reminiscent of Coil. The dialogue is sparse, as Anna is the only character in play for most of the film, so we're even more aware of each sound with nothing to distract from it. Adding the visuals back in enhances them, bringing life to the sound cues and ably growing the tension.

The story itself is relatively simple and far from new. Anna is moving into her dream home, but is left to unpack on her own as her husband Tom has commitments elsewhere once everything has been brought inside.

The camera is fluid and frequently in motion, highlighting to us what Anna is feeling, namely that something else is in the house with her, something that she merely can't see. Things progress roughly how you might expect. Doors open and shut by themselves. There are odd noises. The mellodion starts and stops on its own. There's a superbly executed shot of a mysterious figure in the shadows. The presence really doesn't like Anna's wedding photo. Best of all is the ball of string that rolls itself into view, while Anna ponders things at the kitchen table.

It has to be said that nothing here is new: the ideas, the shocks, the techniques, even the twist. Yet the craft with which John Stead puts all of this together is magnificent, textbook stuff.

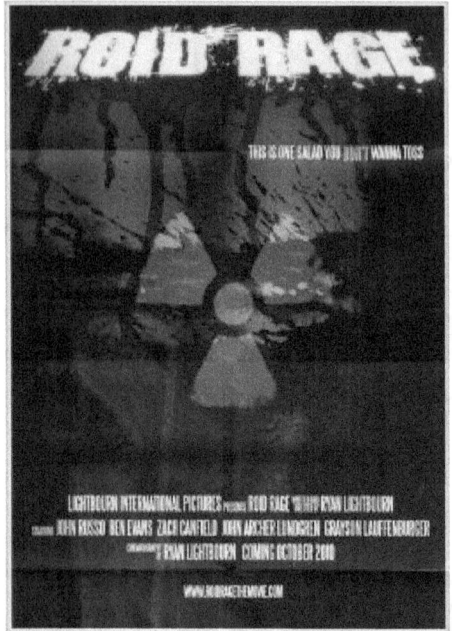

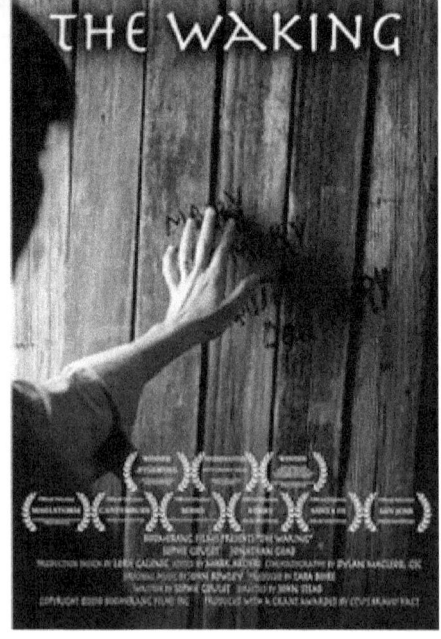

Employee of the Month (2011)

Director: Olivier Beguin
Writers: Olivier Beguin and Colin Vettier
Stars: Catriona MacColl and Manu Moser

If I hadn't seen *Folklore*, then this short Swiss comedy might have played better. As it is, I can't avoid the comparisons and, while it's not a bad little short, it loses out on all fronts except a single key one: it was made first.

Like *Folklore*, it's a set of skits focused around a diverse group of mythical creatures being interviewed by someone working for an agency dedicated to helping them. This time out, it's the B.R.P.M.L., or Bureau de Reconversion pour Mythes et Légendes. Yes, it's in French and it means that the agency provides counselors to help find suitable jobs for the supernatural. Like *Folklore*, some of the actors are better than others, but all are capable and most of them find a moment or two to shine. Like *Folklore*, there's no real attempt to have these creatures interact, instead allowing them to build their characters on their own.

Unlike *Folklore*, however, its laughs are wildly inconsistent. There's funny stuff here, but you have to endure to get to it.

For a start, the names aren't particularly imaginative. *Folklore* wasn't entirely immune from that problem but its vampire was called MaryLane Heth rather than Vlad Pitt and it didn't stoop as low as having a character by the name of Bob Zombie.

British actress Catriona MacColl, who makes far more films in French than she does in English, is capable as the counselor tasked with dealing with all these characters, though her part is little more than a prop for them to work off. They all manage that well, but when we cut away to see their exploits in previous jobs, the cringe factor sets in. A few of the ideas are great, but most are tired and obvious. For every great idea, like having the zombie man a suicide hotline, there are a half dozen bad ones. How long did it take to come up with a vampire having problems in a French restaurant because of all the garlic? And why would anyone think that his being a lifeguard would be a bright idea, pun not intended?

Folklore was consistently funny, in a very dry British sense, and as much as the supernatural beings worked off the interviewers, the interviewers worked right back off them. Here, the counselor has little to do, so much so that she ends up repeating jokes in a short film.

The imagination is solid but the writing is mostly cheap, surprising given that the co-writers have each done better work. Director Olivier Beguin also wrote *Dead Bones*, featuring Ken Foree, which wasn't high art but was still far more consistent than this. His co-writer Colin Vettier wrote *36ème sous-sol*, not a particularly surprising film but a well written one nonetheless. It didn't have to put a ghost in a Hawaiian shirt to make up for a lack of substance.

Folklore was so brimming with character that I found it impossible to pick a favourite. Whenever I picked one, I wanted to switch it to another. Here it's tough for the opposite reason: I couldn't pick one to begin with.

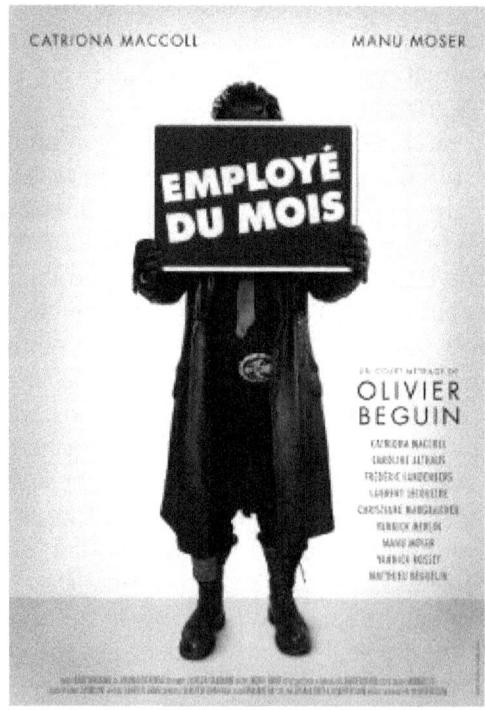

The International Horror & Sci-Fi Film Festival

2012

Sci-Fi Shorts A

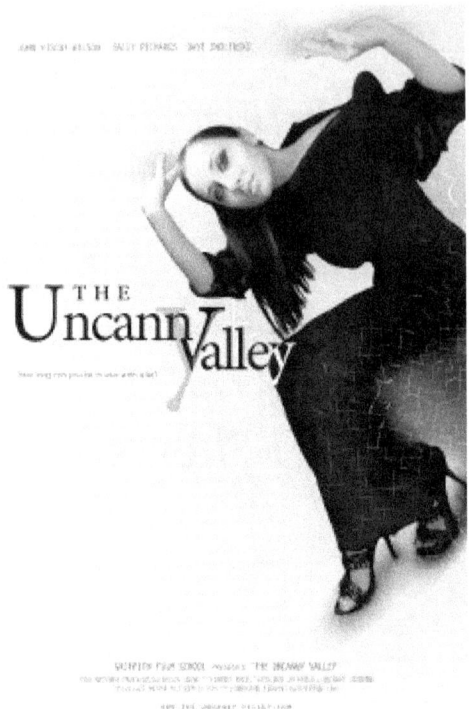

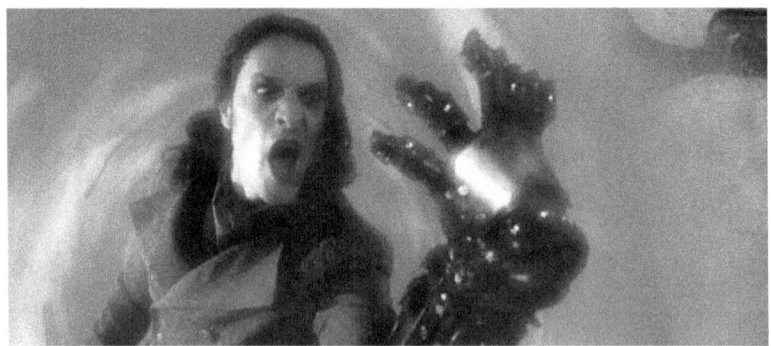

Doctor Glamour

The Uncanny Valley (2011)

Director: Dean Law
Writer: Dean Law
Stars: John Vizcay-Wilson, Sally Richards and Dave Zwolenski

I've been seeing mention of the uncanny valley cropping up all over the place lately, especially in the film world. It frequently accompanies discussion about *The Adventures of Tintin*, a highly realistic animated feature that Steven Spielberg shot using motion capture, as recommended by Peter Jackson. It came up with regards to Jackson again recently, when he screened previews of *The Hobbit* at the usual 24 frames per second because of the negative reaction he received when previewing it at the 48 frames per second he aimed to release the film in. It was too real, people said.

You see, the better technology gets, the closer visuals approach reality, and we as human beings tend to appreciate that; yet when things become almost real but don't quite reach it, we find that revulsion kicks in. Our minds tend to see real as real and unreal as unreal, but "almost real" simply as wrong and that turnoff is what Japanese robotics professor Masahiro Mori termed the uncanny valley.

I was initially a little turned off by what writer/director Dean Law does with this film but the more I paid attention, the more I appreciated just how much he managed to do in a scanty fifteen minutes.

On the first time through, what stands out is the linear storyline that follows Alex, a young man who has always felt a deep kinship to robots. When he was a young boy, his parents bought a robot for the house, a sexy female Asian maid robot to boot. His brother Michael promptly undresses her during a recharge but he's just a curious boy. Alex is attracted on a more fundamental level and he goes on to draw robots for comic books.

This storyline has to do with Alex growing up and it feels unsatisfactory in a set of science fiction shorts because it equates a concept that's dear to the hearts of many science fiction fans with immaturity. Robots are just for kids? That's not as overt as William

Shatner famously telling die hard trekkers to "get a life" but it feels like the same message.

Yet behind this is something much deeper, a meditation on humanity that is deceptively astute. Science fiction has often explored a world in which the non-human has grown so close to human that the two are almost impossible to tell apart. In *Blade Runner*, it took an expert to examine the responses to a set of emotional and empathic questions to tell a replicant from a human being. In Ridley Scott's director's cut, the boundaries between human and non-human are stretched by the implication that Deckard, who hunts replicants, might just be a replicant himself.

What Dean Law adds to the mix here is the concept that Alex, who we are assured is a real live person, somehow doesn't feel quite right, to the degree that even his friends aren't convinced that he isn't really a robot. The outsider status that he feels because of this is mirrored by his choice of profession as comic book artist. Maybe the uncanny valley is all the more uncanny when you're stuck inside it.

I really like this approach that pairs the traditional robot that seems almost human with the more innovative human that seems almost robot. The clinical feel of the film, aided by clever lighting, backs this up to the point that we start to wonder, even with the assurances we're given.

There's a great scene outside a robot brothel where some sort of security guard or cop mistakes Alex for a robot and has to check his eyes before apologising profusely. Imagining that situation helps put Alex's experience into perspective, because he's never been outside of it. No wonder he feels closer to robots than he does to people, but is he any less human because of it?

I'm still not sure about where this film takes us in the end, but the more I watch it, the more I'm fascinated by the journey. There's a lot here in a mere quarter of an hour.

I'd love to see this expanded to feature length, as long as the result asks more questions but doesn't give more answers.

Doctor Glamour (2011)

Director: Andrew W. Jones
Writer: Andrew W. Jones
Stars: Chris Shields, John Charles Meyer and Priscilla McEver

By sheer coincidence, I watched *Doctor Glamour*, starring John Charles Meyer, immediately after watching *The Millennium Bug*, staring John Charles Meyer.

The latter was a fun feature but it was very dark, visually. *Doctor Glamour* was dark only thematically, at least for a while, but it never failed in being less than visually striking. What's more, *The Millennium Bug* was only one thing, even though it had a feature length to run with, while *Doctor Glamour* crams a number of shifts and changes, rather wild ones to boot, into a mere fourteen minute running time. The main one, when it shifts tone and mood utterly a short way in, is fun at home in private but really works in a theatre environment. It truly shocks the theatre audience into paying attention and that helps it to stick it in the mind when it finishes, pressuring you to return to it to see if you really saw what you think you saw. I've now seen it many times and it gets better each time I see it.

It looks a lot better than you might expect a fourteen minute short to look, right from the beginning as some sort of fabulous steampunk airship lands in the grounds of Miskatonic University. It brings the smug Walter Gilman to study the subjects you might expect if you've read Lovecraft, from geometry and history to witchcraft and dimensions. Gilman is initially annoying as he dominates every subject with growing arrogance, but soon enough is dominated himself by a mere girl, Eve Walpurgis by name. Sure enough they fall for each other and so dominate together. Life is bliss. Then, as is prevalent in romances with connections to Miskatonic University, she's absconded to another dimension by some sort of tentacled elder god before he can even propose.

Everything thus far, and Gilman's ensuing attempts to find her, are entirely silent, more accurately voiceless, but then he manages to summon Prof. Jaroslav Gregory Glamour and it all changes.

Doctor Glamour, you see, is the "best transdimensional astronaut this side of Heaven or Hell". He's a bizarre combination of Frank-N-Furter and Zaphod Beeblebrox, with more than a hint of Michael Jackson. He's a rock 'n' roll superhero whose every movement is a pose; Horatio Caine isn't in the same class. He has a techno glove o' love, you dig?

And apparently just because it can, this transforms instantly from silent movie to rock opera, from Lovecraftian dread to comic book inspired graphics demo, from gothic sepia to hallucinatory colour. Unless you worked on the film, and perhaps not even then, this is not a shift you'll see coming. It's impossible to review the film without mentioning it though, because it's the most important thing about it, so I doubt it can be classified as a spoiler. There are other twists and turns of story in and amongst the songs and graphics work but you'll have to watch *Doctor Glamour* to find out about them.

To suggest that this film is a riot is being rather obvious, but it's a controlled riot: it feels like it does exactly what writer/director Andrew Jones aimed it to do. He's racked up a few shorts but he doesn't seem to have any intention to be traditional. I'd see that as a Good Thing and it was only enhanced by following up with his earlier short, *Frank DanCoolo: Paranormal Drug Dealer*, with two of the same leads and even more outrageous shenanigans.

It did take a while for me to be won over to the approach Jones took to this film. Initially I enjoyed the early scenes so much that I felt sad when the tone shift arrived to whisk us off to somewhere else entirely. Everything at the Miskatonic is spot on: the CGI is effective, the editing is sharp and the darkness is palpable. Only with repeat viewings did I begin to appreciate how powerful that tone shift really is. *Doctor Glamour* played partway into a quality set of science fiction shorts at the 2012 festival but it was the most emphatic moment of the set by far. Everyone there immediately paid attention.

As good as Chris Shields and Priscilla McEver are as the pair of starstruck lovers, and they are both very good indeed, the short is entitled *Doctor Glamour* for a reason. John Charles Meyer doesn't even appear until his co-leads are firmly established, yet he stamps his authority on the picture with every pelvic thrust and every facial expression. He's as different from the part he played in *The Millennium Bug* as could comfortably be imagined, but he's solid in both roles, suggesting that he's very much a talent to watch. He's been a busy man these last few years since his first film credit in 2008. Five years has seen him appear in nineteen movies, with five more in post prod, plus appearances on eleven TV shows. Beyond acting, he also produced both films mentioned plus a couple more. Whatever else *Doctor Glamour* is, it's an emphatic demonstration of screen charisma for Meyer. He doesn't need a demo reel; he can just hand out DVDs of this.

I'm still trying to figure out what this short means to me. It's the easiest thing in the world to let it wash over you: the pace of the early scenes, the surreality of the later ones and, of course, the sheer effervescence of the whole thing. I initially compared it to the experience of gulping down a supersize energy drink with triple the normal sugar and caffeine. Your brain immediately shuts down in response and then frantically attempts to quantify what just happened to it. Yet maybe a rollercoaster is a better comparison, because you're likely to want to ride it again as soon as you get off your first run. The thing is that I don't do energy drinks or rollercoasters, so neither really work for me. Instead I ended up going back to the Lovecraftian themes that the film began with.

Perhaps this is as close a translation of his work as I've seen, interpreted as Walter Gilman spiralling into insanity after reading *De Vermis Mysteriis*. That works for me. You dig?

Hollywood Forever (2011)

Director: Amy Ludwig
Writer: Amy Ludwig
Stars: Brian Bogulski and Alana DiMaria

Hollywood Forever is many things beyond merely being the title of this deceptively simple romantic time travel short.

Most obviously, it's the name of the vintage store in Hollywood in which we, along with the lead character, spend the entire picture; it literally begins as Ben walks into the place and it ends when he walks out again. More substantially, it's the entire theme of the piece. The setting emphasises how styles are ever-changing, but the story emphasises that love never does. Ida, the salesgirl, conflates the two by explaining to Ben that the store "hasn't changed in a really long time" and in doing so highlights that neither has the formula that has kept Hollywood synonymous with the movies. A little more subtly, it's surely even a hint to the film industry that Hollywood constantly needs to look both forward and backward. The character of Ida represents both of those views: her job has her living in her past but she's really from Ben's future.

What's more, it's even a nod to first time writer/director Amy Ludwig's reasons for making this short film. She's apparently a thrift store devotee and, like many such people, she has a fondness for romance, not just in the modern meaning of the word that focuses only on love but also in the older meaning that speaks to adventure and imagination. She's a romantic, summed up well in one of Ben's lines of dialogue. His casual suggestion that simply changing clothes is enough to change time is far more than a cosplayer's manifesto, it's a personal statement of individuality, a gentle reminder that we should all be whoever we want to be and the most freeing thing in the world is to simply allow that to happen. That feeling, close to my heart too, is what I took away from this film. We, the viewers, are personified in the character of Ida, whose last line is a notably appropriate quote from classic Hollywood. She merely makes a decision to live it.

The story is less a plot and more a springboard for our minds, which is exactly what a science fiction short should be. Ben is an actor who has come to Hollywood to find work, so steps into Hollywood Forever to buy a suit he can audition in.

Brian Bogulski, who plays Ben, does have one of those faces that transcend time, so it's not surprising to find that it was one of Ludwig's inspirations for the story. He's intriguingly somewhere between Vinnie Jones and George Raft and it would be fascinating to watch him in black and white, especially in a gangster movie or film noir.

By contrast, Ida, the goth salesgirl, is already there. She's dressed entirely in black, which includes her make up, her only colour being the red in her tattoos and the gold in her nose ring. The two characters clash mildly for a little while until they realise that their differences are cultural not personal. You see, she's from 2009 and he's from 1948, and that's where our story really begins.

As a short film, this is pretty good and as a debut for Amy Ludwig, it's very promising indeed. It's short but it has no real need to be longer. The story is basic but achieves everything that it aims to. It draws us in capably and leaves us wanting more, our minds happily conjuring up what happens next. The framework is simple, everything hung on two actors in one location, but those actors are solid and their dialogue is well written, if hardly surprising. While Brian Bogulski may have influenced the film, Alana DiMaria gets more substance to work with, so gets to shine brighter. After all, Ben only needs to open his mind a little between beginning and end but Ida gets a real story arc, gifted with both the opportunity to change and the decision making process to do so. The romance is sweet, albeit swift, and the Ruth Brown song is appropriate. The whole piece is as enjoyable as it's well made, those two attributes not always playing as well together as here.

That's not to say that it couldn't be better. There is notable attention to detail, but there could have been a good deal more. The biggest flaw in my eyes was in how often the camera gave us views out of the front window of Hollywood Forever, something that didn't gel particularly well with the progression of the story, the continually passing cars unwittingly undermining the idea that our characters are isolated in a timeless space. That's tough to avoid in a low budget short, especially given the geography of the store, but it's a problem nonetheless, one that adversely affects the lighting at a couple of points too. If only the fog that obscured the door in one scene could have obscured the front window throughout, but sadly that opportunity apparently wasn't viable.

The good news is that the more romantic the viewer, the less likely they'll care and the more likely this will be the beginning of a beautiful friendship with Amy Ludwig's future work.

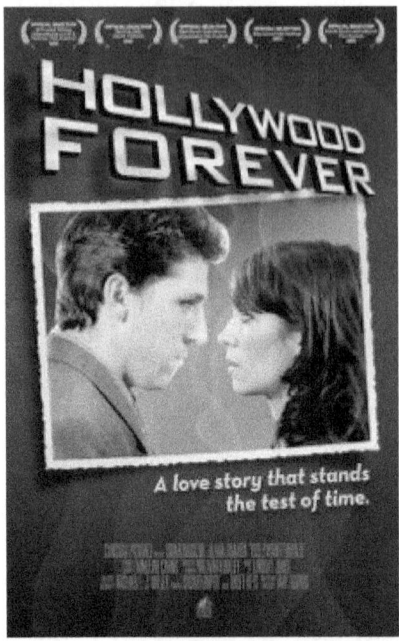

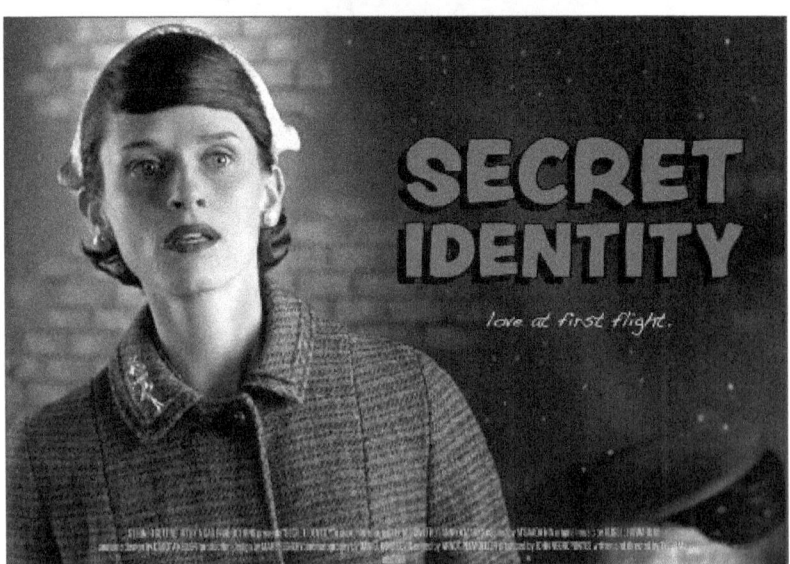

Secret Identity (2011)

Director: Tyler MacIntyre
Writer: Tyler MacIntyre
Stars: Lee Meriwether, Annika Marks and Charles Howerton

Secret Identity had what could be phrased a triumphant screening at the 2012 Festival. I'd been privileged to see it earlier as a festival submission and had been thoroughly impressed, but it simply came alive on the big screen. It hooked its audience early, carried every one of them magnificently along for its near twelve minute ride and left them happier and just a little bit more alive. *Doctor Glamour* had played less well on the big screen, not through any fault of its own, but merely because the sound was more muted than appropriate for that particular film. *Secret Identity*, on the other hand, swelled out at the audience, not just the audio but the emotion too.

You see, this is a lot more than the superhero movie you may have guessed at from the title. It's a romance, one powered by nostalgia but utterly contemporary nonetheless. It's also a subtle commentary on how the flurry of modern life can be summarised as not seeing the wood for the trees.

The lead is a young lady by the name of Janet, who is distracted from the moment she enters our story, chatting away on her mobile as she arrives at the Whispering Oaks Retirement Community to see her grandma, Faye. It looks like a nice place, but Janet is too busy chatting and texting to see beyond the world inside her phone. She has "like a billion things going on", she tells her gran, and her fiancée Darren isn't there because "he's busy", even during the holidays.

We're already siding with grandma, of course, not least because she's played by Lee Meriwether and therefore has to be right. She's as elegant at 75 as she was at 31 when she replaced Julie Newmar as Catwoman in the Adam West *Batman* movie. She's quiet but you just know you should be paying attention to what she says anyway. Faye thinks Janet could do better, and so do we when she asks to use her gran's wedding ring because, you know, it'll be romantic and, well,

Darren can't afford one.

And it's here that Janet comes alive. She does seem to care and she doesn't seem to visit out of duty, but we're not sure if she really sees her grandma at all. Yet, when she discovers that the green tin that contains that wedding ring also contains press clippings about the young Faye meeting Captain Magnificent, she starts to see her in a whole new light. He's a superhero! He's famous! And there's a story in there somewhere, right?

Absolutely! It's the bedrock to the picture, and even Janet pays attention. If Janet is our lead and Faye our star, Janet's phone wants to depose both of them and we can tell that it's as thoroughly pissed off as we are happy that Janet doesn't answer it when Faye prepares to tell her story in flashback. That's a telling moment, showing that she's found her grandma's secret identity and she can see her as a woman who's lived a life, not just a grandma who serves her tea. Her phone exits stage left, forgotten.

Janet is played by Annika Marks, a young actor a decade or so into her career, and she does a good job here. Perhaps the best way to highlight that is to explain that Lee Meriwether is note perfect throughout, as magical as the story she has to tell, endowing her character with more depth in a mere few minutes than many actors manage in entire features. It would take a tough cookie indeed to not get caught up in the gentle emotions of her performance. Yet, her story is only there to underpin Janet's story and it's Marks who ensures that we never lose sight of that.

She has an entire story arc, and she leaves the film a little wiser than she was a mere dozen minutes earlier. Grandma gets the last scene, as she should, and we're treated to a neat, if not too surprising, twist. Like Janet, we leave the film a little wiser than we found it, wondering mostly whether Tyler MacIntyre's direction is a bigger triumph than his writing or vice versa.

The thing is that once you start to think about secret identities, they start to crop up everywhere. It's as if the only thing needed to find is to look, and once you start looking you start finding all sorts of magical stuff floating around in plain sight. It takes a lot of people to make a film, even if some of them wear a few different hats when they do it. MacIntyre's direction is deceptive, as it does everything it needs to without us really noticing until we look.

Arndt Peemoeller's editing is no different, so seamless that we don't realise how good it is until we pay attention. MacIntyre's writing is a lot more overt but it's spot on, even though the realisation that this wasn't written by a woman is a surprising one. Msaada Nia is worthy of mention too for casting so well. That a short indie film can land both Lee Meriwether and Charles Howerton proves that there is much that is right in the world. Both have history in the genre and the talent to play the parts.

The look of the film is notable too, especially in the flashback sequence. Cinematographer Daniel Kenji Levin turns the restriction of space within the care home into an opportunity to focus on the characters, but he plays the flashback scene like a comic book, aided by a simple but very effective alley set. I'm not enough of a comic book geek to know whether MacIntyre and his crew nailed that style or a particular moment in homage, but it feels right.

The story takes us from the busy, complex, detached modern world back to a quiet, simple, connected one, both of an earlier day and an earlier era of comic books. Showing us a young Faye, who wasn't a superhero, with Captain Magnificent, who was, is a throwback to both eras, real and comic book. The different visual styles used make it easy for us to compare the old with the new and to see that nothing has changed, not really, if we'd only allow ourselves to notice.

If only it didn't take a film that tells us to look for us to see.

20th Century Man (2012)

Director: Dustin Lee
Writer: Dustin Lee
Stars: Joseph Adams, Sarah Carleton and Ed Crepage Jr

This short film aims to do a heck of a lot in under twelve minutes. It's a science fiction movie, a romance and a thriller. It's a silent movie. Most of all, it's a drama. One IMDb reviewer suggested that it felt like a two hour picture condensed into a quarter of an hour and that's a pretty good way to look at it.

It is very much the essence of a feature film, condensed so

assiduously that even the dialogue is stripped away. Everything we see has meaning and writer/director Dustin Lee, who shot the film for a mere $2,500 of Kickstarter money, was obviously playing around with cinematic language. It's not just a feature condensed into twelve minutes, it's a film class textbook condensed into twelve minutes too. The use of technique is the greatest success, perhaps aided by the silent approach as the cast and crew were forced to make themselves known and understood without the benefit of words. For the most part, they succeed.

We follow Robert Wallace, a young scientist who's built a time machine to demonstrate at the next World's Fair. It's a simple device, the budget not allowing for the grandeur of the one in George Pal's movie. It's more like an open cage with wires, with a typewriter to trigger it and a flux capacitor to power it, albeit without the need for a DeLorean. We first see Wallace in black and white, as befits 1938, but a device malfunction means that his two week proof of concept trip into the future becomes 76 years and he arrives in 2014 in colour.

I really liked how the last shot of 1938 isn't of Wallace but of his wife, Anna, who is given the much harder task of staying behind. She's dead by the time her husband arrives in 2014, but she never leaves the story and the way it progresses is as satisfying as it is predictable. It doesn't take a rocket scientist, or a time traveller, to see where it's going long before it gets there.

Ironically for a film about time travel, its biggest problem is its sense of time. As a silent movie nut, I liked the opening scenes very much, but they're set a full decade after Al Jolson delivered his death blow to the silent era. Even Charlie Chaplin was done with silent films by this point and he had stuck with the concept longer than anyone.

Maybe the choice of 1938 was tied to the reference to the Buster Crabbe serial, *Buck Rogers*, on the scientist's desk. That was released a single year later in 1939, when the big picture of the year was *Gone with the Wind*, not just shot in sound but in Technicolor too.

The art deco font used in the credits is quintessentially twenties so again is far too early for this timeframe. Only the music really seems to fit. Howard Hanson's *Romantic Symphony* was written in 1930 and was flexible enough to also be used in *Alien*, but it's full of the sort of swell and grandeur so prevalent during the golden age of Hollywood. It's very 1938.

How much you enjoy this short is likely to depend on how much attention you pay to the details and how easily you can overlook them.

As a ride, it's great fun and Dustin Lee speeds us along with panache. You're likely to leave the film full of emotion, not least because of the magnificent way the single word of dialogue is used. I dare your heart not to skip a beat at that point!

With repeat viewings though, you're more likely to notice the details that he speeds us past and if you're the sort of nitpicker that notes plot inconsistencies in the most emotional movies, you'll find a few here.

The timing grated for me the most but there were other issues too. I looked too closely at the props. I thought too long about how Wallace's time travel worked. I wondered too much about why people were waiting for him in 2014, given the device's history in between, as neatly outlined in newspaper clippings. It's all unfair to notice in a $2,500 short, of course.

It's fairer to point out that a number of the actors are too young for their parts, including Joseph Adams as Wallace, though he's otherwise capable in the role. He does everything that's asked of him; it's simply that his face isn't old enough, both in years and eras. I just don't buy that face as being from 1938.

I was impressed far more by Sarah Carleton. She gifted Anna with a echoing timeless quality that was palpable; everything she does in 1938 ensures her prominence in 2014, even though she didn't make it there in person. I bought into how easily her husband could leave her behind but how impossible it was for him to stay away from her, even when the gap between them is time.

After Lee's use of the cinematic toolkit, which any true film fan is unconsciously going to analyse even as the film runs, it's Anna who lingers after the credits roll. We find that we don't want to leave her either; she obviously has much to say, even in a silent movie. That's good acting.

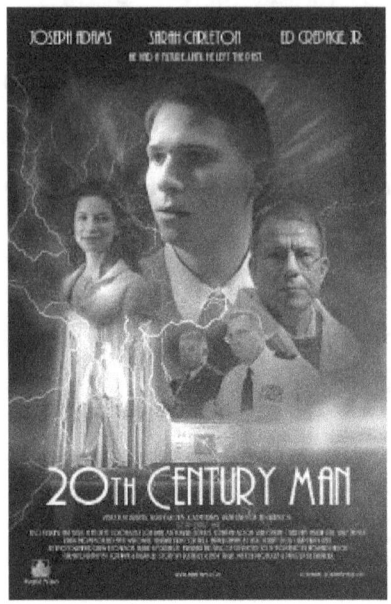
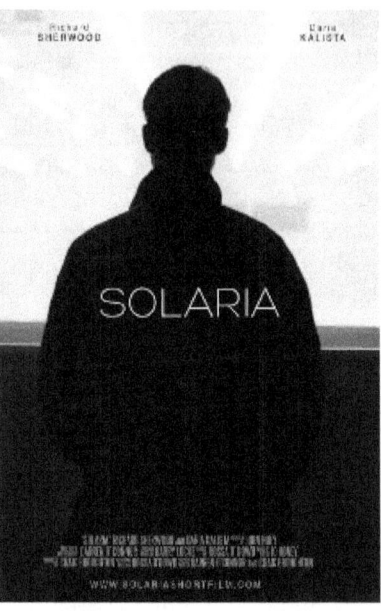

Solaria (2011)

Director: John Hoey
Writer: Darren O'Connor
Stars: Richard Sherwood and Daria Kalista

The biggest problem *Solaria* has is that it's really obvious how it's all going to unfold. You'd have to be one of those people surprised by revelations in *Scooby Doo* episodes to not figure this one out.

That's unfortunate, because almost everything else is really well done. The look and feel is exactly right, beginning with the space photography that accompanies the title and introductory text; it continues looking wonderful as we hop inside the Solaria research station. The first shot inside sets the stage well: obviously futuristic, but very analogue with a cool colour palette. Even when we see the huge digital screen in front of Dr Alex Russell, with its requisite shiny graphics, there's a host of old school physical tech all around him: sockets, cables and industrial material. He shuts stuff down by pulling levers and turning wheels rather than just pressing buttons on his console and the great ensuing physical noises contrast well with the space age computer voice.

Even the story, apart from being obvious, unfolds smoothly. Alex is shutting stuff down because the Earth is so low on resources that it can no longer maintain space research stations. He asks for more time, but he's already had as much as can be given; at least his station is the last of them to go. He wants the time because he shares the station with Rachel, a test subject who fell into a coma decades ago but has ceased to grow old; she's apparently in her fifties but she looks to be in her twenties.

The potential for scientific breakthrough here is astounding, of course, especially for a talented young geneticist like Alex, but it's all about to end because the shuttle coming to pick him up only has room for one passenger. "One has to pay dearly for immortality," he explains, and the full impact of that doesn't take long to be outlined, given that this is a twelve minute short film. The running time and the effective cast of two combines to provide the inevitable surprise ending.

Inevitability aside, this is a strong little short for such an inexperienced cast and crew. There are only two actors, neither of whom have any other credits. IMDb lists five crew members and the film's website adds a sixth, but again, this is the only film any of them seem to have worked on. Yet they all do fine work.

On screen, Richard Sherwood dominates proceedings as Alex, partly because his co-star Daria Kalista has very little to do for the most part except to simply lie there and look cute, but also because he manages to convey both that he's a capable scientist and that he has strong feelings for his subject.

Some may wonder where all the space age gadgetry is but there's no need for it. I liked the old school approach taken throughout that earns this Irish short a kinship with *2001: A Space Odyssey*, though the score is ambient rather than classical.

The film's apparent success bodes well for what John Hoey and his crew will do next.

The International Horror & Sci-Fi Film Festival

2012

Sci-Fi Shorts B

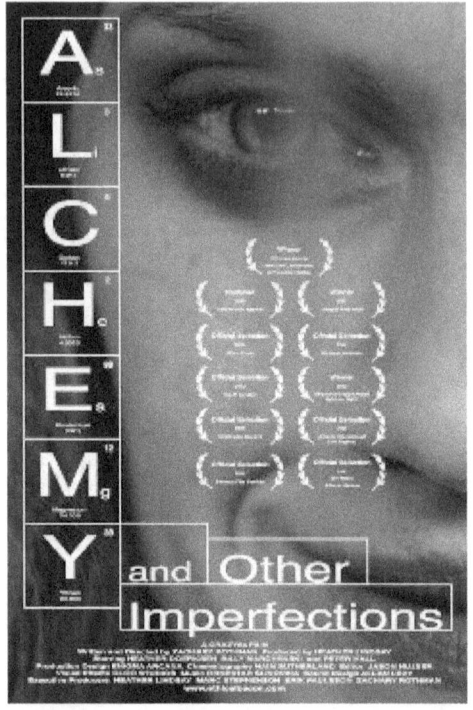

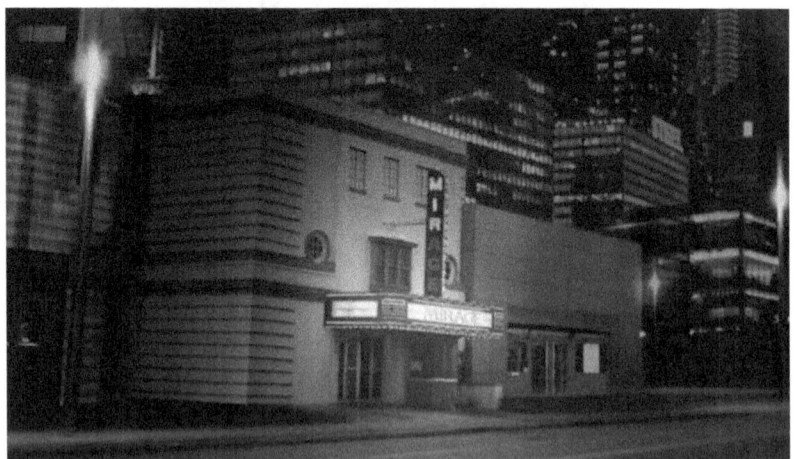

Mirage

Alchemy and Other Imperfections (2011)

Director: Zachary Rothman
Writer: Zachary Rothman
Stars: Heather Doerksen, Billy Marchenski and Peter Hall

What a unexpected treat this was! This Canadian short is a great big slice of fantastic quirkiness from the very outset and it didn't let up until the credits rolled at the end.

It's also many other things in between. It's a silent movie with sound, as there are only two characters, an unnamed married couple who have lost the ability to speak to each other, so there's precisely no dialogue whatsoever. It's a prose poem, as that gap is filled by Peter Hall, whose explanatory contribution cannot be described merely as narration, his voice as delightfully playful as the bouncy Balkan brass score by Vancouver's Orkestar Šlivovica, who must be a glorious riot live. It's a visual treat, the lush colours and fabulous set design enough to bathe in. At heart, it's a fable, less a story and more a cautionary tale with a number of depths to explore.

Oh, and whatever else it is, it's surely the best film ever narrated by a cockroach. That grabbed you, huh?

I find it truly astounding that Zachary Rothman, who wrote, produced and directed, did so on a budget of $800 Canadian. There are Hollywood movies that wish they had as much eye candy as this, ones with four or five more digits in their budgets. I'm not just talking about visual effects like the esoterica that dances around Heather Doerksen's head as she conjures up a plan to fix what can't be fixed. I'm talking about the palpable textures of the set and the costumes, the arcane ephemera that her character dabbles with and the antique mechanics that her screen husband constructs. Surely much of it must have to do with the production design and costumes credited to Enigma Arcana, but it's also in the camera motion, careful choreography and the way that the editing plays with distance and division. This is a movie to feel as much as see and hear, a treat for quite a few different senses.

And all of this means that *Alchemy and Other Imperfections* is less of a short film and more of an experience.

Like most fables, it hints at far more than it says, letting its audience find their own meaning and application, so you're not going to get much of a synopsis. Suffice it to say that this couple have a let a single event bury them so deeply in guilt that they've become isolated both from the world and each other. This fable is triggered by the woman, a practioner in dark arts, deciding on a possible way to fix things.

Naturally it doesn't go quite as she expects. Heather Doerksen and Billy Marchenski do a surprising amount with their characters, especially as they have no dialogue and are deliberately short on background detail. They both approach their roles like paintings, dabbing an impression here and a suggestion there.

I haven't seen either before, but I have seen a film by Rothman: 2006's *Lost*, which I didn't rate highly and don't remember. This one, on the other hand, is a gem I won't forget.

Mirage (2011)

Director: Miao Yu
Writer: Miao Yu and Christopher Amick
Stars: Cory Aycock, Courtney Alana Ward and Andres Acosta

Over the last few years, I've spent a lot of time inside movie theatres and I've seen how difficult it is for them to stay alive in a world of changing technologies and competing attractions. It's not an easy thing today to find a venue screening actual film, for instance, as everything is going digital. By the time you read this, it'll be even less likely that you know a theatre that isn't. I'm sure that writers Miao Yu and Christopher Amick wouldn't expect that what I'd take away from their film is the joy that in 2064 AD there might still be a movie theatre showing real 35mm.

Judging from the posters in the Mirage lobby, all films in the future will be made by the Chinese: *Losing Coconato* is directed by Miao Yu and *The Adventures of Captain Adam* by Sissy Tsu. These are self-referential though. Miao Yu directed and co-wrote this film while Laura Coconato produced. Sissy Tsu isn't in the credits.

Anyway, I wish I could be projectionist Andrew Pan's audience, as he doesn't have one otherwise, perhaps because he's showing just another romcom.

When a bulb blows and the movie stops midstream, nobody notices because he is literally the only person in the Mirage. The popcorn machine has a shroud over it. The counter is covered in dust. Nobody goes to this theatre and Pan must be independently wealthy to be able to keep it open, though this 2064 AD does appear to be a true post-scarcity world. I really wish I could be there for that too.

I'd rather not have to deal with Treasure Island though. While compared with the Mirage, which is retro even today, it's much more like the sort of futuristic vision you might expect for the year, it's still recognisably grounded in today. A physical store where Pan can pick up a physical item, it's bare except for G.E.F., a Genuine Electronic Friend, like Microsoft for Stores. It says, "Have a nice day," when it delivers Pan's bulb, but a call for assistance generates technical difficulties. The more things change, the more they stay the same.

It's here that our story really begins, because the young lady who emerges tentatively from the unseen world behind the store is obviously as uncomfortable being around another real person as is Pan. This is key knowledge, as without it the ending might seem a little insulting.

Pan spends his time in an empty theatre, imagining himself into the role of the leading man in the romcom he's projecting. When the new bulb projects him into the picture and he finds himself having to live that role, it's an eye opener. Initially it's because he has to interact with a woman in a romantic setting, but it becomes more than that and this underlines that the bulb is teaching him a lesson. Without thinking about the young lady at Treasure Island, it feels like a dubious lesson to give to a man who screens movies in a movie for people who watch movies. Yet, I wonder if it's not aiming just at his geeky solitude but at life in a world with no physical interaction. I hope so, but it's still not quite the ending I wanted.

Other than that ending, I liked *Mirage* quite a lot. Current events notwithstanding, there's a certain something about old school movie theatres that feels somehow timeless and they make for glorious environments for futuristic science fiction to play in. This location is a joy.

I liked Cory Aycock's portrayal of Pan, though he does feel rather well rounded for a geek whose only friends are fictional ghosts of the past on his theatre screen. I liked Ashley Pincket even more as Dona, the tentative Treasure Island assistant, enough that I really wish Yu and Amick had gone for the obvious ending for a change. There was room to make it awkward and meaningful rather than just sappy and it would have given Pincket more to do.

I liked the design of Treasure Island, which is half welcoming and half padded cell. In fact the effects are well done throughout.

I even liked the film within a film, though more for how it fit this story than for itself. It looks more rom than com and rather painful to sit through otherwise. This one is much better.

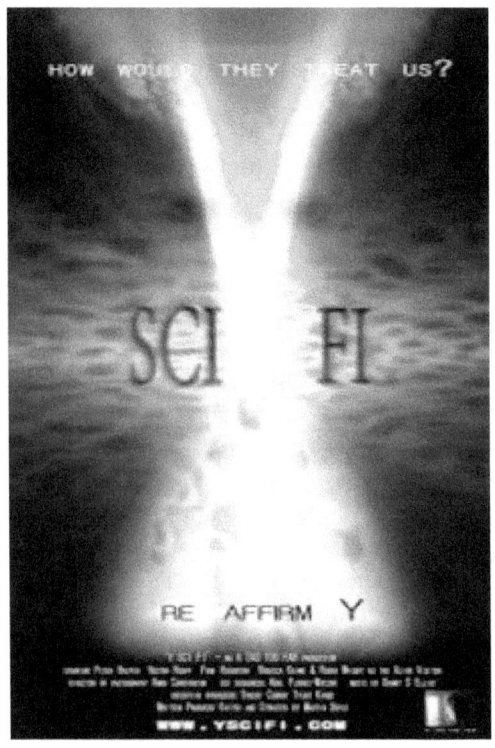

Y Sci Fi (2011)

Director: Martin Doyle
Writer: Martin Doyle
Stars: Peter Halpin, Hester Ruoff, Femi Houghton, Rebecca Keane and Roger Wright

There's a lot of imagination in *Y Sci Fi*, pure science fiction posed through questions by an unseen narrator. It posits that space, as Douglas Adams famously stated, is big, really big, and we're both tiny and relatively new in the grand scheme of things. So, if someone or something is really out there, what would it be like, beyond not being remotely like us? At least, it initially felt like a high concept science fiction piece, these questions addressing the definitions of concepts like time, scale, evolution and, most obviously, intelligence. Visually, it's a lot more generic.

We're tasked with watching a trio of conspiciously diverse young adults being chased through a forest by mysterious lights in the sky. They only get throwaway dialogue because there's no real story to speak of, just the chase and some visual and creature effects to keep us interested until the narrator gets to his point. It's obvious that he's who we should be listening to, not them.

We do play along for a little while, wondering what these aliens are going to look like when they come out from behind the lights and what they're doing. The lights are cool, beams that appear to have numbers within them. When the aliens do arrive, they look interesting, not quite like we've seen elsewhere but with many similarities, both those running the show and the creatures they bring with them. I especially liked the effects as these creatures bounded through leaves. The early views of the aliens are well shot too, keeping suspense alive by bathing them in darkness or light.

But, in the end, we realise that this isn't a science fiction short at all, not really. It's not here to ask questions, it's here to answer them and how it does that feels more like propaganda than science fiction. The fatal flaw isn't the message itself, which is valid, it's the fact that the message is the entire point and the film itself is nothing but a thirteen minute underline.

How to Kill Your Clone (2011)

Director: Jack McWilliams
Writer: Ed McWilliams
Stars: Jamie Kaler, Joseph Culliton and Sasha Feiler

While *Y Sci Fi* was a political message, *How to Kill Your Clone* is a commercial one, albeit fictional right now. With current advances in science, how long will that remain the case?

Well, this short advertising pitch from Clone Killer Corporation aims to take the future into the past. Everything here is done up to seem old school, from the aging effects to make it look like a worn 35mm reel all the way to the wooden corporate spokesman and his mismatched suit. It's like we're back in the fifties, but an alternate universe fifties where clones are an everyday reality for us all.

Our spokesman, Larry, takes us into that reality by showing us lots of Dicks. No, I don't think that was accidental either. Dick has been cloned a number of times and he thinks it's great. For a while, at least. After all, he can sit back and enjoy being waited on by his wife while his clones are doing his job and fixing his car; but soon enough they're doing his best girl and fixing his demise. There's always a catch, huh?

And that's where Clone Killer Corporation comes in. The name is self explanatory and as long as you get to them first, they'll never accept business from your clone. I really like that little touch. I like a lot of the little touches that quickly unfold as Dick and his clones act out the scenarios that will send you rushing to Clone Killer Corporation with chequebook in hand.

How to Kill Your Clone runs a mere five minutes but it's a frantic five minutes that keeps us on the hop as much as Dick. Poor Dick! Every time he turns round, his retro-futuristic clone-filled life has taken another turn for the worse because he doesn't know the tricks that Clone Killer Corporation know. If only he'd got to them sooner!

Well, thank you, McWilliams Brothers, for sharing this valuable information. Now we can be sure that when one of our clones shows that little defect, that little personality quirk, we know exactly where to go to fix the problem. Blammo! Get them before they get you!

It's easy to slip into advertising lingo when talking about this film because its tone and its fast pace bore into your brain, lay down foundations and set up shop, just like every advertising agent back then wished they could do.

Joseph Culliton does a deceptively clever job. Larry feels like a hasbeen, or maybe a never was, who's making a final attempt to pay his rent by hawking a product that might just produce "original casualties". That's much trickier to do than it sounds and he nails it. Jamie Kaler has it even tougher because he doesn't only have to play a character called Dick, he has to play a whole bunch of characters called Dick, all of whom are slightly, if not flagrantly, different from each other. He's on screen a couple of times at once for much of the picture.

Jack McWilliams directed and Ed McWilliams wrote, but maybe that's a Coen Brothers trick and they both did both. Either way, there are flaws here but they hide them well by not allowing us time to blink.

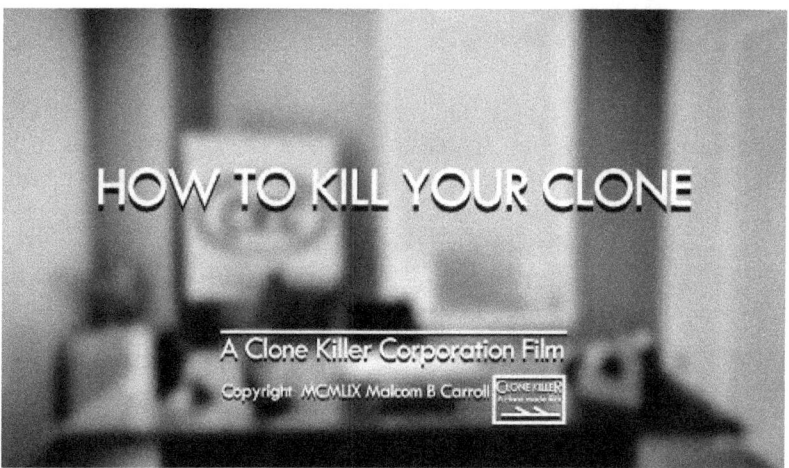

Anaphora (2011)

Director: André Albrecht
Writer: André Albrecht
Stars: Andreas Bendig, Deborah Müller and Stephan Menzel-Gehrke

This long German short is a deceptive creature.

It begins traditionally enough with a few of the usual science fiction triggers. We're not in the future, as the phones are huge and the games are 8 bit; we're in what is more like an alternate recent past, where the Cold War is still raging and very bad things are happening in Germany. The power dies as the news talks of special forces raids so our lead finds his way to a bar.

We wonder why we're watching him, as he's hardly magnetic. In his apartment he played a video game with a cigarette on his lip as if he doesn't know what it's for. He buys a cola at the bar as beer is illegal, even if it's on offer. He shrugs off some chick who tries to chat him up, without even looking at her. Presumably the goal is to set him up as the standard brainwashed citizen/consumer, living as he's told. He smokes Eight Ball cigarettes, the brand on all the billboards. His story arc matches the film. Here we watch; later we care.

We're given some paranoia too. During the blackout, helicopters fly overhead and a bum tells our lead that they're after him. The bar only provides a moment or two of respite before special forces raid the place, decked out in black body armour and black balaclavas, and the place turns into a warzone as they try to find whatever it is that they're tracking. Most of the customers are armed, including the bartender, and we suddenly realise that we only spent a couple of minutes here before it turned into a big action movie.

The testosterone is palpable, though if we have an action hero it's surely our blonde bartender chick. She kicks ass while our lead doesn't, making us wonder again why we're watching him. Sure, the fight choreography isn't quite as slick as it could be but I'm not complaining; Deborah Müller wasn't bad on the eyes even before she disposes of a trio of tough guys without too much effort. She was definitely the focus of my attention here.

All this unfolds so quickly that we have very little time to blink, let alone ponder the meaning of the film.

The feel isn't sci-fi at all, the occasional low budget nods to *Blade Runner* notwithstanding. It feels much more like an action movie, albeit one whose timing suggests that it's meant to be an eighties action movie, presumably set in a pre-unification Germany. I soon started to imagine the bartender as a sort of West German Cynthia Rothrock.

Yet the undertone is all science fiction, dystopian and paranoid and pessimistic, and sure enough, it soon makes itself overt. As our protagonist reaches for another cigarette, he instead pulls out of his pocket what looks like a pocket sized monolith. It glows and generates some sort of mini-black hole. The effects are solid, suggesting that while the budget is obviously low, it's far from non-existent. Both the length of the film and the ambition that soon manifests back that up. As small films go, this is a big one.

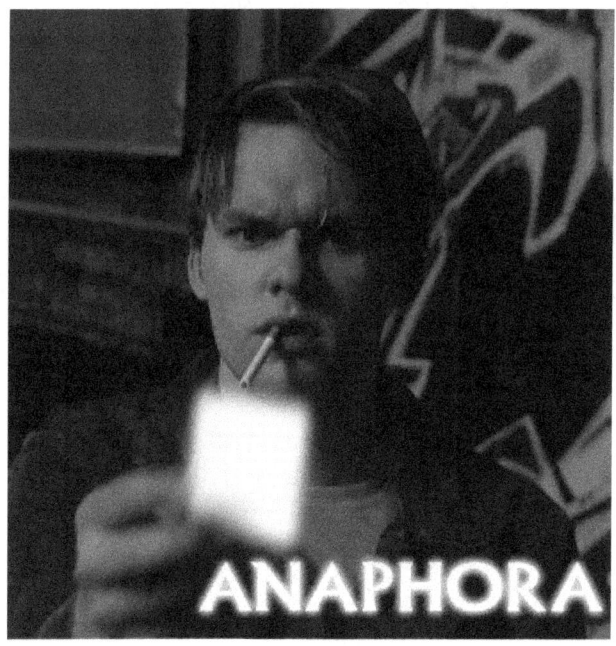

It's a film of two halves. The first half is all about expansion: building the atmosphere, tone and background. It ends with the mysterious death of our bartender in a back alley, but don't worry, she'll be back and that's no spoiler. The second half is all about contraction, as the story takes over and gradually reels in all the little throwaway moments we've seen thus far, explaining how none of them were throwaway in the slightest. It does so through a spiral approach, tightening relentlessly and with a faster and faster pace. The title, a linguistic term for self-reference, is highly appropriate because the spiral of the story is full of them and, like *Pokémon*, each time we think we've caught them all, another one leaps out at us. What's more, the longer the film runs, the quicker they come. The question is merely whether we figure them all out before they're explained. Given how fast it all unfolds that's not too likely. You can't catch 'em all, folk.

I enjoyed this on a first viewing but liked it a lot more on the second. While it's a short that could viably be a feature, keeping it compressed to 22 minutes successfully maintains a pace that a feature probably couldn't, at least without the plot becoming a labyrinth of detail. At this length, it's straight forward enough to understand first time through, but with revelations that will make you want to see the film again. When you do, you'll see a lot more with the benefit of hindsight but it will still remain consistent.

The writer is André Albrecht and he'd deserve most praise here even were that his only role, but he also edited, produced and directed, meaning that it's pretty much his movie throughout. This is his third short film, each time handling those four roles himself (or more), but they're notably spaced out: the first in 2003 when he was 20, the second three years later. Did it really take him five years to make this film? I hope not.

His actors do their job well. This is surprisingly Deborah Müller's only credit. She feels enough at ease here for me to expect experience. Maybe she came to this from the stage, maybe she's just natural. Andreas Bendig, who plays the lead, has a few credits, including the intriguingly titled *The Golden Nazi Vampire of Absam: Part II - The Secret of Kottlitz Castle*. I simply have to track that one down. This appears to be by far his largest part though, and based on the second half of this film much more than the first, he should be moving on to bigger parts generally. The third notable actor is Stephan Menzel-Gehrke, older than his fellow cast members and notably wilder in his role but still effective.

Nobody else lets the side down, though the budget ensures that you wouldn't mistake this for a Hollywood blockbuster, though I've seen worse explosions and gunshots in big budget features. For a short film, they're great, and they sit within a story that's better.

Outsight (2011)

Director: A. R. Madabushi
Writer: Amy Strutt
Stars: Steve Raine, Oihana Garde, Adam Loxely, Frances Allen, Amanda Golding, Gordon Ridout and Dot Smith

Somehow I liked all the component parts of *Outsight* without particularly liking the film itself.

The idea is a good one: one man's rediscovery of colour in a world where people are unable to see in anything but black and white. It's easy to read this both literally and metaphorically, as what we see fits both sides equally. The concept was timely, as I'd recently read about Bruce Bridgeman, a 67 year old neuroscientist whose stereoblindness was cured after watching *Hugo* in 3D.

It's a black and white art piece from the outset, with colour appearing only at key points in the story. Yet that story is also dystopian science fiction, with a traditional small man placed into a traditional big machine, although how Agricorp controls its employees unfolds a little less overtly than usual. Nonetheless Ethan's discovery of colour arrives literally at the same time as his discovery of choice, of viewpoints other than what he's given.

I think my biggest problem was with the feel. I liked the science fiction aspects, the concepts and ideas that are woven into this story without explanation, like Anthony Burgess might do. "Only the company can release people," we hear Ethan tell a company counsellor, though "release" in this instance apparently means "death". We're given no background to the environmental chaos that has presumably led to every employee growing their own plants, which are provided to the company as a quota and distilled into some sort of liquid, unpleasant without a pill, that provides all necessary nourishment. It all simply is, and we're tasked with reading this reality as if we'd been dumped into it by a time machine. It runs 24 minutes and often feels like it ran twice that but lost half of its material. Yet this black and white world misses out on as much emotion as it does colour; that's perhaps deliberate given the metaphor but it's missing nonetheless.

Visually it works very well, though inconsistently. We're treated to some gorgeous shots, though others appear almost throwaway. The colour gimmick is handled well, but the lighting isn't what it could be, some scenes transforming their contents into unintended silhouettes. The actors are capable, Stevie Raine leading the way as Ethan with able support from his peers. Surprisingly it was the more mechanical corporate figures of authority who stood out for me, not those who ought to have provided the metaphorical colour.

In the end, I found myself drawn more to the story than the film. The screenplay was written by the director, A. R. Madabushi, based on a short story by Amy Lydon-Strutt called *Oculus*. That surprises me, because it's such an obvious visual piece that it could easily have been intended from its inception as a short film. Yet it's the ideas that stayed with me, not the gimmick, not the characters and not the visuals.

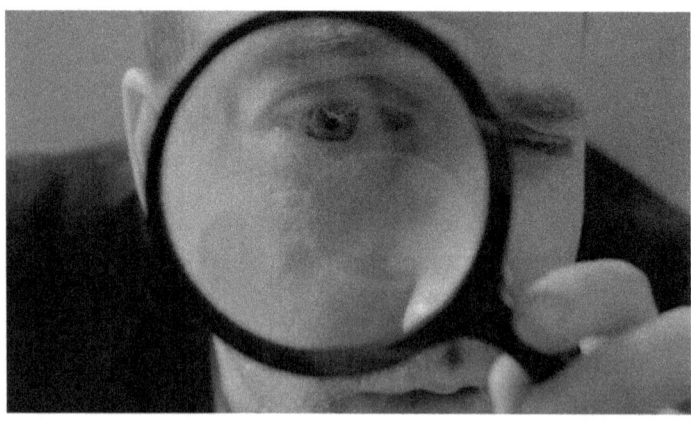

Outsight

Dream Cleaners (2011)

Director: Craig Phillips
Writer: Craig Phillips
Stars: Larrs Jackson, Dave Shalansky and Devan Leos

I found *Dream Cleaners* to be a really frustrating picture. On one front, it's executed superbly, with great acting from everyone involved, gorgeous effects and fun gimmickry. Yet, on another front, it immediately raised a whole bunch of questions and steadfastly refused to answer any of them. There is an ending that offers an explanation to a question actually posed within the film, but that wasn't one of the questions I was asking.

So I sat back and enjoyed the visual aesthetics and the work of the folk we see on screen, while screaming internally at the writer for setting up something that made so little sense. Perhaps Craig Phillips, who wrote and directed, was working entirely in dream logic, which after all is no logic at all. Anything goes, right? In a dream, you can ask a question and a get a fish in reply and it'll make perfect sense until you wake up and try to figure out what the heck you'd eaten the night before to bring all that on to begin with.

We come in as a pair of professional dream cleaners finish off their lunch and prepare to get on with cleaning the dreams of a boy named Fudge, who they've been monitoring for a month. Artie is the experienced one of the pair, brought to life by the suitably grizzled form of Larrs Jackson, who does a great job with the jargon and the "been there, done that, seen it all" attitude. Rex is the new guy, full of pep and confidence but who naturally screws up.

Here, screwing up means a glorious opportunity for the effects guys to take over and paint their clever digital effects over this suburban neighbourhood as they escape from Fudge's dream. They look like state of the art graphics and they're as fun to watch as the delightfully analogue gadgetry in the back of Artie and Rex's van, some of which looks animated too. Visually, this is a treat, courtesy of a team of visual artists, at least one of whom is extremely experienced. If it wasn't for the actors, it would feel like Pixar.

Well, not entirely, because while Pixar are certainly pushing the boundaries of computer-based animation, they're fundamentally about telling stories and, as slick as *Dream Cleaners* seems to be on that front, the story is the weakest link. I've watched this a few times and I still have no conception of what dream cleaners do, why they might be required and who employs them. How can I accept a film without accepting its basic rationale for existing?

I can't even figure out what these guys did in Fudge's dreams as there's no internal consistency here at all. They monitored for a month but Rex is brand new. Artie needs Rex but he can take care of business himself when Rex screws up, without breaking a sweat, The afternoon shift is, what, about three minutes long? How do I get that job?

I understand the ending, honestly, but there just has to be more substance here. We can't merely apply dream logic to everything and expect that to suffice. At least I can't.

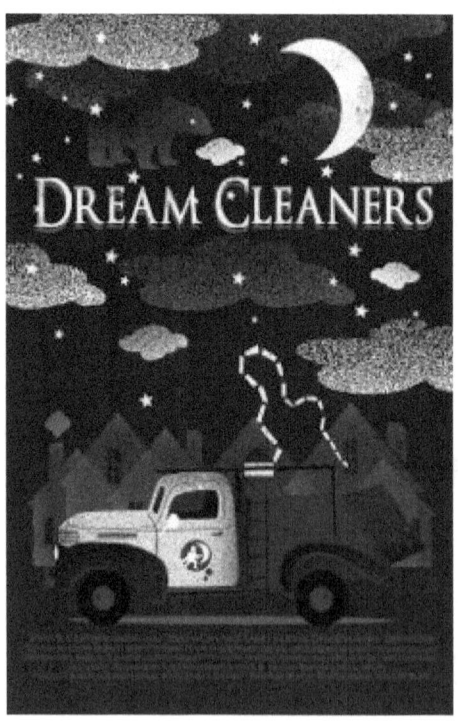

The International
Horror & Sci-Fi Film Festival

2013

Horror Features

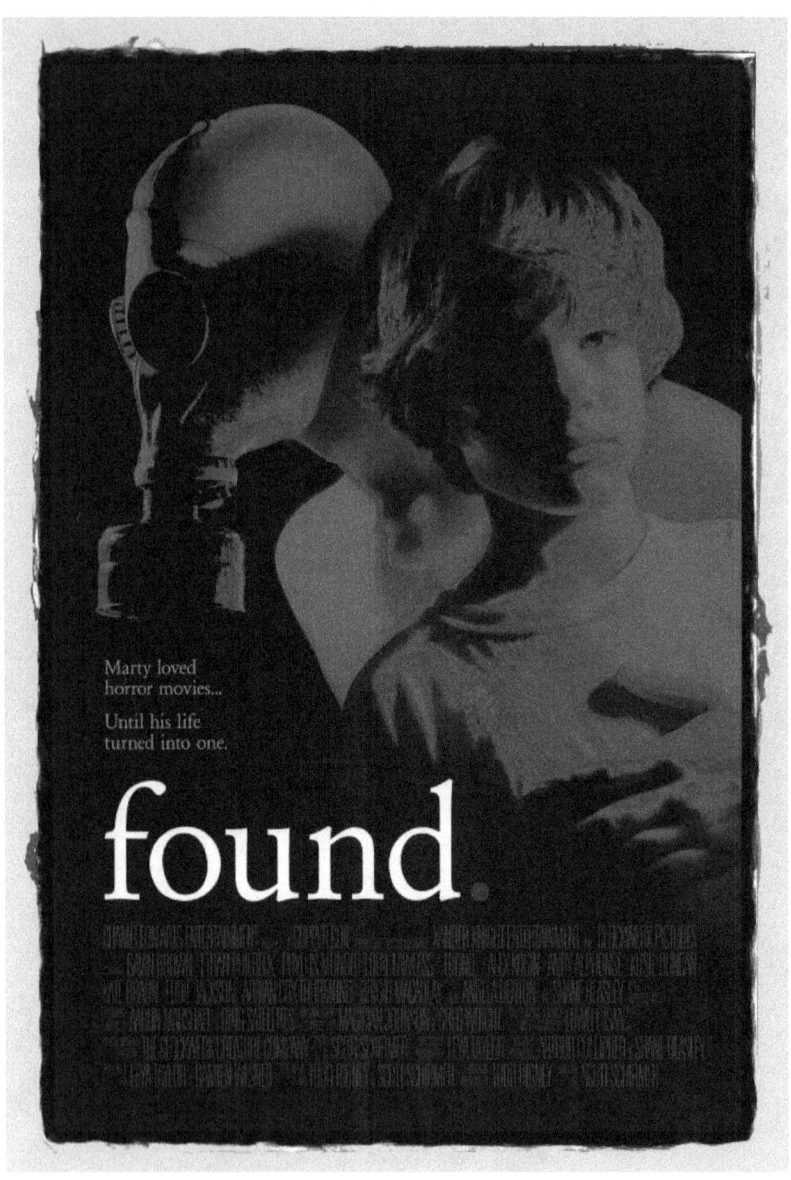

Found (2012)

Director: Scott Schirmer
Writer: Scott Schirmer, from the novella by Todd Rigney
Stars: Gavin Brown, Ethan Philbeck, Phyllis Munro, Louie Lawless, Alex Kogin, Angela Denton and Shane Beasley

Scott Schirmer deserves a lot of respect and not all of it is due to the fact that he made this feature for as low a budget as $8,000. More is because he adapted it to the screen from a self-published horror novella in collaboration with its author, but most is because, two years earlier, he took the effort to write a review of that novella at Amazon.

It's *Found* by Kentucky writer Todd Rigney, who published it himself back in 2004 to "the deafening sound of crickets". Well, one of those crickets was Schirmer, who explains in his review that he found the book "quite by accident" and "could not put it down". He appreciated "the bleakest, most disturbing scenarios you're like to read", but also the "provocative themes and beautiful ambiguities". It's a meaningful review, one that ably highlights just how deeply he was drawn into the piece. "I've read the book three times now," he says, "and new layers keep unfolding before me." Schirmer had made a couple of long short films already, but it's not difficult to see that he felt compelled to adapt this to the screen.

I haven't read Rigney's novella (though I really should remedy that fact soon), but Schirmer's adaptation is magnetic from the very first line. "My brother keeps a human head in his closet," narrates a twelve year old boy called Marty and that's about as engaging as any movie can start out.

Marty is our protagonist, a kid who's being dragged into the adult world whether he likes it or not. He doesn't want to grow up, given that he's been told it'll mean that he won't enjoy horror movies and comic books any more, but he'd sure like to get past the bullying at school. The catch is that he's a curious youngster who wonders about the world and explores it by learning other people's secrets. Mum's are old love letters from some guy called Danny, while Dad's are porn mags in the garage. And, most shocking to us but initially just another adult weirdness to Marty, his older brother Steve keeps severed heads in the bowling ball bag in his closet, a new one every few days. Marty found that out by accident too but can't leave it alone, as you might expect.

Whatever you're imagining the picture to be based on that paragraph, you're probably wrong. This isn't a horror comedy, for a start, a juvenile take on *8 Heads in a Duffel Bag*. It's not a sick and twisted flick that crosses boundaries just to make us grin. It's not even a rapidly paced gorefest where Steve works his grisly way through the neighbourhood like an insane Batman and Marty signs up to be his Robin.

Really, it's a coming of age flick, one that eschews every bit of John Hughes cuteness because it's telling the opposite story. You know all those movies where the kid hero makes it through one adult thing and suddenly is set for life because he gets it? This isn't that, not remotely. Here, growing up is a slow, traumatising process, where everyone is against you in one way or another and nobody gets what you're going through. Gavin Brown, debuting here as Marty, isn't a great actor in the traditional sense but he nails the tone of his role completely and we're with him all the way, as coming of age moves steadily into disturbing horror.

Marty's a relatively normal kid on the surface, one major reason why he's such a powerful lead character, but there are warning signs throughout. He's a quiet kid who only has one real friend, David, with whom he draws notably violent comic books. One of his pictures upset his teacher a year earlier, so he's clearly on that invisible watchlist. His teachers wouldn't like that he watches horror movies too, often borrowed from his big brother, but then all the best kids do. He wants to be accepted, but finds that following the rules don't seem to help. "I get good grades and I do what people ask me to," he pronounces early in the film. "They should just leave me alone." Of course, they don't. He's picked on at school by Marcus Sanders, a bigger kid, and his stooge. Marcus punches him in the stomach one day in the bathroom and only gets a couple of Saturday detentions for it. Marty doesn't have the courage to fight back and his mum pulls him out of school for a couple of days to get over it. You can imagine how well that works.

Marty is rarely off screen and his character is built meticulously, enough that everyone watching is going to recognise something of him in themselves, whether you were bullied or not. Even though he's polite, talented and far from stupid, he's not getting anywhere in a social setting because he's also quiet, awkward and a little nerdy. His parents aren't much help. Dad seems to care, but he's a bigot with a temper; when he hears about Marcus Sanders, he focuses on the kid's black skin rather than what he did. Mum seems to care too, but she's overprotective and babies him.

So it's big brother Steve who he looks up to. Steve is quite a few years older and notably cool to someone like Marty. Just look at the posters on his bedroom wall: of bands like Iron Maiden and Venom and movies like *The Astro-Zombies*, *The Deadly Spawn* and *Wild Zero*. There's even a 27x40 of *The Taint*, one of the more telling ones in this story. The catch of course is that Steve, the cool big brother, the only one who understands him, is also a serial killer. How's that for a tough realisation?

Steve is played by Ethan Philbeck in his only film role and he does a powerful job, especially as he was a last minute replacement for another actor who had to drop out after his family objected to the picture. It's surprising thinking back on the film afterwards at how little he's really in it and how much it revolves around Marty. Even scenes about Steve are often shown from Marty's perspective, even if he's in another room at the time.

One of the most telling early scenes has Steve argue with his dad upstairs, while Marty and his mum silently mirror that argument over the dining room table. To Marty, what's being argued about isn't important, just the fact that they're arguing again. Another scene later on does precisely the same thing and turns out to be all the more brutally disturbing because we can't see anything that's happening. We're focused instead on Marty's face, his horror at what's going down and his frustration at being unable to stop it. The best scene in the film may be the tense one that has us stuck under a bed with Marty.

There are a number of themes here that delve much deeper than most horror movies attempt.

Bullying is the first obvious one, but that isn't just restricted to Marcus Sanders and the responses that are raised to deal with him. Scenes late in the movie suggest that Marty's dad is a bully too, which perhaps highlights why Marty's the way he is and even why Steve's the way he is.

Certainly another theme explores the way that horror movies influence people, a subject close to the heart of anyone who grew up in the UK during the video nasty era. Steve's most overt influence is a fictional (at the time) horror movie called *Headless*, which he appears to be reenacting, but did it and other movies turn him into who he is? I noticed a copy of *Snuff* in his VHS collection, a real film that claimed to do what *Headless* did back in the seventies, with a major furore erupting around its supposedly real act of murder, which of course was no such thing. David Alton and other campaigners against video nasties in the eighties always screamed about copycats, which Steve could well be.

There's a hint at homophobia, but it's only a hint. While Marty has nothing to do with girls throughout, his bullies spread rumours that he's gay and he certainly has hero worship for his big brother, there's no real evidence that he really is gay and Marcus Sanders is committing a hate crime. He's just a bully, throwing out whatever insults are likely to cause impact.

There's more of a hint at racism though, as Steve's collection of human heads are predominantly of black women. Whether or not *Headless* (or *Snuff*) influenced Steve to do what he does, we're clearly led to wonder if his father's bigotry influenced him too, because surely that's where his racism comes from, even if he doesn't realise it. Perhaps the *Daily Mail* could campaign against parents as well as horror movies. Won't somebody think of the children?

At this point, we even wonder if Steve's sexualised violence is sourced from *Headless*, from Dad or some strange conflation of them. As we see this household entirely from Marty's perspective, we know that we're not being told everything and that there's history there.

And, of course, as we wonder about Steve and what really turned him into what he's become, we wonder if we're going to watch Marty going through the same transition. He's bullied already, as Steve may have been earlier in his life. He watches the same movies, perhaps at an even younger age. He's already seen *Headless*, for example, and he overlays his brother's face onto the perpetrator in his mind. He's gradually being alienated from all authority figures (parents, teachers, pastors) except for Steve, his serial killer of a big brother. He starts the film with one friend and ends it without any. If he isn't sexually frustrated yet, he'll surely get there soon, whether he's gay or not. Even without the final scenes which he appropriately interprets as his life becoming a horror movie, he's being screwed up every which way and we can't help but wonder what he'll become. Will he become Steve in the sequel? Will he take the Lovecraftian way out and go completely insane? Or will he just grow up, if this is all traumatising metaphor for coming of age?

I first saw *Found* as a festival screener and I was impressed but not bowled over. It was clearly a capable film, even before I realised how minimal its budget, and it obviously had a lot to say, but it wasn't difficult to bring my own expectations to the table and realise how different this was. It's much slower than horror films tend to be, even down to the music, which varies in style from ambient to noise but rarely ramps up from tracks that include the word "soothing" in their titles. While it was banned in Australia for "prolonged and detailed depictions of sexualised violence", that's mostly restricted to *Headless*, the film within a film, which is ironically far from the most disturbing material, much of which isn't seen but conjured up in our own minds from what Marty has to go through. Watching *Found* again to review, I realised that it had stayed strongly with me from a couple of years ago, so opened up this time around for me to explore more of its admirable depth and realise just how powerful this story is.

And, unlike those Australian censors who couldn't see past the surface, it's the depth that endows it with its power, not the faux snuff antics of the guy in the mask in *Headless*, which incidentally is being made into a feature of its own by Arthur Cullipher, the head of the *Found* effects team.

What's disturbing is the realisation that Marty is so thoroughly everyday but enduring so much as he travels through the rites of passage that lead us to adulthood that we start to wonder why everyone doesn't go batshit insane when they hit puberty. Suddenly we wonder what's going on next door and next door from them. We ask ourselves how we would react to the apparently minor events that lead up to more major ones, all those little details that we denigrate as minor because we've forgotten how worldchanging they are to a twelve year old. We even put on Steve's shoes as Marty muses about his caring, protective big brother and says, "Why do there have to be two Steves?" If that isn't real coming of age, I'm not sure what is.

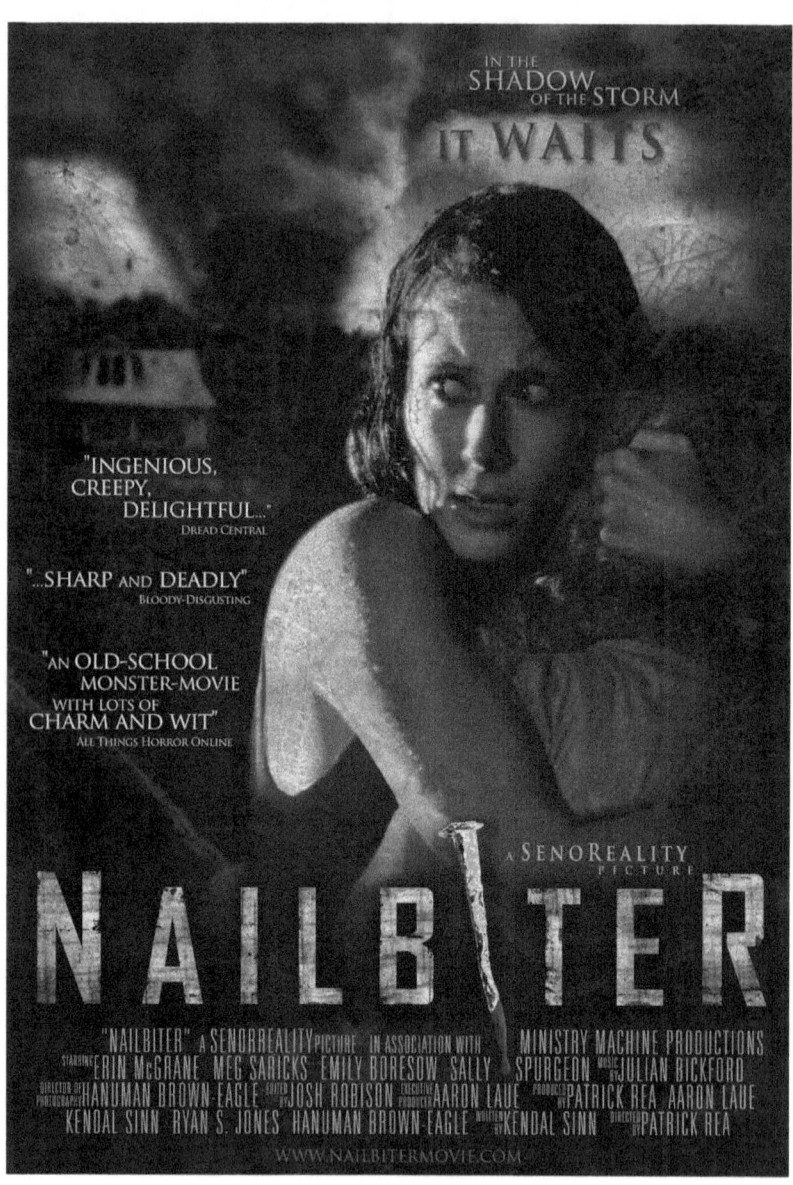

Nailbiter (2013)

Director: Patrick Rea
Writers: Patrick Rea and Kendal Sinn
Stars: Erin McGrane, Meg Saricks, Emily Boresow and Sally Spurgeon

Unfortunately *Nailbiter* screened at the 2013 festival while the theatre was experiencing technical problems with a projector, thus causing issues with the colour balance. Sure, Harkins kindly gave us all a free pass to any movie of our choice, but we chose poorly and discovered that *Nailbiter* with projection issues was still a much more enjoyable experience than *The Incredible Burt Wonderstone* was without them.

Even with these issues, it was quickly clear that prolific short film director Patrick Rea had done something just a little different with a very familiar story. The question of the day is whether he did enough, because the familiar is commonplace throughout; I feel that while he certainly did enough to make this a good film, he didn't do enough to make it a great one.

There are two notable tweaks to the usual: one with regards to the monsters of the piece, who are given a neatly fresh origin and another with regards to the stars, all four of which are female. Rea co-wrote with Kendal Sinn, so there's no overt female influence apparent in the production, but the tone is utterly different from the expected comparisons, which tend to be either testosterone-fuelled or mixed in outlook because they're mixed in actors. Here, it's all about women and their reactions are refreshingly different.

The one nominally in charge is Janet Maguire, a recovering alcoholic whose husband is deployed overseas in the forces. That leaves her to juggle A.A. meetings with bringing up three daughters who are all clearly rebelling against her, as their primary figure of authority, in their own unique ways.

Most overtly, there's Jennifer, a textbook bad girl who's stringing along some dorky young guy because he has a car and he's more than happy to live at her beck and call. We meet them as he drops her off at home, but she keeps him there while she finishes her cigarette, just to emphasise her control over the relationship. Next youngest is Sally, who wants to change her name to Sarah, which is telling in itself. That leaves Alice, who retreats into the world of books and stays very quiet indeed.

Jen may be wearing the rebel card flamboyantly on her sleeve, but all three of them still seem like nice kids who are just stuck in a bad situation and don't know how to reengage with mum now that she's sober. That reading is reenforced as the story progresses and teamwork becomes a must.

They live close to the border between Kansas and Missouri and, as the film begins, they're getting ready to drive up to Kansas City together so that they can be the first people Dad sees when he gets home from deployment. That's something Mum is adamant about and the girls aren't dumb enough to fight her on it, merely selfish enough to bitch about here and there. Instead the backlash is put on hold and the storm that will presumably erupt as Dad finds his family this dysfunctional is mirrored by a more literal storm whose arrival kicks off the movie in impressive style.

Initially the screen is entirely black, while we listen to the radio talk about approaching storms; then lightning splits the sky and our eyeballs engage. Dad's plane isn't going to wait, so the Maguires find themselves heading north in bad conditions that are rapidly deteriorating. Interestingly, Jen has never seen a tornado in her life, even though she's the eldest and she was even born during one; they are a little east of Tornado Alley but not by much, so maybe she's just been lucky. By the time they reach Wellsville, where folk are battening down the hatches and boarding up the storefronts, her luck runs out. With a tornado literally following them up the road, they abandon the car and take shelter in the nearest storm cellar they can find, not knowing or caring to whom it belongs, in order to sit tight and ride out the storm. Unfortunately for them, this is a horror movie rather than a thriller and so this is inevitably just the beginning.

It's been a slow, characterful build thus far, though not a long one, as Rea does initially play the story in thriller fashion. The first enemy is the tornado and the second a tree, which falls onto the cellar door, preventing them from being able to leave. The horror angle kicks in when we, along with the Maguires, discover that the third enemy is human; they realise that there's someone upstairs, someone who not only won't respond to their cries for help, but who actively boards up the cellar from outside to ensure that they can't leave.

We enjoy the very feminine reactions of Mrs. Maguire and her girls, which may be a little underdone, given the circumstances, but are still refreshing in this sort of tense scenario. There's a balance of strength, as Janet faces despair and eyes their unknown host's liquor but recovers as the others band together.

Rea wants to enforce that the story is entering horror territory right before those windows are boarded up, because Sally decides that, with a little assistance, she can climb out through one of them and find help outside. She gets bitten for her trouble, by something that clearly ain't no man. What it is we aren't exactly sure, because Rea wisely only hints at his monsters until it's time for them to come out and play, beginning with the moment that nice deputy Barney discovers the Maguires' abandoned car and comes looking for them. It won't be a surprise to find that he's quickly dragged off and eaten, but what we discover in the moment just before that happens is enough to neatly set the scene for the rest of the movie.

The good news is that this is all different enough to keep us guessing a little as to what's out there with the storms, as the Maguires slowly make discoveries that fill in the background for them and for us. The bad news is that the picture slows down here for a weak, only mildly suspenseful middle act that lasts at least partway into the finalé.

The film's title would dearly like to be an appropriate one in a number of ways and it succeeds in reaching some of them, but the obvious meaning hints at the suspense of the piece and sadly that's not consistently maintained.

The story builds pretty well and we do care about the characters; the arrival of the tornado and the tension sparked by the falling tree are handled very capably too, but here, the suspense begins to fade and the film drags as the Maguires attempt to figure out both what's going on and how they can get out of the cellar to face it. I should emphasise that it isn't particularly bad, and there are some very nice scenes within this part of the film; it's just that they fail to live up to what came before and don't bode well for what we hope is still to come. The framework is still familiar enough for us to build expectations rather easily and Rea delivers some of what we do expect to see, but he keeps it surprisingly low key towards the end, moving back from a horror to a thriller mindset.

All four Maguire ladies are decently played and the family is well nuanced, with each of the actors bringing something different to the table.

Erin McGrane has a surprisingly short filmography, this being only her seventh feature in over two decades, but she brings a believably fragile strength to her role, as befits a mother of three who's struggling with drink.

Meg Saricks, as Jennifer, is brand new to features, with only an anthology segment and a handful of shorts previously to her name, one of those being *Hell Week* for Patrick Rea. Her arc is from bad girl to good then back to bad in the name of survival and she lives up to it reasonably well.

Sally Spurgeon and Emily Boresow as her younger sisters have even less credits to their name but still prove surprisingly capable nonetheless. I wanted to see more from both of them.

Trumping all of them, though, is Joicie Appell, who utterly steals the show as old Mrs. Shurman, a much more important character than she might initially appear. I hate to provide spoilers and this review is as spoiler-free as any I've written, because the twist that comes here doesn't come at the end; it comes with the explanation of what's going on in Wellsville and the various ramifications that arrive alongside it. Rea has a lot more to say after the twist and it's perhaps the biggest success of *Nailbiter*.

There are male characters in the film, but none of them really get to do much of anything. It's as if they all took their lead from Lt. Maguire, Janet's husband, who is referenced both early and often but doesn't even make it on screen until the story is all wrapped up and put to bed. He's there only to underline the solid ending and provide the promise of a testosterone-fuelled mirror image of the movie in imaginary sequel form. Any traditionally male scenes here are handled instead by the women, who prove that though they may be the weaker sex, that doesn't mean they can't take care of business anyway.

It's this surprisingly feminist angle that impressed me the most, along with the mildly subversive concept that while the Maguires may be victims in a stereotypical horror way, the story clearly happening to them, they're also the protagonists of the reverse story, in which they adversely impact the Wellsville community in return. It's a shame that this wasn't taken further, because it's far more interesting than the otherwise routine story it's built on.

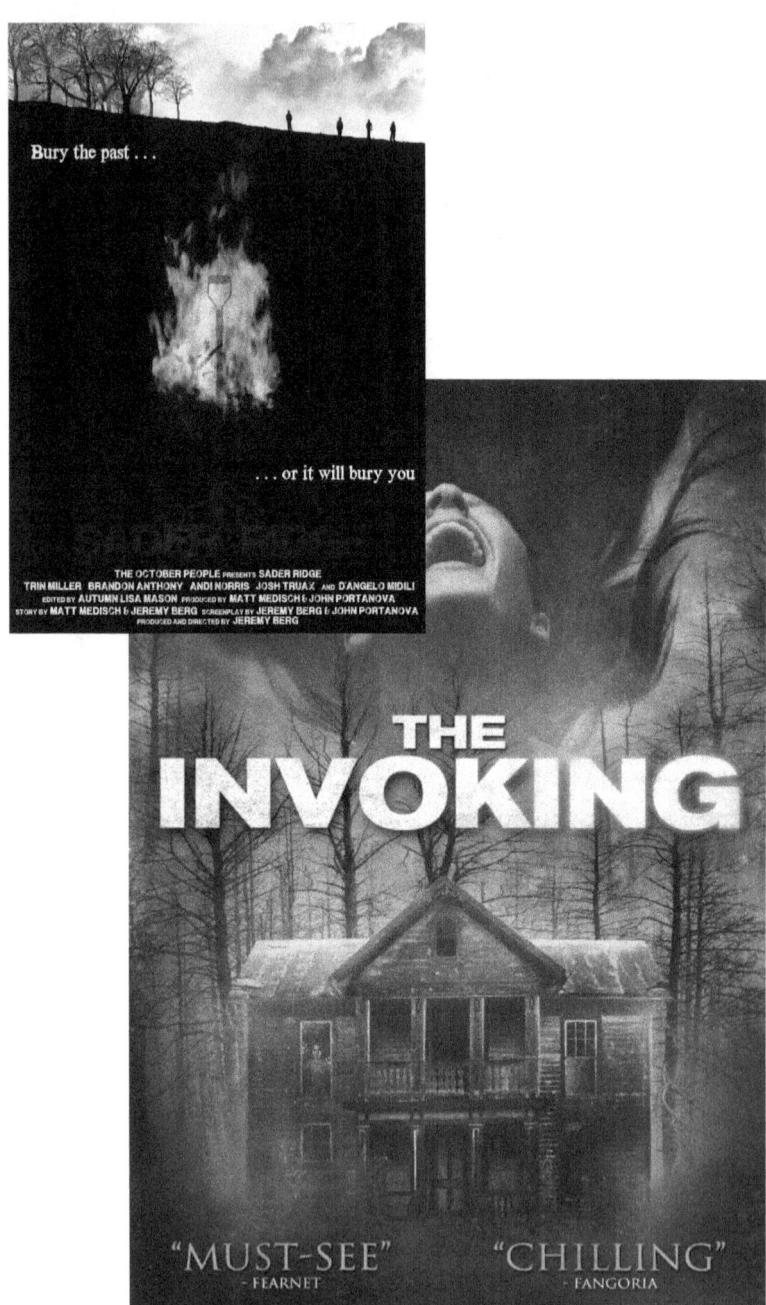

Sader Ridge (2013)

Director: Jeremy Berg
Writers: Jeremy Berg and John Portanova, from a story by Jeremy Berg and Matt Medisch
Stars: Trin Miller, Brandon Anthony, Andi Norris, Josh Truax and D'Angelo Midili

For some reason I can't fathom, *Sader Ridge* is a polarising movie. It quickly garnered a great deal of love and promptly won awards on the festival circuit, from both audiences and judges, and topped at least one end of year list at a genre site. Yet the film was quickly retitled *The Invoking* for home release, which usually means that it failed to capture the audience it aimed for and therefore needed a marketing makeover. Its IMDb rating dropped massively to the point that an army of naysayers debated how low it could go.

Well, I'm in the middle. This isn't close to the worst movie ever made but I wanted a lot more from it than it was able to give me. Most denigrators may have wanted it to get going quicker, because it has a notably slow and subtle build and, especially to viewers used to jump scares every ten minutes, nothing meaningful seems to happen for quite a while. I didn't have a problem with the pace and frankly enjoyed the character building, but I wanted more background. At 82 minutes, it could have done with another eight to nail it down tight at a regular length.

We're here to watch Sam, who's driving into the countryside to take ownership of a house which she's just inherited from an aunt she never knew in the family she didn't grow up with. She's been raised by foster parents, the Harrises, who have refused to tell her anything about the former life that she left at a young enough age to not remember at all.

As you can imagine, that rediscovery of who she was will constitute a good deal of the horror story that she's going to find herself in, but director and co-writer, Jeremy Berg, is eager to avoid clichés. At heart, this is really a drama that wends its way through traditional horror territory, where each scene seems to show us something we recognise from other horror movies approached from a different angle. Yes, this could be read as a cabin in the woods story, but it's far more subtle than that subgenre tends to be. We even open with four young adults in a car, but this thankfully doesn't turn into found footage. The biggest departure from the norm may be that these characters aren't stupid. Thank goodness.

For a young lady who was raised by foster parents, Sam seems well grounded, pondering on her past without ever being overtly inquisitive about it. She realises that they'll lose cellphone signal on their journey, so sneaks in maps and directions to make sure they avoid the usual wrong turn. The car's in good shape, so we don't get the expected breakdown.

Mark, in the passenger seat, is her ex-boyfriend not her current one and we don't feel that they'll be drawn back together even if Jessica dumps him over the phone not far into the film. He's a believable ass, up tight and bitchy but able to apologise. He's bright but socially off a little.

The cute couple in the back seat, Roman and Caitlin, aren't a couple, even if he'd dearly like them to be; she really does see them as best friends. Roman is a young nerd but not stereotypically so, socially capable but interested in capturing odd sounds for his library on an old tape recorder. Caitlin wears the nerdy glasses we might have expected of him, but she's a little tomboyish, a little hyper, a little free spirit. It's easy to see their connection.

I found the four of them refreshing. They're not doing drugs in the car, mooning other drivers or bitching at each other. They're believable people with realistically cool dialogue and it's great fun to watch them, even though they're apparently doing next to nothing. Ten minutes in, the wildcard arrives in the form of Eric, the caretaker of the property who clearly remembers Sam even if she doesn't remember him in the slightest.

He's the one who found Sam's aunt, peacefully dead in her rocking chair, and he's the one who meets them at the gate to show them the property. And, of course, he's the one who's about to introduce us to some of the background that Sam doesn't remember. Her aunt lived here for fifteen years, but took the place over from Sam's birth parents, James and Ellen Sader, who owned most of the land around the house, including the ridge of the title. Sam even lived here too until she was five years old; she played in these woods with Eric, the kid from a property over, five miles down the road.

Thus far, it's a generally believable piece, very old school in its slow character-driven build, the downside being a few darker scenes and the lack of anything except hints at what we might imagine will be coming later. Clearly there's something in Sam's past that she's blocked out, but it takes no less than 41 minutes, literally the halfway mark, for her to finally get round to asking Eric what happened back when she was five and for him to refuse to answer her.

There's some darkness in Mark's background too, based on one offhand comment, and Roman begins to react a little strongly to him getting lost in the woods. It's Roman who gets the first real horror scene too, crouching on the steps to the house too scared to go back inside, pitching some sort of fit about what Sam interprets to be Caitlin's plan to travel for six months before finishing college. Yet, as she calls everyone over, he's not there any more. We're 36 minutes in and suddenly we're in the realm of horror, wondering if Roman is possessed or Sam's having hallucinations. Now's when we need to find out the history of the place, because even if the characters don't think in horror movie terms, we certainly do.

It's certainly the growing shift from banal drama to clear horror territory, a very gradual shift but a strong one, that shines brightest in *Sader Ridge*. Berg doesn't give us anything flash here to distract us from the build and the characters that experience it. He wore a whole bunch of hats on this project, one of the most notable of which was the cinematographer's, but as capable as his eyes seem to be from the well framed rural stills that pepper the minimalist credits, he does keep his visual work very subtle. There are no ambitious camera movements, not a lot of cinematic angles and relatively pedestrian editing, certainly no jump cuts. That's fine, as he's not going for either art film or mainstream horror movie. He's going for that old school disconcerting tone as we gradually question what's real and what isn't and he's relying on the actors to ground their characters so deeply that we can tell when they're being themselves and when they're not. That's crucial here for us to figure out what's really going on and that's the strongest part of *Sader Ridge*.

Trin Miller manages to remain the focus throughout even though Sam is a rather passive lead surrounded by more outgoing, more dynamic characters. Brandon Anthony is particularly impressive as Mark, as he's given two tones to find and he manages to nail both of them, channelling a less comedic Jim Parsons for one and some Alexander Skarsgård for the other. Josh Truax has a similar task as Roman, a more obscure one in which the two tones are a little less distinct, thus a little more unnerving. Andi Norris also has two tones to find but gets less opportunity to do so. As Caitlin, she's the most obvious character in the movie but her other part is more obscure and it took the end credits to let me in on the news that I'd misinterpreted it. As Eric, D'Angelo Midili only gets one character to play and so he seems a little less dominant, even though he's very capable in what he does. I can't say that every actor reached every note, but the way these five act around each other, three of them juggling two personalities, is to my mind a major success.

I was less sold on the story, which Berg conjured up with Matt Medisch and adapted with John Portanova. To be more precise, I was less sold on where it went. I appreciated the basic concept, the way that it built and the ideas that it threw out, but even after a few viewings, I haven't figured out exactly why any of it is happening. I can't talk in depth about this without introducing spoilers, so I'll try to keep it generic.

It felt to me like there were two stories here, one in the present and one in the past, one psychological and one literal, one featuring the characters we're watching and one featuring others. My issue is in how these two stories tie together, because they have to in order to work, but they don't seem to fit. The end result to me was a huge image made up of pieces from two different jigsaws. Now, those pieces may fit together if they happen to be the same shapes, but they're still not from the same picture and thus we can't expect that completed image to make sense. Perhaps I'm still missing something but I don't think so.

In the end, I think that Berg had all the constituent parts he needed to make a memorable feature, but he didn't put them together right. He had a capable eye, a strong cast and a good location. He didn't have a large budget, but this didn't need one. What it needed was some more imagination to the camerawork; a bit more attention to the sound and lighting, especially in outdoor scenes where night is falling; and a lot more work on the script. The location could have been used better, but the script deserved to be polished a lot more than it was.

It felt to me like the first half should have been condensed to be the first third, the second half sped up to be the second third and a whole new emphatic third added at the end that makes some sort of sense within the larger framework. It certainly deserves to be more than it is and I wonder if what was shot matched what was written.

Could Berg have run out of cash in his clearly small budget and so shot a quick ending rather than a third act? Inquiring minds want to know.

The International
Horror & Sci-Fi Film Festival

2013

Sci-Fi Features

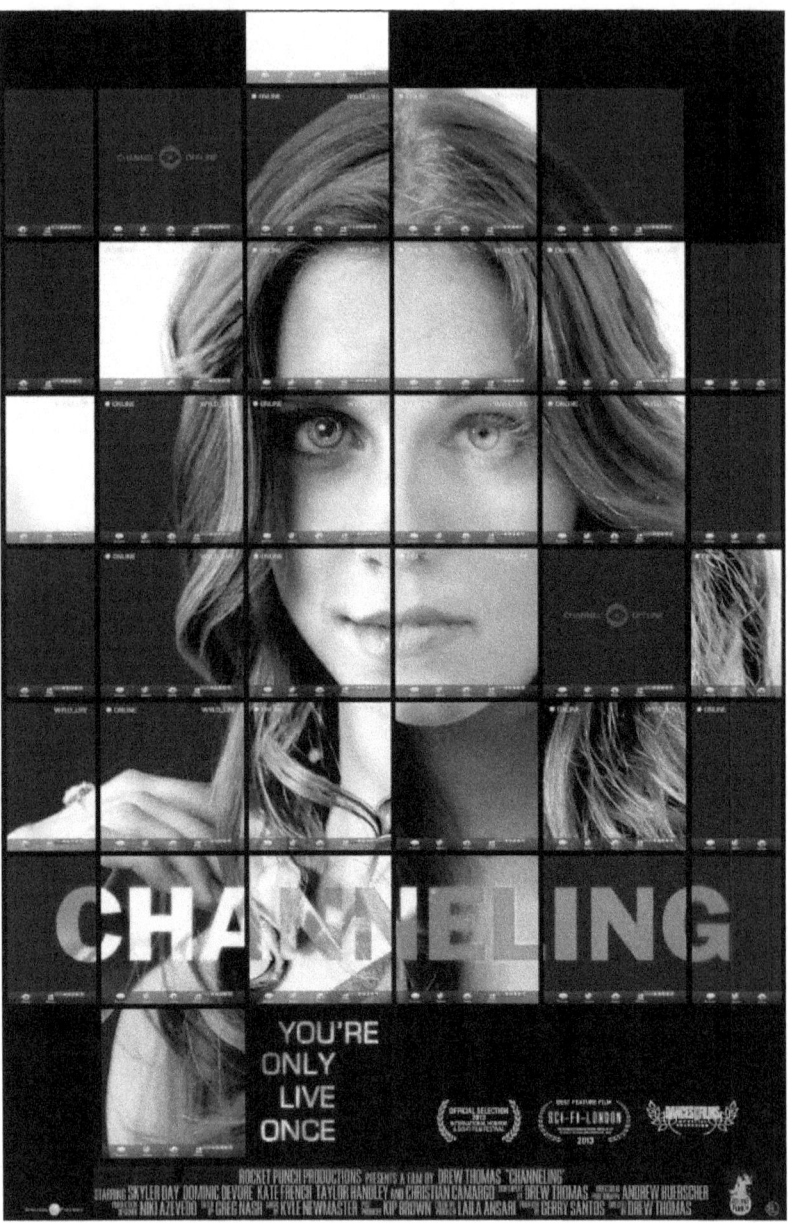

Channeling (2012)

Director: Drew Thomas
Writer: Drew Thomas
Stars: Skyler Day, Dominic DeVore, Kate French, Taylor Handley and Christian Camargo

I'm seeing a lot of movies lately made by people well known for a different role in the movie industry. The cost of entry is decreasing all the time, which means that editors, scriptwriters and effects guys can start to make the artistic statements that they want to make, all while keeping their day jobs and paying their bills.

The man behind *Channeling*, an intriguing sci-fi action flick, is Drew Thomas, who started racking up credits as a cinematographer in 1997, moving up from short films through TV shows to features. Prior to this, his only credits as a producer or director were on *Coachella*, a feature length glimpse of that festival in 2006, and an episode of *Walmart Soundcheck* in 2009. By the way, whatever that suggests, it's really a live music show with interviews that is presumably sponsored by the store. If working for Walmart might mark the low point of Drew Thomas's career, this could easily be the equivalent high point because it's a heck of a lot more ambitious and his integrity remains intact. He wrote, produced and directed.

It opens very well indeed, with a commercial for EyeCast, a high definition camera that's embedded into a contact lens, surely the next step in the technology that's already brought us Google Glass, albeit after this fictional product. "This is your life, live," it says, "because you only live once." The technology is neat material for science fiction, of course, but science fiction isn't just about inventing technology, it's about applying it practically in a social context and building a story out of it.

Fortunately that's precisely what we get here, beginning with Wyld, a young man who oxys up and races a Shelby GT through the countryside, a petrol pump hanging out of the side, broadcasting live all the way on his channel, *Wyld Life*, which has a large number of followers. When a trio of bikers chase after him with guns, also broadcasting through EyeCast, one of those followers pipes Wyld the feed and he takes one of them out by braking hard and letting the biker slam into the other camera on the back of his car. You only live once, indeed, and no, it's not abbreviated.

Switching to Yemen, Sgt. Jonah Maddox of the U.S. Army gets a call from the States. Wyld was his brother, Wyatt Maddox, who has died of trauma. Jonah travels home for his funeral and discovers that Ashleigh, their sister, broadcasts too, if only by looking in the mirror. She's raising to the world the envelope from the coroner that contains Wyatt's stuff and Jonah breaks it up. "This isn't for them," he tells her, but, after watching an old video recording of them as kids, he opens the envelope, discovers an EyeCast and pops it in. This automatically starts the Wyld Life channel and suddenly we have a movie.

Wyld was someone to a lot of people, who are texting, commenting and now ringing. Suddenly Jonah realises that he has a lot more to do than go to his brother's funeral. He goes to EyeCast, masquerading as his brother, who of course was anonymous, unseen on footage broadcast from his POV. EyeCast want "surprise, immediacy, chaos", because, as they pitch to sponsors, "no-one Tivo'd 9/11". And Wyld is all those things.

The potential is obvious here, but it could easily have been lost in the mix. Thomas keeps it focused in all the right directions: porn, first and foremost, as Ashleigh wakes up with Conner who's broadcasting her. I like the nod to the obvious, that EyeCast can be done in secret, which echoes the big privacy fear that's brought up every time Google Glass gets mentioned anywhere, but also that it can happen two ways at once, which I've not seen yet in the Google Glass stories. Maybe it's still too expensive. Blackmail comes up quickly too, with the inevitable money angle. Wyld races stolen cars from which to broadcast and the screen he sees tracks the count of viewers tuning in to watch. It's all about sponsorship, which manifests itself here first in a glorious interruption to the biker's feed during the chase for a diaper commercial. As always, timing is everything, right? And there's the darker side, which we soon discover as Jonah finds his way into the life his brother was leading, which merely starts with what he describes as "a request line for felonies".

Everything takes a back seat to the tech, at least initially. The actors play second fiddle to the contacts in their eyes for a while and the most obvious character is the one who's killed off at the beginning. Jonah is the bland brother when he enters the story, a poor comparison to the cool Wyatt. The story hints at quite a lot, but the tech drives it all. When Tara, Wyatt's partner and broadcast eye candy, explains to Jonah that he was murdered, the fact that he had thousands of viewers at the time but not a single witness is a delicious irony.

Even the cinematography, Thomas's day job, is at its best with the tech at its heart, like that great moment when the biker hits Wyld's Shelby GT. We see the biker hit the car in the rear camera then pan round to watch him land in front of it. It's great enough that we see it twice and we aren't upset in the slightest. Not all the tech is believable, Thomas definitely cutting some corners for cinematic effect, but it's levels above the usual. When Gabriel needs to hack into a website, he tells Jonah and Tara to come back later. This isn't *C.S.I.*

I really appreciated the character of Gabriel. While Wyld and Tara are ramping up numbers to land higher quality sponsors, Gabriel isn't interested in that stuff. Cinematic shortcuts aside, he's the most refreshing screen hacker I've seen in a while. He's a merry prankster who pushes fire-breathing dinosaurs and giant eyeballs through red lights, then hacks into the cameras to grab the images. He's in it for the art not the money, blocking comments let alone sponsors. Much respect to Gabriel for not selling out and to Thomas for including such a character in his movie. I understand that he has to stay firmly in support, backing up the hot chick and the tough guy, but Thomas could have written him very differently and I'm thankful he didn't.

Maybe it's enough to let me forgive him a little for those odd shortcuts and conveniences. Surely the one that rankles the most is that Wyld's continued anonymity relies on him never looking in a mirror, but he's seen most driving stolen cars that have three of them for him to look at frequently.

The acting gets better. Dominic DeVore isn't bad as Jonah and he certainly improves when the character pulls the stick out of his ass and lets him join the story properly. Taylor Handley shows more charisma as Wyatt, with his Leonardo DiCaprio vibe; unfortunately he's not in the picture long enough for us to find out if he can carry one. I liked Kate French a lot as Tara from moment one, because she's believably quick and tough on top of her good looks. Again, I'd like to have seen her do more than she's given the chance to, but her role is what it needs to be.

It's Skyler Day who's the best of the main cast, surprisingly given that she's annoyingly weak at the beginning of the film. Ashleigh's subplot takes quite a while to kick into motion but, in many ways, it's much truer and more resonant than the main one. It doesn't merely take a dive into what the technology does, it's also an exploration of what the technology means to real people, both the positive and the negative. The film finds its emotional peak when it all goes down for her, not for Jonah and Tara.

The biggest problem *Channeling* has is that it's biased too much towards the more commercial angle, to the detriment of the more substantial one. I feel odd bringing this up, because I'm a genre guy and I'm all for the sort of places that the main plot takes us, the snuff, sex tape and gambling angles, not to mention all the driving action. These play out well with a neatly sinister edge to the twists, but they don't hold any surprises because there just aren't enough characters and possibilities for that.

Ashleigh's angle is the one that I wouldn't normally be interested in at all. She's a young lady suffering inside from the constant belittling of her father, parental abuse over decades that leads her to find an online outlet for her anguish. It could all be fodder for a soporific tween drama, especially given the roads it sets her on towards the sort of celebrity reality coverage that makes my brain shut down, but it's really the heart of the technology Thomas turns into fiction in *Channeling* and it's actually the stronger angle to explore. EyeCast is democratised empowerment with a transparent middleman. The demographics create themselves.

With only a hundred minutes to play with, there's much that's missed out. This is Twitter meets YouTube meets liveblogging meets GoPro, of course, but it delves deep enough to capture the trolls on a girl's fashion channel. Yet it misses the legal angle which ought to be massive. How would criminals act if they couldn't be sure if their victims were channeling or not? Surely the N.S.A. is monitoring these feeds. Why wouldn't a serial carjacker like Wyatt not be tracked down through his widely advertised channel? Like cops couldn't monitor that and figure out where he is? Regular people would be capturing streams, whether to relive or remix. Sure, you're only live once, but that doesn't mean captured streams aren't admissable in court as evidence. The insurance industry is why there are so many dashcams in Russia, for a start. There's a lot more depth to this technology than just targetted popups and sponsored ads. I salute Thomas for getting as much of it into his movie as he did, but he inevitably missed a whole heck of a lot.

And this leads to the inevitable talk of a sequel. *Channeling* was well received, enough to win as the best sci-fi feature at the International Horror & Sci-Fi Film Festival in 2013, among other awards. It holds a very strong rating at IMDb, though it's in dire need of more votes. I hope it's doing well enough commercially for a new feature to be a firm possibility in Thomas's mind once he's done promoting this one.

While the suggestion of a sequel is rarely a good one, it seems appropriate here. He wouldn't need to bring any of the cast back, though he easily could, of course. He could fashion an entirely new story around the same technology and explore a host of other angles that he didn't have space for in this film. Maybe the whole surveillance angle would be most timely, after Edward Snowden's revelations utterly changed the tone of everything in the cloud. He could extrapolate the technology much further than video feeds, comments and a little interactivity.

This is a strong film but it deserves to become stronger still in a wider context.

CHAOTIC SEQUENCE PRESENTS

Psychics. Objects. Murder. Time.

FOUND IN TIME

Time isn't what it used to be.

CHAOTIC SEQUENCE PRESENTS MACLEOD ANDREWS MINA VESPER GOKAL KELLY SULLIVAN DEREK MORGAN "FOUND IN TIME" ERIC MARTIN BROWN MOLLIE O'MARA CURT ROBERT BOURIL STEPHEN BRADBURY COSTUME DESIGNER GHISLAINE SABITI CASTING KATHERINE HINCHEY SOUND DESIGN AND MUSIC QUENTIN CHIAPPETTA EDITED BY DANIEL LOEWENTHAL DIRECTOR OF PHOTOGRAPHY BEN WOLF ASSOCIATE PRODUCER ROBERT L. SEIGEL PRODUCED BY CHAOTIC SEQUENCE INC. WRITTEN AND DIRECTED BY ARTHUR VINCIE

Found in Time (2012)

Director: Arthur Vincie
Writer: Arthur Vincie
Stars: MacLeod Andrews, Mina Vesper Gokal, Kelly Sullivan and Derek Morgan

Ironically, perhaps, given the name, it took a while for me to remember *Found in Time*, even though I first saw it less than two years ago. My notes suggested that I liked the concept if not where it ended up, but I had to rewatch to remind myself of why. Perhaps that's partly because it takes a while to ground itself and until it does that it feels rather confusing.

It begins in a field, for instance, where a young man asks an older Peter Fonda hippie type in a colourful shirt to push him back. He isn't a taxi service, he says, but clamps his large hand onto the young man's face until he falls to the grass unconscious, to promptly wake up on a couch looking at a young lady with a laptop.

He's Chris and she's Jina, his fiancée. Well, not quite, because he hasn't given her the ring yet, but he will and they're certainly a couple. He's on meds, somewhat unsurprisingly, but she's his rock so he needs her. And he needs to go to work too, with R.J., who serves coffee from the sidewalk with the aid of a manual typewriter and some electronic gadget.

They're not your usual street vendors, by any stretch. They seem to give people precisely what they need, whether that's exactly the right coffee or a key to a box. Yes, this is a little weird.

Then again, Chris seems to pay more attention to a nail he nearly treads on in the street, standing on its head and waiting for someone to impale themselves on it, than he does his rock and almost fiancée. Clearly he cares for her, but he's more than a little distracted, literally. When he touched that nail, he seemed to transport to another dimension where he found himself putting it down, so it's quite obvious that something is going on here that we aren't being told about yet and Chris and R.J. are at the heart of it.

In this world, people go up to coffee vendors on the street and ask for stamina, humility or confidence rather than cups of coffee.

In this world, people with blood on their shirts and emptiness in their demeanour buy small rocks for arbitrary prices. In this world, people silently present boxes for Chris to unlock with the first key in his tin and refuse to charge a fee for doing so. And in this world, cops take photos of them that mysteriously appear on their cameras as the people they might be thinking about.

Here's where we really understand that we're not in Kansas any more, Dorothy. I don't know if this world is supposed to be an alien planet that looks uncannily like our own or an alternate dimension that's just that far adrift from us.

At this point, it seems bizarrely appropriate that R.J. is played by Derek Morgan whose first regular role on TV was as a character called Thomas Gibson, three years before the Criminal Minds franchise launched, with its lead actor, Thomas Gibson and most prominent character, Derek Morgan. To us, this really ought to be nothing but a meaningless coincidence, but the framework of this film almost wills us to search for weird patterns.

This is disjointed stuff, with clearly deliberate intent, I'll grant you, but disjointed nonetheless. We're stuck at the level of little Billy, for whom Chris fills a little bag with crayons. "What are you doing?" he asks. "How do you do it? You're scary."

Even the explanations don't explain much because everything is either cryptic or surreal, depending on our point of view. That customer who bought a rock? Apparently the cops beat him up because he might have used it, but he comes back for another one, which Chris refuses to sell. The psych cops would take away their licenses and send them to the Mine. The customer doesn't believe that the Mine exists, whatever it is, but Chris claims to be able to see it in the faces of the cops.

Either writer/director Arthur Vincie was dropping some serious acid as he put this together or it's all going somewhere, merely collating confusion factors. Making the lead character a psychic is one, but having his mind experience the days in a different order to his body is another. Having characters swap places, depending on how Chris dreams those scenarios, is a third. Having what might be everyone in the story apparently be there for one reason but possibly a few more besides is what makes it quintessential Philip K. Dick.

Trying to fathom what Vincie was trying to tell us reminded me of Dick stories like *Time Out of Joint*, in which the lead character has a strange profession, lives in a world that's almost but not exactly like ours and who starts to experience weird anomalies that he can't initially explain. In stories like that, what we see tends to be just a front because something completely different is going on behind it and we have to discover what that is.

Here, we're not sure who to look at. Should we be looking at the cops, who are over the top and drawn from a dystopia that this world doesn't quite seem to be? Should we concentrate on vendors, which here seems to be a given role as much as a profession? How about the psychiatrists, like Jina, who do their work from behind masks that are rather like welding helmets fashioned by Apple? Clearly we're supposed to watch the characters who appear in more than one category, but at least three of these are identified quickly, even if their reasons are not. If anything, we wonder about the ones who aren't.

It's around the fifty minute mark that we appear to be given an explanation though, of course, we can't be remotely sure that this reality is indeed reality or just another front. The film's synopsis suggests that Chris, who experiences time like a jigsaw puzzle, finds out that he commits a murder in the future, so he attempts to change his past and present in order to prevent that from happening. This may be true, but it would seem to be a massive oversimplification.

From what I understood of the story, the key to unlocking the confusion is the realisation that not one but two characters, who are connected in a number of ways, are doing exactly the same thing and their respective efforts are undoing each other's. Floating around that are the people who are somehow monitoring this, at least one of which has their own motivations to change this particular future. Then again, what do I know? I'm experiencing this story as a jigsaw puzzle too and, after taking two runs into this particular trip, I'm still only sure that I'm not sure about anything.

With a story this deliberately fractured, multilayered and open to different interpretations, it has to live or die on other factors. It can't simply rely on the story to hook us because after a couple of times through, I still don't know for sure what that story is telling us. I do like the basics that it uses as building blocks, the idea that in this world, wherever it is, there are people with talents and those talents can be used to form and reform that world. I like that the script refuses to answer our questions but is content to pose others in dialogue. "What do we really know?" asks Ayana, one of those double characters, the vendor who sets up next to Chris and who, hardly coincidentally, sees his almost fiancée for psychiatric help. "We think we have some say in how things happen?" I also like how some characters remain tantalisingly unexplained and thus open to interpretation, like the hippie with the spider tattoo on his neck. Is he God? Is he some nature spirit, given that we never see him outside the forest? Is he a humanoid visualisation of a place? Who knows? We can argue that all day.

If the story defies analysis, at least the performances of cast and crew are quantifiable. MacLeod Andrews is a decent lead actor, reminding of Jake Gyllenhaal in both looks and screen presence. He has surprisingly few credits to his name, IMDb suggesting that this is his first feature. Derek Morgan is very capable too, even if his character fades somewhat, to be replaced by Mina Vesper Gokal as the new vendor, Ayana. I'm still not sure about her performance here, as it doesn't seem to find a consistent tone. Andrews acts as if the story revolves around his character, while Gokal seems to react to him and others rather than setting her own stage. I've actually seen her before, in a dubious cannibal vs. zombie movie initially called *Holocaust Holocaust* and later renamed to its tagline, *Destined to Be Ingested*. This is the superior film, but not because she had a bigger part. Kelly Sullivan is better as Jina, though she was much better before we start asking too many questions about who she is and thus what she's doing.

Behind the camera, things are capable enough for us to translate what we see in an attempt to figure out the story. The camera moves oddly, making the whole thing feel disjointed, and the editing enhances the trippy feel. Characters have a habit of moving in a consistent direction, yet suddenly be somewhere else, whether that change can be interpreted as physical, astral or metaphorical. The view often waves around, though in more of a buoyant, floating way than a traditional handheld one. The score is strong, the odd combination of cello, harp and percussion making it memorable.

On the negative side, the footage of Chris and Jina interacting on a New York street was clearly guerrilla style shooting and there are too many people obviously looking at the camera for us to focus. The scenes in the Mine are crazy low budget and unconvincing. And I'm at a loss to explain the ending, which feels to me like a huge copout. I think I've figured out most of the plot after two trips through *Found in Time*, but not all and the ending especially makes no sense to me.

I wish my readers luck in getting further than I did. I'd love to hear what other people read into this film and whether it made sense to them. I'd love to know if the ending felt right to anyone, or if they sat there watching the credits roll wondering whether they'd blipped out for a while just as Chris does periodically in the story.

To be honest, I'm still not absolutely sure what causes Chris to experience the world in the way he does and, if it isn't inherent, who's causing it. There are so many questions here that every time I think I've got it down, I start to argue with myself about whether I've understood any of it.

Found in Time will surely be right up the alley of those who tend to appreciate complexity for its own sake. I enjoy being treated like a grown-up by filmmakers and given something substantial to get my teeth into, but I don't enjoy being led down the garden path by something that can't be explained at the end. I'm not yet convinced that Arthur Vincie understands the story he wrote, but I may well end up giving it a third attempt to figure out.

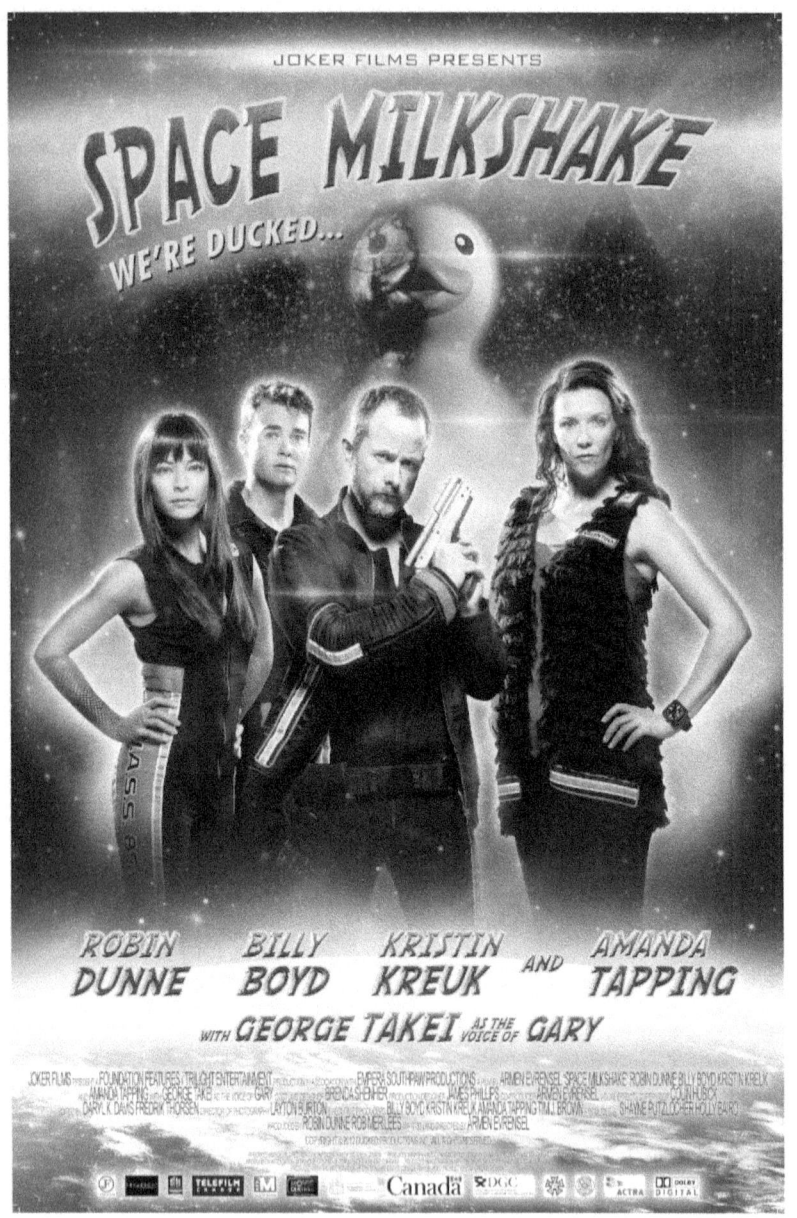

Space Milkshake (2012)

Director: Armen Evrensel
Writer: Armen Evrensel
Stars: Robin Dunne, Billy Boyd, Kristin Kreuk, George Takei and Amanda Tapping

More than ever before, this is sci-fi television turned into a comedy feature film. You might think immediately of *Galaxy Quest*, but that mostly spoofed one show and was cast chiefly with movie actors. As befits its title, *Space Milkshake* spoofs so many sci-fi shows that you'll feel compelled to count them and it's cast from a whole slew of them too.

Out of a cast of seven, three of whom only provide voices, we're provided with two lead actors from *Sanctuary* and one from each of *Smallville*, *Star Trek*, *Stargate SG-1*, *Stargate Atlantis* and *Supernatural*. Amanda Tapping turns out to be most of these on her own, as she was Maj. Samantha Carter in both *Stargate SG-1* and *Stargate: Atlantis*, Dr. Helen Magnus on *Sanctuary* (both the web series and the ensuing TV show), and is now recurring on *Supernatural* as Naomi. Her *Sanctuary* co-star is Robin Dunne, who played Dr. Will Zimmerman; *Smallville* is represented by Kristin Kreuk, who played Lana Lang; and George Takei's voice is here from *Star Trek*.

There's also Billy Boyd from *The Lord of the Rings* movies, which breaks the whole alliterative 'S' motif, but he's clearly trying to be Simon Pegg from *Shaun of the Dead*, just as a Scotsman, so perhaps it all works out in the end.

He's Anton Balvenie, the captain of the Regina, not a galaxy exploring spaceship but an Orbital Sanitation Station, number 8518. His crew aren't astronauts, they're garbage collectors because, in the 22nd century, space debris is a serious problem, as is clear from the ring of rubbish we see around the planet Earth. One collision is enough to prompt space travel to be halted for months, so clearly it's important to make sure that doesn't happen. Tasked with keeping the spacelanes clear, busy and moving are crews like the Regina's, who are entry level techs, one of them seeing orbit for the first time. As you can easily imagine, this is a dysfunctional crew in a barely functional station with an unorthodox set of priorities.

What sparks the plot is a cargo shuttle which takes off from the Quantum Transportation Research Station in Antartica, disappears, reappears and collides with a orbiting screw. Balvenie plays it by the book and refuses to clear the way, but leaps at the chance to salvage the vessel afterwards, even against direct orders. They promptly pick up a power source from the rubble, which you won't be too surprised to discover causes the Regina to travel in ways it doesn't expect.

Next thing they know, they're out of touch with everything and the orbiting trash that they know so well has vanished. Now the crew of four, along with a computer that they haven't even fixed yet, need to figure out where they are and how they can get home. Given that it's often a stretch for them to even talk to each other, it's hardly going to be an easy ride. The bizarre events that start to unfold under their very noses only serve to render that outcome even more unlikely.

And so, as we wait to see how the story will pan out, we watch the characters. The first obvious comparison is *Red Dwarf*, a British show built on characters and wild sci-fi shenanigans. This film and that TV show have much in common: both of them follow a tiny crew of menial workers in a huge spacecraft who have been cut off from the rest of humanity and may well be all that's left. Boyd, looking utterly unlike Pippin from *The Lord of the Rings*, is nominally in charge and he has the same sort of officious, by the book nature as Rimmer in *Red Dwarf*, but his idea of leadership is sticking to a schedule. Everything happens when it's scheduled: from breakfast to bedtime and from calisthenics to Scrabble. He's also perpetually in the middle of whatever is going on, because he finds it difficult to preserve any form of relationship, whether official or personal, as proved by the broken one he has with his second-in-command and former girlfriend, Valentina, played by Amanda Tapping.

Valentina would appear to have precisely nothing in common with Balvenie except the Regina and she's happily trying to leave both. Fortunately she doesn't, because she's the key to getting back home again, through the plot convenience that she used to work at the Quantum Transportation Research Station under Prof. Gary Pinback, who theorised about interdimensional travel to parallel realities. As luck would have it, Gary is on board too, having been thrust into a transdimensional rift and brought on board in the form of a rubber duck that collides with the Regina after it shifts. Here's where the Douglas Adams influences come in. Like the B Ark's captain in *The Hitch-Hiker's Guide to the Galaxy*, Valentina spends a lot of time in the bath. That show explained that "you're never alone with a rubber duck"; this film applies that to a form of *Alien*, right down to the moves of Dr. Pinback's face hugger phase, before he becomes Audrey from *The Little Shop of Horrors*.

Here to battle Gary is Tilda, initially the blasé operations officer who doesn't talk much but soon the parallel universe robot version trying to save infinite universes from destruction. She still doesn't talk much, at least initially, but she looks like Kristin Kreuk, so it's hardly a shock to find the Everyman of the bunch, Jimmy Anderson, falling for her anyway.

He's the new guy, a tech who's on board with faked paperwork to fix Wendi, the ship's computer, another *Red Dwarf* parallel, as it changes sex but not name partway through. "It's not as exciting as I thought it'd be," says Jimmy at one point, talking about life on an orbital station, but needless to say he's soon proved wrong. Robin Dunne has a lot of fun as Jimmy, playing him as loosely as Kreuk is precise as Tilda. There's another *Hitch-Hiker's Guide to the Galaxy* nod when the two find a way to communicate with each other, through a Scrabble board, an appropriate parallel to their situation in many ways.

Surprisingly, given the plethora of British sci-fi references during the build, *Space Milkshake* is a Canadian film, shot in Saskatchewan, whose capital city gave its name to the story's setting, the Regina. Its most notable successes are in channelling those diverse British influences into something new, which is a tough balancing act to keep and one that isn't consistently successful. Almost everything here is derivative, but for maybe two thirds of the film it's kept interesting with fresh characters and neat, quirky situations.

The brokedown machinery, so reminiscent of Ron Goulart novels but more likely sourced from Douglas Adams here, provides neat little touches throughout, like the food outlet that only dishes out sandwiches, even if it's just a reimagining of the Sirius Cybernetic Corporation's Nutrimatic drinks dispenser in *The Hitch-Hiker's Guide to the Galaxy* whose advanced A.I. only ever produces a substance that is "almost, but not quite, entirely unlike tea". I loved the door to the control room which looks like it ought to retract but never does, thus serving mostly to trip up Jimmy on a regular basis, a recurring gag that grounds him for us.

Unfortunately, while the final act is just as derivative, it's far more clichéd. Instead of enjoying the homages and acknowledging their sources with a smile, the later scenes frequently contain less targeted references and far more generic sci-fi moments that are unworthy of inclusion. I didn't find myself cringing at any point during the first hour, however recognisable much of the material was, but that was far from a rare reaction later on in the film, where Armen Evrensel, who wrote and directed, may well have just run out of influences to nod at.

Just like the film as a whole, each of the characters build well but once they reach a certain point, they stagnate into cliché and all of them deserved more. Tilda should have been more than a *Galaxina* clone. Valentina should have had a better crisis of choice. Anton shouldn't have been sidelined. Jimmy, especially, deserved much more of a focus given that Robin Dunne is technically top billed and he's who we're supposed to identify with.

In fact, the entire crew take a backseat once Gary the tentacled rubber duck shows up, not because he's a classic screen villain but because the voice work of George Takei utterly steals the show. I remember Takei well from the original series of *Star Trek* and even more from the movies, but he was merely a good part of a good ensemble cast at that point in his career. Since his reinvention in the internet age, he's become a bona fide star, thus far resisting becoming a caricature of himself like William Shatner, even if that's perhaps inevitable. He simply has fun here, as he apparently does in everything he puts his name to. Since his last *Star Trek* feature in 1991, I've enjoyed him having a blast in *Bug Buster* and two *Oblivion* movies and I absolutely want to watch him play the sensei being rescued by the title characters in *Ninja Cheerleaders*.

Unfortunately, he doesn't always pick the best movies to have fun in. This one is certainly better than *Bug Buster*, but it needed to raise its game to match his contribution and unfortunately it fell apart instead.

The International
Horror & Sci-Fi Film Festival

2013

Showcase Features

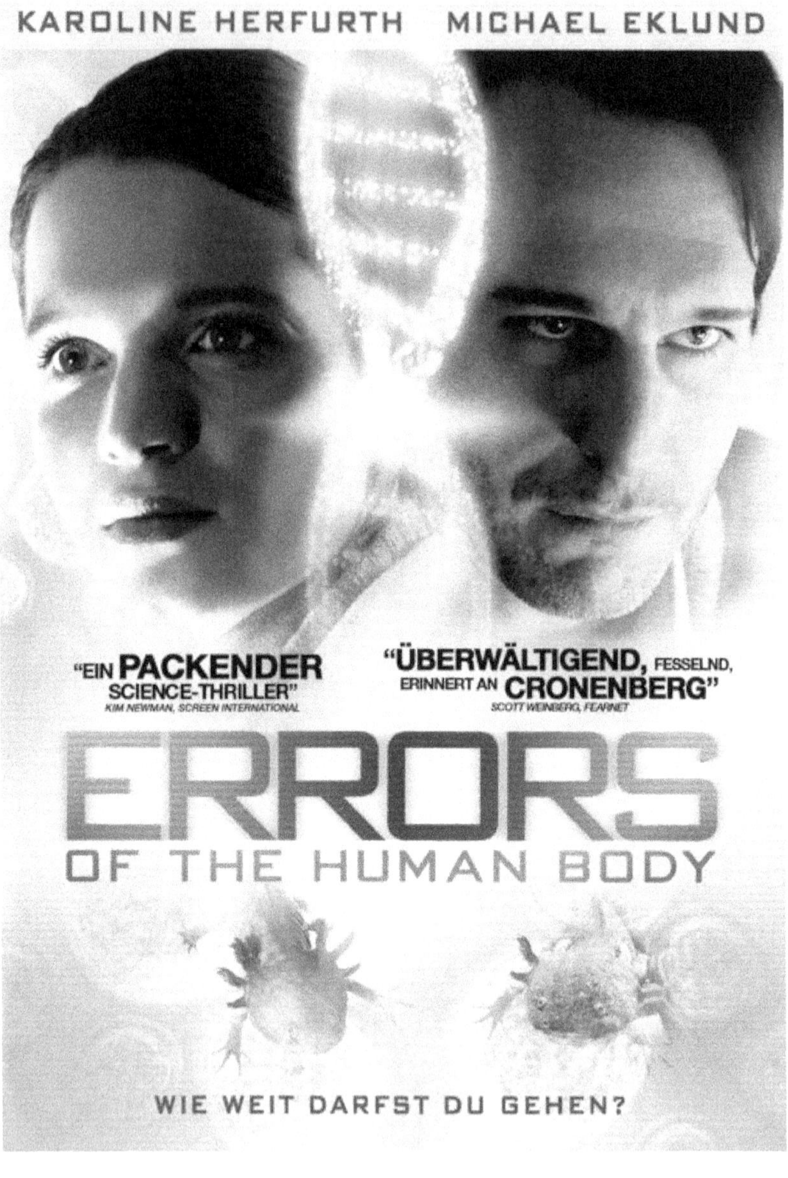
KAROLINE HERFURTH MICHAEL EKLUND
"EIN PACKENDER SCIENCE-THRILLER"
KIM NEWMAN, SCREEN INTERNATIONAL
"ÜBERWÄLTIGEND, FESSELND, ERINNERT AN CRONENBERG"
SCOTT WEINBERG, FEARNET
ERRORS
OF THE HUMAN BODY
WIE WEIT DARFST DU GEHEN?

Errors of the Human Body (2012)

Director: Eron Sheean
Writer: Shane Danielsen, from a story by Eron Sheean
Stars: Michael Eklund, Karoline Herfurth, Tómas Lemarquis and Rik Mayall

This multinational science fiction thriller, shot in Germany by an Australian with a Canadian in the lead and prominent supporting roles for German, Icelandic, British and Japanese actors, takes a worthy new approach to its genre and gets a lot right.

Like all the best science fiction, it tells a quintessentially human story within its scientific framework, this one centered around communication, which here goes a lot further than merely the ability of people to talk to each other. The film's director, Eron Sheean, within a Q&A during the picture's US première at Austin's Fantastic Fest in 2012, explained that it was "about a breakdown in communication, both on the surface in the characters and internally with the cells." If our innate ability to communicate is what moves us forward as individuals and as a race, the lead character, Dr. Geoff Burton, quickly sets the stage to move in the opposite direction as he's socially broken, unable to talk to his ex-wife, his ex-mistress turned new co-worker and, well, pretty much anyone else.

The good news is that Burton is played by Michael Eklund, who turns in a stunning performance one year before *The Call* but two after his role in Xavier Gans's *The Divide*, surely cast here because Sheean wrote and produced that picture, even though it's this one which promptly became his demo reel.

Initially he's a little reminiscent of Aaron Hotchner in *Criminal Minds* in the way that he's clearly very bright and capable but also very insular, as well as in how he loses that clinical air as the script lets loose on him with brutal irony. As the plot escalates, Eklund's acting escalates with it so that his character falls apart with starkly believable effect. Before we get to that point, of course, we're supposed to see his potential both as that future nightmare waiting to happen and as simply the new research scientist at the Max

Planck Institute of Molecular Cell Biology and Genetics in Dresden, Germany. He was invited here by its head, Samuel Mead, in the form of a very serious Rik Mayall, looking more like a politician here than he ever did as Alan B'stard, M.P.

Burton has moved to Dresden for two reasons.

One is that he's a very talented scientist, notable for pioneering work at the University of Massachusetts on the early detection of embryonic abnormalities. Originally he was a bacterial biochemist, but was drawn to genetics because of his son, who suffered and died at the age of a single week from a rare genetic mutation that now bears his name, Burton's Syndrome.

The other is that his work had become entangled in what Mead describes as a "politicised environment" back in the States, where he couldn't be fired outright because of tenure but could have his funding progressively restricted until he quit of his own accord.

He'll have a lot more freedom at the Planck Institute to pursue his work, though he's quick to explain to audiences that his pre-screening of embryos does not mean that he's practising eugenics. This is Germany, after all.

Of course, this is a movie so there are plot points waiting for him in Dresden too, less believable but more cinematic in their ability to spin a yarn around Burton and his work.

The one he knows about is Rebekka Fiedler, his former intern and mistress, presumably a strong reason why he's no longer married to his wife, who is now pregnant by her new man. What he doesn't know yet is exactly what Fiedler has been doing in her work to regenerate limbs or what a previous partner, Jarek Novak, has spun that work into in a secret lab in the bowels of the institute.

Naturally, he'll find out soon enough, given that the reason Mead reached out to him in the first place is the condition of her research. She's been achieving wonders with axolotls, regenerating limbs at rapid speed, but she's been unable to transfer that success over to mice, which are Novak's specialty. Of course, it's not rocket science to see where this is going to take us, but it unfolds against the backdrop of two key ideas, both outlined during Burton's first lunch at the institute. The first comes from an odd but endearing duck called Chiba, while the second comes from Novak himself, keen to the degree of fanatical.

Chiba reconstructs the skeletons of the fish that he eats in the cafeteria, because he likes to see big pictures. Too many of us talk about food but not how it got to us, naturally echoing how many of us talk about the cures that medical science can provide but not the research it takes to perfect them. In other words, the end does not justify the means, even if we shroud the means in mystery and pretend that the end was always the beginning.

Novak plays up how he's the same as Burton, because of "taking risks, whatever it takes, new brave world." His personal dream is to harness the distribution power of mosquitos to spread vaccines to the populace rather than the usual disease. Rather than eradicating the problem, why not use science to transform it into the solution? It's an enticing concept, but while Chiba feels grounded but still interesting, Novak, with his stereotypically sinister bald head and expressive eyes, feels overly eager and freakish. What works is the combination of these two ideas, which ground the film neatly.

There are other strong aspects to the film. The pace is slow but measured, somewhat like Burton himself and the work he does. I've read that *Errors of the Human Body* is unparalleled in the accuracy with which it depicts "the look and feel of a high level research lab", to quote an IMDb review. This is surely mostly due to Sheean's access to the real Max Planck Institute as an artist in residency. He developed the film over six years at the institute and was gleefully happy when they agreed to let him shoot it there.

This is why the colours are so interesting, very clinical in tone. We might expect gleaming white everything from generations of hospital shows on television, but these shades are more blue and green; much of the look is the colour of brushed steel with a little bit of light against it. However, that accuracy surely owes some of its success to the pace, which refuses to leap from breakthrough to breakthrough like levels in a game and unfolds instead with the patience of clinical testing in which every negative result is important as well.

The varied cast help to ground this too. Just because this is a German institute doesn't mean that each of the scientists working there has to be German. Eklund is Canadian, but his odd accent is appropriately a hard one to place, given that Burton presumably moves wherever the work takes him. Karoline Herfurth is German, though she's fluent in the English language and starred in English language productions before this, such as Tom Tykwer's *Perfume: The Story of a Murderer* and the Kate Winslet movie, *The Reader*. It's somewhat telling that Herfurth buries Rebekka so deeply in her work that we don't think of her outside it, even though she once again hooks up with Burton in Dresden. By comparison, Tómas Lemarquis screams for attention as Novak, not only because he escalates him well up the fanatic scale, but because he's cast so stereotypically. This Icelandic actor without a hair on his head is the very image of science unbound, but he deserves praise for his acting rather than just what he looks like.

The negative side begins with the convenience. Even if I can admire the irony that pervades later scenes and the particularly blistering realisation of the past that comes along with it, I have to acknowledge that it only works because of a stacked set of plot conveniences that are too contrived to buy into.

The scientific grounding of the film, which extends so far as a useful PDF download, is seriously stretched by the later scenes that are grounded by their cinematic impact rather than their science. Of course, many will prefer the thrills of the third act to the slower build which aims for coldness, clinicality and distance rather than eye candy. I recently revisited *The Astronaut's Wife*, a picture which ultimately fails because it achieves the sense of alien detachment that it aims for and so detaches the audience as well. Sheean keeps us more engaged, but he still doesn't seem sure who we are.

This doesn't work as a horror movie, as neatly horrific as a few moments are, and it doesn't offer the tension of a thriller. Even as sci-fi, it's more sci than fi, then more fi than sci.

In the end, it's really a drama, albeit one that's so drenched in science that it ought to shimmer with dry ice like the experiments in the Planck Institute labs. The technical details gradually reveal themselves to be background as the themes take over, and most prominent among them is the guilt that's haunted Burton since the death of his son. Perhaps he was a great scientist before that, but we can only presume that it led to his adultery, his divorce, his banishment from American science and the errors he makes in this film both as a scientist and a human being.

The title serves double duty, highlighting not only the mutations that drive his work but also its lead character with all the little obsessions that chip away at his genius. It ends up as a character study, brilliantly portrayed by Michael Eklund. The science which drove the film's creation simply can't keep up with him, perhaps why it eventually disappoints as a story but not for a moment as a performance. Sheean showed a good deal of promise here, but Eklund's career should skyrocket.

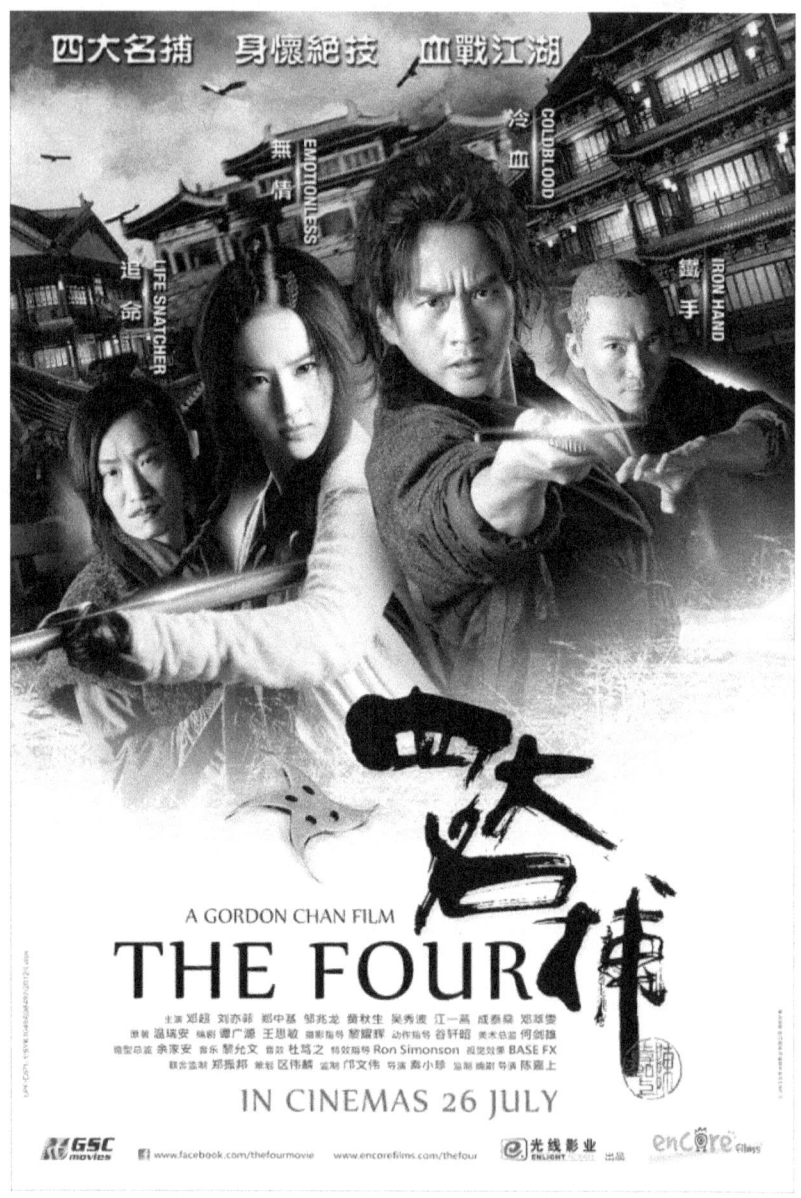

The Four (2012)

Directors: Gordon Chan and Janet Chun
Writers: Gordon Chan, Maria Wong and Frankie Tam, from the novels by Woon Swee Oan
Stars: Deng Chao, Liu Yi Fei, Ronald Cheng, Collin Chou and Anthony Wong

The Four, one of many adaptations of a series of novels by Woon Swee Oan, is an infuriating picture that throws so much at us that multiple viewings are required to avoid getting quickly lost. I was notably confused during my first time through, less so on a second and not at all on a third, by which point the film was a lot of fun. I'm fond of it now, as flawed as it is, but it really shouldn't take three times through to grasp a plot.

Much of the problem boils down to it being a sort of Chinese *X-Men*, introducing us to so many characters so quickly that it's tough to keep track of them. Some of that was definitely deliberate on the part of the filmmakers, as if they wanted us to have to watch it twice to figure it all out. For instance, we catch a glimpse of many of the lead characters in the sprawling opening sequence, a one shot CGI deal with a camera swooping and soaring like a bird, literally as we're vaguely following a pigeon for surveillance purposes. They appear like featured extras, enough to stand out from the crowd, marked as people we should notice, but only for a moment before they're gone again and the pigeon moves on.

However, while we see most of the primary characters during this opening sequence, we have to wait until the first action scene to be introduced to who they are, what they do and why they matter, albeit so quickly that it's tough to keep track.

They all head over to the Drunken Moon, a rather delightful inn, to watch Jia San try to sell a fake coin cast that presumably ties to the rampant forgery going on in the town. A debt collector known as Life Snatcher meets him, but when he realises that their wine is poisoned, all hell breaks loose. Life Snatcher battles another martial arts master, while others use wilder talents to stop Jia San escaping through the use of body duplication magic. One young lady in a wheelchair hurls things around telekinetically, while her boss uses qigong power to pull people towards him like a tractor beam. We watch this all unfold at lightning speed until they all end up outside, trapped by the constabulary known as Department Six, who descended en masse on the inn and aim to arrest everyone. Only now do we get to the point, that we have a clash of authorities going on.

Department Six are the standard police force in this city and they scare most people silly because they exude brutal and militaristic power. They're fond of intimidation tactics and shows of force, which inevitably lead to demonstrations of overkill like the one we've just witnessed. Their uniforms are dark and fetishistic, as are their headquarters which are vast, echoing and arrogant in their overt worship of power. Their commandant is Lord Liu who runs Department Six through a standard chain of command with four supreme constables.

It took me a long while to realise that these characters, who were introduced much earlier than this point, are *not* the Four of the title. Then again, this is an origin story, so we're watching how the real Four come together and where they fit in the grand scheme of things. At this point, only one them works for Department Six; he's Cold Blood, the master who fought Life Snatcher at the Drunken Moon. He's about to be publicly fired by Lord Liu but secretly tasked with infiltrating the Divine Constabulary, the secret organisation which we've also just met without realising it.

The Divine Constabulary couldn't be any more different than Department Six if it tried and I loved everything about them except the contradiction which sets them up. Apparently, they're a secret police force, small and select, which reports directly to the emperor through their calm, polite and humble leader, Zhuge Zhengwo, the man with the tractor beam power.

Department Six haven't heard of them, so plan to arrest them at the Drunken Moon until the Prince arrives and orders Zhuge to show Lord Liu his imperial badge of office. Yet this secret police force hitherto unnoticed by everyone has their own headquarters in town with a sign on the door reading 'Divine Constabulary'. That anomalous sign notwithstanding, it's a glorious place. It's utterly organic, a light and inviting home full of wood and paper, space and curves. Nobody wears uniforms and nobody barks orders. They just wouldn't fit, as the atmosphere is one of trust and the group of people who live and work there feel far more like a family than a police force.

Having saved Life Snatcher from arrest by Department Six, Zhuge invites him to stay, to become one of them. He wants to leave, but is suckered into staying through flattery and wine. Lots of wine. Aunt Poise from the Drunken Moon brings good wine and they drink for free. With Life Snatcher under their roof, the Divine Constabulary now have three of the Four within their organisation, the other two being Iron Hands and Emotionless. Are you keeping up?

Emotionless is the more obvious; she's the telekinetic girl in the wheelchair, who sees into people's thoughts and therefore quantify the strength of their qigong power. To go where she can't, she has a bird companion, Skywings, the very pigeon who led us through that merry dance through the sky to show us the key players during the opening credits. Iron Hands is the blacksmith and carpenter, who forges no end of magnificent gadgets for the group, including a wonderful wheelchair/Segway for Emotionless to power with her mind. Presumably he also built the various secret doors and the awesome steampunk library too. I want.

There are many others, but those are the major players because they're ranked among the Four, even if that doesn't seem to be official nomenclature. The rest are colourfully named, of course: Big Wolf, Dingdong and Guts, not to mention Bell, who in the form of Tina Xiang may just be the cutest creature I've ever seen.

And into their ranks comes Cold Blood to shake everything up. He isn't merely a Department Six constable undercover, he's also some sort of moody beast man who was raised by wolves and he quite obviously has the hots for Emotionless, wheelchair or not.

Other key players include Ji Yaohua, the leader of the ladies hired into Department Six at the beginning of the film, on the orders of the Prince, and Lord An Shigeng, the God of Wealth, who she's really working for and who's clearly highlighted as the villain of the piece very soon into the picture. Lord An has the coolest moves yet: the ability to freeze people or burn them alive at a single touch. Stopping a martial arts master from killing you with his sword by catching it in your teeth is a pretty neat trick too.

Whew! With this dizzying array of characters finally introduced in entirety after about a quarter of the film's two hour running time, we can finally start to watch their dynamics click into gear like a clockwork plot.

Unfortunately, while this plot does unfolds against an agreeably cool background of imaginative locations, wirework fights and Machiavellian intrigue, it really isn't that interesting in itself. It's obvious after twenty minutes that it's all going to come down to a big battle with the big boss, Lord An, and, given that this is the first part of a planned trilogy, we surely know that the good guys at the Divine Constabulary are going to win.

This knowledge lessens the tension and renders some of the subplots meaningless, like the battle between Department Six and the Divine Constabulary. Like the heroes of the franchise are ever in danger of losing their mandate to the local guys? To be frank, at this point, do we even care about the rampant forgery plaguing the town? Again, we know that's all going to get taken care of one way or another. We're too busy watching the people.

Ronald Cheng is the most engaging of the Four as Life Snatcher. He's a prolific actor who always provides good entertainment and he works well as the will he/won't he outsider who is always going to join in the end. Collin Chou has promise as Iron Hands and absolutely looks the part. He's the least used of the Four, so it's the writing that lets the character down rather than the actor. The moody stylings of Liu Yi Fei and Deng Chao as Emotionless and Cold Blood respectively might endear them to a particular demographic but I found them less interesting because they're a notably emo couple.

Fortunately, above the Four, is Anthony Wong as Zhuge Zhengwo. He's by far the most experienced member of the cast, typecast for years as notably outrageous villains, not least in his first Hong Kong Film Award winning role as the serial killer who baked his victims into meat pies in *The Untold Story*, a Category III *Sweeney Todd*. He steals every scene he's in here by being the opposite of outrageous, making us very aware that he has immense power but keeping it constantly in check.

On the side of the villains, Wu Xiu Bo is delightfully cocky as Lord An, at his best when commanding an army of reanimated corpses.

Jiang Yi Yan is much more vanilla as Ji Yaohua, not particularly memorable until her featured fight with Emotionless, which is highly entertaining.

As an origin story, there's less attention given to the villains and far more to those little dynamics between the characters that will no doubt work as ongoing subplots throughout the sequels. Lord An is more apparent here than the villains in *Guardians of the Galaxy*, another origin story with an ensemble cast of characters, but he and his minions clearly don't get the attention that the ongoing heroes do.

It's a real shame that there's so much shoehorned into the script, because we'd appreciate so much of this all the more if we didn't miss it by blinking. It's fine for us to miss little background details, because that sort of thing will draw us back to watch again, but losing introductions and key plot points like explaining the title is unforgiveable.

And, at the end of the day, the speed at which this unfolds is both what is most memorable about the film and its biggest flaw. The fights are cool but they're so frantic that we often can't catch what's going on. It took me two viewings to nail down who some of the minor characters were, why they were in the picture and what purpose they served, all because they're skipped over so quickly. Here's a key scene in the plot, but don't dally on it because here's another one and, if you didn't catch the first one, the next three won't make any sense at all.

On one level, this would have worked much better had it been slowed down to fit a four hour mini-series instead of a two hour feature. Perhaps I should seek out the TV series on the Hong Kong channel TVB, also titled *The Four*, which ran for 24 episodes of 45 minutes each. Then again, if we could easily figure out what's going on in a slower version of this film, its other flaws would become much more apparent and those are even more problematic.

Put simply, while this is a Chinese wuxia movie whose trappings couldn't be mistaken as being from any other culture, it's notably reminiscent of western superhero movies. The fact that I much prefer the look and feel of pictures like this to anything I've seen in any Marvel superhero movie thus far doesn't mean that it isn't acutely derivative. In what is starting to become a sad trend, this is a Hollywood action movie in Chinese clothes, for all that the source material was penned by a Malaysian Chinese novelist who studied in Taiwan and lives in Hong Kong.

It's formulaic stuff which tries to cloak its unoriginality in its blistering pace but fails because the more interested we become in the characters, the more we realise that their powers really aren't traditionally Chinese, they're just mutant powers from *X-Men* and its like translated into vaguely Chinese characteristics. Zhuge is Professor X, the Divine Constabulary is his school for mutants, Emotionless is a Rogue/Phoenix hybrid and so on.

If you can get past that, this is fun action fluff. After enough viewings.

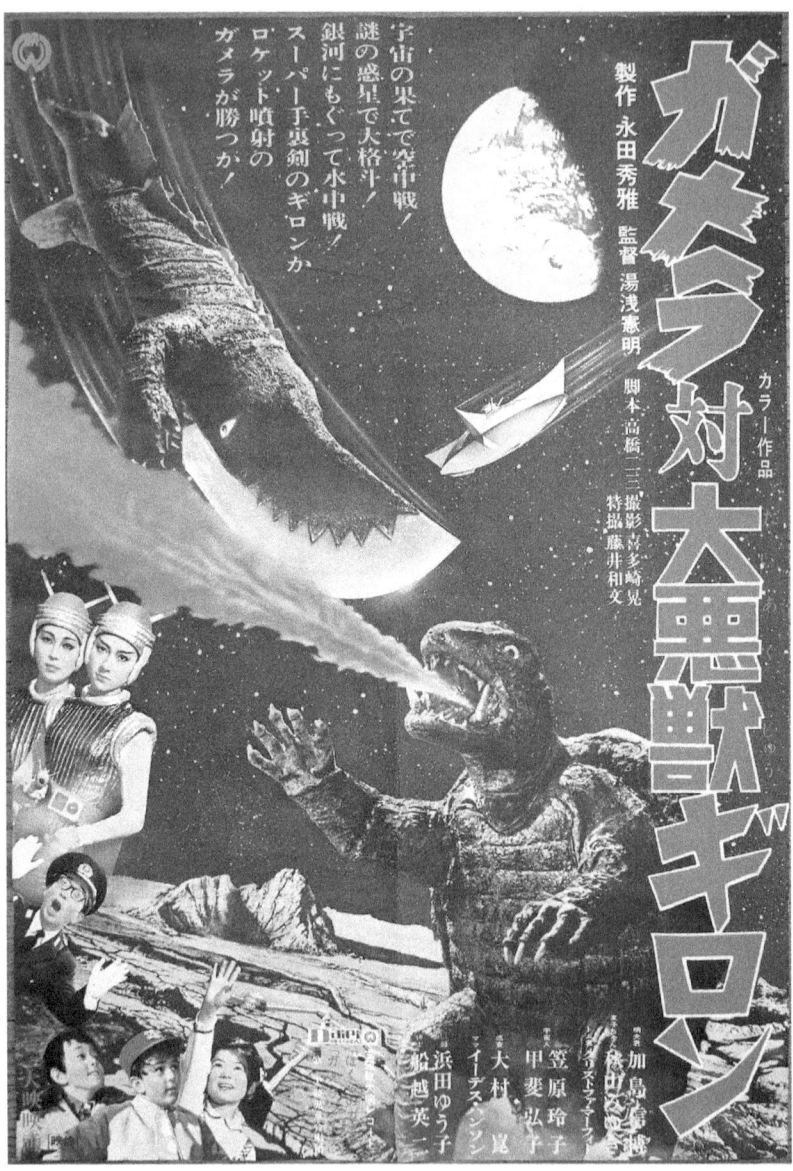

Gamera vs. Guiron (1969)

Director: Noriaki Yuasa
Writer: Nisan Takahashi
Stars: Nobuhiro Kajima, Miyuki Akiyama and Christopher Murphy

Tonight we went to the drive in for free movie night, but we left after *Guardians of the Galaxy* as the other half of the double bill was the reboot of *Teenage Mutant Ninja Turtles*. Once through that mess of a movie was enough for me, so I avoided a second viewing by heading home instead to watch a memorable turtle picture, *Gamera vs. Guiron*.

This is the fifth movie in Daiei's original Gamera series which was released Stateside by American International Pictures as *Attack of the Monsters*. Even in their television print, in a full screen ratio with an English dub and notably faded colour, it's still a great deal more fun than that latest Michael Bay debacle. Seen as it should be seen, in the widescreen version issued by Shout! Factory on DVD in the original Japanese and with crisp colour, it's a real treat. It's also a wilder ride because it restores the fight scene between Guiron and Space Gyaos to its full glory, one of those gloriously inappropriate moments in Japanese children's entertainment that force us into wondering whether we're watching a movie or dreaming one.

Now, let's be clear before we begin. This is an awful movie by most standards and it's not surprising that *Mystery Science Theater 3000* riffed on no less than five of the eight Showa era Gamera movies. In fact, it did so twice, firstly with a five episode marathon during its initial run on KTMA in Minneapolis, coincidentally the earliest surviving episodes of the show at present, and then again during episodes scattered throughout season three of the regular syndicated show, its debut season on Comedy Central. They riffed on a third version of this film, one dubbed into English so poorly by Sandy Frank Entertainment that its voice acting became a running joke in itself.

However awful the film is, we shouldn't forget that this was a movie for children, with a pair of boys in the lead roles, and, kaiju fans aside, it's easy to see how it would play much better to a young audience. Akio and Tom go on a great adventure, flying a spaceship to an alien planet, where they watch monsters fight, meet strange ladies, get saved by Gamera and return home safely. What glorious fun!

Bizarrely, given how great that sounds, it begins in a completely boring fashion, especially for kids, with no less than three sections before we can finally be introduced to Akio and Tom and get down to business.

First up is a brief introduction that effectively lets us on in the scientific secret that space is big, before pointing out to us that a star is in trouble. Then we get the opening credits, which unfold over some sort of lava flow, which I really hope isn't supposed to be the star in trouble. Finally, we meet Dr. Shiga, in the form of Eiji Funakoshi, who returns to the series after playing the lead, Dr. Hidaka, in the first Gamera movie. He's supposedly here to explain to the assembled press that the strange waves from space they're receiving aren't the same ones that the Brits are getting. This is an excuse to play us delightfully squeaky space age sound effects, courtesy of some delightfully squeaky analogue technology. Really Shiga is in the movie to explain to the kids watching why none of the planets in our solar system are viable candidates for the source, which is nonetheless somewhere nearby!

Fortunately, we have Akio and Tom on the case. They've been trying to figure out where the waves have been coming from too, using the portable telescope they keep on Akio's balcony.

Akio is highly believable as a boy scientist, as Nobuhiro Kajima ably captures that magic combination of knowledge, optimism and discovery; surprisingly, this was his only film. Tom, on the other hand, who is as Japanese as the name suggests, is very much stuck playing the role of Akio's sidekick, Christopher Murphy proving endearing but apparently not capable of displaying emotion on screen. He does appear to be fluent in the Japanese language; if he was dubbed, it wasn't by Sandy Frank Entertainment!

The kawaii factor is reserved for little Tomoko, Akio's younger sister, left behind when the boys embark on their adventure for no reason other than to be disbelieved when she explains to mum that they tracked a spaceship on their telescope to the vacant lot where they play, cycled over in the morning and promptly flew away in it. And I thought that was routine behaviour for Japanese kids!

The spaceship is an obvious model, of course, but it's a cool one with huge fins and a revolving top. It's designed in a minimalist style with a few abstract wall designs and a preponderence of triangles, but few actual controls, navigational or otherwise. Then again, the ship is apparently flown by remote control, even if we're supposed to believe for a moment or two that the kids successfully launched it themselves.

We are asked to buy into a great deal here! Given that they're hurtling into space at ludicrous speed, the sparkly meteor that quickly threatens to fly into them must really have been flying backwards at just less than ludicrous speed. Either that or the laws of physics don't apply and we don't want to go there yet, given the early emphasis on 'hard science'.

Fortunately for them, Gamera is apparently cruising in their immediate vicinity and he promptly steps in to save them, before flying in convoy for a while so that we can sing along with the Gamera theme song. Sure, this is a kids' movie, but these plot conveniences aren't just ridiculous, they're blatant too.

Then again, we shouldn't argue too much about little details like this when we're watching a movie starring a giant, jet-propelled, spacefaring turtle, hardly the most grounded character in Japanese cinema; even Godzilla seems completely believable by comparison.

However Gamera was one of the major box office successes of Daiei, one of a half dozen great studios of postwar Japan. They produced Akira Kurosawa's *Rashomon*, the first Japanese film to win an international award: it won both the Golden Bear at the Venice Film Festival and an honorary Academy Award (the Best Foreign Language Film award hadn't been introduced yet). They produced Teinosuke Kinugasa's *Gate of Hell*, the first Japanese film to screen internationally in colour; it also won an honorary Oscar and the Palme d'Or at Cannes. They also produced such legendary Japanese films as Kenji Mizoguchi's *Ugetsu* and *Sansho the Bailiff*, Yasujiro Ozu's *Floating Weeds* and the long running Shintaro Katsu series featuring Zatoichi, the Blind Swordsman. Gamera was certainly in good company.

Akio and Tom soon find themselves in bad company. Landing on an alien planet, the first thing they see is Space Gyaos, an alien version of Gamera's most popular enemy painted silver. Gyaos is a giant airborne monster with a triangular head who had been introduced in the third movie, *Gamera vs Gyaos* and would return later, both in the first Heisei era movie, *Gamera: Guardian of the Universe*, and the Millennium era film, *Gamera the Brave*.

These eras don't denote period Japanese settings, by the way, just the different series that Gamera has appeared in thus far: seven Showa films from 1965 to 1971 and an eighth in 1980 as the studio was facing bankruptcy, three Heisei titles in the late nineties and one Millennium picture in 2006. Gamera is portrayed differently in each of these eras, with a different design and different powers. The Showa era saw him released by a nuclear explosion from natural cryogenic storage in the Arctic circle to apparently fly around and save children. He retracts his legs to ignite his jets and is able to breathe fire.

Here's where we get that amazing fight scene that was censored for *Attack of the Monsters*. It's not a long battle, as the very first blow is a self inflicted injury, with a laser from the eyes of Space Gyaos bouncing off Guiron and severing its own leg. Guiron is an odd monster, not only in how it looks but also in how it fights. Space Gyaos looks like the standard Japanese actor in a big rubber suit, but Guiron mostly restricts itself to crouching on all fours, its huge knife shaped head apparently weighing it down. Then it leaps into the air when the time is right to slice something off its enemy, like the wing it neatly removes from Space Gyaos's body in mid-air, sending it into a spin and a crash landing. Then it jumps again to sever the other wing on the ground, leaving the monster with only one of its four limbs left.

Our eyes are already wide as we're not used to seeing severed kaiju limbs wriggling on the ground or spurting purple kaiju blood, but it continues. Guiron decapitates his rival, then proceeds to chop off more slices. Remember, kids' movie!

Of course, we're going to end up with Gamera battling Guiron as the title has to mean something, but it'll take a while before we get there. First, we need to watch Akio and Tom explore the nearby alien city until they run into the only two inhabitants left on the planet. Naturally, they're cute Japanese ladies, but that's amazingly explained, as is their ability to speak fluent Japanese. Now, it isn't explained well, I grant you, but it is explained!

They're Barbella and Florbella, names which translate to Sweet as a Bird and Pretty as a Flower, ironically given that they're planning to eat our heroes' brains and invade the planet Earth with the advanced tech from their dying civilisation. They have plenty of that: teleportation wigwams, a remote control spaceship and a device that allows them to change their speech into any language, really useful when you're the only two people left on the entire planet. Guiron is their watchdog, who protects them from other giant monsters; beyond a giant knife shaped head, he can also hurl shuriken through telekinesis. Remember, kids' movie!

I don't know about you, but when I was six, I'd have fallen in love with a movie where kids accompany a jet propelled turtle to an alien planet in their hijacked spaceship, teleport around an alien city, narrowly avoid having their brains eaten by cute alien women and yet still get home in time for supper. Having a set of monsters like Gamera, Guiron and Space Gyaos is just icing on the cake, especially as it's notably gory icing. For some reason, we just don't see bizarre monsters counting down to the moment where they decapitate an enemy on *Teletubbies* or *Bob the Builder* and they don't feature a single drop of spurting alien monster blood. I could argue that the western world might be a much more interesting place if they did.

Don't get me started on Japanese TV shows where child actors get to shoot guns in the holy name of saving their country, their world and their universe. Sure, Japanese children get to spend way more hours at school cramming for exams, but they get wildly imaginative wish fulfilment television, so that's a fair trade off.

Now that I'm much older than six, it's impossible not to see the wild flaws, leaps and conveniences that pervade this movie, and frankly I'm sure that my grandkids would see them too. Perhaps I need to introduce them to Gamera movies like this one to see if they find the magic or the stupidity. It would be worth it to hear them singing the Gamera theme song instead of Carly Jepsen or Justin Bieber.

I have no idea at all why *Gamera vs Guiron* was screened at the International Horror & Sci-Fi Film Festival, as it didn't tie to anyone attending or any apparent theme. It merely followed another out of the blue classic selection at the 2012 festival, *The Brain That Wouldn't Die*. That slot didn't exist in the much smaller 2011 event and it wasn't continued into 2014, when the showcase features had plenty of interesting new movies to screen instead. The only classic shown in 2014 was *Cujo*, with Dee Wallace-Stone there to give a Q&A.

Now, I'd have gone to *Gamera vs Guiron* if Christopher Murphy had been there to talk about it!

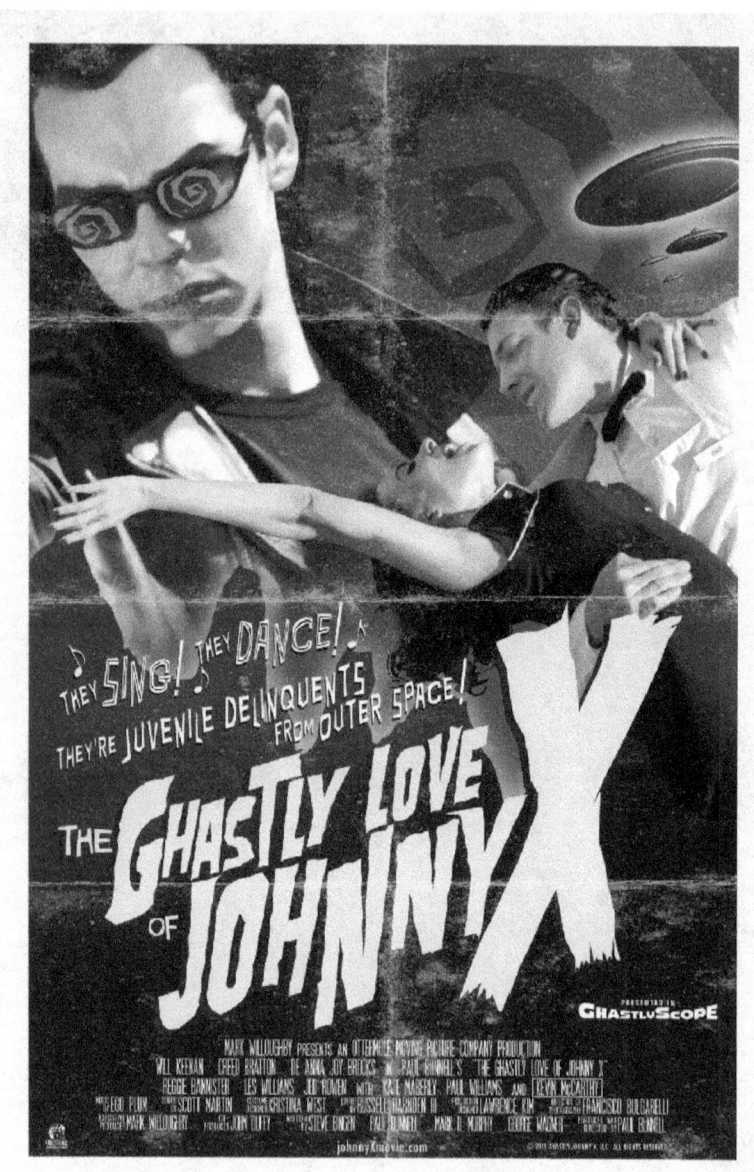

The Ghastly Love of Johnny X (2012)

Director: Paul Bunnell
Writers: Steve Bingen, Paul Bunnell, Mark D Murphy and George Wagner
Stars: Will Keenan, Creed Bratton, De Anna Joy Brooks, Reggie Bannister, Les Williams, Kate Maberly and Kevin McCarthy

I've been to a lot of film festivals and I've heard a lot of Q&As, but I've never seen a movie that its own cast and crew apologised for as much as this one and that really didn't bode well.

Director Paul Bunnell is a bouncy, eager and enthusiastic soul who clearly loves film. He doesn't just love movies, he loves that film stock feel enough that he collects 16mm and 35mm prints and bought up the very last Eastman Plus-X 5231 Safety stock after production of it was discontinued so that he could shoot this in glorious black and white 35mm. He also spent over a decade of his life making this movie, the earliest scenes being shot as far back as 2002 with production stopping every time funding ran out and starting up again every time he managed to secure more. His cast and crew didn't believe it would ever get finished, but he stuck with it and here it is at last on the big screen. Yet his enthusiasm while presenting it was all for his next film, *Rocket Girl*, which he promises will be so much better than this one.

For a while, it's actually pretty good. The perpetually hip and thoroughly defiant Jonathan Xavier has been arrested and hauled in front of the Grand Inquisitor for, well, being perpetually hip and thoroughly defiant or some crime like that. The judge stands tall and strong, resplendent in his decorated Devo hat, but Johnny X waggles his eyebrows and manipulates him like a voodoo doll. And so he and his followers are exiled to the planet Earth, with one single hope that "an unselfish act will bring you home."

A year later they walk out of a cave, a not so magnificent seven looking rather like a gang of juvenile delinquents from the fifties. There are four guys and three chicks, each gender with its own finned out Thunderbird to spin up desert dust. Meanwhile, into some diner in the middle of nowhere walks a bunch of curves called

Bliss. She's Johnny's girl and she needs the help of Chip the soda jerk because the lizards are hot on her trail.

It's wild and it's wacky, with characters who are colourful even in black and white. As it becomes a musical, with lots of catchy refrains layered over each other, it feels like a winner. There's a strong *Forbidden Zone* vibe, with catchy music from Ego Plum, who coincidentally is working alongside Danny Elfman on the upcoming *Forbidden Zone* sequel. It's lively stuff, with a host of characters to keep us intrigued: the wicked cool Johnny with three varied stooges and a bevy of beauties with initials on their jackets to back him up, all to take on his dangerous dame who's stolen a dastardly device from him called the Resurrection Suit. All he has left to spark up a confrontation in the diner is an electric glove, but it's enough to keep him on top for now. Caught in the crossfire is King Clayton, a dubious promoter who reacts when the news on the diner TV highlights that Mickey O'Flynn, the Man with a Grin, the King of Cactus Rock, has disappeared.

In short we're thrown into this all at once, rather like Chip the soda jerk, and like him we're tasked with finding it in ourselves to leave our comfortable lives and embark upon a journey through whatever musically twisted retro-wasteland Paul Bunnell has conjured up for us. Frankly, at that point, we're all for it, and if we weren't, having the bountiful bosom of Bliss thrust into our face at an empty drive in as she sings a sultry salsa called *Hips That Never Lie* is enough to persuade us.

We're reminded of a slew of cult musicals, only beginning with *Forbidden Zone* and including *The Rocky Horror Picture Show, Repo! The Genetic Opera* and *Phantom of the Paradise*, films that maintain an enthusiastic following however many years it's been since they were originally released. I saw *Repo!* in a packed theatre before the shadowcasters took control and the promise in the air felt like the calm before a storm. For a little while, the same promise hung in the air here, but unfortunately only for a little while.

The point at which the film starts to fall apart is after we discover a dead Mickey O'Flynn on King Clayton's stage being manipulated, very badly, as a puppet. The flashback scene that explains how he died during a business discussion is a long, slow one that doesn't contribute much of anything to the movie except to take all the momentum built thus far and beat it to death.

Suddenly we start to notice a whole host of problems that only become more apparent as the picture runs on. I honestly never thought I'd say this about a musical but there aren't enough songs. What's more, the best ones are the early ones, meaning that any of the energy generated early on gradually dissipates. Scenes that ought to rage merely whimper, like the catfight. Plot convenience rears its ugly head in a number of ways all at once, not all of which I feel comfortable outlining in a review. A third of the way in is certainly an odd time to throw out a crucial plot twist though.

Perhaps the largest and most abiding problem is that *The Ghastly Love of Johnny X* is a product of its evolution. Creating a movie by patchwork over a decade doesn't bode well for consistency and having no less than four writers massage the script during that time bodes even worse.

Even the title becomes rather meaningless, not only because we can never really be sure what the ghastly love of Johnny X is but because the story gradually ceases to be about Johnny X at all. Even as we discover that Chip is Clayton's nephew and so bringing the Resurrection Suit to him means that it gets handed right over to Johnny, we switch focus to Mickey O'Flynn, rather bizarrely given that he's dead. But hey, the suit is so named for a reason and it inevitably sets up the rest of the film. The only reason that we can't write the rest in our heads is because suddenly Sluggo decides that he needs a rebel moment and turns from Johnny X stooge to James Bond villain.

Early on, Will Keenan was notably solid as Johnny X, pouting and posturing as if he's a cartoon version of Marlon Brando in *The Wild One*, a great character for someone who started out as Tromeo in *Tromeo and Juliet*. However he's consistently not fed the material he needs to maintain the persona, so as the film runs on, he simply fades, baby, to black.

Instead we watch Mickey O'Flynn, as patchwork a character as the movie he finds himself in. When he's still alive, he's a hybrid of Johnny Cash and Crispin Glover, with plenty of Roy Orbison thrown into the mix and maybe some Grandpa Munster too. After he dies and is brought back by the Resurrection Suit, he becomes either John Wayne as a zombie Bill Murray or Bill Murray as a zombie John

Wayne, one or the other. Creed Bratton, best known for the American version of *The Office*, is fascinating to watch as the King of Cactus Rock, but we continually wonder why we're watching him, even as we start to forget about Johnny X.

The second half of the film would be a complete train wreck, if only there weren't a host of magic moments to enjoy liberally sprinkled amongst the dreck.

As good guys turn bad and bad guys turn good, weak characters become strong and strong characters become weak, all without explanations offered, we start to despair. As plot conveniences, questionable decisions and unfathomable script directions multiply, we wonder why we're still watching. But we can't stop watching Mickey O'Flynn, whatever inappropriateness he's getting up to.

We certainly can't resist Cousin Quilty, a quirky talk show host played by the wonderful Paul Williams. He was originally cast as O'Flynn, but couldn't dedicate the time needed so was thankfully shifted over to Cousin Quilty, a gift of a part for him that he nails to perfection.

The costumes, sets and dialogue occasionally get it very right indeed. "The party isn't started," says Clayton to his girl Lily, "until I see the whites of your thighs."

It's entirely clear where this film went wrong, not just to us but to the people who made it. If Paul Bunnell had secured enough funding to make this in one shot, whether back in 2002 or in 2012, it would likely have been a riot, if not the cult favourite it obviously dreams of being. If it had been written by one writer, instead of being rewritten by four, it would surely have had more coherence and consistency. The actors did their best, but the conditions were tough. Keenan isn't fond of his work here and he does vanish from our attention after a strong start. He raves instead about De Anna Joy Brooks, who does the same to a lesser degree as Bliss. The first twenty minutes would be a great short for them, but the feature isn't theirs at all.

A film with this much imagination and flair, with actors like Keenan, Williams and Bratton, not to mention Kevin McCarthy in his last screen role as the Grand Inquisitor, should have resonated but now I want to forget it and go see *Rocket Girl* instead.

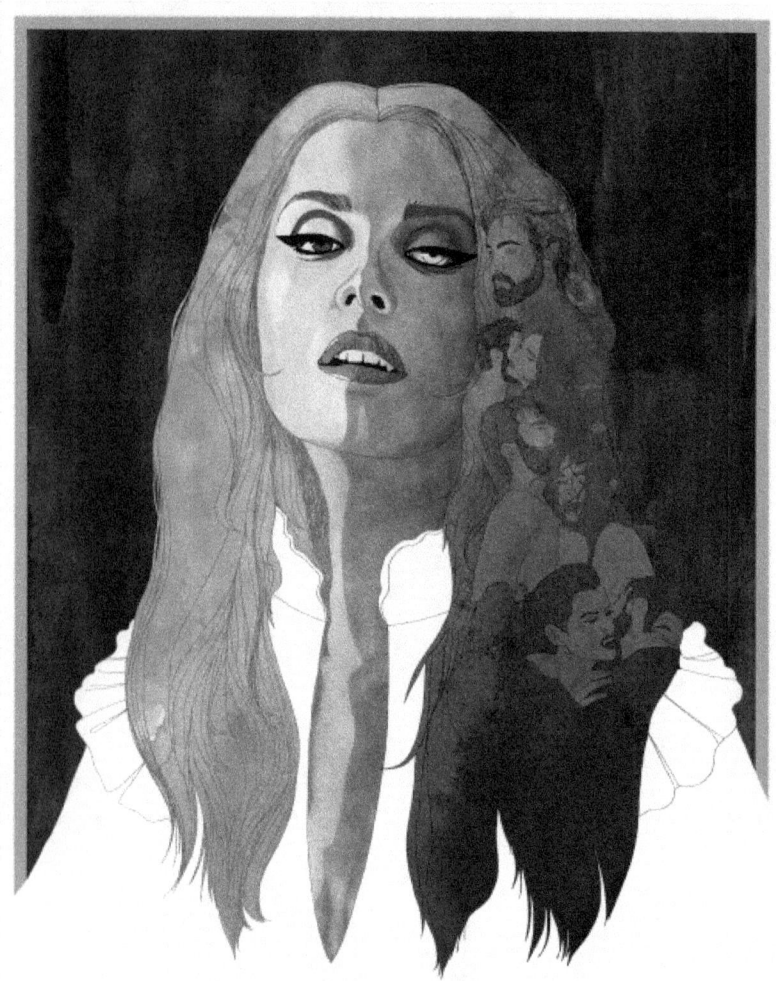

Kiss of the Damned (2012)

Director: Xan Cassavetes
Writer: Xan Cassavetes
Stars: Josephine de la Baume, Roxane Mesquida, Milo Ventimiglia, Anna Mouglalis, Michael Rapaport and Riley Keough

When you happen to be the daughter of pioneering American indie filmmaker John Cassavetes and his wife, the award-winning actress Gena Rowlands, anything you do in film is going to bring up that connection. Surely, therefore, one reason why Xan Cassavetes wrote and directed *Kiss of the Damned* as her feature debut is because it's as far away from anything her father made as could be imagined.

John made exceptionally personal pictures, usually in a cinéma vérité style, that were often uncomfortably realistic, constructed out of grit and sweat and sheer acting ability. This is nothing of the sort, instead being a throwback to the sort of arthouse horror movies that only the Europeans made, auteurs like Jean Rollin, Dario Argento or Jess Franco. Like so many of the films that carry Rollin's name, this is mostly style over substance, telling its simple story mostly through visual style, building a dreamy atmosphere out of blood, sex and architecture. Casting mostly European actors helps ensure that it sounds authentic to that approach too.

That's not to say that this would be mistaken for a Rollin picture. While a great deal of care and attention is given to make the film feel older than it is, not through artificial aging but through stylistic choices, the anomalies can't be accidental. The very first shot of Djuna has her firmly occupying two eras: watching a classic Vittorio de Sica movie from 1953 while working on a modern Apple laptop. Before long, she visits a video rental store apparently entirely stocked with VHS tapes, but she's returning DVDs. Clearly, the message is that the movie is contemporary but consciously made in an old fashioned style.

This style is everywhere as the film begins, immediately and deliberately setting down its goalposts. The font used for the title is one borrowed from Rollin's 1979 feature, *Fascination*, in decadent purple. We're shown still shots of the countryside, as we listen to a calmly pulsing soundtrack that quickly gives way to some Italian prog rock beats, a soft flute and soon just the wind. Whatever else this is, there's no false advertising to be found.

It's also notably sparse on dialogue, as Rollin's movies usually were, like a silent movie with speech, if that apparent contradiction makes sense. When Djuna catches sight of Paolo in the video store, she says nothing but runs outside as if to escape his charm; of course he follows. Forced to a stop as it's pouring with rain, they swap names and we leap forward to a bar. In a rare talky scene, they swap more in depth introductions: he's in isolation to write a script, while she's staying at a friend's house, translating poetry and literature into different languages, as quintessentially European as her French accent suggests. She also explains that she has a skin condition that prevents her from experiencing sunlight. Then it's off to her house, where they watch *Viridiana* silently and get close. This unfolds without a word until she says, simply, "No". She makes him leave, even though she clearly doesn't want him to go, then cries in the huge bathtub as the camera backs away to leave her be. All the dialogue could have been seamlessly provided in intertitles.

The biggest problem the picture has is the way that we're clearly supposed to buy into pretty much any aspect of Paolo's character. Initially it was his naïveté which annoyed me but soon it became his motivation.

All the lesser moments early on tie to the characters, who are poorly written, while all the great ones are visual. I loved the look of the piece: the very deliberate lighting choices, whether they're to make a scene lush or stark; the composition of frame, some shots looking rather like old paintings; the fluid camera motion, such as when Djuna floats down the stairs; the choice of camera angles, like when we look down on the pair of prospective lovers devouring themselves through a chained door.

Yet I hated the characters: the way that Djuna and Paolo fall in both love and lust with each other at literally first glance; her weakness and his one track mind; the way he refuses to leave, even when every fibre of his being must have been telling him to get the hell away from this lunatic woman.

She even tells him that she's a vampire fifteen minutes into the picture; he doesn't believe her, of course, so she lets him chain her onto the bed so she can't hurt him. We're enjoying the choice of camera angles and motion even as we completely fail to buy into either character's motivations. Naturally, she changes, fangs and bright contacts betraying who she really is. Yet he doesn't leave; he unchains her instead and walks around in slow motion, exuding alpha male power even as he sets himself up completely to be her victim. He pretty clearly bares his throat for her too as they're reaching the moment. "I would have done anything to be with you," he tells her, "however insane."

I presume we're supposed to be feeling the love and the fantasy and the romance of it all, but we're really just trying to figure out why he'd be so ridiculously foolish. There's thinking with your pecker and there's not walking away from an admittedly gorgeous young lady when you've known her for five minutes and she's shedding tears over how she's going to kill you.

What follows is as clichéd as it is stylish. To underline Paolo's naïveté, he apparently has no clue what a vampire is, so Djuna explains it all without a single surprise on our part. I can appreciate that they don't sparkle, but everything is so utterly traditional that we wonder what Cassavetes is going to bring to the table, given how rich the genre is.

Even here, everything we appreciate is visual, like the way we're given scenes so colour saturated that they could be black and white with hand tinting. I actually wondered at this point if none of this was real and we were really watching a visualisation of Paolo's writing process, all extrapolated from that one glimpse of Djuna in the video store. Maybe he's writing a vampire movie but doesn't have the imagination for it.

I do like the idea that a vampire and a human can fall in love, but you know, maybe there should be a little more build to it than, "You're cute, please bite me." There must be a way for them to do lunch first, at least, perhaps romantically out under the stars with her conspicuously only drinking a rare vintage of red wine.

Given how cloying and clichéd it had already become, I found myself aching for something new and not just the abstract blur of Paolo's first kill. I wondered if it was finally going to arrive when a new character drives up to the house 27 minutes into the picture.

She's Mimi, another French vampire all dressed up in the *Sunglasses After Dark* aesthetic, in from Amsterdam to stay for a week on her way to a sort of rehab ranch for vampires in Phoenix. "She's a disturbed creature," Djuna tells Paolo, "a crazy freak". Now we're ready for all that cutesy stuff to get completely shaken up, because if Djuna is the epitome of a romantic vampire, Mimi is clearly the animalistic flipside of the race and there's no chance that they'll peacefully share the same roof for long. While Djuna is all elegance, poise and control, Mimi is raw, wild and emotionlessly nihilistic. It does bode well for improvement, but sadly, we're only inflicted with an acute bout of bitchy vampire self loathing, which doesn't help the story in the slightest.

There are good moments to come, but bizarrely none of them are tied to any of the characters to which we've been introduced thus far. We've spent half an hour, almost a third of the running time, watching a pair of characters we don't care about wonder if another character we care about even less will cause a problem for them. At this point, I was mostly wondering if I could ask the projectionist to switch to French language and English subtitles.

Most of the good moments revolve around Xenia, a vampire actress who owns the house that everyone else is staying in. At least with her we get something new, a neat vampire take on Alcoholics Anonymous because Xenia, like Djuna, feeds on animals rather than people. It's been forty years without a taste of human blood for Xenia and Mimi's "a disturbed creature", remember? I adored that whole sequence, which is as capably and enticingly written as the rest is cheap and clichéd. Up to then, the best part is that Irene, the housekeeper, is safe from her hosts because she has a rare blood disorder.

The reason I keep harping on about the writing is that it quickly jeopardises the film and eventually sinks it, the ending proving even more dissatisfying than the beginning. What's so frustrating about the writing is that everything else around it is strong, especially the visual aesthetic which nails its goal to replicate the old Rollin feel. It's telling that even the vampire threesome is boring, not because it isn't shot well but because we have so little connection to anything except the camerawork at this point that we just don't care. Mimi is apparently a centuries old creature of the night, a talented predator, but she acts more like a pouty little thirteen year old girl. At points I seriously wondered if I'd blinked during her sparkling scene.

If the primary goal Xan Cassavetes had with this picture was to make something so utterly unlike her father's body of work, so as to firmly establish herself as a filmmaker of her own, she succeeded magnificently. He avoided style and delivered substance; here, with *Kiss of the Damned*, she did the exact opposite.

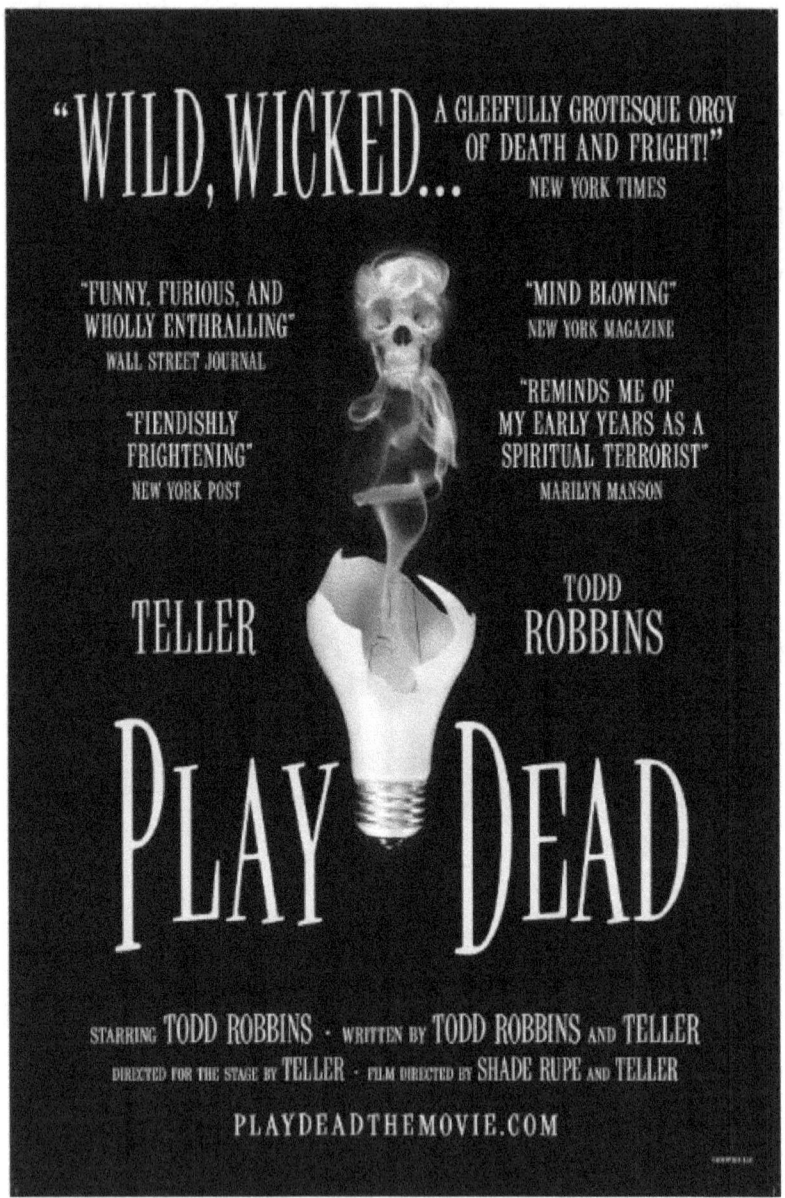

Play Dead (2012)

Directors: Shade Rupe and Teller
Writers: Todd Robbins and Teller
Star: Todd Robbins

Play Dead is a particularly odd film to see at a film festival, given that it's really not a film at all; instead it's a filmed record of a stage performance.

Now, you might be imagining a teacher sitting at the back of a school hall with a camera on a tripod documenting kids performing their summer play, but this is much more imaginative than that, both as a stage performance and a recording of it. That's not too surprising, given that Teller (of Penn & Teller fame) directed the stage show and co-directed this film version of it with Shade Rupe. However, the same flaw applies equally to this and the school play, namely that we can't interact with a recording.

That's by far the biggest problem with this picture, as this stage show featuring magician and carnival showman, Todd Robbins, is emphatically a participatory one. It sets up all sorts of gimmickry that is surely a riot for those attending in person, but we're stuck on the other side of the fourth wall so get to merely watch the reactions of the audience members who showed up in person. We can't experience a rollercoaster on television.

Teller is a magician, of course, well known for performances where he explains his tricks to us at the very same time that he's bamboozling us with them. He's also known for his TV show, *Penn & Teller: Bullshit!* which allowed the dynamic duo to debunk dishonesty wherever they could find it, including in such fields as professional mediums. It's therefore no surprise at all to find him interested in Robbins's interactive throwback to the "spook shows of the 1940s" where he does both of those things at once, setting up apparent connections to the spirit world and then clearly debunking them as carnival tricks.

Robbins's own background fits the material too just as well. He discovered the art of magic at the age of ten and gradually progressed up through the ranks, but it wasn't paying the bills, so he sidestepped into the carnival scene, working in a Coney Island sideshow working all the traditional acts: swallowing swords, hammering nails into his nostrils and eating fire and light bulbs. He kicks off this show by chewing up a light bulb with gusto.

Well, technically he kicks off the show by building up the theatricality of the performance, because we're never able to forget that this is a stage event. His first act is to plunge the entire theatre into darkness, right down to switching off the exit signs. Needless to say, there are young ladies in the audience who scream. Then, to introduce "an evening of spooky entertainment", he gives audience members the opportunity to leave by turning over an hourglass. Once that runs out, the doors are locked.

He wasn't kidding either: if you're in, you're in; you don't get to skip out halfway through, whatever happens up there on stage. We recognise gimmickry like this from movie showmen like William Castle, but he only brought it to cinema from the same spook shows that Robbins took influence from here. The sold out audience at the Players Theatre in Greenwich Village in the last days of the show's run in New York weren't passive observers, they were part of the show itself and locking them in merely ensured that they couldn't forget it.

At this point, Robbins was almost a year into the show. After a couple of weeks worth of workshop performances in Las Vegas and preview shows in New York, it officially opened off Broadway on 21st October, 2010 and ran until 24th July, 2011. However, it felt like he'd been working it for decades, stalking the stage and the theatre floor like a Satanic car salesman, in complete control of everyone in the audience and everything that might happen either to them or around them.

He's a massively talented storyteller, which allows him to keep his audience captivated as he selects an apparently random file box from the stacks of them that provide the stage's backdrop and make it look like a bizarre underground museum. He then explores the history of the character whose effects are kept within it, a character with a particularly strong association with death: a child murderer, a carnival geek, a fake medium at a society sex party. Of course, that exploration isn't in the form of merely a lecture, it's a full on participatory experience.

The obvious success of what Robbins does here makes me wonder why these shows no longer pepper the landscape, but that's a wider subject than this review should cover. Sure, the elements that he brings to the stage are time honoured ones: Grand Guignol effects work, spook show shenanigans, carnival magic tricks and spiritualistic explorations. Robbins approaches them all from a modern framework though, one that's reminiscent of Penn & Teller but with the technical aspect toned down in favour of more of the human connection.

The material leaps all over the place in tone, but that only serves to keep the audience on the hop, unsure of where it's going to go next. One moment they're subjected to broad slapstick haunted house humour, the next focused in on poignant remembrance, only for nudity to appear out of nowhere. In less able hands, this would have been problematic, but with Robbins in charge, it's merely another way to emphasise how showmen can manipulate emotion. He does it impeccably even while he's talking about it.

Of course, it can't hurt that he talks about it with a clear voice that doesn't merely cajole and command, it even ventures into Vincent Price impersonation as he introduces some of the dead folk who inhabit his file boxes.

Perhaps my favourite part arrives when he adds a new one, an audience member called Alan who writes his names and dates onto one of the boxes. I won't spoil how he bites the big one, because it deserves to wait for you to experience it yourself, so let's just say that it's a brutal and bloody act. What I appreciated most was how Robbins harangues the audience afterwards for their reaction to this heinous murder, given their rather different reaction to an earlier trick in which he apparently devoured a live rat. Everything in this show revolves around faith and how it can be manipulated by people with the will and the talent to do so. This is a show; everyone in the audience knows that Alan is alive somewhere, waiting to be reintroduced, but maybe the rat wasn't a trick. The light bulb wasn't, was it? How about the rat?

I won't spoil the other stories either, because they're also worthy of being experienced, but I will highlight that to do that properly, you really need to go to the show rather than find a way to see this recording of one. If anything, it might be worth seeing the show live, then following up with this film, because there are a few aspects included in this recording that you won't get from the live experience.

Most obviously, there are a number of points where the theatre is plunged into complete darkness, not only to allow for Robbins's team to scare the crap out of the audience by cleverly exploiting their fears, but to allow us at home to witness what's really going on through the use of infra-red cameras. Shade Rupe recorded the show with panache before sending the footage on to Teller who edited it into its final form with the comedian and professional athiest, Emery Emery. Clearly video wouldn't work too well with scenes of utter darkness, so the infra-red approach was a key one to make the project possible.

There is a DVD for *Play Dead*, because I certainly watched one as a film festival submission but, to the best of my knowledge, it isn't available for sale. I wonder if the goal is to restrict screenings to the festival circuit as an advert for the ongoing live show, perhaps suggesting that this will be released as and when the show ceases to be performed live. It would seem viable that it could be sold after the shows as a souvenir that adds a little extra insight to the experience people had just been through.

It would also seem that there's not just a show here, there's a message too, one that Harry Houdini gave a century ago. Robbins wants us to know that anyone who claims to communicate with the dead is a liar and a cheat; this show helps him to debunk their tricks by repeating and then exposing them in front of a live audience. That message is one that deserves to be shouted from the hilltops and a DVD would reach a lot more people than would eight shows a week. Given the choice, go see the show rather than the film, but this is a good follow up.

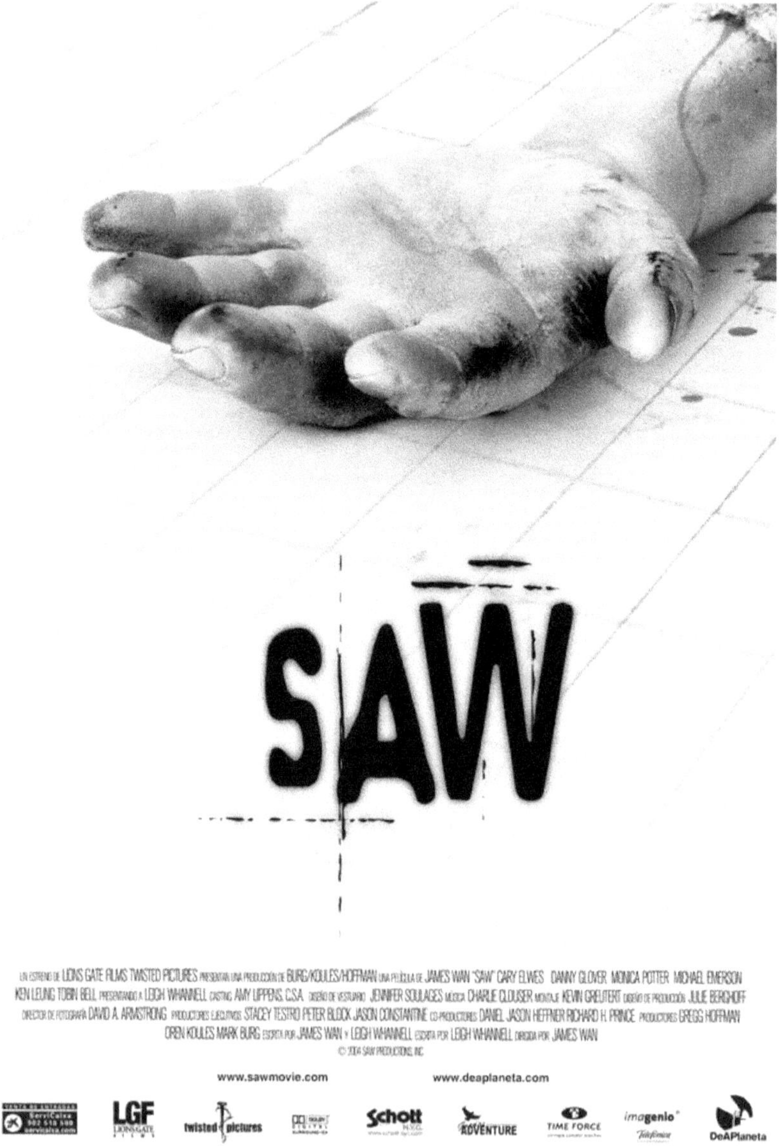

Saw (2004)

Director: James Wan
Writer: Leigh Whannell, from a story by James Wan and Leigh Whannell
Stars: Cary Elwes, Danny Glover, Monica Potter, Michael Emerson, Tobin Bell, Ken Leung, Makenzie Vega, Shawnee Smith, Dina Meyer, Benito Martinez and Leigh Whannell

It had been quite a while since I last saw *Saw*, so revisiting it was an odd experience.

It was originally released in 2004 and I saw it in 2005, probably soon after the word of mouth that quickly built around it had become substantial. While it cost a little over a million dollars to make, making it hardly a big budget film, it grossed over a hundred times that and its six sequels gradually built the franchise into the most successful at the box office of any horror series, a massive achievement given how many such creatures there are today.

I was impressed with it, though the sequels gradually fed on each other incestuously and I haven't yet made it all the way through to the latest, *Saw 3D*, the seventh and currently final film in the series which was released in 2010. I've only got as far as *Saw V*.

I hadn't revisited it since, until doing so around the time of its screening at the 2013 festival, which tied in to the attendance as a guest of its executive producer, Peter Block, who had become the C.E.O. of FearNet. Eight years was long enough that plot details had either faded from memory or become blurred with the sequels. I remembered the final twist which is famously vicious, but I didn't remember the many others that preceded it.

What I discovered was that it remains an impressive film, notably better than the sequels I've seen thus far, though it hasn't entirely stood the test of time.

The fundamental concept still stands up well, a neatly twisted one that has a couple of men wake up in a bathroom, chained to separate walls with hacksaws provided to free themselves, not ones strong enough to sever their chains but ones that will cut through their legs. This is only the first sadistic torment with which they're faced as they gradually discover why they're there, how they're connected and what else might be going on that they can't yet see from their perspective.

This concept stands up today, even if it served to introduce the world to the modern and much maligned torture porn genre. This first film isn't as gory as its sequels and the complexity isn't overwhelming, remaining close enough to the simple vision of its twisted mastermind to ring true. I agree with creators James Wan and Leigh Whannell that it wasn't torture porn yet, even if I don't agree that it didn't get there later.

As a standalone film, which it originally was, it tells two stories that gradually become one.

The first revolves around the bathroom, with its two questioning captives and the bloody corpse between them in the middle of the room that they can't reach. It's a intriguing puzzle, not merely for Dr. Lawrence Gordon and Adam Stanheight, the two men inside it, but for us watching as well. Of course, Lawrence and Adam have more motivation than cinematic inquisitiveness pushing them to figure out why they're there but their actions are cleverly tailored not only to drive their story forward but to draw us into the wider picture as well.

There are two realisations that accomplish this very well indeed. Dr. Gordon suggests that there's a purpose behind their kidnapping and captivity as, after all, they could easily have been killed too, but they weren't. "They must want something from us," he points out, sending our imaginations off to figure out what. Then he notices that the clock on the wall of this notably wrecked room is brand new, meaning not only that time is important but also that we need to look as much as think.

The other half of the story ties to a police investigation, in which a couple of detectives try to find the Jigsaw Killer, an odd criminal because he doesn't actually kill anyone, merely places them into darkly ironic situations where they die more often than not.

Paul, a man who had attempted suicide by cutting his wrists, was put into a cage of razorwire and given two hours to tunnel a way through it to escape. Mark pretends to be ill to get other people's money, so wakes up with a poison running through his veins that he can counter by taking the antidote that's merely feet away in a safe. There are catches, of course: the combination is on the wall, but there are a heck of a lot of numbers to work through, the floor is covered in broken glass and he's doused in a flammable substance but has to use a candle to read what's on the walls. There has only been one survivor thus far: Amanda, a drug addict, who could only escape the reverse bear trap attached to her head by carving the key out of the stomach of the paralysed man in her makeshift cell.

We soon find that there's already a tie between the two stories, beyond the obvious fact that this pair of captives are clearly going through the latest of the Jigsaw Killer's ironic setups. By this point, we've been let in on how this one will work: Lawrence has been given until six o'clock to kill Adam or his wife and daughter will be murdered in his stead. The tie is that Dr. Gordon was a former suspect in the police investigation. Sure, he was quickly cleared of being the Jigsaw Killer without any doubt, but the real mastermind behind these cruel acts of irony still chose to set him up.

Certainly putting his family on the line is ironic because the alibi that cleared his name also exposed his infidelity; the wife he can now only save by commiting murder is the wife he's been cheating on. And so we watch Lawrence and Adam try to figure out a way to escape while hoping that former Det. David Tapp, now clearly obsessed with the case, will find them first. And we try to figure out the connections before Wan and Whannell show us their finished puzzle.

However much they reject the suggestion that this film is torture porn, it's impossible to talk about *Saw* without talking about the sadistically intricate but ingenious traps that the Jigsaw Killer constructs. Frankly, they dominate the film far more than its stars, the acting or any other cinematic angle. The outrageous success of the film prompted immediate talks of a sequel and the traps were always going to be the logical focus.

They turn this film into an odd hybrid of horror and thriller that's never entirely comfortable in either genre. It's more gory and sadistic than thrillers tend to be, which has led to frequent and fair comparisons to David Fincher's *Seven*, and it doesn't play up the tension as a thriller would; we rarely see the clock, for instance. However, it's not a conventional horror movie either. It's not scary, for a start, even if the jump scares are clearly supposed to catch us unawares. In fact, I'd venture to suggest that it's better as a thriller than a horror movie, especially given that Wan and Whannell play it straight throughout, even if a couple of elements do threaten to send it screaming into the territory of camp horror: mostly Adam's occasional attempts at poor humour and a freaky puppet unnamed in this film but known outside it as Billy.

There are major actors in the cast, but nobody really shines on the acting front. I appreciated the choice to tell this predominantly from the victims' point of view, an unusual but highly successful angle, but that means that as Dr. Gordon, Cary Elwes is the closest thing we have to a lead and he's done far better work elsewhere.

Critics have lambasted Elwes for overdoing it here, but it isn't really that. Dr. Gordon is a notably flawed character, a cheat who's been caught cheating and a liar who isn't particularly good at lying, and this makes him seem deceptive all the time. No wonder Det. Tapp never buys into him not being the Jigsaw Killer, even though he isn't, as his cop's instinct would be to immediately distrust him. Sure, Elwes doesn't appear to be endowing this role with what we know his talents allow, but then he's playing a duplicitous character whose every word and action is, by its very nature, a performance. If Dr. Gordon was a better actor, then I might buy into Elwes not doing his job. As it stands, I'm unsure as to whether he doesn't do his job or whether he does it too well.

Leigh Whannell's acting isn't up to his writing, as his script is much more successful than his performance as Adam. He was the first actor cast, having played the lead of David in the original 2003 short, also titled *Saw*, in the role that became Amanda in this feature. Much of the reason that the film stayed independent is that director James Wan wasn't willing to lose Whannell as Adam; while another actor might have been better in the role, that choice indirectly led to many of the successes of the film.

With Wan unable to do much of what he wanted because of the restrictions of budget, cast and time, he found himself gradually forced to use his imagination to make everything work instead. Unusable shots were transformed into still photographs or footage from a surveillance camera. The end result was something that's "more gritty and rough around the edges", which helped it feel real. No wonder the underlying theme is one of control; Wan and

Whannell were constantly fighting to keep control too, firstly of their project and then of the film that they wanted to make.

If Cary Elwes got the opportunity to depict a man who believes he has control over his life, even though it isn't deserved, and who rails the most against the Jigsaw Killer taking that control away from him, the rest of the cast didn't get those chances.

Danny Glover shot all his scenes as Det. Tapp in two days; while he's far from bad in the role, it deserved to be more substantial. I like that Tapp isn't the lead character, as he would have been in most takes on this story, but he deserved better than he got. Dina Meyer is hardly in the movie as another detective and neither is Tobin Bell, who would soon come to dominate and epitomise the franchise. Michael Emerson is far too overt as Zep Hindle, one of Gordon's orderlies who gets hauled into the mix too. It's Shawnee Smith and Ken Leung who impress most in smaller roles as Amanda and Det. Sing respectively. Each of these characters returned in future films, though sometimes only tangentially. Bell is in all seven pictures; Smith, Meyer and Emerson four each, Glover and Leung three and Elwes in two.

One sure reason why the film did so well is its ending, which is one of the great twists of the modern era. It's been torn apart by many critics and with possible good reason, but I believe that it's easy to explain it without venturing into the dubious logic of conspiracy theorists. Then again, if I'm right, it would counter the general tone of control that pervades the picture.

There are other things I'd complain about first. One is how it's impossible for the audience to figure everything out from the little information we're given early on; we're reliant on a steady stream of information throughout to fill in gaps. Another is the complexity of the film's structure which unfolds in an overly complex set of flashbacks, mostly to keep the stream of information flowing. That leads to the next, which is that the script is effectively playing with us just as much as the Jigsaw Killer is playing with his victims. Most annoying to me was how Wan and Whannell task us with figuring out their puzzle but deem us incapable of reading the periodic notes. In fact, that's not just annoying, it's insulting.

I stand by my rating of *Saw* as a capable and original thriller, especially considering its budget and even if its many and varied issues become more and more apparent with repeat viewings. I'm hardly going to complain much about a movie that spurs us to think that earned close to a hundred times what it cost to produce.

This first film (and this first film alone) certainly deserves to be judged on its own merits and not merely as part of a franchise which soon came to value the cruel ingenuity of its traps over its stories and its characters, which are less believable as the films ran on.

It also shouldn't be judged on its legacy, which directly led to more overt examples of the torture porn genre than this ever was.

I firmly believe that it's been mostly forgotten in favour of its even more successful sequels and the wider picture of which it became a mere part, like a single piece in a jigsaw. I wonder how it'll be received when it's re-released in theatres this Hallowe'en for its tenth anniversary. It may bring some respect back to the franchise, which is far more successful commercially than critically, but it may disappoint people used to the more extreme material in the sequels.

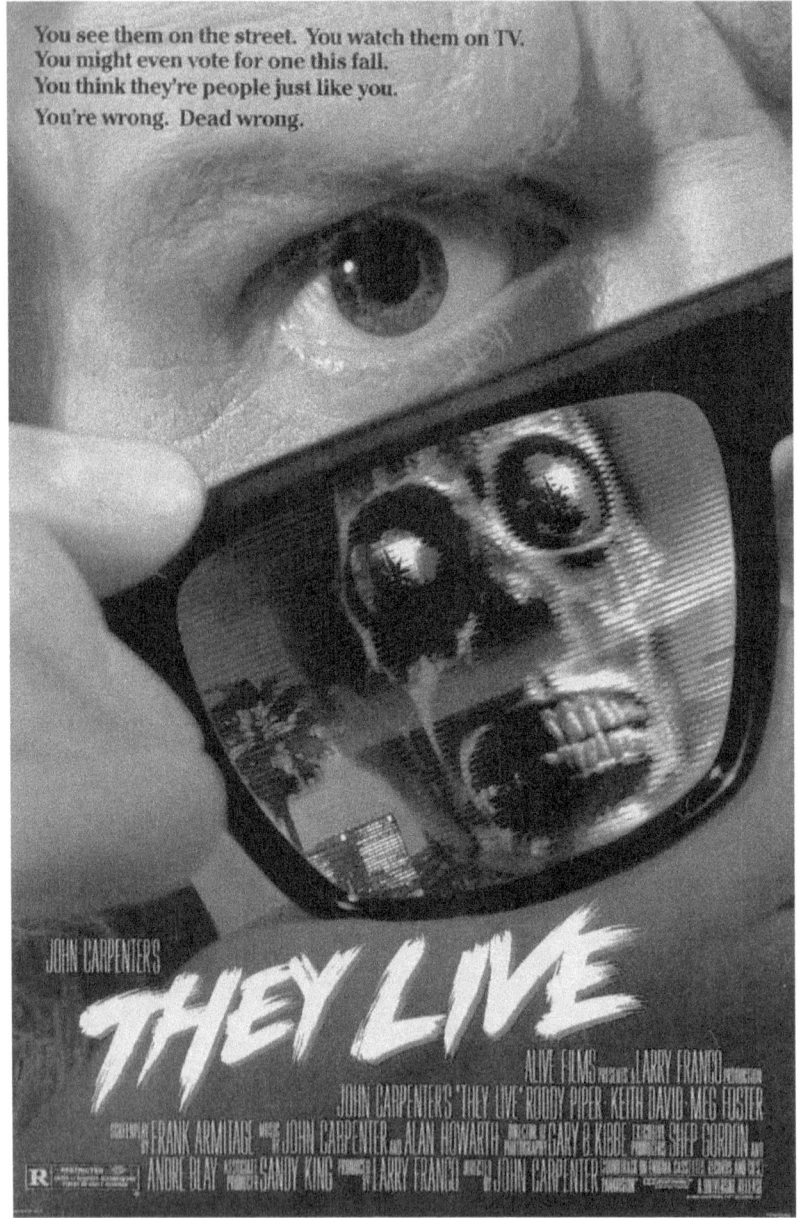

They Live (1988)

Director: John Carpenter
Writer: John Carpenter, from the short story by Ray Nelson
Stars: Roddy Piper, Keith David, Meg Foster, George "Buck" Flower, Peter Jason and Raymond St Jacques

Back in the eighties, when I found the money to go out and discover a wider variety of movies than were broadcast on the four TV channels we had in England at the time, John Carpenter was surely the biggest name in genre cinema.

He seemed to be most highly regarded for two hits, *Halloween* and *Escape from New York*, both of which did very well at the box office and strongly resonated down the years. Yet today, it's his less heralded features that stand up best for me, especially *Big Trouble in Little China*, which lost money at the box office, and *They Live*, which made a profit but hardly a spectacular one. If I had to pick a third place, it would be *Assault on Precinct 13*, Carpenter's update to *Rio Bravo*, as *Halloween* feels simplistic now and *Escape from New York* wears some of its more convenient scenes heavily on its sleeve. By comparison, *They Live* feels more and more relevant with each year that passes. It's horrifying to realise that it often feels like we're living in this world that Carpenter created in 1988. How do we shut down the source?

At the time, *They Live* was quintessentially about the eighties, perhaps why many critics didn't see much value in its message; they needed to skip forward a few decades to see how it would all evolve. In truth, Carpenter was railing against a number of things, one reason why *They Live* doesn't feel like a one note message, but at its heart, it's anti-consumerism. He told *Starlog* that he'd started to watch TV again and that he quickly realised that everything was designed to sell us something, but he also noticed the reflection of this trend in the thriving yuppie movement, which tied success specifically to money, and the Reaganomics of the time.

Carpenter naturally polarised this in his script to become a clear "them and us" scenario, but as he phrased "them" as alien free enterprisers and "us" as the human race, he tapped into a set of wider truths about modern America that have become more obvious with each year that passes, a recognition that the class system of the British is present in the United States too, merely manifested in a different form.

Today, yuppies and Reaganomics have gone by the wayside, but *They Live* feels more contemporary than ever because it's phrased vaguely enough to be universally applicable. When I rewatched it at home in 2012 and again at the 2013 festival, it felt like Carpenter was writing specifically about the Occupy movement, the 99% and venture capital firms like Bain Capital. Watching once more in 2014 to put this review together, it's suddenly reminiscent instead of Ferguson, police brutality and the erosion of the middle class.

I'm sure Carpenter looked backwards to history for references to McCarthy's communist witchhunts and the civil rights movement, but he also presaged climate change, subliminal advertising and modern corporate America. He certainly adapted one of the most telling lines in the entire film, "We all sell out every day," from an anonymous executive at Universal. Since then, Universal has not coincidentally sold out to a whole string of global multinationals and is currently owned by Comcast.

I first saw *They Live* on British TV as a presentation of *Moviedrome*, in which Alex Cox introduced me to a stunning range of films and, in many ways, placed me on the road to what became Apocalypse Later. I remember that Cox highlighted that the primary character is homeless, hardly a common scenario for the leading man in an action movie. He's also never named, his credited name of Nada meaning "nothing" in Spanish, and he's the product of a broken home too, from which he ran away at the age of thirteen.

The movie's title on screen is sourced from graffiti, initially scrawled underneath a bridge, and it opens with Nada walking past it, literally travelling from the other side of the tracks in search of work; he ends up in a shanty town for the homeless quite a distance away. However, Nada is never once phrased as a victim. While the government's job centres have nothing for him, he's an able bodied man with his own tools and he finds work on a construction site himself. "I believe in America," he explains to a bitter co-worker. "Everybody's got their own hard times these days."

His optimism isn't reflected in anything else we see or hear, as is hammered home in the early scenes. The lady he meets at the job centre clearly doesn't care and, what's more, doesn't want to listen; the loudspeakers explain that the food stamp programme has been suspended; a man in a wheelchair rolls past him, shaking his head. Out in the streets, a preacher asks, "Why do we worship greed?" before a cop shows up to shut off his words. Frank, that bitter co-worker, hasn't seen his wife and kids in six months; they're back home in Detroit, but he had to leave because the steel mills closed down. Nada himself came from Denver where "things just seemed to dry up."

In other words, it's not just here, it's everywhere. The only way out is through television, where you can watch and dream, even if it's in a shop window. Maybe that simply means that the dreams are bigger. It doesn't address the problems of society, of course, but it serves as a temporary escape from them. On television, as we hear during a commercial, you'll never, never grow old and you'll never die. No wonder people stop trying, even in the shanty town; it's much easier to escape than to try.

Then, breaking into that TV signal comes an old bearded hacker, ironically because he's utilising their own medium to rail at the complacence of the people. He isn't received well, partially because his message is nowhere near commercial (how about catchy zingers like, "We are living in an artificially induced state of consciousness that resembles sleep" or "Their intention to rule rests with the annihilation of consciousness") and partially because interference from his meagre signal literally gives them headaches. The truth hurts, right?

His more effective words are very familiar, but here's where the setup ends and our story really begins. Clearly something is going on at the African Methodist Episcopal Free Church over the road from the homeless town and our hero is an inquisitive soul. He wanders in to find that it's a front for a group of scientists who discovered the truth behind all the proselytising and want to wake up the populace. Talking at them doesn't help, but what has a chance are the sunglasses they're manufacturing that show things as they really are.

Given that *They Live* is now over a quarter of a century old, that the point at which Nada puts on a pair of these sunglasses is only half an hour into the movie and that what he sees has passed into pop culture to the degree that street artist Shepard Fairey's Obey campaign was deliberately inspired by it (and arguably his iconic Obama Hope poster was too), it seems fair to talk about it. Heck, it's even spoiled on the movie's own poster!

When wearing these sunglasses, the world of colour that we know is transformed into black and white, partly because it works metaphorically and partly because Ted Turner was prominently and controversially colorising classic movies for TCM at the time and it seemed like a good way to make him out to be "a monster from outer space". Images and words vanish too, replaced by simple subliminal slogans on every advertising hoarding, every page of every magazine and every sign in every window. Many contain only a single word: "Obey", "Consume" or "Conform", while others are more complex, like "No Independent Thought" or "Do Not Question Authority". Paper money reads "This is Your God".

What's more, while some people look identical, others are utterly different, like a mass of bruises without skin. That's because they're the aliens who own us and the message becomes crystal clear. The first alien we see is an affluent white businessman but the first human is a black newspaper seller; in this world, we call them "sir" and that concept is reinforced over and over. Masters are alien, but their servants are human. Aliens get promoted, while humans don't. Some cops are human but most aren't, something that echoes today in the maxim that good cops protect bad cops.

Stumbling around town in a daze because he's been rooked between the eyes by the truth, Nada decides that he'll do something about it and the rest of the story falls easily into place, the social comment stronger early on but not lost as *They Live* turns into an action movie. The most telling moments arrive late, such as the transformation of "Buck" Flower's character, a lazy nobody from the shanty town who's now gussied up in a suit and bow tie as the epitome of the nouveau riche. "We all sell out every day," he says. "Might as well be on the winning team."

For a movie that carries a whopper of a message, much better constructed than the hacker's diatribe that is primarily received as "just that idiot licking his nuts again," it's a highly enjoyable piece. The source was a story called *Eight O'Clock in the Morning* by Ray

Nelson, which was published in *Fantasy & Science Fiction* in 1963 and it's surprisingly close to Carpenter's adaptation to the big screen. In the story, George Nada wakes up to a similar revelation after being hypnotised on stage, finding that our world is ruled by Fascinators who breed us for food but control us through subliminals. It ends with an extra twist that isn't in the film, surprisingly given that it's even shorter than this review, under two thousand words, but Carpenter does a magnificent job of turning them into 94 minutes of visualisation and social analogy, not least through how he set up the characters. Nada is far from the only unusual primary character and, even a quarter of a century on, this stands surprisingly alone in its varied heroes, right down to the heavily tattooed biker with his long beard.

Playing the homeless, nameless hero is Roddy Piper, who is definitely a better actor today than he was in 1988 but is perfectly cast nonetheless as the everyman; as Carpenter told *Starlog*: "Unlike most Hollywood actors, Roddy has life written all over him." At the time he was best known for his career as a W.W.F. wrestler, but he was starting to dabble in movies, first being noticed in this and the much lower budget *Hell Comes to Frogtown* in 1988.

Playing opposite the white guy is a black guy, Keith David, clearly a much better actor, who had impressed Carpenter during the making of *The Thing*. In fact, he wrote the part of Frank specifically for him, as he "wouldn't be a traditional sidekick, but could hold his own." Just as prominent in a smaller role as a blind, black street preacher is Raymond St. Jacques, who had broken down a boundary on his own in 1965, as the first black actor to become a regular on a western series on television, playing cattle drover Simon Blake on *Rawhide*. It's appropriate that he was a noted civil rights activist in real life. He sells his role well.

"Buck" Flower is perfectly cast as the drifter who finds his way up the food chain by selling out. It's notable that unlike most of the homeless folk in the shanty town, he never seems to do anything except sit back and watch television. His creaky voice is perfect for the role, as are his notably unkempt looks. As Gilbert, whose part in running the shanty town is mostly a front for his more subversive operations in the underground, Peter Jason is strong too, even if he's one of those actors who we remember visually without ever letting his name sink into our skulls. He was also in Carpenter's previous picture, *Prince of Darkness*, another of his underrated gems.

And that leaves Meg Foster, whose unique blue eyes have never been more overt. She has an odd role, in that she doesn't show up until almost halfway through the picture and even then does so as a hostage. She plays Holly Thompson, network executive, as cool, composed and conciliatory. "You have two guns," she tells Nada. "You're not sorry. You're in charge." Yet the moment she can act, she does so, quickly and powerfully.

There's so much to discuss in *They Live* that any review can easily run away and become a book of its own, something impossible to even conceive of happening with most eighties action movies, which we often look back at today as guilty pleasures, the nostalgia overriding the cheese.

That cheese isn't entirely absent though, as we can't forget the film's most famous line and most famous scene, both of which are remembered far more than the substance and depth that pervades *They Live*. The line, of course, is Nada's oft quoted, "I have come here to chew bubblegum and kick ass and I'm all out of bubblegum." Piper apparently ad libbed the line, but he certainly didn't ad lib the long alley fight he worked with Keith David, all to get him to put on sunglasses. Carpenter had them watch *The Quiet Man*, with John Wayne battling Victor McLaglen, then they designed and built up the choreography over weeks.

It's arguable that fight credibility is lost whenever a suplex is added into it, but if it's bringing new people to *They Live* after 26 years, it's well worth it.

The International
Horror & Sci-Fi Film Festival

2013

Horror Shorts

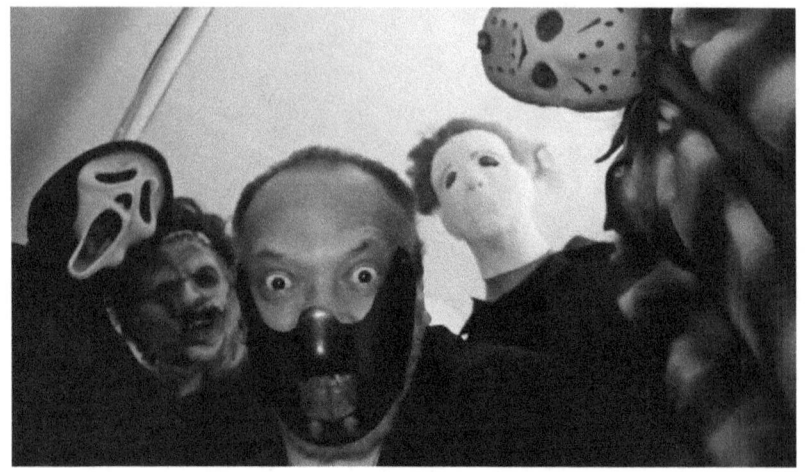

Diecons

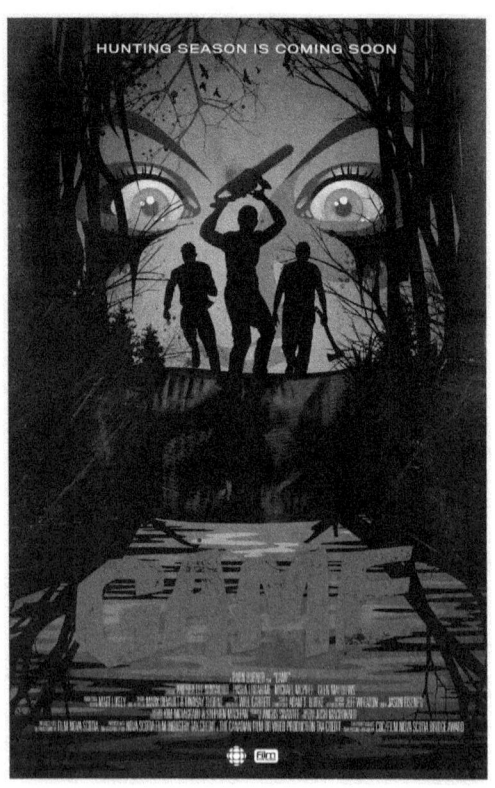

Diecons (2012)

Director: Lomai

A highly appropriate way to kick off a set of horror shorts at a genre festival, *Diecons* is a trailer for a nonexistent feature.

It stars the cinematic equivalent of a slasher supergroup, most of those iconic monsters from eighties movies attempting to make a comeback in an era that sees them as camp and doesn't take them remotely seriously. There's only a hint of a story but that hint only puts it in parity with many of the movies to which it pays homage.

The puppeteer behind them appears to be a psychiatrist with a Hannibal Lecter fixation, who gets most of the dialogue, perhaps appropriately given that he was one of the few modern monsters to get any (and this is an odd moment for me to realise that most of the great monsters of the eighties were just as silent as those of the twenties). "They do not see you as I see you," he pronounces, sliding a new mask over to Michael Myers. If I caught his masked dialogue correctly, he sees them as "proud slayers of the degenerate mongols that plague this plane of existence."

And so you can write the rest of the script yourself. He talks up their collective achievements and how they're unjustly forgotten, their legacies bastardised, timely with the *Hannibal* series and a host of modern day franchise reboots. Pop culture sucks in his view, which is mirrored in the response of one victim who points out that it's all about paranormal activity nowadays (and you can make that genre a movie title if you wish)

"You must let them know who the real icons of death are," Lecter tells his oversized iconic minions. "Take your weapons and carve their flesh!" I can't resist quoting this overblown dialogue, which is one of the best reasons to watch this short, but unfortunately the sound quality is a little murky so I wasn't able to catch all of it.

That's surprising, as the piece was put together by musicians, a collective of Chicago rappers known as 21st Century Hip Hop. Even there the horror influence is apparent, as director Lomai surely takes his name from Lo-Mai, the cat/man hybrid in *The Island of Dr Moreau*, rather than the Fijian rugby team.

Given that this is a faux movie trailer, it has to be judged from the perspective that the imaginary feature it promotes isn't quite so imaginary after all. Would this entice potential viewers away from the Hollywood eye candy on offer on the other multiplex screens?

Well, maybe. It has a vision that's as fun as it is cheesy. There are fan films out there, such as *Freddy vs Jason vs Ash*, that cover this sort of territory and they're popular with a certain flavour of horror hound, even if they screen at parties and cons rather than national theatre chains. Certainly to succeed, they need to be made by fans rather than studio executives, but even *Freddy vs Jason* made back three times its budget and its ending still prompts discussion whenever its name is dropped.

This is definitely on the party scale, as the acting is poor to mediocre, the action is generic (though phrased knowingly) and the technical side is capable at best. After the idea, it's the dialogue that keeps us, as overdone as anything given a mad doctor in the forties. Ed Wood would mouth it all.

Game (2013)

Director: Josh MacDonald
Writer: Josh MacDonald
Stars: Andrea Lee Norwood, Pasha Ebrahimi, Glen Matthews and Michael McPhee

Josh MacDonald's credits are mostly as an actor, with a growing string of roles in short films and features with titles as engaging as *Suburban Zombie Christmas*, *Foam Drive Renegades* and, well, even *Time Farter*, but he remained behind the camera for this, his directorial debut. He also wrote and produced, so even offscreen it's clear that this film, along with the lion's share of its success, belong to him.

I wasn't sold on it the first time I saw it, as a festival screener, but it played well on the big screen and it gets better with time, as the craft of the piece shines out. It's a deceptively solid little picture, one that takes the stereotypical, turns it neatly on its head and ratchets everything up a few notches for good measure.

Its biggest problem is surely that nothing much seems to happen for a while. I should emphasise that it really does; it merely doesn't seem to because two thirds of the film is taken up with a chase that's bereft of dialogue and relies entirely on the tension woven around characters we know nothing about.

What becomes clear with repeat viewings is that it's deceptively well crafted. The pastoral flute that bookends the film and the way the piece is shot, especially in the wetlands scenes towards the end, mark it clearly as a throwback to the seventies. Films were slower back then, with more emphasis on character, and that's what we're given as a young lady runs for her life through a Nova Scotia forest, encumbered as she is with duct tape, hand ties and chains.

The credits call her a businesswoman but we know just as much about her as we do about the three hillbillies chasing her, which is to say next to nothing; what we know we have to conjure out of what we see. They're patient men on the hunt for game, in one of the various meanings of the title. Jubal has a lumberjack shirt, a chainsaw and horrific burn scars on his face. Gabe favours an axe and his running make up, from the lipstick their quarry dropped, shows that he's as scarred inside as Jubal is out. Prior merely has bad teeth and an earring.

On the side of the victim, we see that the businesswoman doesn't scare easily, as a beautifully shot scene with her and a spider ably demonstrates. She also has the gumption to try to free herself with what she finds, which lends us to believe that this isn't going to be quite as simple as the proto-torture porn we might expect.

The feel of the piece remains quintessentially seventies, evoking both backwoods hillbilly horrors and rape revenge movies. What it ends up delivering remains true as an homage to those genres but also adds something very new and refreshing. The very last shot, in particular, is particularly haunting. It's a gorgeous ending, with a deceptively peaceful scene sitting above a powerful undercurrent of menace.

The pace is measured throughout, with three strong up periods each followed by corresponding quiet down periods, the last of which leaves us ready for more. The editing is by Jason Eisener, of *Hobo with a Shotgun* fame, and it's as deceptively strong as anything else here. Just make sure to watch it more than once.

The Root of the Problem (2013)

Director: Ryan Spindell
Writers: Ryan Spindell and Mark E. Davidson
Stars: Alison Gallaher, Ptolemy Slocum, Brea Grant and Chad Jamian Williams

Ryan Spindell, who wrote, produced and directed this short film, clearly likes period settings. His 2007 film, *Kirksdale*, which was an International Horror & Sci-Fi Film Festival selection back in 2008, was set in the sixties at a rural Florida mental instutition; this one is a decade older, set in the unmistakeable America of the fifties.

He also seems to be building a common theme in his films about helplessness. *Kirksdale* was full of it, beginning with a young lady being driven to an asylum by a cop who tries to rape her within the first minute. *The Window* has an old man abandoned in a care home and the title of *Bully* speaks for itself. Here, the helpless character is Mary, waiting in the dentist's chair for Dr. Clayton to pull her wisdom teeth.

Spindell does a lot here with very little, happy to let the story wait so he can torment Mary by peppering her boredom with odd distractions: a noisy water pipe, some bizarre screaming from next door and a fly who we follow into the room through ducting behind the opening credits.

Eventually, as her growing fear persuades her that it's time to leave, Dr. Clayton finally shows up, as genial and full of calming jokes as you might expect. Ptolemy Slocum and Brea Grant, playing Nurse Su, bounce well off each other in what believably seems like the hundredth enaction of an old routine to politely break down the resistance of their patients. Everything is completely normal, but of course it doesn't take long for Spindell to ratchet up the tension. He starts with a cringeworthy anaesthetic jab, guaranteed to have any audience squirming in their seats, but follows it up with Clayton's recounting of the original tooth fairy legend, all about grues who ate bones and teeth, utterly out of place in the doctor's calming routine so clearly setting us up for something.

We're left to figure out how to read it all: as a literal piece or as a manifestation of Mary's existing fear, perhaps one enhanced by anaesthesia. It could even be a riff on snake oil, sparked by the use of Dr. P. Q. Finkelman's Ultra-Calming Tablets.

Really, of course, it's all the above: it's all about the common fear that many of us still have when visiting the dentist, built by a few choice impressions conjured out of the surroundings and given focus by an unfortunate choice of words. Or is it?

Spindell is very good at letting our imaginations loose, placing a lid on them to rein us back in to reality and then leaving just a little hint that maybe we were right all along. He also clearly plays on our fear of authority, whether that be the people who run an asylum, a care home or the dentist's surgery we see here.

He uses talented effects folk to launch our fantasies but equally talented actors to tamper them back down. Slocum and Grant, both vastly experienced in film and television, are excellent here, while the much less experienced Alison Gallaher does a fair job of staying within our focus of attention while anaesthetised and in the presence of scene stealers. The humour is solid too, even if it begins with an outrageous pun: Mary's appointment is for 2.30.

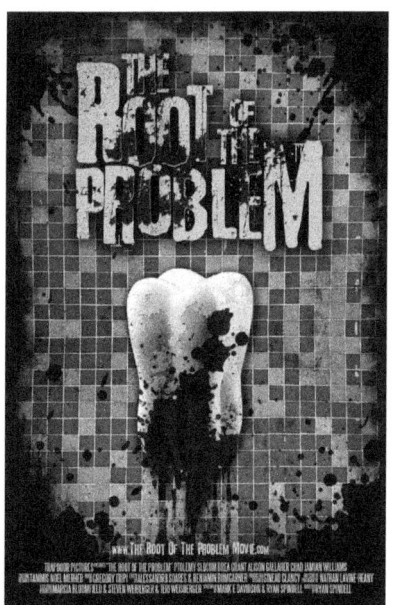
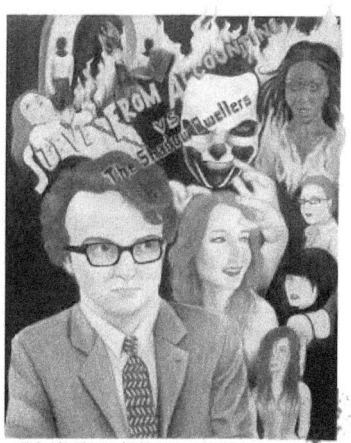

379

Steve from Accounting vs. The Shadow Dwellers (2012)

Directors: Patrick and Paul Gibbs
Writers: Patrick and Paul Gibbs
Stars: Zachari Michael Reynolds, Rosalie Bertrand, Mary Etuk, Terence S. Johnson and Chris Henderson

With an outrageous title like *Steve from Accounting vs. The Shadow Dwellers*, this was never going to be a serious affair, but humour is tough to get right in horror movies. This year's horror shorts at the International Horror & Sci-Fi Film Festival did pretty well on that front, *Killer Kart* and *The Root of the Problem* especially nailing it.

This one is more overt with its laughs, eschewing the subtleties of those films in favour of a Walter Mitty-esque lead character who constantly veers off into flights of fantasy and a ludicrous story that may or may not be one of them. It's never clear, for instance, how many of the 24 minutes we spend in the company of corporate drone, Stephen H. Burrows, take place at Kensington Enterprises, his workplace of three years, and how many unfold entirely within his imagination. The most obvious reading is that only the first couple of minutes are reality: his dressing down because of a rough disciplinary report and then his interaction with a few colleagues immediately afterwards.

We do have some sympathy for poor Steve. He's stuck in a dead end job in accounting, tasked with little more than carrying boxes; no wonder he starts fantasising about the three hot secretaries who share his lift to the fourth floor. He's lost whatever enthusiasm he ever had and he's got lost in small office feuds like tormenting Earl who may or may not have stolen his chocolate. What's more, he's about to turn thirty without ever having been laid, so it's hardly surprising that his psyche is screaming out for something more or that his happy place turns nightmarish.

What's fun is how that happens. He simply walks out of the lift and stumbles into a satanic cult performing a ritual human sacrifice on company time. His bosses clearly owe their success to a long habit of killing off their own staff; Kerri is just a stopgap until the great upcoming virgin sacrifice the next day when the victim turns thirty. I wonder who that could be? Well, we have twenty minutes to figure out what Steve has to do to avoid that inevitability.

Patrick and Paul Gibbs, who wrote and directed, were well aware of their limitations, as they countered each of their weaker points.

Steve's guardian angel clearly has no martial arts training, unlike some of the heavily muscled shadow dwellers like Phil Sevin, so the fight choreography is carefully edited and plays up the humour. So does the dialogue; as Steve escapes his first encounter with Sevin, he hurls feebly back, "I'm so sorry I ruined your murder party, scary skull man!"

The shadow dwellers' chant is backwards talk: "Sacul! Grebleips! Nosirrah Drof!" highlights *Indiana Jones and the Temple of Doom* as a more overt influence than any horror movie, emphasised by Randin Graves's epic score. Like that film, this is an enjoyable ride, a desk jockey's fantasy action adventure to counter his failures in life. This framework invites us to forgive the low budget, flawed acting and sync issues and sit back to enjoy the ride. Steve from Accounting is no Dr. Jones, but we're more likely to know a Steve than an Indy.

Sybling Rivalry (2011)

Director: Tara-Nicole Azarian
Writer: Tara-Nicole Azarian
Stars: Tara-Nicole Azarian, David Topp and Carrie Marshall

I was a little disappointed with *Sybling Rivalry*, but only because it tells a simple tale without a single surprise.

Young Sybelle, as outrageously capable as she apparently is, lives in her brother's shadow. She's merely insurance, nothing but "a spare in case anything ever happened to the heir." Whatever she achieves, it's never enough to prompt her mother to stop fauning over Kobe, who is utterly aware of the situation and smarmily plays it up, David Topp carrying the role with charm.

And so, fed up of being effectively invisible, Sybelle decides to reframe her situation as a challenge. "Solve a problem," her mother tells her dismissively. Well, every problem has a solution, right? As you might imagine by this film's inclusion in a horror shorts set, the solution Sybelle finds is a violent wish fulfilment fantasy that many an overlooked young girl might confide to the attentive pages of her diary, while remaining afraid to take such an emphatic leap to the dark side in reality.

From the very beginning, as Sybelle writes in her diary about fear and motivation, musing about how fear can empower a step beyond, we know she's about to do something outrageous. Once we realise what her situation is, it's clear what that something is going to be; from that point, it's just a case of watching the script already in our head unfold on the screen. It's agreeably gruesome, I'll give it that, but it isn't surprising.

However, on most other fronts, *Sybling Rivalry* is a surprisingly capable film. For a start, it was shot in only one day, even though there were obviously multiple setups in each of four different rooms within a single house. That suggests a thoroughly effective shooting schedule and the results suggest a capable crew. While the camera is never still, it avoids the usual pitfalls of the handheld camera and attempts a couple of more ambitious angles to boot. The entire film is well lit and the sound is excellent, with a suitable score to back it up. Technically, it's solid.

Most obviously though, the young lady behind the film is clearly a talent to watch. She's Tara-Nicole Azarian, who graduated from high school this year at the age of fourteen. She wrote and directed this, currently her second of five short films, and she also took the lead role of Sybelle for herself. As befits an overdone character, she overdoes the acting, well grounded as an invisible girl but clearly relishing every moment of her dastardly scheme to be noticed, all the more obvious compared to the matter-of-fact portrayal singer Carrie Marshall gives to her mother. It's grand guignol in suburbia and Azarian plays to the audience more than just through her narration; this could work even better on stage.

This is a rare approach for her though, as the fifty plus roles she's played on screen are highly varied and her other personal films each focus on social issues: *My Name is Anna* dealing with anorexia, *Cardboard* with homelessness and *ROTFL* with teen suicide. In such company, this is fluff but at least it's capable fluff.

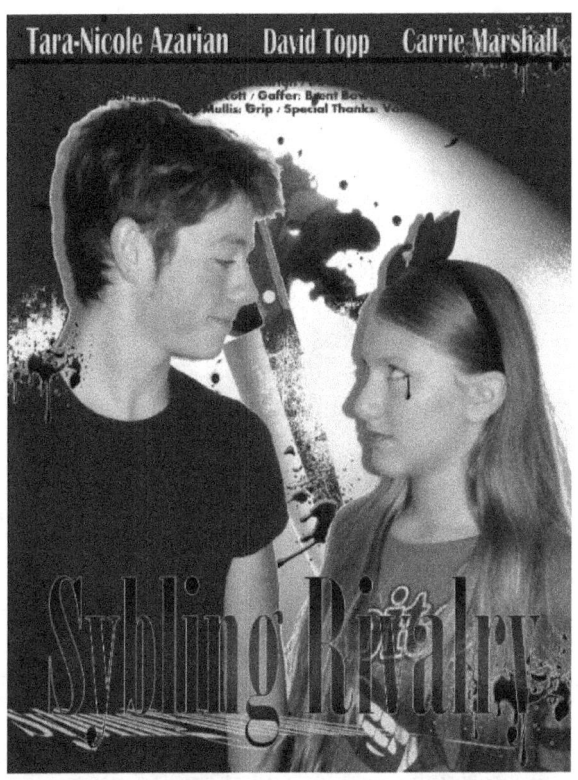

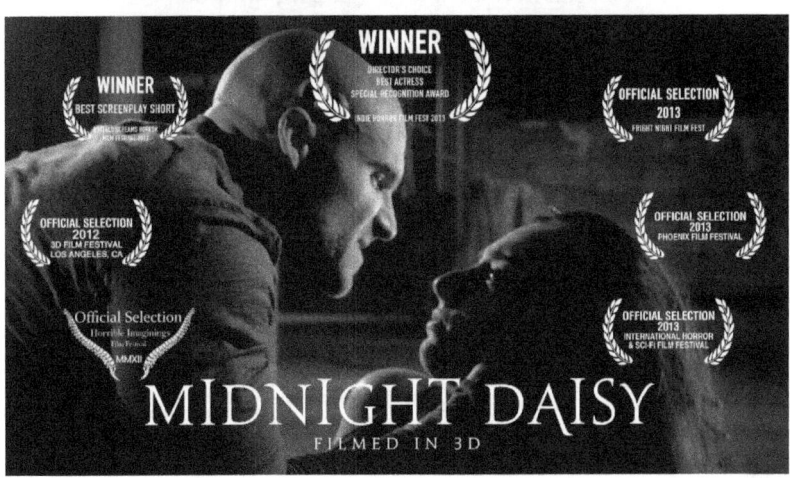

Midnight Daisy (2013)

Director: Asa Shumskas-Tait
Writer: Jesse Vigil
Stars: Najarra Townsend, Raymond Stefanelli, Daniel Roberts, Mark Cirillo, Henry Le Blanc and Claire Scott

The winner of the Best Horror Short at this year's International Horror & Sci-Fi Film Festival was *Killer Kart*, a ridiculous homage to ridiculous eighties slashers that was played delightfully straight. It was a great film, but had the judges looked past the laughter, this would surely have been the film chosen.

It plays perfectly as a short film, only fifteen minutes in duration, but it has enough substance to be easily expanded to feature length, as indeed, unsurprisingly, the folk at the awesomely named Psychic Bunny production company plan to do.

It's a lot of different types of movie all wrapped up into one neat package: it isn't the torture porn that the opening scene might suggest, but it is a supernatural movie, an urban legend movie and a ghost hunter movie, with hints at a conspiracy theory movie to boot. What makes it so impressing is that all of this plays out precisely as it should, without ever feeling like the filmmakers had to shoehorn material in to achieve what they wanted.

It starts as it means to go on with a great camera movement. Initially we watch the Reverend Billy Mason preach, but then the camera pulls out to show that he's on TV, then back again in an elliptical curve until we see that it's leaned up against a pillar in a underground garage at an angle, being watched by a young lady on the floor.

Her hands are bound with duct tape but she isn't gagged, because her captors want her able to talk. They're initially what you might expect (one threatens her with a knife and another waggles his tongue provocatively in her face) but she isn't. She may have been in the wrong part of town but she's not entirely unarmed because she knows how to summon the help of Midnight Daisy, a "vengeful spirit" in local urban legend who supposedly comes to the aid of women in distress, women just like her. It just takes a particular symbol drawn in blood and a particular chant, all within the right circumstances. And if this all seems a little deliberate, we soon find out why: Dom and his men are ghost bounty hunters.

I really like the concepts in play here. Director Asa Shumskas-Tait aimed at "a new campfire story", the sort of local ghost myth that's most commonly explained around campfires in horror flicks, but he wanted it to have more substance than the usual take where nobody believes the story but the spirit shows up anyway and slaughters everyone. Adding the ghost hunter idea was a good one, a way to tie the new paranormal investigator trend to the tried and tested old urban legends.

Dom, the lead bounty hunter, is a fascinating character, with enticing subdermal implants that would stand out all the more if seen in the stereoscopic 3D in which this was filmed. Of course, he plans so well that we know his target is going to shake things up and so she does.

This short film is certainly enough to whet our appetite but it'll take the full feature to really define this urban legend, as well as to explore who Dom is and what drives him. I've seen features with less substance than this short; it ought to expand superbly.

Welcome Wagon (2013)

Directors: Jessica Lee Wright and Sadie Shaw
Writer: Sadie Shaw, Jessica Wright and Dave Malloure
Stars: Maitress Madeline, Bryan Coons and Mineko Brand

OK, I didn't get this one at all, unless its point is scarily obvious. It's a short film by the Wooden Lens, working in collaboration with Everyday's a Holiday, and it markets itself appropriately as "a dark comedy from the most twisted parts of Jessica Lee Wright's and Sadie Shaw's brains."

It may just be the definition of "it seemed like a good idea at the time," given that it was shot as part of a 24 hour film challenge over one Friday night and Saturday morning. 48 hour films are tough enough, but 24 hours is surely enough to only throw out wild ideas for five minutes to see which ones stick before getting down to business. Apparently this one stuck.

It appears to rail against the normal world by pointing out that what goes on behind the front doors of those quintessentially nice folk in small town America is wilder than you're likely to imagine. Maitresse Madeline certainly ought to know that, given that she's a professional dominatrix, fetish model and B.D.S.M. performer, but as Mary Lou Blue from number 259, she's saccharine sweet with a cherry on top.

I don't need to have watched *The Andy Griffith Show* to know why Grand Mayberry sounds so decent and all-American. Here it's a down home town full of other down home locations: Sunnybrook Lane, Strudel Street and Chesapeake Lane. You just know that if you moved into this neighbourhood, you'd have neighbours pounding on your door with apple pies to make you welcome.

Well, Mary Lou brings cupcakes and lemon meringues instead, but she's just as wholesome with her striking red hair and gleaming smile. She even has a dog that's as tiny as you might expect. What you won't expect is who moved into number one to spark such a welcome.

It's a panda. Well, really it's some dude wearing a panda suit, but Mary Lou takes it entirely in stride and never even mentions it. The script has no concerns with the concept either, suggesting that furries moving in next door is so unremarkable that it isn't even worth commenting on. They're just neighbours.

And so it goes. Quite why this sprang out of the imagination of Jessica Lee Wright and Sadie Shaw, who directed and co-wrote the film with Dave Malloure, I have no idea. How they happened to have a professional dominatrix and three panda suits immediately to hand, I have no idea either, but I'm sure the aftershoot party must have been memorable.

What they were trying to say here, I have just as little idea: either it's that old chestnut that the people who seem the most vanilla are secretly the wildest of the bunch or it's a call to action to rid the world of the furry menace. From glancing at their other films on Vimeo, I have a feeling that The Wooden Lens are non-commercial absurdists who enjoy the process of filmmaking and like to see things on screen that they've never seen before. For my part, I'm all for it. They succeeded here on that front, but that's about all.

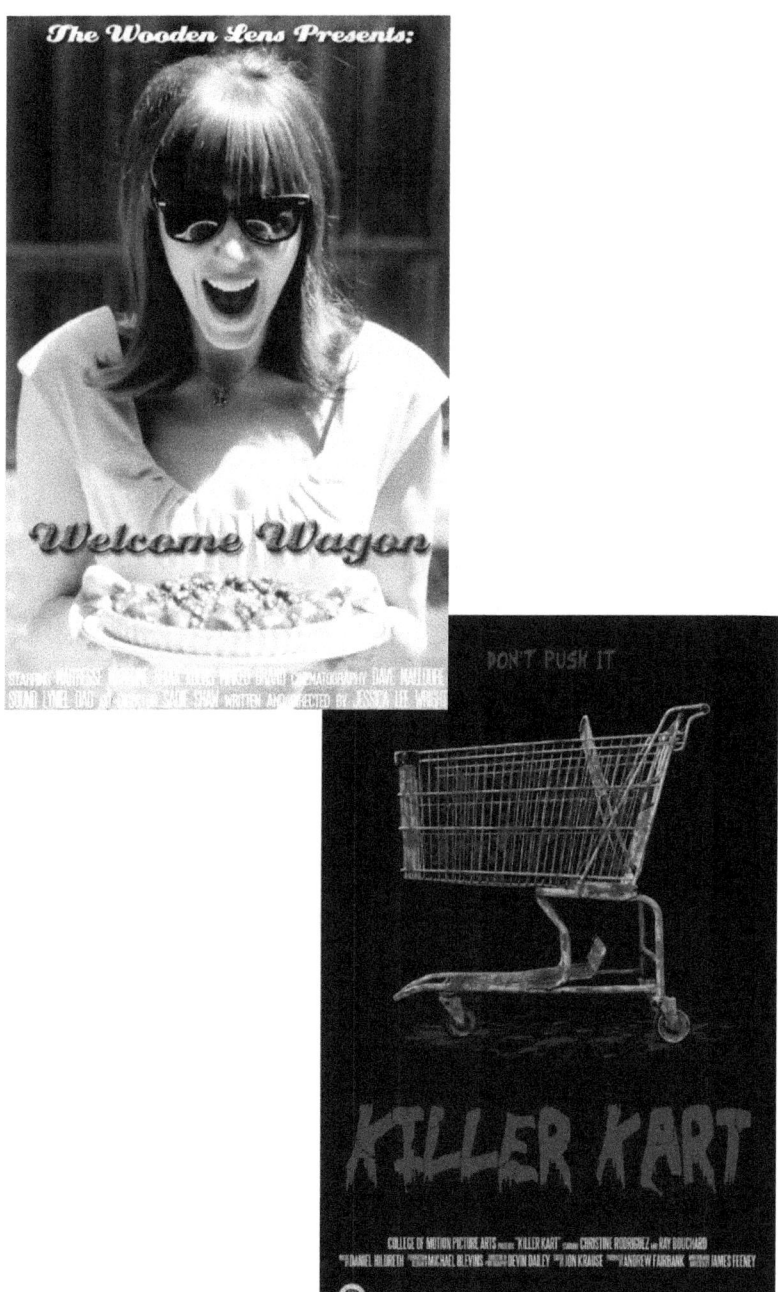

Killer Kart (2012)

Director: James Feeney
Writer: James Feeney
Stars: Christine Rodriguez, Ray Bouchard, Elly Schaefer and Britt Michael Gordon

I don't know what they're putting in the water down there in the Sunshine State (except alligators), but the horror filmmakers who are emerging from Florida State University's College of Motion Picture Arts are making themselves rather noticed. at least in my household.

There was only one set of horror shorts at the 2013 festival, but two of the best films in it have ties to F.S.U.: *Killer Kart* was made there and *The Root of the Problem* was made by an alumnus of the school who shot *Kirksdale* there, a festival selection in 2008.

This one works as a companion piece to Quentin Dupieux's *Rubber*, but its questions about technique are not posed on screen, only in our minds. The goal, of course, is to make a slasher movie with a plainly ridiculous antagonist but to play it so straight that we can't help but be affected even against our better judgement. In *Rubber* that antagonist was a car tyre, able to explode its victims through some sort of psychic power; here it's a shopping cart seeking revenge on mankind for years of abuse.

To explain how well this fifteen minute short was constructed, I should point out that there isn't one thing in the entire movie that you haven't seen before, merely with a different villain. The whole thing is so archetypal that you could easily use it as a template. Conjure up a new monster, then take this script, change the location and character names and shake up the dialogue until you're not going to get sued for plaguarism. You'll then have a framework on which to build your horror movie. Rinse and repeat and you'll have a dozen of them ready to go. Don't feel too bad about it either, as it's nothing new: Charles B. Griffith reused some of his scripts for Roger Corman three or four times.

Of course, to make a generic script worthy, it takes a crew to make it work and a cast to make it shine. Fortunately those aren't problems here. The crew hit their beats so well we could set our watches by them and the cast play their roles delightfully straight, however many takes it must have taken them.

We follow Cass, a young lady working her first night as closing manager at the Victory supermarket. It's not going well for her: the phones are failing, the comm system is broken and the lights go out while she's in the bathroom. Her boyfriend Ryan, a shelf stocker, wants to get frisky in the aisles. Bailey, the only cashier who's still working, disappears with her till open. That leaves Hale, who's been the maintenance man forever and looks like it. "There's a lot of years there," suggests Cass, "and they weren't all good."

He gives good jibe though and he's a joy from his first moments on screen. Ray Bouchard channels a Bill Moseley vibe as he delivers the serious lines, putting the case for the abused carts with such a straight face that it deserves our admiration. His performance would play well next to Christopher Bradley's in *Black Gulch* and for most of the same reasons. It's hard to pick a favourite line, but I'd have to go with the one he throws out after realising Bailey is still alive. "Jesus!" he cries. "I thought she'd be the first to go!"

Elly Schaefer does well as Bailey, although she has little to do except scream. She's good at that and she is in the ice cream aisle, making it all a bad pun too. Christine Rodriguez comes out best as Cass, because, surprisingly for a short film, she grows believably throughout. In the beginning, she's just a nervous young store manager but, by the end, she's ready to kick ass and take names, as nervous but now able to work past her fears to do what has to be done. When she screams, "Shopping carts can't kill people!" it feels right and, given the line, that's pretty astounding.

Of course the main characters in slasher movies always take a back seat to the monster, even more the case here because of what it is. Writer/director James Feeney obviously had a great deal of fun contrasting wild reactions with benign motion; Cass's pans across the parking lot to find the killer are hilarious. He had even more fun modifying his cart to pay homage to *Jaws* or *Alien*.

And at the end of the day, that's what this is all about: pure, unadulterated fun.

The International Horror & Sci-Fi Film Festival

2013

Sci-Fi Shorts A

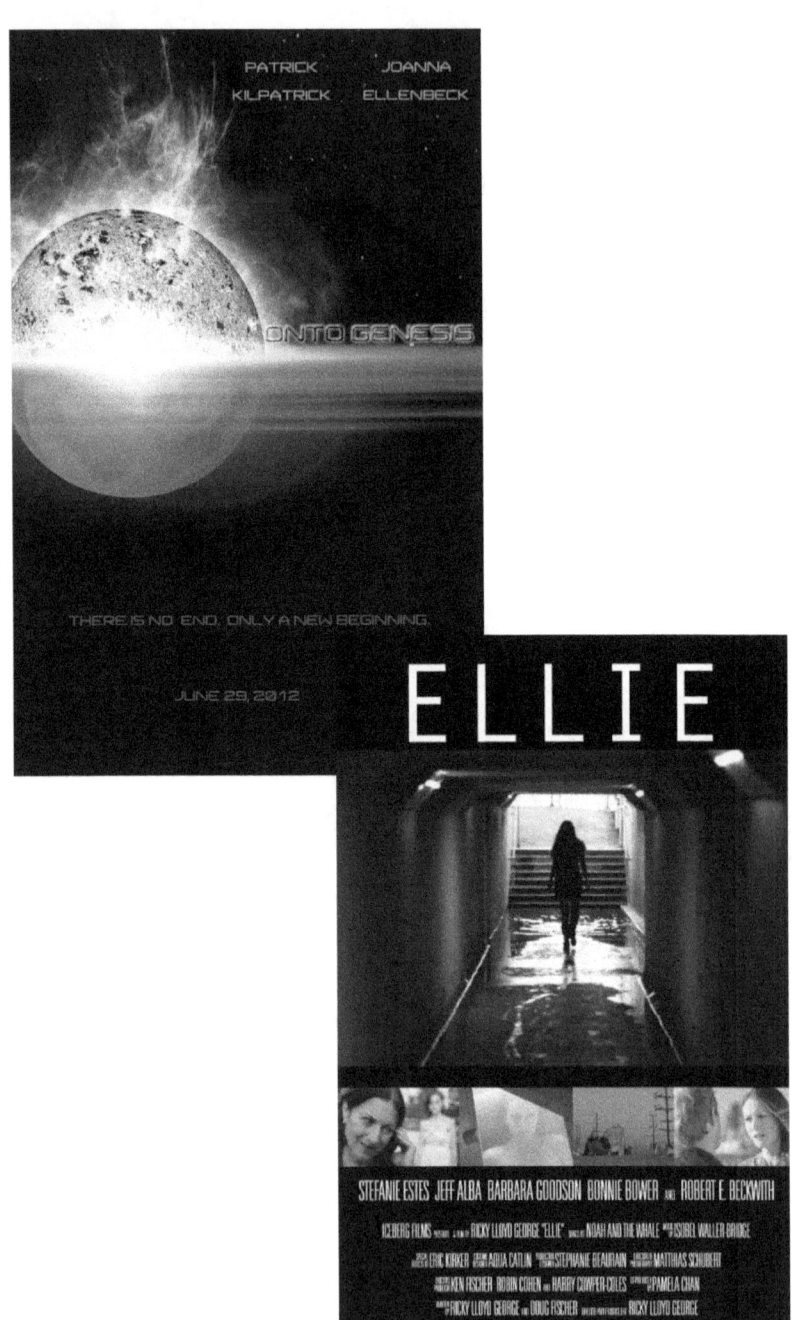

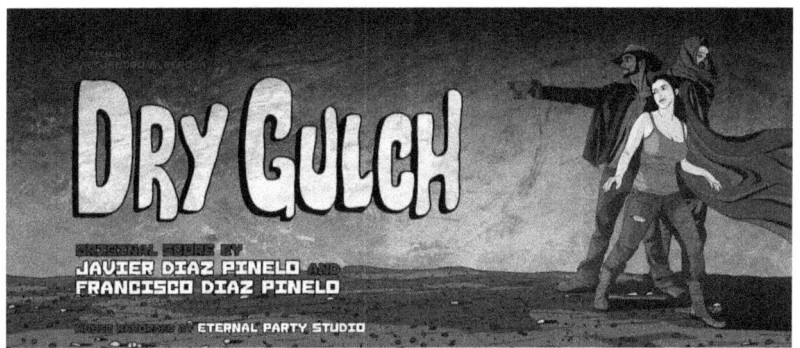

Dry Gulch (2013)

Director: Alejandro Alberola
Writer: Alejandro Alberola

This was a subtle choice by programmer Mike Stackpole to kick off the first Sci-Fi Shorts set in 2013. Not only is it an animated film, it's one without a single word of dialogue, the only vocal sound we expect to hear being a scream that escapes its owner's throat in the form of searing guitar. It even starts slowly, but the stunning visual design on display was certain to grab everyone's eyeballs and turn them to the screen.

The films that populated two sets of sci-fi shorts this year were of unparalleled quality, hopefully because filmmakers are starting to realise that science fiction doesn't have to equal special effects, and those still playing with CGI are finding it easier to make it look good. Selections during the past few years have been inconsistent, as the quality of submissions has varied so much, but this year's pleasant surprise of consistency is outweighed perhaps only by the pleasant surprise of variety, this being its epitome.

It's a Mexican short, which is quintessentially science fiction and quintessentially western all at the same time. We're in Chiseler's Burg, which the film's IMDb synopsis calls "an old town on a dying planet in a long forgotten region of space". It's clearly influenced by the movie *Heavy Metal* and in turn by the organic work of artists like Jean Giraud aka Mœbius, who had co-created *Métal Hurlant*, the

French comic book whose legacy led to it.

Perhaps uncoincidentally, Mœbius, who is still mostly known for fantasy and science fiction work, had started out in westerns with a series called *Blueberry*. He worked occasionally in film, including concept designs for *Alien*, which grew out of the legendary failed adaptation of *Dune* by Chilean auteur, Alejandro Jodorowsky, with whom he'd created comic books in France, such as *The Incal*. The reason I mention all this is that *Dry Gulch* is clearly so influenced by titles like *The Incal* that they could almost be seen as part of the same universe.

If you've ever seen anything drawn by Mœbius, I'm sure you'll be instantly intrigued by that. *Dry Gulch* was brought to life by six animators, who share no less than twenty names between them, so I'm not going to list them here, but they channel Alejandro Alberola's vision into a striking world.

As we follow a silent story from murder and hanging to revenge, we can't help but bathe in the highly organic visuals: a spaceship that reminds of a giant flying centipede, snow that makes it seem like the stars are dancing, huge mushrooms that serve as bridges.

While this is clearly a western, that concept is fully translated to this alien world. In place of horses there are giant spiked warthogs or huge birds. Instead of carriages, there are hovercars with neatly retracting steps. The sniper rifle looks like a dieselpunk antique. Yet the archetypes are still here and eerily familiar: the wanted poster, the windswept duster and the fire to keep people warm out in the middle of nowhere in the desert.

The music is another archetype, but less traditionally American and more like an Italian prog rock improvisation on spaghetti western themes by Ennio Morricone. The choice to to make this rather universal by eschewing spoken words in favour of themes is a good one, the English words on the wanted poster really as much art as the images they accompany. The lack of words highlights the prominence and importance of the music, by Javier and Francisco Diaz Pinelo, and also underlines that connection to *Heavy Metal*. I really enjoyed the score, which accentuates the visuals but also survives them, as it would be much easier to listen to this outside the framework of the film than most soundtracks.

If I'm navigating Spanish websites appropriately, it would seem that both play for a Mexican hard rock band called Ravenscar, who I will now need to explore. Now all these guys need to do is make more films like *Dry Gulch* and we'll have a Mexican *Heavy Metal* to enjoy.

Ontogenesis (2012)

Director: Joanna Ellenbeck and Jason Neudecker
Writer: Joanna Ellenbeck and Joseph Ruggieri
Stars: Joanna Ellenbeck and Patrick Kilpatrick

Perhaps the best way to highlight how consistently good the selections for the Sci-Fi Shorts A set were in 2013 is to point out that *Ontogenesis* is probably the worst of them.

It's far from a bad film; in fact I've seen sets of sci-fi short films at festivals where this would have been the best rather than the worst, but it just didn't spark for me, playing a little on the wrong side of the simple vs. deep conflict. Otherwise it's a promising piece, with decent actors in front of the camera, competent crew behind it and a thoughtful idea underpinning it all.

It isn't as pretentious as the title would suggest, though it neglects, perhaps deliberately, to tell us what ontogenesis actually means. The dictionary says that ontogeny or ontogenesis is "the origin and development of an individual organism from embryo to adult." The poster puts it more simply: "There is no end. Only a new beginning." The broad sweep of the film is ambitious enough to apply this to our entire species.

Within that stunningly broad framework, we get little pictures to focus on. Joanna Ellenback, who wrote, produced and directed the picture (each role with a different collaborator), also plays Aria, who has survived the end of the world by the time the film begins. What apocalyptic event triggered it is never mentioned, but she's part of a small band of survivors eking out their existence as best they can given the circumstances, struggling against similarly wary bands of survivors in the process.

When Aria returns alone from a vaguely outlined mission, maybe to parlay with one of these bands, she's confronted angrily by the apparent leader of hers, Nathan. What happened to everyone else, he asks? How come she survived? And when she tells him what really happened, he doesn't believe her in the slightest. If what she says is true, why was she let in on the secret? Why not him, the powerful leader who does so much to keep his people alive?

I like the way that *Ontogenesis* attempts to explore such a broad concept with such a small story, clearly one of many such stories ongoing on this world at this time. Ellenbeck proves capable as Aria, really the leading lady though she's soon lost in the noise when the film begins to incorporate wild and beautiful footage from NASA's Hubble telescope website, directed by Oli Usher. Contrasted with the majesty of creation in the form of an exoplanet orbiting Fomalhaut and a space artist's impressions of a vampire star, people we've just met can't help but fade from our memories as if they were never there to begin with.

Patrick Kilpatrick, a massively experienced actor who has appeared on what might just be every dramatic TV show of the last decade and a bit, makes more of his brief appearance as Nathan, endowing his character with a surprising amount of depth given how long he doesn't get to do it, but just like Aria, once that space footage takes over, Nathan is lost too.

I'd like to have liked this film more, but while it has a great story wanting to come out, Ellenbeck and her co-writer Joseph Ruggieri can't seem to find a way to phrase it. Instead we're given some good scenes but little to tie them together. The impressionistic bundling of realistic scenes is not particularly successful, though the impressionistic bundling of impressionistic scenes is far better, in a sort of intergalactic *Koyaanisqatsi* sort of way.

Perhaps appropriately, given where the story takes us, it felt like the film had two completely different approaches that were pulling each other apart. Had Ellenbeck chosen either of those, the result would probably have worked better than choosing both of them within a mere nine minute running time. That was only fitting if her goal was to demonstrate how jarring the events she recounts would be, but that isn't the best way to entertain an audience.

Ontogenesis is a capable film and it has much to offer, but it should have been much more and it was outclassed by the rest of the short films in this particular set.

Ellie (2013)

Director: Ricky Lloyd George
Writers: Ricky Lloyd George and Doug Fischer
Stars: Stefanie Estes, Jeff Alba, Barbara Goodson, Bonnie Bower and Robert E. Beckwith

I liked *Ellie* from moment one, because of the colours. They're lush: natural greens and yellows at an outdoor photoshoot and red indoors at a bar, where the model goes to drown her sorrows. The music finds a way to mirror that in sound too.

She's the Ellie of the title, of course, and she's not quite who we might think. The first hint comes when she introduces herself to the gentleman next to her at the bar and the lights dim, but we discover that she's not human when she swipes the back of her neck to open her belly, so she can empty out three glasses worth of Jack Daniels through a tube in her mechanical innards. Back at the bar, we realise that she's magnetic, both literally, as cutlery on the bar occasionally moves towards her, and figuratively, because the bartender immediately recognises her on the commercial that shows on the bar's TV while she's in the bathroom. That's for Spirit, which could be anything from the abstract beach scene we see.

There's a vast amount of depth here, going far beyond the romance at the heart of the film which sparks up between Ellie and Roger, who feels as suffocated in his job as she does in hers. I found this romance as meaningful as any screen romance between two people who are separated only by convention.

I don't know if Ricky Lloyd George, who directed and co-wrote, deliberately aimed to comment on relationships between members of the same sex or different races, but given how much else he's obviously commenting on here, I'd assume that he did. For a story named for and following a robot woman, it's packed to the seams with an exploration of human drives, what we might reference as making us human: the need to be happy and to make others happy, the joy of being wanted and the fear of not being wanted any more, the drive to do what's expected for no better reason than the fact that it's expected. This is an amazingly human story.

Even moving past Ellie and Roger, there's a lot of commentary here about society and especially about the power of advertising, which is a central part of the story. The purpose of advertisers is to convince us what's best for us and for everyone else, to explain to us in every detail how we should live and how we should act. That's also the realm of another occupation, that of gods. The two merge here in another way too, namely the ability to create life in our own image.

There's a great deal of debate about ethics in advertising, as it's easy nowadays to enhance reality through magic powers known as PhotoShop plugins, to remove blemishes and improve features, and so create false impressions of reality that can have both positive and negative real world effects. Nina and the advertisers in Ellie go a step further to create 3D models to serve their campaigns, not using graphic manipulation but using robotics. Ellie herself is completely artificial but passed off as real.

And with that, the story goes full circle and asks us that time honoured science fiction question of how to define humanity. What makes us human? How can we measure it? What line can be drawn that uniquivocally divides what is human from what is not?

Everything that Ellie does feels human, even though she clearly isn't by any obvious definition we may conjure up. So we have to begin to examine her motivations. Is she doing all these human things because that's how she feels, or is it because that's how she's been programmed, whether literally through code or figuratively through the advertising that aims to program us incessantly from every billboard, magazine and television set?

This film, like its thematic cousin, *Blade Runner*, makes us think not only about the characters we watch but about ourselves too. And in an homage to another classic film, *Some Like It Hot*, the last line brings us neatly back down to earth.

What a wonderful short film this was!

A Conversation About Cheating with My Time Travelling Future Self (2012)

Director: Pornsak Pichetshote
Writer: Pornsak Pichetshote
Stars: Bobby Campo, Haley Webb and Lauren Kruse

Surely the best title in play at this year's International Horror & Sci-Fi Film Festival (or indeed the last bunch of them) was this one: *A Conversation About Cheating with My Time Travelling Future Self.*

Given that the first short film made by writer/director Pornsak Pichetshote was intriguingly called *Women Who Eat Meat*, I'm very tempted to build a time machine just to find out what other films he's going to make in the future.

Perhaps he already built one and used it to go back in time to persuade Hollywood producers that the titles they had weren't the right ones. Was it Pichetshote who persuaded Clint Eastwood to rename *The Cut-Whore Killings* to *Unforgiven*? Maybe it was he who talked the adapters of a newspaper article called *The Tribal Rites of the New Saturday Night* into calling it *Saturday Night Fever* instead. If he was the one responsible for changing the title of that obscure, unpublished stage play, *Everybody Comes to Rick's*, when Hollywood began to adapt it for the screen, into *Casablanca*, I'll buy him a drink or three.

"It's never just one thing, but you know that, right?" That's what the narrator tells us, as we watch Stan dance rather suggestively with a gorgeous blonde who is clearly not the dark haired lady in the image on his phone. He's talking about all those little moments we could have played in other ways or those decisions we could have taken differently.

What makes this special, as Stan knows already and we're about to find out, as he leaves a guaranteed sexual conquest with this smoking hot blonde, is that he's the narrator too. And as the title hammers home, that doesn't mean his inner voice needling for attention, his conscience screaming to be heard or a pair of those little angels and devils that show up on shoulders in animated movies to figure out the best plan of action, it's that he's literally the narrator.

He's in a nearby room ready to explain. "I have travelled exactly one year back in time," he says, "to tell you to cheat on your girlfriend with that slut in the other room."

Now, as setups for science fiction stories go, that's a pretty good one. It doesn't quite reach the epic stature of Fredric Brown's *Knock*, but it's a peach nonetheless. Bring it on, I say!

And Pichetshote does. Like any story about cheating, everything here boils down to trust and selfishness, but that usually means the trust that exists (or doesn't) between a couple and the selfishness that leads at least one half of that couple to stray. This nine minute short goes a notable step further by making it all about Stan.

It may be difficult, and perhaps even counterintuitive, to trust another person a hundred percent (which is why love has to step in to do the job), but how hard can it be to trust yourself? What if "yourself" is outwardly manifest and has your unlived next year of future lived and outlined so that you can make better informed decisions? Even he might have ulterior motives, after all. But who knows him best?

Where Pichetshote goes with this is consistently fascinating and provocative. It's rare that I get to see a new twist on the tired time travel trope that short sci-fi filmmakers like to explore so much.

Haley Webb and Lauren Kruse get a little to do here but not much. Almost the entire running time revolves around Bobby Campo and Bobby Campo, the current and future versions of Stan talking to each other in a hotel room, thus proving that capable science fiction doesn't have to have CGI up the wazoo, it merely has to have ideas.

Pichetshote describes this as a "theatre piece that can only be done on film" and I find that a pretty solid way to see it. Given that what we see relies on what Campo does, it's good to see that he does good work here, ensuring that each version of his character is slightly but believably different, not only because a year makes everyone just a little different but to help us keep track of which one's which. Their conversation feels natural because he really is replying to himself, merely a recorded version, which in a way is a microcosm of the story as a whole. Even without a spectacular title, this one is worth coming back to.

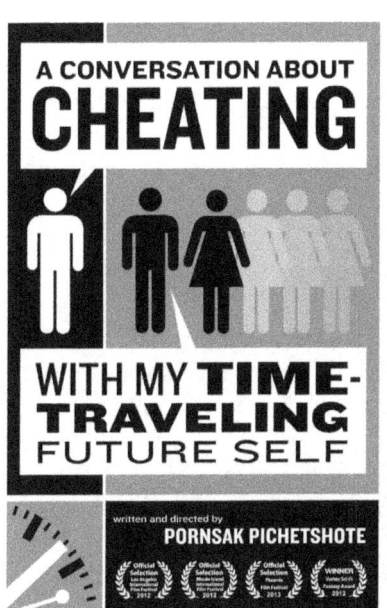
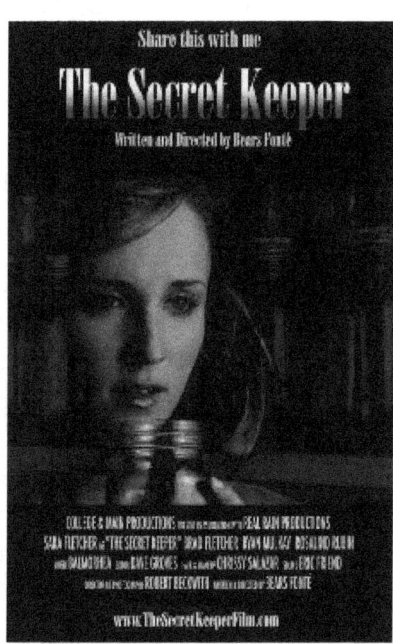

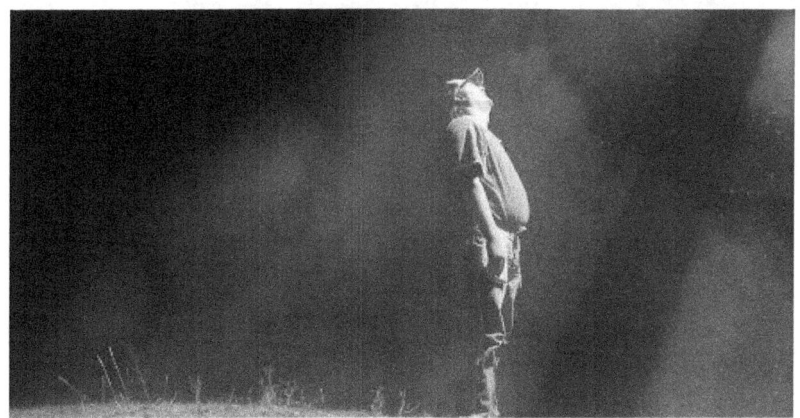

Low Tide in the High Desert

The Secret Keeper (2012)

Director: Bears Fonté
Writer: Bears Fonté, from a story by Bears Fonté and Sara Fletcher
Stars: Sara Fletcher, Brad Fletcher, Rosalind Rubin and Ryan Mulkay

Around the time *The Secret Keeper* began, partway into the Sci-Fi Shorts A set, the projector began to misbehave, thus rendering the colours notably off. Given that, even with this hindrance, *The Secret Keeper* was without a doubt my favourite short in this set, I'm very happy to report that it looks a lot better when not filtered through a malfunctioning projector.

That said, the colours are still faded, as old fashioned as are the clothes, hair styles and feel of the piece. We're never told where we are, but it's some sort of alternate universe 1940s America, with a lot that's very recognisable but things here and there that are completely alien.

One of the latter is the mention of the Open Zone, in which our story takes place and from which our characters aim to flee. The other is the neat little concept at the heart of the story and which provides its title. Alice, the leading lady, is a secret keeper, which is a profession in this world.

We watch how she works as the film begins, dealing with a client in such a way that invites a clear parallel with another profession. Alice works from home and her client feels nervous in even being there. It's his first time, apparently, and he's not sure how it's all supposed to work. He's Calvin, but she doesn't need his name. She takes his money and asks him to wait for her in the bedroom. When she joins him, they can begin.

No, she's not a prostitute, though she serves a similar purpose, to take good care of a mental urge that has a physical manifestation. However, there's nothing sexual in either the source of the urge or the way in which she satisfies it, making her more like a confessor, who can relieve burdens and allow people to move forward with their lives, happier with their secrets shared and not festering away inside. There's a literal transference, making Alice akin to a sin eater (or a prostitute again), but the secret doesn't stay in her; she's a physical conduit who transfers it on again into a glass jar.

I adored this concept, which merges the world's oldest profession with perhaps its next oldest. There are ties to prostution beyond the clearly outlined parallels, in that secret keeping is hinted at not being a respected profession, perhaps one to which people come out of desperation and doubt, their visit a secret in itself. Yet there are continued parallels to the priesthood too, such as the ritual and litany of the event. "Share this with me," Alice asks each client to formally begin the process; "Go and let the peace surround your soul," she recites after it's over.

This is an enticing concept and Sara Fletcher is magnificent in both aspects, simultaneously carnal and consecrated. Magnetically gorgeous even in dowdy attire, she would surely be the favourite in any brothel. Yet she carries herself impeccably, with a inherently trustworthy, almost holy air, making her a natural confessor. One client calls her a saint, but she prefers martyr.

What makes *The Secret Keeper* such a great film instead of just a great concept is that there's also a strong story wrapped around it, unfolding consistently and believably over an unrushed eighteen minutes. I'm getting close to spoiler territory, so I'll be extra careful and merely say that another client comes to her with a secret to unburden which affects Alice directly and so tests her integrity as a secret keeper.

With both prostitutes and confessors, there's a substantial level of trust inherent in the exchange and that's no different here. While there are clear sides drawn, with Alice the justified heroine, the underlying theme of the piece is Juvenal's old standard: "Quis custodiet ipsos custodes?" This literally means "Who will guard the guards?" but, courtesy of Alan Moore, is more commonly translated nowadays as "Who watches the watchmen?" The Latin for "Who will keep the secrets of the secret keepers?" is remarkably similar: it just adds the word "arcana" for 'secrets'.

This film really has everything. It starts with a great concept, which it then fashions into a great story, courtesy of Fletcher and director Bears Fonté. Underneath it all is a great theme which keeps us thinking, not only about what we see but the ramifications of it as well.

The production is pretty solid too, with Fletcher's acting most notable. The other two actors with substantial screen time are Ryan Mulkay and Rosalind Rubin, both of whom do solid work as well, Mulkay looking especially right for the period.

If there's a downside, it's the lighting. While it looks much better without projection issues, it aims at a muted palette in deference to the forties feel and some scenes play out in light that's a little too dim and with colours that are a little too faded.

That's not much of a downside for a powerful short and I really need to track down *iCrime* now, a feature which Bears Fonté wrote and directed in 2011 with Sara Fletcher in the lead. If it's half as good as this, I'll be impressed.

Low Tide in the High Desert (2011)

Director: Stanley Ray
Writer: Stanley Ray
Stars: Chris Ranney and Steve Corona

Sometimes just mentioning the location is enough to set the scene. This one's set in Roswell, New Mexico. Now tell me what it's about?

Well, you're not going to be far wrong, but Stanley Ray's script has a great deal of charm to it and it's cleverly written as a dialogue driven piece. Almost the entire picture unfolds in the form of a conversation between a pair of cousins, Gary and Chuck, who are camped out by a lake. Gary is like a redneck who can reason, while Chuck is mildly retarded. They contrast strongly in almost every way, perhaps the best example suitably being in dialogue during an early exchange. "You're so unprepared for life," Gary tells Chuck, who pouts and replies. "You're such an assface!"

The most important difference for this picture is that Gary doesn't believe in UFOs at all, while Chuck believes in pretty much everything Fortean: Bigfoot, the Loch Ness Monster, Princess Leia's virginity, you name it. And from that extra hint, I'm sure you can tell precisely where this is going.

Shot in seven days with a mostly student-based crew, *Low Tide in the High Desert* is capably done. For an outdoor shoot, most of which took place at night, the lighting and sound are surprisingly good. When the effects show up, they're minimal but effective. The acting is precisely what it needs to be: Chris Ranney grounds the film superbly as Gary, while Steve Corona overplays Chuck with wild abandon.

Chuck is the sort of character which Eddie Deezen would have played back in the eighties, outrageously nerdy and with a whole collection of social issues to suit every occasion. He's the sort of character who you'd hate to be around unless you have a nerdy streak yourself, in which case he would be your best friend forever. Well, until that inevitable argument about something completely meaningless culturally that turns you into mortal enemies. Ray plays in that pond a lot here, deliberately stirring up sacred cows in both the *Star Trek* and *Star Wars* universes, often as part of the very same sentence.

The dialogue that handles this sort of shenanigans is by far the best thing about this picture. Corona and especially Ranney bring it to life well, but it's the writing that stands out. Stanley Ray, who wrote and directed here, has six short films to his name; he wrote all of them and directed four. Based on what he does in this one alone, he has a knack of writing simply but effectively, not merely as the means of moving his story forward but also to build his characters and engage his audience at the same time. I wonder how many audience members at genre festivals talk to him afterwards, not to comment on his film but to debate him on one of the cultural points he riffed on in it.

This isn't the most substantial sci-fi short you'll have ever seen, not even the most substantial in this particular set of sci-fi shorts, and you certainly won't be surprised at how it turns out in the end, but it's fun and engaging and it sits very well halfway through a set of generally serious short films. It'll definitely raise some chuckles and they're always welcome.

Restitution (2013)

Director: Justin O'Neal Miller
Writer: Justin O'Neal Miller
Stars: Jason MacDonald, Luke Donaldson, Catherine Dyer and Jasmine Burke

Restitution was another sci-fi short that knocked my socks off at the 2013 festival. There's a lot going on in this one, some of it very subtle, and I don't know if many of the audience members really caught the particularly brutal key twist, which stayed with me for a long while after I'd left the theatre.

At heart, it explores the point at which humanity and technology meet, using two very different examples. First up, Preston Sanders finds out the hard way that his wife, struggling with the loss of one of her two sons, had the survivor cloned without even raising the idea to him first. That's as emotional as the other is prosaic, but it's sprung on us as ruthlessly as having twins in the house again is sprung on him. It's simply the user interface he uses in his work as an architect, but it's perhaps the best, most seamless, imagining of such I've ever seen in film. It's just a pen and a sheet of paper, but they're digital and manipulated by an abacus on his desk.

It's the seamless nature of both of these that stands out for me. Sanders plays with his son for a little while without ever realising that it wasn't his son at all. Instead of Timmy, it was his cloned twin, Tommy. Given that they call each other "poppa" and "son", there's surely comment here on the lack of emotional connection Preston has to his family, especially given Susan, his wife, is quite clearly devastated, but it's also a commentary on this seamless use of technology. Susan simply went to a doctor's office one day, did the necessary and came home with a new son, that her husband is unable to distinguish from the real one. That's precisely the same trick that writer/director Justin O'Neal Miller plays on us with the "computer" in Preston's office. We see him doodling away at the outset, but only later in the film do we even realise that he's using a computer. Lost in thought, his pen leaks all over the paper, but he makes an effortless gesture and the ink blot disappears.

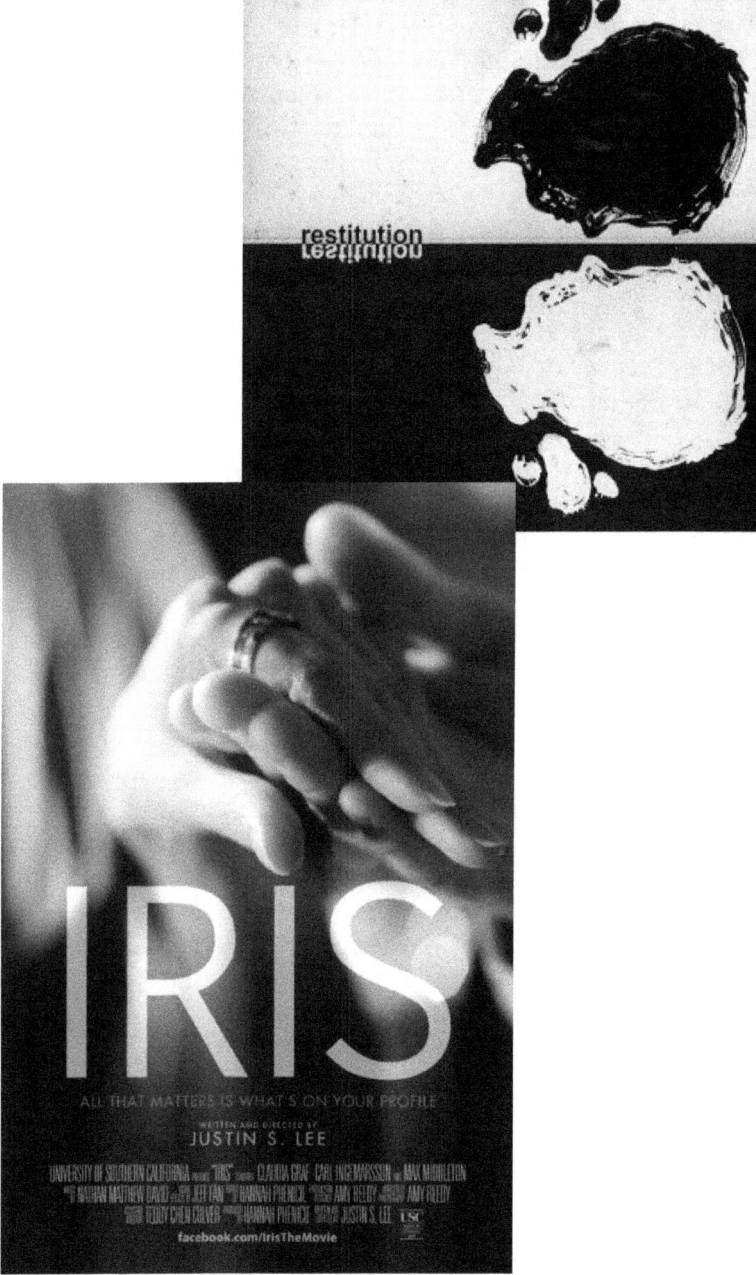

The impact here is substantial. Because I work in IT for a living, I've spent years hating what gets thrown on screen under that banner. Often it's pure ignorance on the part of a filmmaker, but still more often it's a deliberate misrepresentation of technological reality to shortcut a story. This film, hand firmly on heart, is the first time I've ever seen future technology on screen and not only not hated it, but been actively stunned in a good way by what I saw. This future version of a digitiser tablet used for computer aided design is never once even commented on, because it's routine in this man's life. To apply an overused tech phrase in its truest context, "it just works". It's invisible, background, not worthy of mention. The technology takes a back seat, so that the human beings in the equation can do what they do best, to create. And with that established, Miller applies the precise same thing to another technology: human cloning.

Cloning in films tends to be seen as science gone mad, the one step too far category that started with *Frankenstein* and never really went away, merely updated itself again and again to the next year's breakthrough instead. If I counted right, the word "clone" is only mentioned once in this script, though the entire picture is about cloning and the very title of the film is a euphemism for one step in that process, a returns policy and undo button all in one.

Just like the invisible computer Sanders uses, we never see the technology in play, just its interface, which in this instance is a doctor's office. "I was just expecting it to be more difficult," Sanders says but, as illustrated so well with his computer, that's the entire point of technology. It just works. The unasked question to the audience, especially as we know something that Sanders doesn't at this point, is whether that's always a good thing. Do we really want some things to be so easy that they can be done without thought?

Miller surely crafted this film as impeccably as someone crafted the spiral staircase in Sanders's office out of wood. He's building up a solid amount of experience as a set designer, on TV shows like *The Walking Dead*. That occupation doesn't surprise me in the slightest, as the opening of the film showcases the set design over everything else and it was the interface design that blew me away first. Perhaps it's the incessant attention to detail in that function that helped him to make this film so seamless as a writer, producer and director. He also did the digital effects.

The acting is consistently solid, whether it's the experienced adults or young Luke Donaldson playing twins, but nobody stands out above anyone else here, whether they're in front of the camera or behind it. Everyone plays their part in support of ideas that wait for us to notice them. How many clones did you see in this film? This is impeccable stuff, worthy of many return visits.

Iris (2012)

Director: Justin S. Lee
Writer: Justin S. Lee
Stars: Claudia Graf and Carl Ingemarsson

This is the sort of story that I expect to be made a lot over the next few years. Like *Restitution*, its story is set within those points where people and tech meet, but it doesn't have the philosophical depth of that film. Instead it becomes a cautionary tale, albeit a very timely one in these modern times when social media is king.

Read any tech site on a regular basis and you'll see the cycles of discussion, where proponents of a particular solution vie against its opponents again and again as each incremental change is released. One of those basic discussions has to do with trust: how to define something so that it can be absolutely trusted and, once there, how it can be hacked. What comes out of those discussions is that there are very few absolutes, which is what this film outlines. It tells a similar story to the Israeli short film, *Sight*, which I adored at this year's Jerome Indie Film & Music Festival, but it's focused onto one particular app rather than encompassing an entire experience.

This app aims to confirm an identity. Touch someone's ring and it'll provide you with certain data that you care about. Now, that doesn't sound particularly sexy, but technological solutions can be applied in different ways, which can be.

While this could easily be used to provide authentication, so you can access your work office or your bank account, here it's used for dating and the opening scene, which is accompanied by the elegant accompaniment of strings, could easily be used as a commercial. A lady and gentlemen meet in a bar, they share a mutual physical attraction and they touch rings to ensure that they're not picking up someone, you know, unsuitable.

Yes, it's inappropriate to reduce someone to a few key data, but isn't that's what people do in bars when searching for a one night stand anyway? Is there any difference between instantly defining someone by the size of their breasts and doing it by their education history or current employment?

This opening scene introduces Iris Johnson, with degrees from both Harvard and Stanford and who serves as an executive director at Goldman Sachs, to William Preston, whose degrees were earned at Princeton and Yale and who is a managing partner at his family's law group. Satisfied with their good fortune in finding each other, they walk out hand in hand, without either saying a single word. Such is the magic of technology! What could possibly go wrong?

Well, three weeks later when the sound kicks in for us and reality kicks in for the characters, we discover what went wrong in no uncertain fashion. None of this is particularly surprising, but it's handled well and it combines the latest in technological wizardry with the oldest payment method in the book. It's not a long short, running only six minutes and with the first couple taken up by that silent commercial meeting, but it covers exactly what it needs to cover and leaves us with a neat little twist to keep us thinking.

Justin S. Lee, who wrote and directed, is a student at the University of Southern California's School of Cinematic Arts, at which this was a student project. To aid the learning experience, the task at hand wasn't to make your own film, but to rotate through three different projects with a different role in each. I like that concept, because it provides the perspective not only of different aspects of the filmmaking process but by ensuring that you work on other people's pictures just as they work on yours.

As with any student, the real test is when you take all this to the next level, after graduation. It looks like Lee is starting to do that, having interned on *Atlas Shrugged: Part I*, but I hope he continues to make shorts outside of that career path. I'd have to go with *Sight* over this one, because it covers more ground and explores more depth, but this is strong on its own merits and it held its own against tough competition at the 2013 festival.

Odokuro (2011)

Director: Aurelio Voltaire
Writer: Aurelio Voltaire
Star: Gary Numan

Aurelio Voltaire, professional Cuban weirdo supreme and cultural superhero, may be best known today for dark and quirky songs that liven up episodes of the children's TV show, *The Grimm Adventures of Billy and Mandy*, but he started out in stop motion animation, inspired by the classic films of Ray Harryhausen, a first love that he's never forgotten.

He began as a kid, using a Super 8 camera he bought at the age of ten, then at seventeen he ran away to New York and worked his way up the ladder animating anything he could animate, usually commercials and station idents. He's also taught the subject for two decades at New York's School of Visual Arts, where this film was shot, or anywhere anyone might pay attention, like a panel I saw at Phoenix's première horror film festival, Fear Fest, in 2010. Over the last decade, he's been creating a series of stop motion animations called *Chimerascope*, each merging a suitably Voltaire vignette with an unwieldy title and a narration by a musician.

How unwieldy do you want to get? The short he played at Fear Fest was *DemiUrge Emesis*, with a narration by Danny Elfman of Oingo Boingo and now, of course, movie soundtracks galore. Before that was *X-Mess Detritus*, narrated by Gerard Way of My Chemical Romance and *Transrexia*, with narration by Richard Butler of the Psychedelic Furs. Perhaps the first in the series or perhaps more of an influence on it, there's also *Rakthavira*, going all the way back to 1994, with Debbie Harry of Blondie providing the narration.

Those early shorts were only a minute long, but this one hits the seven minute mark. The title is a real word, sourced from Japanese mythology where it means a starving skeleton. These particular skeletons are fifteen times taller than the rest of us, because they're amalgamations, constructed from the bones gathered from regular sized folk who died of starvation, and they like nothing more than biting off our heads, presumably to get bigger still.

Voltaire naturally gifts us with a skeleton here, partly because of the title and partly because what Ray Harryhausen fan could pass up using a skeleton in his stop motion animated short? This one's a Sumatran rat monkey freed from a bell jar by a typewriter. We're conditioned to see him as the villain of the piece but he's really a beleaguered hero, tormented by a cavalcade of curiosities and obsolete technology.

It's a gorgeous collection, crammed full of old fashioned radios and cameras, typewriters and adding machines, LPs and cassette tapes, one of which I noticed was *Replicas* by Gary Numan and the Tubeway Army, not uncoincidentally the beginning of his machine era. It looks like the display window of my sort of antique shop, right down to the mounted jackalope heads. Because this is a Voltaire short, these objects aren't there merely to make me drool, they're also haunted, starting with a cursed tape deck that springs to life and speaks in the voice of, you guessed it, Gary Numan.

It muses enticingly on the philosophical origins of life, what it actually means and how it evolves, but Numan's soft voice and the sheer range of his thought mean that it's difficult not to let this narration wash over us, playing out as just another instrument in a lively score by Gregory Hinde.

However, it refuses to be relegated to the background, because there's such a strong tie between the audio and the video, albeit Voltaire's impish stop motion work interpreting literally what the narration clearly intends to be metaphorical. That escalates until Numan mentions the wind being knocked out of our sails and Voltaire hits us with the twist.

Even more than *DemiUrge Emesis*, this is a short film that's worth watching over and over again, just to see which different moment leaps out at us each time. First time it'll be the typewriter letter eyes, then perhaps the steampunk look to the skeleton and... well, you go find out for yourself. You can thank me later.

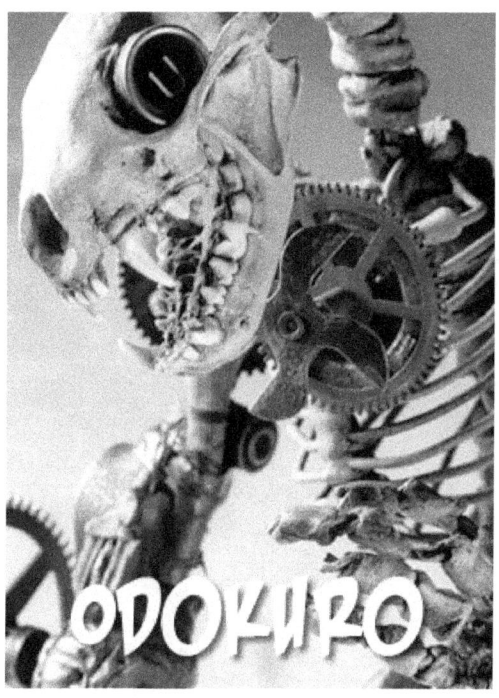

The International Horror & Sci-Fi Film Festival

2013

Sci-Fi Shorts B

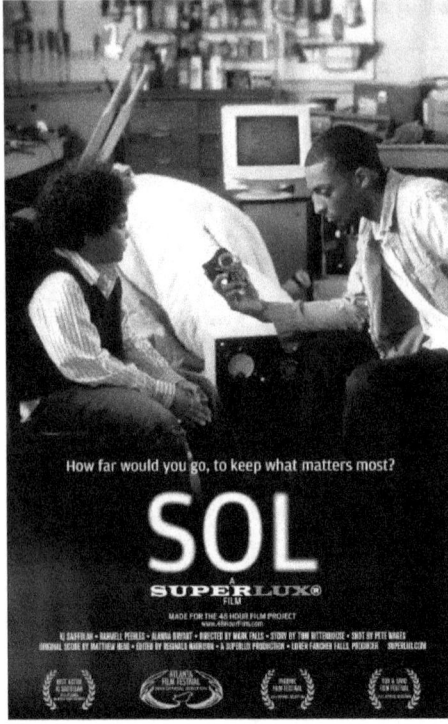

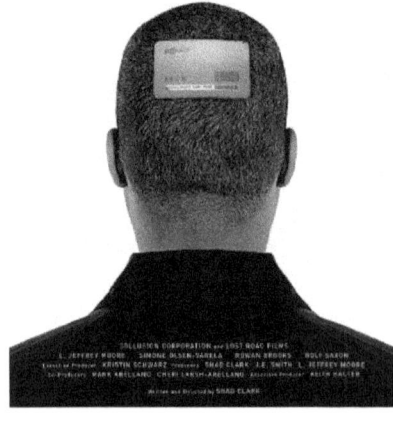

Sol (2013)

Director: Mark Falls
Writers: Mark Falls and Tom Rittenhouse, from a story by Tom Rittenhouse
Stars: K. J. Saifullah and Rahmell Peebles

I've been reviewing a lot of 48 hour films lately but they tend to be home grown ones, shot here in Arizona for the IFP Phoenix Beat the Clock challenge. This one, which opened the Sci-Fi Shorts B set in 2013, comes from a little further afield, made by Superlux for the Atlanta 48 Hour Film Project in 2012, for which it won K. J. Saifullah the Best Actor award.

He's a young boy who starts out the film enthusiastically reciting statistics about a baseball player called Jackie Lewis to his father. Dad's clearly proud: "You're perfect," he tells him, but he carries sadness in his voice as well as pride and to discover why in the eight minute running time, we're gradually given not only their personal back stories but the end of the world to boot.

This is a refreshing post-apocalyptic story, because you won't be able to find a single zombie, mad scientist or sociopolitical message anywhere. What we get instead is believable and realistic, filtered through a very personal little story.

That story was conjured up by Tom Rittenhouse, who turned it into a script in collaboration with the film's director, Mark Falls. Neither one of them appears to have much experience, if their scant IMDb credits are anything to go by, and they certainly didn't have much time to work on it. Until a 48 hour film has a script, everything else is on hold and if it's left that way for long, the time limit is going to kick your ass.

Yet this is an accomplished script, one that builds cleverly and carefully all the way to the admirable grand irony that ends the picture. Reflecting back on the short after it's done, it feels unrushed and confident that it has the space to tell its story, even though it resorts to voicemail and flashback to make that happen.

Perhaps Saifullah's cheerful smile sets us in the right mood to watch the apocalypse unfold and his father's carefully PG choice of words keeps us there. Rahmell Peebles certainly has the sort of voice and demeanour that we instinctively trust, so it's an easy ride.

If the script is accomplished, I'd need another word to describe the acting. Saifullah is a joy to watch and even more a joy to hear. Peebles matches him well, utterly attentive throughout. The third great performance is by Alanna Bryant, who plays the boy's mother. We don't meet her at all, but we hear her voice bubble at us over the phone and it's as nuanced as those of the rest of her screen family.

I see that none of these actors have many credits either, Saifullah surprisingly having the most. I'd have been impressed if this was a regular short film that its creators took their time to produce, but for all three of them to be this note perfect in a 48 hour piece, which was shot in a day before hitting post, I'm a long way beyond impressed.

I enjoyed *Sol* when I first saw it, but it's such a smooth ride that it takes a couple more times through to really appreciate how pristine it really is, even surrounded by the best sci-fi shorts this festival has seen in years surely.

All I Think of is You (2012)

Director: Shad Clark
Writer: Shad Clark
Stars: L. Jeffrey Moore, Simone Olsen-Varela, Rowan Brooks, Rolf Saxon and Jeremy Kaller

We might be excused for thinking that the pained and bloodied gentleman dying on a gurney as this film begins is too busy to think about anything. Either that or he's seeing his entire life flash before his eyes; that's the cliché, right? Well, every movie has a title for a reason and we find out about this one soon enough.

This man is Nate and he's dead by the time we see that title. What he really thinks of as he dies is his wife, Claire. In fact he tells her that in the very next scene when he calls her on the phone. Yes, that is the chronological order of events, as this is a sci-fi short and we're here to watch the results of technological advancement.

Scientists, led by a Tim Curry clone and notably including Nate himself, are working on what they call reconstructions through serial sectioning microscopy but we're far more likely to call mind uploads. And, as he starts to question what they're doing, he finds himself in a fatal car accident and his mind uploaded into a different body. Now he's Subject 0001.

There are a number of ironies and contrasts here, as this story aims to cover a lot of ground in a mere eight minutes. Clearly it's a shock for Claire to receive a phone call from her dead husband but that's only the first (shock and phone call). When he shows up at their house to surprise her when she gets home, she discovers an equally obvious change: he's not a thin white guy any more, he's a chubby black man, who had died of a pulmonary embolism at only 36. Nate died at a particularly convenient time for his team's debut reconstruction and the consequences of that soon test him as much as they do his wife.

This grandest irony was shared by a few sci-fi shorts at the 2013 festival, most obviously this and *Flashback*: that the man who makes something technologically possible is the only one not to benefit from it. In a flashback, Nate explains to Claire that it's her that drives him. "All day at work, all I think of is you," he tells her. That scene resonates throughout the rest of the film.

This is a good story to begin with and writer/director Shad Clark takes it exactly where it needs to go, but it also feels too crammed into this short a running time. One of the most common comments I hear after watching festival short sets is that people want to see good shorts expanded to feature length. It's rarely appropriate, as most shorts have stories to fit their running time, but this one is a notable exception: it absolutely would benefit from an expansion to feature length because it's far from a one idea piece; many of the ideas here deserve more attention that only more time can allow.

I certainly wanted more background about the scientists, Nate's conflicts and the convenient timing of his death; I wanted a lot more about Claire and her reactions to the events that unfold; and I wanted more about the shells being inhabited by orphaned minds, a darker aspect to donating your body to science. The circles we see here are fascinating, but there should be circles in the circles too.

While we would benefit from such an expansion, each of the

actors would benefit even more. The film as it stands doesn't give them much opportunity, as they all play second fiddle to the script. They do good work but unfortunately they each discover that their wings are clipped as soon as they try to fly.

What's more, I have a feeling that some of the depth they try to explore goes beyond the script as it exists here. I wonder if Clark has a wider story written and whether his actors got to see it before they shot this short. With the benefit of hindsight, I believe that actors like Simone Olsen-Varela, who plays Claire, are reacting to material that would logically show up in a longer picture but isn't actually in this one.

Perhaps its a whole new irony that in writing a story about technology that can cheat the ultimate limit of death, the film's biggest flaw is that it can't cheat the inherent limit of its running time, a sort of equivalent to death for a filmed piece of fiction. Let's hope Clark can achieve that with a feature.

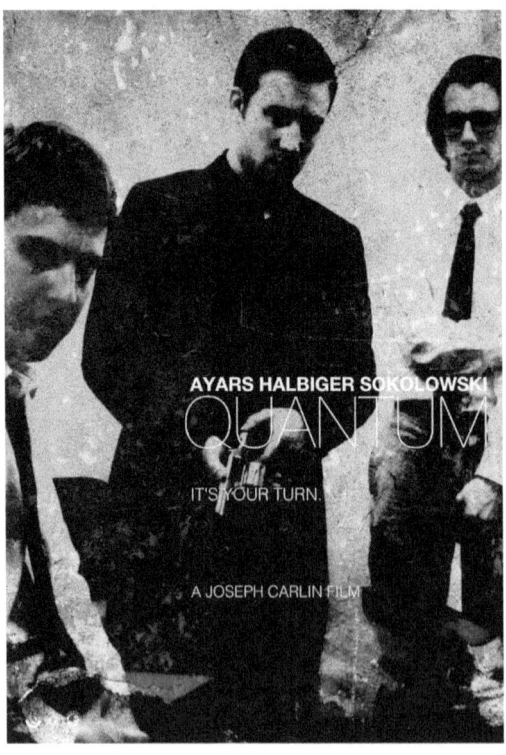

Quantum (2012)

Director: Joseph Carlin
Writer: Joseph Carlin
Stars: Jeffrey R. Ayars, Frank Halbiger and Mike Sokolowski

A lot of people avoid science fiction films, especially Russian ones or short ones, because of a general assumption that they'll be called upon to think, as if that would be a bad thing. It does mean that they miss out on a lot of great movies but it also means that they safely avoid what they hate and fear: the possibility that an idea might take root in their head and throw their safe, boring lives out of whack.

It could be said that *Quantum*, a short film from writer/director Joseph Carlin and Transfixion Films, is the epitome of that fear, as it's fundamentally about taking an idea, releasing it into our skulls at fast speed and letting it ricochet around until we drive ourselves batty. Its story is effectively torture for physicists, the sort who can paint themselves into a corner, all the while meditating upon what a corner really is and whether it still exists after they close their eyes. It's based, you'll be utterly unsurprised to note, on the famous Schrödinger's cat experiment, but with a number of enhancements to make it cinematically viable.

For a while it's tedious, as we just follow a man on a long walk into a library, the glitchy soundtrack and odd angles not adding much to proceedings. We merely want to know why a man, before we're even given opening credits, placed a gun to his chin.

The walker, Tyler by name, holds the key because everything ties to a study he wants to perform. He tells Robert that he aims to "push the limits of quantum theory, human understanding" and Brandon that "by the time we're done, we'll have lifted the veil of reality as we know it."

It's an odd experiment, as we expect from his voice which is half soporific college lecturer and half persuasive used car salesman. That voice is the principal reason why we buy into some of what follows, because the logic is dubious, even though it's rivetting.

In most films, the quick bout of Russian roulette that we're soon treated to would be the drama that underpins the story, but this is certainly not most films. In this one, it's just the beginning, as the real story is in the participants then arguing about what the result really means.

Inevitably, the more we think about this one, the more it falls apart on us. I'm a realist: If I shoot myself in the head and survive, then I'm alive. However, because this story is is inextricably rooted in quantum theory and the characters are students of the subject, we can't help but watch from their perspective. In other words, if Brandon shoots himself in the head and survives, how can he know whether he's alive or dead? How can Robert prove the outcome in numbers written on the white walls of their box like room? Here's where the true value lies, as a clear vision of what most of us tend to see in the subject of quantum mechanics: men in white shirts torturing themselves over whether black is white or vice versa.

All three of the actors are believable in this intellectual torture, even though they're otherwise completely different: Jeffrey Ayars is an infuriatingly calm Tyler, Frank Halbiger a quintessential nerdy genius as Robert and Michael Sokolowski a less disciplined wildcard as Brandon. The film relies on them all and they deliver.

Mostly, of course, it relies on the story, which is a clever little bugger that's always careful to make itself about the characters' interpretation of quantum theory rather than about that quantum theory itself. That way we stay sane while they don't and we follow proceedings clearly even without a grounding in the subject.

After all, quantum theory tends to trump cryptography as the archetypal example of the science most fundamentally inaccessible to the layman. At least we know cryptography works, even if we haven't a clue how.

This approach is why Carlin could get away with such a minimal set; most of the film unfolds in a closed room with white walls and almost no props because everything is conjured out of words. The budget ran around a thousand dollars, most of which went into building that room.

The beauty of a film that revolves around a cryptic thought experiment is that it keeps us thinking and it's the easiest thing in the world to think round in circles. I bet the three of them are still in that room doing just that.

Golem (2013)

Directors: Patrick McCue and Tobias Wiesner
Writer: Tobias Wiesner, from the novel by Stanislaw Lem
Star: Cyrena Dunbar

If *Quantum* was torture for physicists, *Golem* is surely torture for technologists because it raises the potential that once a computer becomes more intelligent than those who built it, it will diverge from us in ways that we cannot predict.

This animated short is a beautiful thing, notably organic in its visuals, but it's also an overwhelming and almost inpenetrable one, especially without the necessary background, which, in the most puzzling choice of the two filmmakers, Patrick McCue and Tobias Wiesner, is not provided.

We are told that *Golem* is a short adaptation of a novel by Polish philosopher and science fiction author Stanislaw Lem, for instance, but not that it's told by a computer. The book *Golem XIV* riffs on one of Lem's regular themes: the inability of mankind to communicate with truly alien intelligence, the title character here being exactly that, an artificial intelligence created for military purposes which becomes conscious and quickly outstrips its creators. It initially lectures to them but eventually ceases communication altogether for no provided reason.

Like the book, this film is told by the Golem XIV AI in the form of one of its lectures. It's a deep and dense talk, one which covers so much ground that it's exceedingly difficult to keep up. In the end, we surely fail to do so and the narration by Cyrena Dunbar becomes nothing but white noise to accompany the eye candy. I've lost the plot every time through, though repeated viewings do help. I also know that I'm not alone; when I talked to other audience members after its screening in 2013, they reported the same effect.

Initially it's relatively simple, as Golem XIV recounts a tale about rats in a labyrinth, probability ensuring that at least one should escape it, even if not through its own talent. This quickly becomes an analogy for the human race and the process of evolution, which allows us to choose our own fate. So far, so good, but it continues to expand outward, explaining how we limit ourselves by imposing religion and culture. At some point this discussion of rationality gets too obscure.

While I'm not qualified to say whether this philosophising has meaning or not, it clearly ceases to do so to most viewers within this film's framework. Those ambitious enough can watch and rewatch to figure out if they can fathom it all; everyone else can at least enjoy the audiovisual treat, which continues on unabated.

The visuals begin with what looks like slow motion footage of the sun, even though it's computer generated and morphs into less recognisable and more abstract forms. Presumably the tendrils are the thoughts of human beings and the ice cages reflect how we bind them. Eventually we're led backwards into a mechanical structure, presumably Golem XIV itself. The score is an ambient electronic piece that is pleasant to the ear with gentle pulsing beats, courtesy of composer Cliff Martinez. Dunbar's soft voice becomes another instrument, playing along with it.

I applaud the filmmakers for their ambition and I'm not going to ask anyone to dumb their work down, but I can't help stating that this particular one lost me.

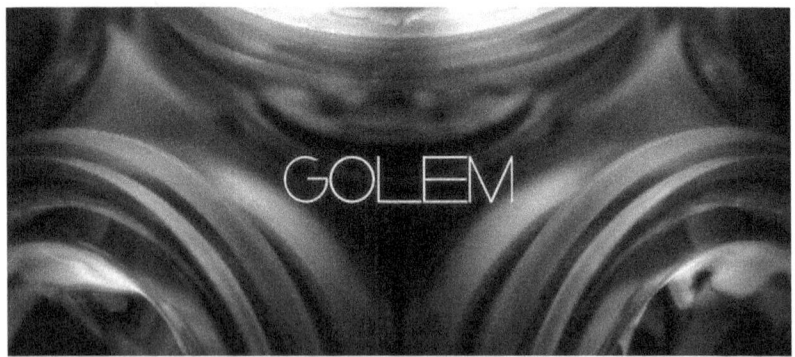

Sunset Day (2012)

Director: J. A. Duran
Writers: J. A. Duran and Ferran Grau
Stars: Ramon Novell, Jordi Llordella, José María Blanco, Laura Motos, Roberta Pasquinucci, Roser Boladeras and Ariadna Minguell

I wanted to like *Sunset Day* more than I found I could. I loved the concepts in play and the ramifications that spring from them, but it felt to me like they weren't explored as well as they could be, in favour of a safer and lesser approach.

The key idea is similar to the old time travel trope where people go back to a critical point in time to change that one seemingly insignificant event that will alter the course of history and prevent a particular future. You know it by heart from *The Terminator* and *Twelve Monkeys* and dozens of others. Well, this is the same thing, but in reverse.

A shadowy organisation known only as the Corp has a mysterious ability to see far enough into the future to identify when and where the apocalypse is going to happen. Here it's codenamed Sunset Day. They then send an agent to make an insignificant change and deny that potential future its chance to unfold. Great, you might think. Well, insignificant changes may not feel insignificant; would you crash a train, for instance, killing 236 people, if you knew that it would delay the end of the world for a mere 18 days?

That's what our hero does at the beginning of this film, explained through the deep and resonant narration of David Seys. To add an extra level of impcat, it's the 36th time he's saved the world. In a nice touch, the apocalypse is a constant foe to the Corp. They can't just save the world and be done with it; they have to keep doing it, time after time.

There are so many ramifications to this great idea that a whole feature could easily be dedicated to exploring a bunch of them. Surely trust would be a major concern; how could each agent sent on such a mission be sure, absolutely sure, that they were doing the right thing? Just one shred of doubt would be enough to cause psychological torture. Well, unless you hire sociopaths. Surely the knowledge that they will be called upon to do the same thing again next week would be enough to spark that shred. The conspiracy angle is vast; shadowy organisations inherently attract conspiracy theories anyway, but the Corp wouldn't just be a gift to the tin hat brigade, it would be a conspiracy to everyone who worked for it.

Yet those angles are mostly jettisoned here in favour of a very personal story. We learn about our hero, how he was brought into the fold as a child and how the friend he lost in an explosion comes back into his life and changes his thinking. It's not a bad direction, but it's a far safer one than director Josep Antoni Duran and his co-writer, Ferran Grau, could, or even should, have taken with their script. I wanted so much more from their story, given that the film itself had so much more to back it up.

We visit more than one time, as we see our hero, credited as Owl, as a child and an adult, but the look of the film is believably dated, not just through costumes and sets but by the use of a wonderful orientation video that takes the form of a cartoon. There are neat hints back at history, like the Hindenberg disaster being a means to avoid Sunset Day, for example. The CGI is too crisp and artificial but it's suitably spectacular and it's ably backed up by Roger Costa's excellent score. Technically, this is mostly an accomplished piece.

The acting is also solid, even from the child actors like Ramon Novell and Laura Motos, who play the young Owl and the unnamed friend at the orphanage who he believes is lost. They're only tasked to act physically, as the entire fifteen minute running time is devoid of dialogue.

The piece unfolds well as an almost silent film with narration, possibly to aid international distribution. It's a Spanish film, but just as silent movies were able to simply swap out intertitles for each market, this could easily swap out the narration, along with a few minor details to reach a whole new country. Sunset Day also comes in a Spanish language version and it wouldn't surprise me to see other languages follow.

I wouldn't mind seeing that original version to see if anything was done differently, but I doubt it. What I really want to see is a longer, tighter, more complex, story that attempts a lot more than this one and covers a lot more background. Sunset Day gives us a glimpse into a fascinating world; now I'd like to explore it.

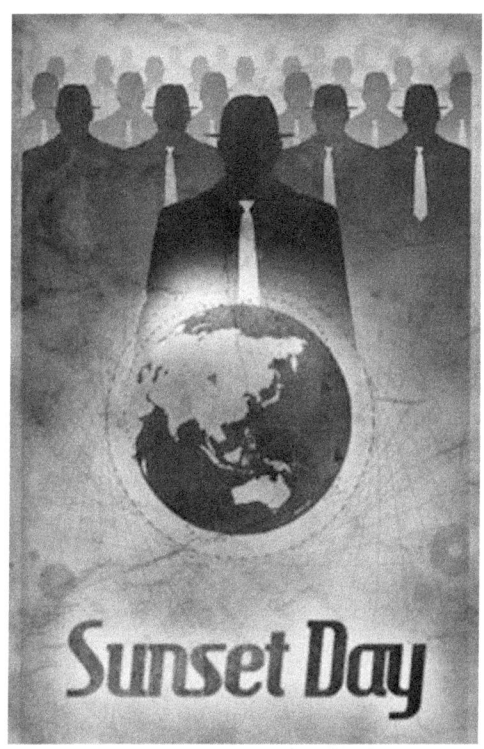

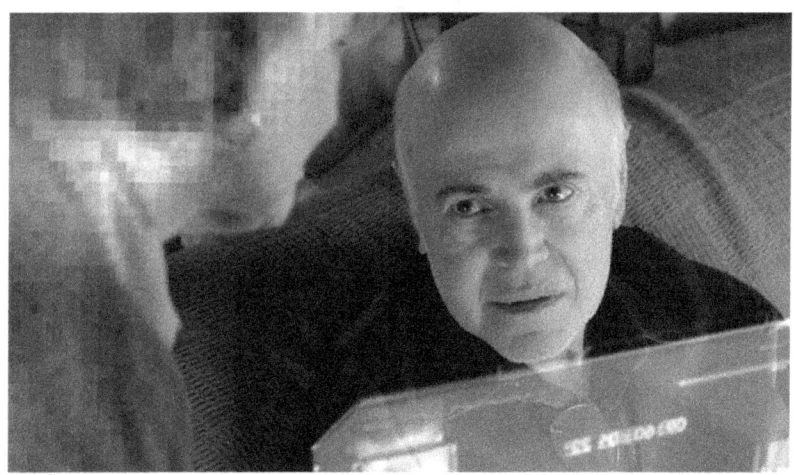

Flashback

Flashback (2013)

Director: Steve Petersen
Writer: Steve Petersen
Stars: Walter Koenig, Judy Levitt, Tom Biagini, Shannon Murray and Karla Osella

The science fiction shorts at the 2013 festival were notable both for their consistent quality and for the emotion they drew out of the audience. Films like *Ellie*, *Restitution* and *The Secret Keeper* nailed both the science fiction aspects of their stories and the emotional ones. It may be that *Flashback* is the most emotional of them all, especially because of the searing performance of the lead actor, Walter Koenig, who proves emphatically here that he deserved a much bigger role to play in *Star Trek*.

It revolves around our personal connection to new technology, another common theme running through the festival selections in 2013, especially *All I Think of is You*, *Restitution* and *Iris*. The new technology here, the Flashback Device created by Dr. Joseph Griffin, Koenig's character, is reminiscent of the slow glass of Bob Shaw's superb short story, *Light of Other Days*, but with the control given to the user. Griffin dedicates his life to perfecting this device, only for irony to strike in the cruellest fashion.

As befits a story about a gadget which allows people to relive moments of their lives, we're whisked back into the lives of the Griffins, Joseph and his wife, Greta. We watch them as a young couple, decorating their house with all the open possibility that the future can hold, but Joseph is already distracted by his work. His boss suggests that he has the potential to change the world and he believes him. We soon find that he manages it too because, back in the present, he's living on Mars with his perfected device selling in the billions.

The catch comes in how he got there. Even as a young man he tells Greta that he loves his work more than anything and we see her understanding of that, in her eyes as the truth of it registers and also in the moment to which he flashes back over and over with his own device, of her leaving him as an old woman. It hasn't been a good life for her, living it alone while he works, so she leaves just as he finds the time to spend with her and regret that he can't do it any more because she's gone.

Koenig is magnificent here, his eyes full of sadness and regret, as he interrupts a TV interview to flash back to Greta leaving him yet again. "Is there anything I can do to get you to stay?" he asks her, knowing full well that there isn't because she only exists in the memory with which his device provides him. The ability for him to converse with it is little solace.

The ironies are palpable. The time that he spent developing the device stole the opportunity for him to spend valuable time with his wife, only for her to leave and force him to use his own gadget to relive what may well be the only moment of time he captured before she left, which in turn nails home again and again what he could have had but lost through dedication to the device. It's an ever decreasing circle, which we can see in Koenig's eyes and hear in his broken voice. Here is a man who has achieved wonders, lives among wonders and has given wonder to billions, but he's a broken man because of it all.

Like many of the sci-fi shorts in 2013, surely the biggest problem *Flashback* has is that it's only six minutes long. Apparently there is an intention to expand it to feature length, which I'd dearly love to see, but there's precious little information available online about this goal. It deserves more time to breathe, to draw each of the characters out, even if that's by expanding to a longer short film of twenty minutes or so.

Koenig gets the most screen time but there's surely a lot more to Dr. Griffin than we see within that. Judy Levitt is excellent as the elder Greta, but again there's a great deal more possibility to her character than just a repeated exit in Griffin's repeated flashback. Their younger versions have possibility too, both Tom Biagini and Shannon Murray believably ready for the world ahead of them. Murray in particular gets that one moment but not the opportunity to make more of it.

I have no doubt that, given the ironies that Steve Peterson shoehorned into the six minutes he had, he could layer it more with the flexibility of time. Here's to hoping we see more of *Flashback*.

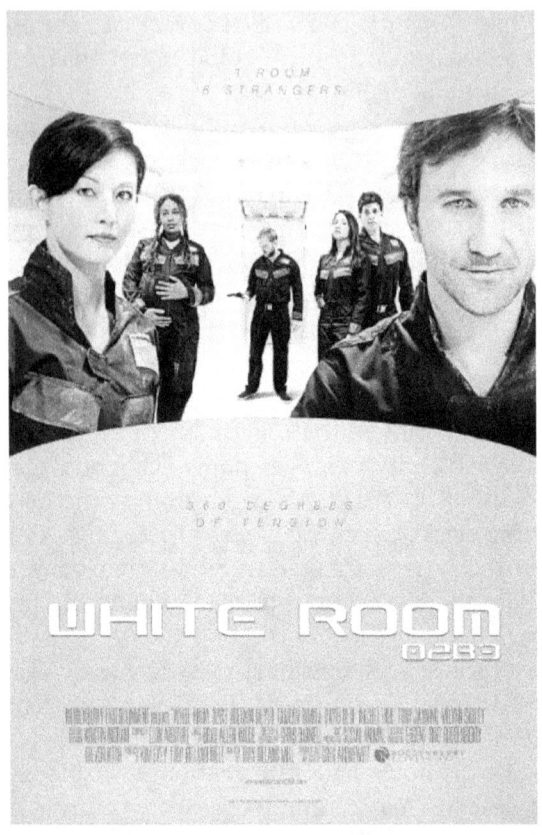

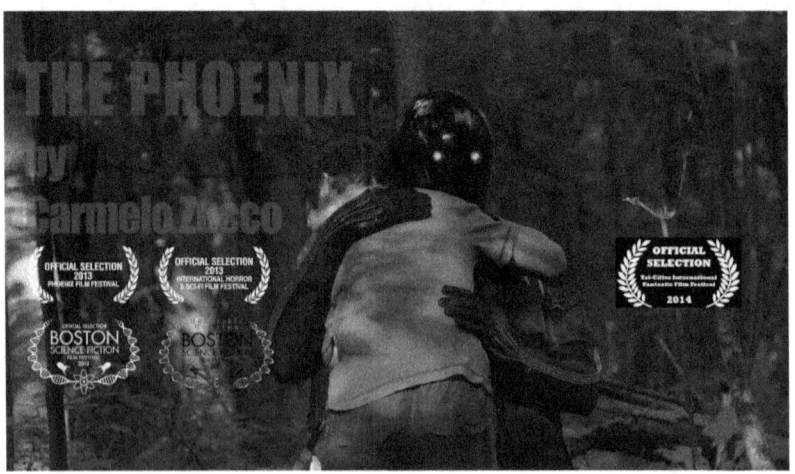

White Room: 02B3 (2012)

Director: Greg Aranowitz
Writer: Tony Mell
Stars: Breckin Meyer, Tamlyn Tomita, Rachel True, David Blue, Tony Janning, Milynn Sarley and Doug Jones

I wasn't surprised when the cryptically titled *White Room: 02B3* was awarded Best Science Fiction Short at the 2013 festival. After all, it checked off every possible box.

The story by Tory Mell was intelligent, thoughtful and resonant, even though he hasn't written any of the enviable list of films that he's worked on. There are cool special effects everywhere, from the gorgeous auto-retractable seats to, well, let's just highlight that Doug Jones is in the movie and he's about as visually recognisable as usual. The set is so shiny and white that it could easily be an iSet with an Apple logo displayed prominently. The cast are strong and generally established actors, most recognisable to a genre audience through TV shows or webseries: Breckin Meyer is a *Robot Chicken* stalwart, Tony Janning was Neil in *The Legend of Neil*, Milynn Sarley was on *Team Unicorn* and *The Guild*, Tamlyn Tomita was perhaps most obvious on *Eureka* and David Blue was a regular on a couple of the *Stargate* shows. Only Rachel True is new to the genre. Oh, and it carries the name of Roddenberry Entertainment: produced by Rod Roddenberry, Gene's son.

What surprised me was that it was only after enjoying the film at the Harkins CineCapri that I learned that I hadn't seen it as it was designed to be seen. No, it's not one of those pointless modern 3D movies that serve mostly to inflate the ticket price; it's a great deal more unique than that.

It was shot using a camera system that shoots 360° footage, with the camera placed in the middle of the set to catch everything that goes on, even if characters aren't directly engaged in what's happening. If I wanted to watch in a true immersive environment, I couldn't go to a Harkins, an AMC or any other multiplex, let alone any of my favourite indie theatres; none of them have the required technology. Instead I'd have to go to a dome theatre, where I can effectively sit in the set and watch the action unfold all around me. There are only three compatible venues within 120 miles of my house: a science centre, a community college and a charter school. Of the mere six in Arizona, one is the Lowell Observatory in Tucson.

That would be a serious movie night, but fortunately, the film doesn't require such rare technology to be enjoyed; when screened on a regular movie screen it plays like a regular movie, albeit one that swaps explosions for tension.

It grabs us immediately, with a strange beginning that sets up a mystery and prompts us to ask questions about it. Six people wake up around a table in what must be a spaceship, given that it's built out of the same moulded white plastic that we know from movies that all spaceships are built from. The colour here comes from the people, dressed in uniform black outfits. They're suitably varied as to race, sex and age; one is even pregnant. They're as confused as we are about what's going on and there's little to help them; merely a gun on the table and numbers over their hearts. The one who's missing his glasses is the first to pick up the gun and wave it around in a hope for answers. He's number 6 and number 6 is always the first to go, some say. And so he does. It all fades to white, then starts again with the five remaining players. And on we go.

For all the the technological hoopla and recognisable faces (or recognisable voice, in the case of Doug Jones), it's the script by Tory Mell that makes this work so well. It feels rather like something we might have seen on a black and white episode of *The Twilight Zone*, an overtly science fiction exploration of human nature. The initial mystery is ramped up a few times with fresh revelations and we learn much before we're gifted with the why of it all at the finalé, only to realise the true scope of events and how this means that the end is merely another beginning. It's quality writing and it keeps proceedings very tight indeed.

The actors are as reliable as you might expect and I wonder how much more depth we'll get from them in a dome theatre where all are on screen simultaneously. If there's a flaw, it's that the theme that eventually manifests itself is perhaps a little closer to what Gene Roddenberry aimed to achieve with the original *Star Trek* than his son should probably play if he wants to stand on his own two feet. Of course, many might see that as an asset.

The Phoenix (2012)

Director: Carmelo Zucco
Writer: Carmelo Zucco
Stars: Alex Cardillo, Jim Bradford, Brie Barker and Howard Rosenstein

Perhaps I think too much about science fiction shorts, but isn't that the point of them?

Here's another one that I liked but had problems with for entirely uncinematic reasons. The core of the film revolves around a concept that's gradually easing into the mainstream, namely that cybernetic technology will improve to the point where we can effectively, for the most part, conquer death.

This near future film explores a small human story after that point has been reached, in which "cybernetics have done away with the fragility of the human body" and little Ben's grandpa, his sole companion, doesn't have to die.

He's old and frail and his body is failing, but instead of just giving up the ghost to leave his grandson all alone, he can merely check into wherever and swap out his human shell for a nice shiny metal one, in which he can continue on and, presumably, feel a heck of a lot better while he does so. He isn't rejuvenated, he isn't cloned and he isn't fixed; instead he's replaced, all except his consciousness and his clothes.

Before this happens, we see an old man, presumably actor Jim Bradford, with worried eyes and wildly receding white hair. After the change, after he's risen again like the phoenix of the title, we discover why he was really cast in this role: we're not going to get to experience any more of him than his voice, which is perfect for the task, the sort that we intrinsically want to trust. If he doesn't voice a lot of commercials already, he should. "It'll still be me," he tells young Ben before his rebirth, "on the inside." Now Ben has to adjust to that reality, as do we.

I can totally buy into all the concepts thus far, because we're already doing this today to a lesser degree, just a smaller scale. After all, what are pacemakers, hearing aids and prosthetic limbs, if not primitive cybernetic replacements for faulty or dying flesh? I can also, having lived for the last decade in the United States with their reliance on health insurance rather than healthcare, easily buy into a scenario where the rich get better care than the poor. Again, we're already doing this today too.

What I don't buy is those two facts manifesting themselves here in Grandpa coming back in a *Tron* suit and a huge birdlike helmet with googly eyes. As the main thrust of the film runs on and this unlikely couple hike into the wilds so Grandpa can toss his ashes into a waterfall and Ben can come to terms with his only relative being the sort of robot we tend to laugh at in serials from the forties, I couldn't get past this.

Fine, make his new human suit uglier than the one that will go to the boss of the company that makes them, but why so much so that he can't even lean over without stabbing himself in the chest? This is just tech; you can buy an expensive phone with all the gimmicks or a cheap one with crappy battery life, but both are going to look current generation. The cheap one is still going to fit in your pocket; it's not going to be a ten pound monsters with an antenna the size of your kid sister.

I don't know if I'm alone with this issue, but it was an important one for me. Even neat and far more believable little touches like Grandpa's batteries coming in different flavours couldn't get me past it. And that's a shame, because the human side of this story is explored well, if inevitably limited by the film's sixteen minute running time.

There's surely a great movie somewhere in these ideas, especially nowadays as the artificial controversy over Obamacare prompts the American people (or, more accurately, the entire rest of the world) to wonder why the U.S.A. is the last civilised country on the face of the earth without nationalised healthcare. Unfortunately that great movie isn't this one, which is relegated to the level of merely being promising.

While I can't buy into this particular robot Grandpa, his rather stunning change of appearance is more than enough to highlight what writer/director Carmelo Zucco clearly aimed to do, which is to starkly contrast the before with the after to explore how little Ben reacts to the wild change. He asks all the right questions and

Alex Cardillo, who plays him, does so with an appropriate mixture of wary adjustment and youthful tolerance. With Jim Bradford's reassuring voice to guide him, it's a safe bet that Ben will find a way to deal. What isn't explored is how long Grandpa will, along with a whole heck of a lot more.

I like the way that *The Phoenix* asks questions. I just wanted more of them and I don't agree with all the answers.

Afterword
by Andrea Canales

I started volunteering with the International Horror & Sci-Fi Film Festival in 2005 on the promotions team: handing out and delivering flyers all over the valley. Being a huge horror movie buff and just getting in to program my own film events under the Midnite Movie Mamacita moniker, this was the perfect way to satisfy my appetites for film and volunteering. In 2006 I helped bring *A Nightmare on Elm Street* scream queen Heather Langenkamp in as a special guest. From then I was hooked.

In 2008 when founder and local valley horror icon Brian Pulido stepped down from the festival director position, I was honored to be offered the position. Seeing the festival's evolution - moves to different venues, different sponsors, partners and new volunteers - has been really motivating. We've gone from being an independent event to becoming part of the Phoenix Film Festival. Over the years we have shown some really outrageous films, had some amazing guests and entertained thousands of festival-goers. It's been an amazing ride.

2012 was a special year for the International Horror and Sci-Fi Film Festival. In its eighth year and second year as part of the larger Phoenix Film Festival, we were out to make it bigger and better. But on a personal note, I was six months pregnant, so that added a new aspect to my usual duties.

Luckily things got off to a great start when we were put in contact with Jennifer Blanc-Biehn and then Michael Biehn through a mutual friend. Excited to play to a home-town crowd, Michael and Jen agreed to come out to the festival and première their new feature, *The Victim*. Meeting Michael's mother and family was a great joy and sharing that special screening with the festival crowd and the Biehns was a true delight.

One of my primary roles with the festival is to program the showcase films and coordinate the talent. It's always a lot of fun, but also a challenge finding new genre films (and some cult classics) that fit within the scope of the festival, which is run by a non-profit organization, the Phoenix Film Foundation.

One feature that I was dying to bring to the festival because I knew it would be incredibly divisive was *Beyond the Black Rainbow*, a synthetic nightmare set to a stellar soundtrack with stunning visual imagery. Sitting in the dark theater with it on the big screen, I saw a few people walk out, heard the muttered gasps of confusion when the film finished and was thrilled that I could bring a film that made people think and wasn't your standard mainstream fare.

Another highlight was premiering *With Great Power: The Stan Lee Story* and *F.D.R.: American Badass!* Filmmakers came out for both these screenings and entertained the crowds with fun antics and their recollections of making their films. Interacting with truly independent filmmakers and being able to showcase their work, which are labors of love, to an appreciative crowd is always a thrill. The festival is always a whirlwind and 2012 was no exception.

I met Hal at the 2007 festival (mistakenly thinking he was a Kiwi after hearing him talk after one of the screenings); he is one of the vast community that this festival has created. I'm blessed to have met and worked with some really amazing people. If Hal's appetite and passion for all things film and especially this festival are anything to go by, you are in for a real treat with this book.

Andrea Canales
October 2014

Award Winners

During the Transition Years from 2011 to 2013, the International Horror & Sci-Fi Festival handed out awards in four categories: best feature and best short for each genre of horror and sci-fi.
Here's a list of the winners of each.

2011

Best Horror Feature Film	*Absentia*
Best Sci-Fi Feature Film	*Triple Hit*
Best Horror Short Film	*Bugbaby*
Best Sci-Fi Short Film	*Picture Show at the End of the World*

2012

Best Horror Feature Film	*It's in the Blood*
Best Sci-Fi Feature Film	*Pig*
Best Horror Short Film	*Brutal Relax*
Best Sci-Fi Short Film	*Secret Identity*

2013

Best Horror Feature Film	*Found*
Best Sci-Fi Feature Film	*Channeling*
Best Horror Short Film	*Killer Kart*
Best Sci-Fi Short Film	*White Room: 02B3*

Bibliography

While movie reviews are inherently based on personal opinion, there's also a factual side that has to be covered by research and I tracked down details about these films from many sources.

IMDb and Wikipedia are always useful but never absolute; they fill in filmographies and highlight ties to other movies.

I always talk to as many filmmakers as I can at festivals and have corresponded with many more afterwards, especially as I've sought permission to screen some of these films at Apocalypse Later mini-film festivals. Not one has ever said no, incidentally; the creators of short films are generally most interested in their work being seen.

I also took notes during the Q&As of any filmmakers who came out in person to this particular festival, which is especially known for that aspect.

I garnered useful information from a few official websites, some of which no longer exist. The Wayback Machine is our friend.

I found Kickstarter or IndieGoGo campaign pages, as some of these short films were crowdsourced. It's often interesting to see what the goal of a film was, especially when compared to what it eventually became.

Some articles and interviews, whether in print or online, proved useful in providing background information.

In addition to the above and to sources cited within the reviews themselves, the following sources were especially useful in writing this book:

For *The People vs. George Lucas*, George Lucas's 1988 testimony to the United States Congress which is preserved online with some additional context, at *Saving Star Wars*, an important site in the fight to preserve culture.

For *I am Nancy*, many entries by Heather Langenkamp on the *I am Nancy* blog, especially *Freddy on My Street*, as well as the *Heather Langenkamp Interview* at BellaOnline by Steven Casey Murray.

For *Stakeland*, an article by Eric Kohn in *The New York Times* called *A Kingmaker in the Realm of Cheapie Horror* and an interview by Fred Topel at Crave Online, *Stake Land's Jim Mickle Talks Vampires*.

For *Last Seen on Dolores Street*, an interview by "thehorrorchick" at Dread Central called *Shriekfest 2011: Exclusive Q&A with Filmmaker Devi Snively*.

For *Cell Phone Psycho*, the website of the Noisician Coalition.

For *Roman's Ark*, the film's profile page at Short Film Central.

For *Earwigs*, Robert Hood's article, *There's a New Bug in Town*, on his own blog, where you can also hear the film's amazing theme tune, *My Baby Left Me for an Earwig* by the Hot Rod Daddy Oh's.

For *The Hollow Men*, Ashley Denton's *How We Did It* on the *Who are the Hollow Men* website.

For *Below Zero*, a Slate article entitled *"A Terrible Evil": Edgar Allan Poe Writes About His Wife's Illness and Death*.

For *Beyond the Black Rainbow*, an interview with Panos Cosmatos by Phil Brown at Dork Shelf imaginatively titled *Interview: Beyond The Black Rainbow Director Panos Cosmatos*.

For *Found*, an interview at iHorror.com by Chris Crum called, just as imaginatively, *Exclusive: An Interview With 'Found' Director Scott Schirmer*.

For *They Live*, the source story, *Eight O'Clock in the Morning* by Ray Nelson.

Where to Find These Films

Given that one of the primary focuses of this book is to highlight films in danger of being forgotten, it seems appropriate to identify which are commercially available, which are available to watch online and which are not currently available in any form.

Obviously, as this is a print book, this static information is likely to be out of date as soon as it's published. This should therefore be seen as a baseline only; please search yourself when you need to do so to ensure fresh information.

Features

All the features reviewed in this book have been commercially released and are generally available from all the usual stores or providers in both physical (DVD or BluRay) and multiple streaming formats, with the following exceptions or notes:

Folklore, Found in Time, Pig and *Space Milkshake* are currently only available to stream. They have not yet been released commercially on physical media.

The Brain That Wouldn't Die and *Gamera vs. Guiron* are in the public domain so can be legally downloaded for free from the Internet Archive and/or other sites.

Sader Ridge is available in both physical and streaming formats but only under its new title of *The Invoking*.

Channeling and *Slumber Party Slaughter* have not been released to the public at this time.

Shorts

The following short films can be watched for free at Vimeo:

20th Century Man, Alchemy and Other Imperfections, All I Think of is You, Antedon, Bad Moon Rising, Brutal Relax, Cell Phone Psycho, Doctor Glamour, Dream Cleaners, Dry Gulch, Ellie, Follow the Sun!, Game, Golem, The Hollow Men, I Rot, Killer Kart, Low Tide in the High Desert, Midnight

Daisy, Restitution, Secret Identity, Sol, Solaria, Shoreditch Slayer, S.N.A.F.U., The Turing Love Affair and *Welcome Wagon.*

The following short films can be watched for free on YouTube:

Anaphora, All I Think of is You, Bad Moon Rising, Brutal Relax, Bugbaby, Diecons, Dream Cleaners, Earwigs, Employee of the Month, Flashback, Game, The Island, Killer Kart, Odokuro, Ontogenesis, The Recipient, Steve from Accounting vs. The Shadow Dwellers, Sunset Day, The Table and *The Waking.*

Brutal Relax is also available to watch for free at DailyMotion.
Red Umbrella is available to watch for free on ViddSee.

Earthship is available to watch on YouTube but for a rental fee.
Last Seen on Dolores Street is available as an extra in the two DVD release of *Trippin'.*

The following short films were not available to watch online at the time of publication. Hopefully this situation will change over time so that these films can be seen by the wider public.

Ambush, Carry Tiger to the Mountain, Cold Sore, A Conversation About Cheating with My Time Travelling Future Self, The Escape, Hollywood Forever, How to Kill Your Clone, Iris, Last Seen on Dolores Street, Mirage, Outsight, The Phoenix, Picture Show at the End of the World, Quantum, Roid Rage, Roman's Ark, The Secret Keeper, Sybling Rivalry, The Uncanny Valley, White Room: 02B3, Y Sci Fi and *Zombiefication.*

Websites

Daily Motion	http://www.dailymotion.com/us
Internet Archive	http://archive.org/
ViddSee	http://www.viddsee.com/
Vimeo	http://vimeo.com/
YouTube	http://www.youtube.com/

About Hal C. F. Astell

While he still has a day job, Hal C. F. Astell is a teacher by blood and a writer by inclination, which gradually transformed him into a film critic. He mostly reviews movies at his own site, Apocalypse Later, but he also reviews books at the Nameless Zine and provides film festival coverage for Nerdvana, among others.

He also runs mini-film festivals at Arizona and California cons including Phoenix Comicon, San Diego Comic-Fest, Wild Wild West Con, Phoenix FearCon, Gaslight Gathering et al, screening award-winning international sci-fi, horror and/or steampunk short films.

Born and raised in the rain of England, he's still learning about the word "heat" after a decade in Phoenix, where he lives with Dee, his better half, in a house full of assorted critters and oddities.

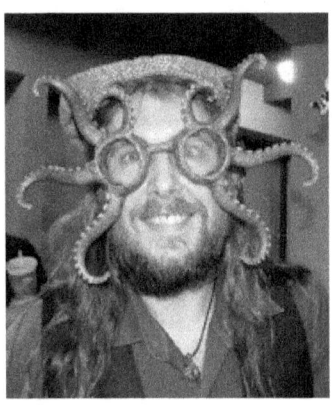

Photo by Dee Astell

Just in case you care, his favourite movie is Peter Jackson's debut, *Bad Taste,* his favourite actor is Warren William and he thinks Carl Theodor Dreyer's *The Passion of Joan of Arc* is the greatest movie ever made. He's always happy to talk your ears off about the joys of odd films, whether precodes, fifties B-movies or Asian horror flicks.

He's usually easy to find at film festivals, conventions and events because he's likely to be the only one in a kilt. He's friendly and doesn't bite unless asked.

About Apocalypse Later

Initially, Hal C. F. Astell wrote film reviews for his own reference because he could never remember who the one good actor was in otherwise forgettable entries in long crime series from the forties. After a year, they became long enough to warrant a dedicated blog.

As he was reviewing his way through every movie in the IMDb Top 250 for a project tentatively titled Apocalypse Later, that name promptly stuck. Originally it was just a joke with a punchline of reviewing *Apocalypse Now* last but, hey, there are worse names.

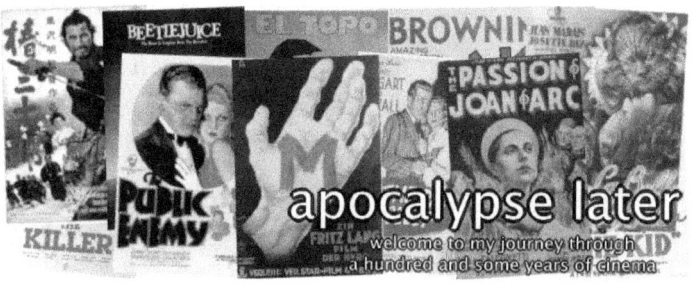

Over time, it became something of an anomaly, a movie review site full of reviews of movies most reviewers don't review. There are reviews of silent films, classic films, foreign films, indie films, short films, microbudget films, obscure films, genre films, festival films... pretty much everything except modern mainstream films. It's also one of the rare sites reviewing new microbudget horror movies that doesn't kill your eyes with white text on a black background.

Think of it this way. If you want to read about *Frankenweenie*, the $39m Tim Burton animated feature from 2012, you can go to Roger Ebert's website or any one of a thousand others. If you want to read about the other *Frankenweenie*, the black and white short film that Burton made for Disney in 1984, you'll find that Apocalypse Later is one of a few that'll help you out. And if you want go back to the odd movies that Burton made before that with a bunch of colleagues at Disney who all needed to blow off steam, then there might just be somewhere other than Apocalypse Later but I wouldn't count on it. If there are any, they'll probably be good reads too.

www.ingramcontent.com/pod-product-compliance
Lightning Source LLC
Chambersburg PA
CBHW060818170526
45158CB00001B/16